CONVEYANCING 2015

CONVEYANCING 2015

Kenneth G C Reid WS

Professor of Scots Law in the University of Edinburgh

and

George L Gretton WS

Lord President Reid Professor of Law in the University of Edinburgh

with a contribution by Alan Barr of the University of Edinburgh
and Brodies LLP

Avizandum Publishing Ltd
Edinburgh
2016

Published by
Avizandum Publishing Ltd
25 Candlemaker Row
Edinburgh EH1 2QG

First published 2016

© Kenneth G C Reid and George L Gretton, 2016

ISBN 978-1-904968-75-7

British Library Cataloguing in Publication Data
A catalogue record for this book is available from the British Library.

Typeset by Waverley Typesetters, Warham, Norfolk
Printed and bound by Bell & Bain Ltd, Glasgow

CONTENTS

Preface   ix

Table of statutes   xi

Table of orders   xv

Table of cases   xix

PART I: CASES

Missives of sale   3
Servitudes   10
Real burdens   17
Variation etc of title conditions by Lands Tribunal   18
Tenements   23
Property factors   23
Competition of title   24
Land registration   26
Barony titles   35
Community right to buy   37
Residential right to buy   39
Leases   41
Standard securities   56
Solicitors and surveyors   57
Special destinations   60
Boundaries, encroachment and prescription   61
Insolvency   65
Criminal property law   69
Miscellaneous   69

PART II: STATUTORY DEVELOPMENTS

Legal Writings (Counterparts and Delivery) (Scotland) Act 2015 (asp 4)   75
Community Empowerment (Scotland) Act 2015 (asp 6)   75
Consumer Rights Act 2015 (c 15)   78
Finance Act 2015 (c 11) and Finance (No 2) Act 2015 (c 33)   78
Mortgage Credit Directive   78

The Land Register: fees and completion   80
Private rented housing panel   81
Fees for registration as a property factor   82

PART III: OTHER MATERIAL

Land Reform (Scotland) Bill   85
Private Housing (Tenancies) (Scotland) Bill   91
Consultation on a code of practice and training requirements for
    letting agents   93
Registers of Scotland   93
Aronson and postponed standard securities: the RoS response 102
Conversion of ultra-long leases into ownership   105
Significant changes to Law Society's Property Law *Guidance*   105
Letters of obligation and the Master Policy   105
ScotLIS   105
10-year property-market report   106
Standard securities: restriction on the right to redeem after 20 years 106
CML *Lenders' Handbook*   107
Consumer protections in conveyancing cases   108
The Scottish New Build Standard Clauses   110
New PSG styles for residential conveyancing   111
Exploring the barriers to community land-based activities   111
Statutory guidance to local authorities on 'missing shares' in tenement
    repairs   113
Scottish Vacant and Derelict Land Survey 2014   114
Impact evaluation of the community right to buy   115
Land reform – from the House of Commons   116
Housing Statistics 2014–15   117
Books   118
Articles   118

PART IV: COMMENTARY

Execution in counterpart   125
    The basics   125
    Last-minute alterations   128
    Assembly, probativity, registration   130
Retention at settlement: beware!   133
    Introduction   133
    What happened in *Sneddon*   134
    The appeal to the Inner House   135

Real burdens and amenity areas   137
  Three models for amenity areas   137
  The owner-manager model: effective in theory   138
  But ineffective in practice   147
  Practical implications   149
Promises, promises: is a bank's word worth its bond?   151
  Carlyle case: bank 0, customer 1   151
  Alexander case: bank 1, customer 0   154
Building on someone else's land   158
  Introduction   158
  Minor encroachment   158
  Major encroachment   161
Electronic delivery of paper documents   167
  Introduction   167
  The standard case: delivery of a copy of the document   167
  A special case: delivery of a copy of part of the document   168
Exercising options: the importance of words   169
Fraud   171
  Faking law firms   172
  Impersonating owners   174
Exercise of servitudes – by whom?   176
  Grant v Cameron   176
  The underlying law   178
  Reid v Aberdeen Cafe Co Ltd   178
  Access rights under the Land Reform (Scotland) Act 2003   180
Buying from a discharged bankrupt   180
  Background   180
  The litigation in *Fortune*   183
  Some conclusions   185
Tenements and other developments   187
  Common parts: repairs or alterations?   187
  Appointing factors   189
  Recovery of repair costs: 5 years or 20?   190
Debtor protection and the enforcement of standard securities   193
  Introduction   193
  Westfoot: the protection of corporate debtors   193
  Swift Advances: debtor protection and negative equity   197
The secret flat   200
  The facts   200
  The law   201
  The result   202
  The future   203

Property taxes in Scotland   204
    Land and buildings transaction tax   205
    Scottish landfill tax   209
    Tax administration   210
    UK taxes on land   210
    The Scotland Act 2012 and the Scotland Bill   213

PART V: TABLES

Cumulative table of decisions on variation or discharge of title
    conditions   217
Cumulative table of appeals   228
Table of cases digested in earlier volumes but reported in 2015   233

PREFACE

This is the seventeenth annual update of new developments in the law of conveyancing. As in previous years, it is divided into five parts. There is, first, a brief description of all cases which have been reported, or appeared on the websites of the Scottish Courts (www.scotcourts.gov.uk) or of the Lands Tribunal for Scotland (www.lands-tribunal-scotland.org.uk/records.html), or have otherwise come to our attention since *Conveyancing 2014*. The next two parts summarise, respectively, statutory developments during 2015 and other material of interest to conveyancers. The fourth part is a detailed commentary on selected issues arising from the first three parts. Finally, in Part V, there are three tables. A cumulative table of decisions, usually by the Lands Tribunal, on the variation or discharge of title conditions covers all decisions since the revised jurisdiction in part 9 of the Title Conditions (Scotland) Act 2003 came into effect. Next is a cumulative table of appeals, designed to facilitate moving from one annual volume to the next. Finally, there is a table of cases digested in earlier volumes but reported, either for the first time or in an additional series, in 2015. This is for the convenience of future reference.

We do not seek to cover agricultural holdings, crofting, public sector tenancies (except the right-to-buy legislation), compulsory purchase or planning law. Otherwise our coverage is intended to be complete. It has been possible to include a small number of cases from England.

We gratefully acknowledge help received from Alan Barr, Sarah Duncan, Roddy Paisley, Catherine Reilly, David Robertson, Andrew Steven, Ann Stewart, and Scott Wortley.

Kenneth G C Reid
George L Gretton
29 March 2016

TABLE OF STATUTES

1870 Apportionment Act 45
1882 Bills of Exchange Act 193
1890 Partnership Act
    s 20 ff 71
    s 21 200
1892 Allotments (Scotland) Act 77
1894 Heritable Securities (Scotland) Act 193,
                                 195, 197
    s 5 196
    s 5A 195
1906 Marine Insurance Act 193
1924 Conveyancing (Scotland) Act
    s 44(4) 182, 184, 185, 186
1940 Law Reform (Contributory Negligence)
   (Scotland) Act
    s 3(2) 51
1964 Succession (Scotland) Act
    s 30 61
1970 Conveyancing and Feudal Reform
   (Scotland) Act 45, 193, 195, 197
    s 19A 194
    s 24(1A) 195
       (5) 197
       (5)(b) 199
       (7)(b) 199
       (7)(e) 195
    s 24A(3), (4) 198
    s 26(1) 102–03
    sch 6 form BB 194
   Taxes Management Act
    s 12ZB 212
1973 Local Government (Scotland) Act
    s 75 90
   Prescription and Limitation
   (Scotland) Act 17
    s 1(1) 35
    s 6(1)(a) 192
    s 9(1) 192
    sch 1 para 1(ac) 191
         para 1(g) 191, 192
         para 2(e) 191

1974 Land Tenure Reform (Scotland) Act
    ss 8, 11 106
1978 Interpretation Act
    s 16(1) 29, 30
    s 23A 29
1979 Land Registration (Scotland) Act
    s 3(1)(a) 12, 201, 202
    s 6(2) 12
    s 9(3)(a) 26, 27, 35
       (iii) 34, 203
    s 17 139
    s 25 . . . . 28, 29
   Sale of Goods Act
    s 14(2) 137
1980 Solicitors (Scotland) Act
    s 43 108
       (3)(a) 110
1984 Inheritance Tax Act
    ss 8D–8M 212
   Roads (Scotland) Act
    s 151 62
1985 Bankruptcy (Scotland) Act
    s 12(3A) 56
    s 14 . . . . 182–84, 185, 186
    s 14(3), (4) 182
    s 31 . . . . 181, 186
      (1A), (1B) 181
    s 32(4) 185
      (8) 181–82, 185, 186
    s 39A 183
   Law Reform (Miscellaneous
   Provisions) (Scotland) Act
    s 4 53
1987 Housing (Scotland) Act
    s 61B 40
    s 62 39
    s 65(2) 39
    s 68 40
1988 Housing (Scotland) Act 91
   ss 24, 27, 34 92

1992 Taxation of Chargeable Gains Act
  ss 2C, 2D 211
  ss 14B, 14F, 14G 211
  ss 222A–222C, 223A 212
  sch B1 para 4(1), (3)–(11). 211
  sch 4ZZB 211
1995 Proceeds of Crime (Scotland) Act . . 69
  Requirements of Writing (Scotland)
  Act 1995
    part 3 (ss 9A–9G) 126
    s 1(3), (4) 163
    s 2(1) 129
    s 3(1) 132
    s 5(1) 129
    s 6 130
    s 7(1) 131
      (3) 130, 131, 132
    s 8(2) 131, 132
    s 9E 167
    s 9F(2) 167
    s 9G 130
    s 12(2) 130
1997 Town and Country Planning
  (Scotland) Act 10
1998 Competition Act
    s 18 . . . . 145, 146
  Scotland Act
    s 80M 214
2000 Abolition of Feudal Tenure etc
  (Scotland) Act
    s 63 36
2001 Housing (Scotland) Act
    s 23(5) 41
    s 36 54
    s 49 39
  Mortgage Rights (Scotland) Act . . 193,
                               195, 197
2002 Land Registration Act
    s 58(1) 176
    sch 8 para 1 176
  Proceeds of Crime Act 69
2003 Finance Act
    ss 44–45A, sch 2A 207
  Homelessness etc (Scotland) Act
    s 11 194
  Land Reform (Scotland) Act 88
    part 1 (ss 1–36) 90, 180
    part 2 (ss 37–61) 75, 76, 115
    part 3 (ss 62–73) 76, 77
    part 3A (ss 97A–97Z) 75
    s 1 140

2003 Land Reform (Scotland) Act (cont)
    s 6(1)(b)(iv) 180
    s 7(5) 180
    s 9(f) 180
    s 20(1) 90
    s 28(7A) 90
    s 33 75
    s 34(1)(a) 38
    s 34(1A), (1B), (4A), (5) 76
    s 37 37
    s 38 39
    s 38(1)(a), (b) 38
    s 39 77
    s 51A 77
    s 56(3)(a) 77
    s 60(1A) 77
    s 60A 77
    s 61 37
    s 97C 75
    ss 97F, 97G 75
    s 97H(1) 76
    ss 97S, 97V, 97W, 97Z1 76
  Title Conditions (Scotland) Act . . . 139
    part 9 (ss 90–104) 145
    s 1(1) 140
    s 2(5) 148
    s 3(1)–(3) 140
    s 3(6) 143, 145, 146
    s 3(7) 141, 142, 143
    s 4 139
      (2)(a) 148
      (c)(ii) 149
    s 5 148
      (2) 148
    s 6 139
    s 8 18
    s 14 148
    s 18 192
    s 26(2) 189
    s 28 . . . . 142, 143, 189
    s 56 148
    s 61 145
    s 63 . . . . .142, 143, 148, 189
    s 64 . . . . 142, 143
    s 65 190
    s 75 14
    s 90(1)(a)(ii) 139
    s 90(7)(a) 20
    s 95(a) 19
    s 100(a) 20, 21
      (b) 20, 21, 22

2003	Title Conditions (Scotland) Act (*cont*)	
	s 100(c)	18, 20, 21, 22
	(e)	20
	(f)	18, 20
	(g), (j)	20
2004	Tenements (Scotland) Act	
	s 4	187
	(4)	189
	s 4A	113, 192
	s 7	187
	s 11(9)	191
	s 12	191
	(3), (4)	192
	s 13	192
	(3)	192
	s 16	188
	s 29(1)	191
	sch 1	188
	r 1.2(a)	188
	r 2.5	188, 189
	r 3.1(a)	188
	r 3.1(c)	189
2005	Income Tax (Trading and Other Income) Act	
	ss 272A, 272B, 274A, 274B	213
2006	Commons Act	
	s 15	16, 17
	Companies Act	
	ss 1012–1014	54
	s 1020	55
	ss 1024–1034	54
	s 1028	54
	s 1032(1)	54
	Housing (Scotland) Act	
	s 23	81
	ss 28A–28C	81
	s 120	43
2007	Bankruptcy and Diligence etc (Scotland) Act	181
	s 17	186
	Income Tax Act	
	s 6	213
2010	Home Owner and Debtor Protection (Scotland) Act	193, 195, 197
	Interpretation and Legislative Reform (Scotland) Act	
	ss 15, 16	29
2011	Private Rented Housing (Scotland) Act	
	s 35	81
	Property Factors (Scotland) Act	
	part 2 (ss 16–27)	23

2011	Property Factors (Scotland) Act (*cont*)	
	ss 1–12	82
	s 22	24
2012	Land Registration etc (Scotland) Act	28, 35, 107, 202
	s 12(2)	31
	s 14	105
	s 23	105
	s 27(3)(b)	80
	s 48(3)	99
	s 48A	88
	ss 63, 64	105
	ss 67(2), 69(1), 70(1), 71(1)	81
	s 80	30, 32, 103
	s 84(1)(a)	32
	s 103	28
	sch 4 para 14	28
	paras 17–24	29, 30
	para 17	30
	para 18	29, 30
	para 22	203, 204
	para 23	204
	Long Leases (Scotland) Act	102, 103
	Scotland Act	
	ss 25–27	213
2013	Finance Act	
	part 3 (ss 94–174)	210
	s 99	211
	schs 33–35	210
	Land and Buildings Transaction Tax (Scotland) Act	
	s 14(1)(c)	207
	sch 5	209
	sch 10A para 4(1)(a), (b), (3)	208
	para 7	208
	paras 9, 10, 13–15	209
2014	Bankruptcy and Debt Advice (Scotland) Act	
	sch 4	57
	Finance Act	
	ss 109, 110	211
	Housing (Scotland) Act	
	part 4 (ss 29–62)	93
	ss 25–27	81
	s 85	113
	(1)(b)	193
	s 93	106
	Revenue Scotland and Tax Powers Act	210
2015	Community Empowerment (Scotland) Act	75–78, 86, 89

2015 Community Empowerment
(Scotland) Act (cont)
    part 5 (ss 77–97) 76
    part 9 (ss 107–138) 77
    s 36. 75
    s 37(4), (6), (7). 76
    s 41. 39
    s 42. 77
    s 49. 77
    s 54(a) 77
    s 56(a) 77
    s 57. 77
    s 74. . . . . 75, 115
    s 79. 76
    s 82. 76
    s 84(2) 76
    s 85. 76
    s 94. 76
    s 102 77
    ss 111, 112 77
    s 117 78
    ss 119–121. 78
    s 144(2) 39
    sch 3 76
    sch 5 39
Consumer Rights Act 78, 158
    part 2 (ss 61–76) 9, 46, 78, 144
    s 2 157
      (2), (7). 78
    s 61(1) 78, 145
    s 62(1), (4) 78, 144
    s 63(1) 144
    sch 2 144
      part 1 78

2015 Finance Act 78
    ss 37, 38 211
    s 39. 212
    s 70. 211
    sch 7 211
      para 43 212
    sch 8 211
    sch 9 212
Finance (No 2) Act. 78
    s 9 212
    s 24. 213
Legal Writings (Counterparts and
Delivery) (Scotland) Act 75,
                      125–33
    s 1 . . . . 75, 128
      (2)–(4). 126
      (2). 128, 132
        (a). 131
      (3). 130, 131
      (4)(a) 130
        (b) 130, 131, 132
      (5). 127
        (b) 127
      (6), (7), (9) 127
    s 2(3), (4), (5) 127
    s 4 . . . . 75, 127, 167, 168
      (2)(a) 167
        (b) 168
      (3). 169
      (4), (5). 167, 169
      (6). 127
      (7). 168
      (9). 167

TABLE OF ORDERS

1980 Land Registration (Scotland) Rules 1980, SI 1980/1413
      r 9(1) 201, 202
1993 Act of Sederunt (Fees of Solicitors in the Sheriff Court) (Amendment and Further
      Provisions) 1993, SI 1993/3080 23
1994 Unfair Terms in Consumer Contracts Regulations 1994, SI 1994/3139. . . . . 46, 158
      reg 4(1). 145
      reg 5(1), (5) 144
      reg 8(1). 144
      sch 2 144
1999 Consumer Protection from Unfair Trading Regulations 2008, SI 2008/1277. 9
      part 4A (regs 27A–27L) 8, 9
      reg 6 8
      reg 27C 9
      reg 29 8
      Unfair Terms in Consumer Contracts Regulations 1999, SI 1999/2083. . . . . 46, 78
2002 Housing (Scotland) Act 2001 (Scottish Secure Tenancy etc) Order 2002, SSI 2002/318 . . . 39
2009 Company and Business Names (Miscellaneous Provisions) Regulations 2009,
      SI 2009/1085
      sch 2 para 1(a). 52
2010 Applications by Creditors (Pre-Action Requirements) (Scotland) Order 2012,
      SSI 2010/317. 198
      art 3(1)(e) 196
2011 Tenancy Deposit Schemes (Scotland) Regulations 2011, SSI 2011/176 . . . . 41, 42, 43
2012 Homeowner Housing Panel (Applications and Decisions) (Scotland) Regulations 2012,
      SSI 2012/180
      reg 3 24
2014 Land and Buildings Transaction Tax (Scotland) Act 2013 (Commencement No 1)
      Order 2014, SSI 2014/279. 204
      Landfill Tax (Scotland) Act 2014 (Commencement No 1) Order 2014, SSI 2014/277 . . . 204
      Registers of Scotland (Fees) Order 2014, SSI 2014/188
      art 4 81
      Revenue Scotland and Tax Powers Act 2014 (Commencement No 1) Order 2014,
      SSI 2014/278. 210
      Revenue Scotland and Tax Powers Act 2014 (Commencement No 2) Order 2014,
      SSI 2014/370. 210
2015 Community Empowerment (Scotland) Act 2015 (Commencement No 3 and Savings)
      Order 2015, SSI 2015/399. 76
      Community Right to Buy (Scotland) Regulations 2015, SSI 2015/400
      reg 1(3). 77
      Consumer Rights Act 2015 (Commencement No 3, Transitional Provisions, Savings
      and Consequential Amendments) Order 2015, SI 2015/1630. 78

2015   Devolution of Landfill Tax (Consequential, Transitional and Savings Provisions)
           Order 2015, SI 2015/599 204
       Housing (Scotland) Act 2014 (Commencement No 2) Order 2015, SSI 2015/122
           art 2 . . . . 113, 193
       Housing (Scotland) Act 2014 (Commencement No 3 and Transitional Provisions)
           Order 2015, SSI 2015/272. 81
       Income Tax (Limit for Rent-a-Room Relief) Order 2015, SI 2015/1539. 213
       Land and Buildings Transaction Tax (Open-ended Investment Companies) (Scotland)
           Regulations 2015, SSI 2015/322 209
       Land and Buildings Transaction Tax (Scotland) Act 2013 (Commencement No 2)
           Order 2015, SSI 2015/108. 204
       Land and Buildings Transaction Tax (Sub-sale Development Relief and Multiple
           Dwellings Relief) (Scotland) Order 2015, SSI 2015/123
           art 7 208
           arts 8, 9 209
       Land and Buildings Transaction Tax (Tax Rates and Tax Bands) (Scotland) Order 2015,
           SSI 2015/126
           arts 2, 3, 4 205
           sch, tables A, B, C. 205
       Landfill Tax (Scotland) Act 2014 (Commencement No 2) Order 2015, SSI 205/19 204
       Landfill Tax (Scotland) Act 2014 (Commencement No 3 and Transitional Provisions)
           Order 2015, SSI 2015/109. 204
       Legal Writings (Counterparts and Delivery) (Scotland) Act 2015 (Commencement)
           Order 2015, SSI 2015/242. . . . . 75, 125, 167
       Mortgage Credit Directive Order 2015, SI 2015/910 . . . . 78, 157
       Mortgage Credit Directive (Amendment) Order 2015, SI 2015/1557. 78
       Private Rented Housing Panel (Landlord Applications) (Scotland) Regulations 2015,
           SSI 2015/403. 81
       Private Rented Housing Panel (Tenant and Third Party Applications) (Scotland)
           Regulations 2015, SSI 2015/369 81
       Private Rented Housing (Scotland) Act 2011 (Commencement No 7) Order 2015,
           SSI 2015/326. 81
       Property Factors (Registration) (Scotland) Amendment Regulations 2015,
           SSI 2015/217. 82
       Registers of Scotland (Voluntary Registration, Amendment of Fees, etc) Order 2015,
           SSI 2015/265. . . . . 80, 99
           art 3 81
       Revenue Scotland and Tax Powers Act 2014 (Commencement No 3) Order 2015,
           SSI 2015/18 210
       Revenue Scotland and Tax Powers Act 2014 (Commencement No 4) Order 2015,
           SSI 2015/110. 210
       Revenue Scotland and Tax Powers Act (Fees for Payment) Regulations 2015,
           SSI 2015/36 210
       Revenue Scotland and Tax Powers Act (Interest on Unpaid Tax and Interest Rates in
           General) Regulations 2015, SSI 2015/128. 210
       Revenue Scotland and Tax Powers Act (Postponement of Tax Pending a Review or
           Appeal) Regulations 2015, SSI 2015/129 210
       Revenue Scotland and Tax Powers Act (Privileged Communications) Regulations 2015,
           SSI 2015/38 210
       Revenue Scotland and Tax Powers Act (Record Keeping) Regulations 2015,
           SSI 2015/130. 210

2015   Revenue Scotland and Tax Powers Act (Reimbursement Arrangements) Regulations
         2015, SSI 2015/131 210
       Scotland Act 2012, Section 29 (Disapplication of UK Stamp Duty Land Tax) (Appointed
         Day) Order 2015, SI 2015/637 204
       Scotland Act 2012, Section 31 (Disapplication of UK Landfill Tax) (Appointed Day)
         Order 2015, SI 2015/638 204
       Scottish Landfill Tax (Exemption Certificates) Order 2015, SSI 2015/151 209
       Scottish Landfill Tax (Qualifying Material) Order 2015, SSI 2015/45 209
       Scottish Landfill Tax (Standard Rate and Lower Rate) Order 2015, SSI 2015/127. 209
2016   Community Right to Buy (Scotland) Amendment Regulations 2016, SSI 2016/4. 77

TABLE OF CASES

AMA (New Town) Ltd v Law [2013] CSIH 61, 2013 SC 608 7
Aberdeen Varieties Ltd v James F Donald (Aberdeen Cinemas) Ltd 1939 SC 788 148–49
Advice Centre for Mortgages Ltd v McNicoll [2006] CSOH 58, 2006 SLT 591 165
Akram v Ahmad 2015 GWD 6-128 52
Alexander v West Bromwich Mortgage Co Ltd [2015] EWHC 135 (Comm), [2015] 2 All ER
   (Comm) 224 . . . . 57, 155–58
Alvis v Harrison 1991 SLT 64 178
Anderson v Brattisanni's 1978 SLT (Notes) 42 159–60
Anderson v Dickens [2008] CSOH 134, 2009 SCLR 609 70
Arnold v Britton [2015] UKSC 36, [2015] AC 1619 . . . . 45, 47
Aronson v Keeper of the Registers of Scotland [2014] CSOH 176, 2015 SLT 122 102–03
Auld v Hay (1880) 7 R 663 63

BAM Buchanan Ltd v Arcadia Group Ltd [2013] CSOH 107A, 2013 Hous LR 42 49
BNP Paribas Securities Services Trust Co (Jersey) Ltd v Mothercare (UK) Ltd [2015] CSOH 47,
   2015 Hous LR 42 48
Balfour v Keeper of the Registers of Scotland 2015 SLT (Lands Tr) 185 31
Bank of Ireland (UK) plc v Knight Frank LLP [2015] CSOH 157, 2015 GWD 40-627 59
Barton v McAllister, April 2015, Stranraer Sh Ct 10, 177
Beatsons Building Supplies Ltd v Trustees of the Alex F Noble & Son Ltd Executive Benefits
   Scheme 2015 GWD 15-271 49
Ben Cleuch Estates Ltd v Scottish Enterprise [2008] CSIH 1, 2008 SC 252 170
Blemain Finance Ltd v Balfour & Manson LLP [2012] CSIH 66, 2013 SC 160 174
Boyle v South Lanarkshire Council 2015 SLT (Lands Tr) 189, 2015 Hous LR 99 (merits),
   2015 SLT (Lands Tr) 205 (expenses) 39
Brand's Trs v Brand's Trs (1876) 3 R (HL) 16 166
Brown v Stonegale Ltd [2013] CSOH 189, 2014 GWD 2-27 . . . . 66, 67
Brown v Stonegale Ltd [2015] CSIH 12, 2015 SCLR 619 65
Burgerking Ltd v Rachel Charitable Trust [2006] CSOH 13, 2006 SLT 224 50
Butt v Galloway Motor Co Ltd 1996 SC 261 62

Campbell-Gray v Keeper of the Registers of Scotland 2015 SLT (Lands Tr) 147 (merits),
   31 March 2015 (expenses), Lands Tr 30, 62, 65
Candleberry Ltd v West End Homeowners Association [2006] CSIH 28, 2006 SC 636 10–11
Carr-Glynn v Frearsons [1998] 4 All ER 225 61
Chalmers v Chalmers [2014] CSOH 161, 2014 GWD 38-699; *revd* [2015] CSIH 75, 2015, SLT 793,
   2015 Hous LR 82 . . . . 24, 200–03
Cheltenham and Gloucester plc v Krausz [1997] 1 WLR 1558 199
Cheshire Mortgage Corporation Ltd v Grandison [2012] CSIH 66, 2013 SC 160 174
Collins v Hotel in the Skye Ltd 2015 GWD 12-200 3

Cordiner v Al-Shaibany 2015 SLT (Sh Ct) 189 43
Cumbernauld Housing Partnership Ltd v Davies [2015] CSIH 22, 2015 SC 532,
    2015 SCLR 459. . . . . 23, 189–92
Currie v Campbell's Trs (1886) 16 R 237. 65

Dem-Master Demolition Ltd v Healthcare Environmental Services Ltd [2015] CSOH 154,
    2015 GWD 38-604 52
Dickens v Anderson [2015] CSOH 161, 2016 GWD 3-63. 70
Dodd v Southern Pacific Loans Ltd [2007] CSOH 9, 2007 GWD 21-352 202
Douglas & Angus Estates v McAllister [2015] CSIH 2, 2015 SC 411 25
Dunvale Investments Ltd v Burness Paull & Williamsons LLP [2015] CSOH 32,
    2015 SCLR 567. 58

ELB Securities Ltd v Love 2014 GWD 28-562. 55
ELB Securities Ltd v Love [2015] CSIH 67, 2015 SLT 721, 2015 Hous LR 88 54
East Lothian Council v Keeper of the Registers of Scotland 2016 GWD 4-91 32
Ellice's Trs v Commissioners of the Caledonian Canal (1904) 6 F 325 17
English Welsh and Scottish Railway Ltd v E.ON UK plc [2007] EWHC 599 (Comm) 146

Ferguson v Gunby 2015 SLT (Lands Tr) 195 18
Ferguson v Paul (1885) 12 R 1222 . . . . 165, 166
Fortune's Tr v Cooper Watson Ltd [2015] CSOH 140, 2015 GWD 34-553 . . . . . . 68, 180, 183–86
Fortune's Tr v Medwin Investments Ltd [2015] CSOH 139, 2015 GWD 34-552 . . . 68, 180, 183–86
Fowlie v Watson, 9 July 2013, Peterhead Sheriff Court 14, 177

Gardner v Kerr, 27 July 2015, Airdrie Sh Ct. 12, 177
Gibson v Royal Bank of Scotland plc [2009] CSOH 14, 2009 SLT 444. 165
Gilchrist v McClure Naismith LLP [2015] CSOH 134, 2015 GWD 33-533 . . . . 59, 165
Glasgow City Council v Chaudhry 2015 SLT (Sh Ct) 107 56
Gloag v Perth and Kinross Council 2007 SCLR 530 180
Gordon's Trs v Campbell Riddle Breeze Paterson LLP [2015] CSOH 31, 2015 GWD 12-216. . . . 58
Grant v Cameron 1991 GWD 6-328 . . . . 176–78, 180
Grant v National Trust for Scotland, 5 May 2015, Lands Tr 22
Grant & Wilson Property Management Ltd v Egbuka 2015 SLT (Sh Ct) 193,
    2015 Hous LR 30 23
Greenbelt Property Ltd v Riggens 2010 GWD 28-586 . . . . 141, 147
Greig v Davidson [2015] CSOH 44, 2015 SCLR 722 57
Grove Investments Ltd v Cape Building Products Ltd [2014] CSIH 43, 2014 Hous LR 35 . . . 5, 47
Gyle Shopping Centre General Partners Ltd v Marks and Spencer plc [2014] CSOH 59,
    2014 GWD 18-352; [2014] CSOH 122, 2015 SCLR 171; [2015] CSOH 14, 2015 GWD 6-127. . . . 49

Hamilton v Campbell Smith WS 2015 GWD 10-174 60
Henderson v Foxworth Investments Ltd [2014] UKSC 41, 2014 SC (UKSC) 203 154
Heritage Fisheries Ltd v Duke of Roxburghe 2000 SLT 800 149
Homebase Ltd v Grantchester Developments (Falkirk) Ltd [2015] CSOH 49,
    2015 Hous LR 38 50
Homebase Ltd v Hammersons (Kirkcaldy) Ltd [2015] CSOH 50 50

Ikbal v Sterling Law [2013] EWHC 3291 (Ch), [2014] PNLR 9 173
Inverclyde Council v McCloskey 2015 SLT (Sh Ct) 57, 2015 Hous LR 14 53
Ireland v Dundee City Council 2015 GWD 40-635 39
Islington Council v Panayi, 16 October 2015, Blackfriars Crown Court 69

Jack v Jack [2015] CSOH 91, 2015 Fam LR 95 71
Jenson v Fappiano 2015 GWD 4-89 41
Johnson v Old [2013] EWCA Civ 415, [2013] HLR 26 43
Jones v Muir 2015 GWD 11-183 . . . . 61, 161

Kennedy Ptrs [2015] CSOH 103, 2015 GWD 25-436 4
Kenwright v Stuart Milne Group Ltd [2015] CSOH 86, 2015 GWD 22-389 10
Kinch Ltd v Adams 2015 GWD 5-105 . . . . 3, 170–71
Kirk v Singh 2015 SLT (Sh Ct) 111 42

Lee v Highland Council 2015 GWD 38-601 40
Leonard v Lindsay (1886) 13 R 958 158
Letham Grange Development Co Ltd (Liquidator of) v Foxworth Investments Ltd [2014]
    UKSC 41, 2014 SC (UKSC) 203 68
Lloyds TSB Bank plc v Markandan & Uddin [2012] EWCA Civ 65, [2012] 2 All ER 884 . . 172, 173
Lock v Taylor 1976 SLT 238 25
Lorimer Homes Pittodrie Ltd v Greig 2011 GWD 33-697 57
Lundin Homes Ltd v Keeper of the Registers of Scotland 2013 SLT (Lands Tr) 73 138

Macallans v W Burrell Homes Ltd 2015 SLT (Sh Ct) 243 70
McGraddie v McGraddie [2013] UKSC 58, 2014 SC (UKSC) 12 154
MacKay v McGowan 2015 SLT (Lands Tr) 6 22
McKenna v Keeper of the Registers of Scotland, 21 Aug 2015, Lands Tr 33
Mackenzie v British Linen Co (1881) 8 R (HL) 8 202
McLellan v J & D Pierce [2015] CSIH 80, 2015 GWD 37-594 . . . . 61, 159
McManus v City Link Development Co Ltd [2015] CSOH 178, 2016 GWD 6-126 55
MacPherson v MacQueen [2015] CSIH 60, 2015 GWD 26-449 5
Magistrates of Edinburgh v North British Railway Co (1904) 6 F 620 17
Malin v Crown Aerosols UK Ltd [2015] CSOH 58, 2015 GWD 17-290 43
Mannai Investment Co Ltd v Eagle Star Life Assurance Co Ltd [1997] AC 749 170
Mapeley Acquisition Co (3) Ltd (in receivership) v City of Edinburgh Council [2015] CSOH 29,
    2015 GWD 13-234 48
Mark v City of Edinburgh Council 2015 SLT (Lands Tr) 157 40
Marks and Spencer plc v BNP Paribas Securities Services Trust Co (Jersey) Ltd [2013] EWHC
    1279 (Ch); [2014] EWCA Civ 603; [2015] UKSC 72, [2015] 3 WLR 1843 44–45
Marriott v Greenbelt Group Ltd, 2 Dec 2015, Lands Tr 9, 17, 46, 138–51
Mather v Alexander 1926 SC 139 25
Menking Ptr 2015 SLT (Lyon Ct) 21 36
Miller Homes Ltd v Keeper of the Registers of Scotland 2014 SLT (Lands Tr) 79 138
Mitchell v Reilly, 11 July 2006, Glasgow Sh Ct 23, 177, 187–89
Muir's Exrs v Craig's Trs 1913 SC 349 202
Munro v Finlayson 2015 SLT (Sh Ct) 123 . . . . 61, 160

Nationwide Building Society v Davisons Solicitors [2012] EWCA Civ 1626, [2013] PNLR 12 . . 173
Nicol v Keeper of the Registers of Scotland 2013 SLT (Lands Tr) 56 33
North British Railway Co Ltd v Park Yard Co Ltd (1898) 25 R (HL) 47 14
Norwich Union Life Insurance Society v Shopmoor [1999] 1 WLR 531 50
Nova Scotia Ltd (3052775) v Henderson [2015] CSOH 126, 2015 SLT 691 67

Omale v Barcenas 2015 GWD 8-157 42

PDPF GP Ltd v Santander UK plc [2015] CSOH 40, 2015 Hous LR 45 . . . . 75, 167
PIP 3 Ltd v Glasgow City Council [2015] CSOH 119, 2015 GWD 29-486. 48
PMP Plus Ltd v Keeper of the Registers of Scotland 2009 SLT (Lands Tr) 2 . . . . 138, 149–51
Park Ptrs (No 2) [2009] CSOH 122, 2009 SLT 871 . . . . 75, 167
Playfair Investments Ltd v McElvogue [2012] CSOH 148, 2012 GWD 30-611 193
Pocock's Tr v Skene Investments (Aberdeen) Ltd [2011] CSOH 144, 2011 GWD 30-654 108
Portobello Park Action Group Association v City of Edinburgh Council [2012] CSIH 69,
    2013 SC 184 90

R (Newhaven Port & Properties Ltd) v East Sussex County Council [2015] UKSC 7,
    [2015] AC 1547 16
Rainy Sky v Kookmin Bank plc [2011] UKSC 50, [2011] 1 WLR 2900 5
Ramsden v Santon Highlands Ltd [2015] CSOH 65, 2015 GWD 20-332; [2015] CSOH 66 8
Reid v Aberdeen Cafe Co Ltd 2015 GWD 12-205. 178–80
Reid v Haldane's Trs (1891) 18 R 744 65
Rivendale v Clark [2015] CSIH 27, 2015 SC 558 . . . . 26, 63
Rivendale v Keeper of the Registers of Scotland, 30 Oct 2013, Lands Tr 26, 64
River Clyde Homes Ltd v Woods 2015 Hous LR 33 (relevancy), 2015 GWD 33-542 (proof) 54
Royal Bank of Scotland plc v Carlyle [2010] CSOH 3, 2010 GWD 13-235 . . . . 70, 151–52
Royal Bank of Scotland plc v Carlyle [2013] CSIH 75, 2014 SC 188. . . . . 70, 151, 153
Royal Bank of Scotland plc v Carlyle [2015] UKHL 13, 2015 SC (UKSC) 93, 2015 SLT 206. . . . 69,
                                                                                                151–54
Royal Bank of Scotland plc v Wilson [2010] UKSC 50, 2011 SC (UKSC) 66 . . . . 45, 102–03

STV Central Ltd v Semple Fraser LLP [2014] CSOH 82, 2014 GWD 16-299 51
STV Central Ltd v Semple Fraser LLP [2015] CSIH 35, 2015 SLT 313 50
Safeway Stores plc v Tesco Stores Ltd 2004 SC 29 31
Santander UK v RA Legal Solicitors [2014] EWCA Civ 183, [2014] PNLR 20 173
Schubert Murphy v The Law Society [2014] EWHC 4561 (QB), [2015] PNLR 15 . . . . . 60, 172–73
Scott v Muir 2012 SLT (Sh Ct) 179 53
Sebry v Companies House [2015] EWHC 115 (QB), [2015] 4 All ER 681 35
Shetland Islands Council v BP Petroleum Development Ltd 1990 SLT 82 166
Shilliday v Smith 1998 SC 725 163
Sinton v Lloyd, 11 June 2014, Lands Tr 19, 148
Sipp (Pension Trustees) Ltd (@) v Insight Travel Services Ltd [2014] CSOH 137,
    2014 Hous LR 54; [2015] CSIH 91, 2016 SLT 131 47
Smith v Duke of Gordon (1701) Mor 16987 125
Sneddon v Scottish Legal Complaints Commission [2015] CSIH 62, 2015 GWD 26-458 . 60, 133–37
Sturzenegger Ptr (No 2) 2015 SLT (Lyon Ct) 2 35
Swift Advances plc v Martin [2015] CSIH 65, 2015 Hous LR 50 . . . . 56, 197–99

Tailors of Aberdeen v Coutts (1840) 1 Rob 296 141
Tenzin v Russell 2014 Hous LR 17; [2015] CSIH 8A, 2015 Hous LR 11 41
Thomas v Santon Highlands Ltd [2015] CSOH 67 8
Trustunion LLC, Noters [2015] CSOH 38, 2015 GWD 13-223 69

United Investment Co Ltd v Charlie Reid Travel Ltd 2016 GWD 1-13 22
University Court of the University of St Andrews v Headon Holdings Ltd [2015] CSOH 113,
    2015 GWD 27-464 9

Van Lynden v Gilchrist [2015] CSOH 147, 2015 SLT 864. . . . . 54, 163, 165, 166
Voudouri v HM Advocate 2003 SCCR 448, 2008 JC 431 69

West Dunbartonshire Council v William Thompson and Son (Dumbarton) Ltd [2015] CSIH 93,
   2016 SLT 125. 51
West Register (Property Investments) Ltd v Lord Advocate, 11 March 2015, Selkirk Sh Ct 37
Westfoot Investments Ltd v European Property Holdings Inc 2015 SLT (Sh Ct) 201, 2015
   Hous LR 57 . . . . 56, 194–97
Whitelaw v Acheson, 29 Feb 2012, Lands Tr 19
Wight v Keeper of the Registers of Scotland 2015 SLT (Lands Tr) 195, 2015 Hous LR 93 28

Yule v Tobert 2015 GWD 39-620 (merits), 4 Dec 2015 (expenses), Lands Tr 20

PART I

CASES

CASES

MISSIVES OF SALE

(1) Kinch Ltd v Adams
2015 GWD 5-105, Sh Ct

An e-mail which purported to exercise a right to withdraw from missives was held to be too vague to take effect. See **Commentary** p 170.

(2) Collins v Hotel in the Skye Ltd
2015 GWD 12-200, Sh Ct

This was a dispute arising out of the sale of the Flodigarry Country House Hotel on the Isle of Skye. The missives provided, in clause 8.1, that:

> With effect from the Completion Date, the Seller will (a) procure the transfer or novation of such of the Business Contracts (where the contracts are capable of transfer or novation) as are listed at numbers 1 to 4 inclusive in Part 2 of the Schedule and (b) the Business Contracts listed in part 6 of the Schedule and in all cases the Buyer shall accept all responsibility for and obligations under such contracts with effect from the Completion Date, all at the Buyer's own cost.

As it turned out, there were some difficulties with this clause: the contracts were listed in part 3, not part 2, of the schedule, and none was listed in part 6. The dispute, however, concerned a contract which, the parties accepted, *was* covered by the clause. This was a contract between the seller and Peninsula Business Services Ltd for the provision of services including employment advice and health and safety advice. The total fee was £14,400, payable monthly. The contract ran for five years, beginning in March 2011, so that at the time of the completion of the sale, in June 2013, the liability for the remaining period stood at £6,400.

In the event, Peninsula refused to allow the buyer to take over the contract but instead offered new contractual terms – at double the original rate – which the buyer refused to accept. That refusal left the original contract still in place. Peninsula was entitled to payment, but who had to pay? In a question with Peninsula, liability was of course with the seller. But in this action the seller sought to recover this amount from the buyer by virtue of clause 8.1.

In the interpretation of a business contract, provisions fall to be construed according to the commercial purpose of the contract and in its overall commercial context. There is ample authority for this approach, and it was accepted by both sides as applying. As, however, this was a debate and not a proof, the sheriff (N A Ross) was limited in identifying the commercial context to the terms of the contract itself; and as these terms did not give any clear guidance on the point at issue, the matter ultimately rested on the wording used in clause 8.1.

At least with hindsight, clause 8.1 was less clear than might have been wished. 'It is this kind of late-night, red-eye drafting', said the sheriff (para 13), 'which is frequently found to obstruct, sometimes to the point of confounding, the efforts of courts in attempting to bridge the gap between the principles to be applied to inferring the parties' intentions and the perplexing reality of how the parties have expressed themselves.' That 'perplexing reality', however, now fell to be interpreted.

The clause was in two distinct parts. In the first, the seller bound itself to procure the transfer or novation of the contract; in the second, the buyer bound itself to accept the obligations under 'such contracts' with effect from the completion deed. The crucial question was the relationship between the two parts. Was the buyer to be liable for all contracts, whether transferred (or novated) or not? Or, rather, was the reference to 'such contracts' a reference only to those contracts which were transferred (or novated)? Naturally, the seller argued for the first interpretation and the buyer for the second.

In a long and careful judgment, the sheriff ultimately came down in favour of the second interpretation. If the parties had intended the buyer to indemnify the seller in respect of all contracts, 'one would expect the language of indemnity to be used' (para 32) – which it was not. Furthermore, for the buyer to have liability even for contracts which were not transferred – contracts which could not be enforced against the buyer and in respect of which the buyer had no say – would be an uncommercial result. The seller's action was dismissed.

(3) Kennedy Ptrs
[2015] CSOH 103, 2015 GWD 25-436

A development company, Dickie & Moore Holdings Ltd ('DMH'), concluded missives to buy land (6.293 hectares at Doonholm, Alloway, Ayrshire) with a view to building houses on it, if planning consent could be obtained. Later DMH withdrew from the missives but continued to pursue a planning application in the hope that funders or other developers might show interest. Keen to recover the cost of the expenditure involved, DMH then entered into a minute of agreement with the sellers in the following terms:

> [I]t has been agreed between the parties that in the event of the Sellers concluding unconditional ... missives with a third party for the sale of the said subjects ... during the shorter of the period when the Planning Consent obtained or to be obtained by DMH for the development of the said subjects remains extant and the period of five years from the date of these presents, as the case shall be, the Sellers will reimburse DMH the full amount of the said professional fees together with any further professional fees (up to a maximum of £10,000) incurred by DMH in obtaining such Planning Consent.

In the event, no planning consent was obtained.

When the site was sold on to Miller Homes Ltd within the five-year period, DMH sought reimbursement of its costs. A dispute then arose as to the meaning of the minute of agreement. For the sellers it was argued (i) that the resale must occur within the *shorter* of two periods, ie the duration of the planning consent and five years, and (ii) that, as no planning consent had been obtained, the duration of the planning consent was zero. Therefore resale had not occurred within the stipulated period. For DMH it was argued that planning consent and the five-year period were alternatives so that, if the first period did not apply, then matters were governed by the second.

The Lord Ordinary (Lady Stacey) accepted that the minute of agreement was ambiguous and hence that cases such as *Rainy Sky v Kookmin Bank plc* [2011] UKSC 50, [2011] 1 WLR 2900 and *Grove Investments Ltd v Cape Building Products Ltd* [2014] CSIH 43, 2014 Hous LR 35 (*Conveyancing 2014* Case (41)) applied. The effect of these cases was agreed by counsel (para 73):

> I accept the submissions made by both counsel to the effect that the task of the court is to consider what the reasonable person, armed with the information that the parties reasonably had at the time of entering into the contract, would consider was meant by the words of the contract. I accept that the construction should, if there is a choice, favour a commercially sensible outcome. I am bound by the case of *Grove Investments* to proceed in that fashion. The words of the contract are to be read as a whole, and if possible meaning given to all of them. I am not concerned to find out what the parties intended to agree, but rather what in the context of the facts agreed or proved, their words show that they did agree. I have reached my view by considering all of the circumstances known to both parties. I have not relied on internal communications known to only one of them.

After a proof, which was concerned with the background to the minute of agreement, Lady Stacey found in favour of DMH's interpretation (para 79):

> I find that the petitioners [the sellers] agreed to make payment to the respondents [DMH] of the sum in the Minute of Agreement because they wished to encourage the respondents to proceed with their planning application during the period when the petitioners were looking for a third party to purchase the site. The agreement does not, however, provide that the payment will be made only if the respondents are successful in obtaining planning permission. If that had been the intention then it would not have been drafted as it has been drafted. It would not have been difficult to draft an agreement which stated plainly that payment was dependent on the respondents obtaining planning permission. It would not have been difficult to draft a condition putting a time limit on liability.

Accordingly, the sellers were liable to make payment to DMH.

(4) MacPherson v MacQueen
[2015] CSIH 60, 2015 GWD 26-449

The defenders concluded missives to buy property (at North Connel, by Oban) from the pursuers after which, so far as we know, the transaction proceeded to settlement without incident. The present litigation concerned clause 7 of the contract, by which the defenders agreed in turn to convey a strip of land (which they already owned) to the pursuers and to grant a servitude in respect of another area. This was in order to allow the pursuers to develop adjacent land, on which they proposed to build houses.

Clause 7 was in the following terms:

> Subject to the approval of our clients' [ie the defenders'] mortgage lenders they will convey to your clients the strip of ground coloured yellow on the title plan and grant a servitude right of access in favour of your clients [ie the pursuers] over the strip shown coloured green on the plan which two strips of ground form part of the subjects owned by our clients at 35 Lora View, North Connell, by Oban however this is a separate matter and it is not a condition of the Missives that it be completed prior to the date of entry.

The action was for declarator and specific implement, which failing for damages of £200,000. The main defence was that the two years provided for in the supersession clause having passed, clause 7 had ceased to be enforceable.

The contract was subject to the Combined Standard Clauses, clause 22 of which provided that:

> The Missives shall cease to be enforceable after a period of 2 years from the Date of Settlement except insofar as (i) they are founded upon in any court proceedings which have commenced within the said period or (ii) this provision is excluded in terms of any other condition of the Missives.

The 'Missives' were defined as '... the contract of purchase and sale concluded between the Purchaser and the Seller of which the Offer incorporating reference to these clauses forms part'.

The question to be determined was whether clause 7 was a term of the 'missives' (as so defined) or whether it was a completely separate contract which just happened to be included in the same contract letters as the missives proper. If the former, the supersession clause applied and the obligation was at an end; if the latter, the supersession clause did not apply and clause 7 remained in force.

At first instance, the sheriff opted for the second interpretation. In doing so, he was influenced by the rider at the end of clause 7, although the rider supported that interpretation only in the incomplete and inaccurate version quoted by the sheriff ('this is a separate matter and not a condition of the missives'): see *Conveyancing 2014* Case (2). The defenders appealed.

An Extra Division of the Court of Session has now allowed the appeal. Its reasons for doing so are cogent. The obligations on the defenders in clause 7 were as much part of the consideration as the payment of the purchase price itself. If that were not so – if clause 7 were truly unconnected with the sale of the property – then the obligations in that clause would fall to be performed, without payment, even if the sale itself had fallen through. 'That seems so unlikely, if not absurd, an outcome that we consider it strongly supports the construction urged on us by the defenders' (para 26). Finally, when the rider to clause 7 was quoted correctly and in full, it gave no support to the view of a separation of obligations. '[I]t is not the obligations themselves that are not a condition of the missives. Rather, what is not a condition is that they required to be performed prior to the date of entry' (para 25).

The decision is noted by Gordon Junor in 'Non-supersession clauses – the continuing story' (2015) 83 *Scottish Law Gazette* 53.

(5) PIP 3 Ltd v Glasgow City Council
[2015] CSOH 119, 2015 GWD 29-486

In December 2011 the parties entered into an agreement which gave PIP 3 Ltd an option to buy a brownfield site in the east end of Glasgow from Glasgow City Council. A year later PIP 3 exercised the option but failed to pay the price at the settlement date (11 April 2013). When the Council rescinded the agreement, on 4 July 2013, PIP 3 challenged its right to do so. In this action PIP 3 claimed £15,372,790 in damages for its loss of the profit which, it was said, the completed development would have brought. The Council denied any breach of contract, arguing that it had been fully entitled to rescind.

PIP 3 explained its failure to pay the price on the basis that, as at the settlement date, the Council had been in breach of (i) clause 4.1 of the agreement, and (ii) condition 8.7 of the 'missives' (ie the provisions in part 1 of the schedule to the agreement which governed the exercise of the option). The Lord Ordinary (Lord Woolman) rejected both arguments and dismissed PIP 3's claim insofar as it related to breach of contract.

In relation to (i), Lord Woolman emphasised that clause 1.7 of the missives, which prevented rescission where the Council was itself in breach, applied only in respect of breaches of the seller's obligations under the missives. Clause 4.1 was contained in the agreement proper. But in any event, it had not been breached. Clause 4.1 provided that

> In so far as not already done, as soon as reasonably practicable after the Effective Date and in any event no later than the Settlement Date, the Council shall instruct the Remediation Consultant to undertake the Materials Classification Exercise and to prepare the Site Waste Management Plan and the Materials Management Plan. The Council will provide PIP 3 with a copy of both the Site Waste Management Plan and the Materials Management Plan as soon as reasonably practicable upon receipt thereof.

According to the PIP 3, the Council was in breach by failing to provide either plan by the settlement date. But that was to misread the clear words of the clause. The Council's only obligation was to 'instruct' the plans by the settlement date, and that had been done. To uphold PIP 3's construction would involve 'the rewriting of the contract' (para 27).

In relation to (ii), condition 8.7 required delivery of the disposition, titles and other documents 'in exchange' for the price. In *AMA (New Town) Ltd v Law* [2013] CSIH 61, 2013 SC 608, the Inner House interpreted missives of sale as requiring that the price should be paid *before* the seller delivered the disposition – in other words, that performance should be sequential and not simultaneous. That view seems open to question (see *Conveyancing 2013* pp 126–31), but it was binding on, and so followed by, Lord Woolman in *PIP 3 Ltd*. As, therefore, PIP 3 had to pay first but did not do so, there could be no breach by the Council in failing to deliver the disposition and other documents. We would observe that the result would have been the same even if, as we think the law to be, the reciprocal obligations of the parties are to be performed simultaneously. In order for one party to be bound to perform, the other must also, simultaneously, perform.

Even if PIP 3 had succeeded in establishing a relevant case for breach of contract, it would have failed, Lord Woolman held, in respect of the measure of damages sought. That measure was based on the supposition that PIP 3 would have carried out the development. Yet PIP 3 had a detailed alternative case, the relevance of which was not challenged, for misrepresentation, averring that it would not have entered into the agreement in the first place – far less exercised the purchase option and proceeded with the development – had it known of certain facts (the depositing of significant amounts of hazardous waste) which the Council failed to disclose. PIP 3 could not have it both ways (para 54):

> I agree with Mr Dunlop [senior counsel for the Council] that the whole thrust of PIP 3's pleadings indicate that this is a 'no transaction' case. It is not compatible with substantial justice to allow it to proceed to proof based on one sentence in Condescendence 11 that contradicts the rest of the pleadings. The Council is entitled to know the case it faces: *Morrison v Rendall* 1986 SC 69. The corollary is that PIP 3 is not entitled to embark on an expedition based on hope.

(6) Ramsden v Santon Highlands Ltd
[2015] CSOH 65, 2015 GWD 20-332

(7) Ramsden v Santon Highlands Ltd
[2015] CSOH 66

(8) Thomas v Santon Highlands Ltd
[2015] CSOH 67

All three cases arose out of the sale by a developer, Santon Highlands Ltd, of plots of land at Courtyard Cottages, The Highland Club, Fort Augustus. In terms of each set of missives, purchasers were to receive, in addition to the plot in question, a right of common property in certain common areas. Later it turned out that parts of the common areas were contaminated land. In each of these actions the purchasers sought reduction of the missives and disposition. The basis of their actions is not entirely clear but seems to have been (i) that the purchasers were consumers; (ii) that, accordingly, Santon Highlands was subject to the Consumer Protection from Unfair Trading Regulations 2008, SI 2008/1277; and (iii) that, in terms of reg 6 of the 2008 Regulations, Santon Highlands had been bound to disclose that the land was contaminated.

The actions were dismissed as irrelevant. Regulation 29 of the 2008 Regulations stated that: 'Except as provided by Part 4A, an agreement shall not be void or unenforceable by reason only of a breach of these Regulations'. (Part 4A did not come into force until 1 October 2014, which was long after the missives were concluded. To this we would add that, in any event, Part 4A does not apply to immoveable property, with the exception of assured tenancies and holiday lets: see reg 27C.)

(9) Marriott v Greenbelt Group Ltd
2 December 2015, Lands Tr

This is the first case in Scotland to consider the application of the Unfair Terms in Consumer Contracts Regulations 1999, SI 1999/2083, to contracts for the sale of heritable property. The contract comprised builders' missives, the terms of which had not been individually negotiated. In the event, the clause under scrutiny was held not to be 'unfair'. See **Commentary** p 138.

It may be noted that with effect from 1 October 2015, the Unfair Terms in Consumer Contracts Regulations 1999 were replaced by part 2 of the Consumer Rights Act 2015: see p 78 below.

[Another aspect of this case is digested at (17) below.]

(10) University Court of the University of St Andrews
v Headon Holdings Ltd
[2015] CSOH 113, 2015 GWD 27-464

Various landowners and a developer entered into a joint-venture agreement for the purposes of obtaining planning consent for development of land ('an area of land to the west of St Andrews') and of optimising its sale. Later it turned out that one of the owners (a Mr Headon) held the land on a latent bare trust for another of the owners. On discovering this, the remaining owners raised an action for reduction of the joint-venture agreement on grounds of (i) misrepresentation, and (ii) breach of a duty of disclosure. They argued that they would not have entered into an agreement which gave Mr Headon equal rights of participation and control if they had known that he was no more than a bare trustee for the other owner. The Lord Ordinary (Lord Tyre) rejected both grounds and dismissed the action.

In relation to (i), the statements relied on – essentially that Mr Headon 'owned' the land in question – could not be regarded as misrepresentations because they were true. Mr Headon did indeed own the land. Lord Tyre continued (para 21):

 If it is correct to describe a person with a registered title to land as 'the landowner', then none of the statements objected to on the ground of the use of the word 'landowner' is inaccurate. The same applies to statements to the effect that the first defender [Mr Headon] had purchased land from the Cuthills; as narrated above, that was indeed the case. What the pursuers complain of is that the land was purchased, and title taken to it, subject to an agreement of which they were unaware regarding entitlement to the proceeds of the ultimate sale to the developer or a third party. That does not, however, of itself render what was said a misrepresentation. In my opinion there is no misrepresentation inherent in describing the first defender as the owner or landowner in respect of the Headon land; it was the holder of title to the land, and no-one else answered to that description. Specifically, it does not amount to a representation that the first defender was 'beneficial owner' in the sense in which that term is used by the pursuers.

In relation to (ii), parties entering into contracts were, the Lord Ordinary noted, not normally subject to a duty of disclosure and, while there could be exceptions such as in partnerships and contracts of insurance (Gloag on *Contract* (2nd edn, 1929) p 496), the present facts did not engage one of the exceptions.

(11) Kenwright v Stuart Milne Group Ltd
[2015] CSOH 86, 2015 GWD 22-389

This was a fact-specific case about the interpretation of an indemnity letter granted by developers to the owner of fields in respect of which a purchase option applied. The letter covered obligations due by the owner in respect of a s 75 agreement under the Town and Country Planning (Scotland) Act 1997. One obligation under the agreement was to convey an area of land to the Council. The developers accepted that they were liable to the owner for the costs of the conveyancing. What was in dispute was whether the indemnity letter extended to the value of the land which was to be conveyed (which was said to be £292,800). It was held that it did not.

SERVITUDES

(12) Barton v McAllister
April 2015, Stranraer Sheriff Court

By a disposition recorded in 1966, Kapemi Investment Co Ltd disponed to the Secretary of State for Scotland five separate and discontiguous areas of land. Two of those areas (Areas 1 and 2) came to be owned by the defenders. A third (Area 3) came to be owned by the pursuers. The present litigation arose because of the stated intention of the defenders to abstract timber from Areas 1 and 2 and transport it over a road within Area 3. The pursuers sought to prevent this by interdict. The defenders' case was that they were entitled to take access by virtue of a servitude.

The defenders had two main arguments. The first was (a) that the 1966 disposition created a servitude over the road in Area 3; (b) that such a servitude could not take effect for as long as all five areas were in the same ownership; but (c) when Areas 1 and 2 were separated off and disponed, in 1996, the disposition expressly conferred the rights of access and egress contained in the 1966 disposition, so that a servitude must be regarded as having come into existence at this point. *Candleberry Ltd v West End Homeowners Association* [2006] CSIH 28, 2006 SC 636 (discussed in *Conveyancing 2006* pp 12–13) was a case in point.

This was an enterprising argument. In *Candleberry* the servitudes were set out in a deed of conditions and so were plainly intended to burden and benefit the individual properties on severance. The same could not be said in the present case where a disposition had been used.

In the event, the sheriff, in an *ex tempore* judgment, was 'not impressed with this argument'. This was partly because a disposition was not the same as a deed of conditions. And it was also because, unlike in *Candleberry*, no new servitudes were set out in the deed. On the contrary, the disposition did no more than convey the land subject to the existing servitudes. Not only was there no specification as to what these servitudes might be, but 'it is inconceivable that it was in the contemplation of the parties that amongst these was a prospective servitude right of access in favour of the future proprietors of Auchness Moss [Area 1] and Grennan Moss [Area 2] over the future proprietor of Blackloch Plantation [Area 3]. That is nothing more than speculation.' We have not seen the disposition, but if the sheriff's account of it is accurate then his conclusion would appear to be correct.

The second argument turned on the terms of the title sheet in respect of Area 3 (WGN 179). In the D (burdens) section, the 1966 disposition formed the second entry; the first burden listed there was:

> All existing rights of way or access over the said subjects or over any roads, paths or rights of way forming part of the said subjects including without prejudice to the foregoing generality the route indicated by the brown tint on the Title Plan.

The route indicated by the brown tint was the route in respect of which the defenders claimed a servitude. This reference was reinforced by the third entry in the burdens section in respect of what appears to be the split-off disposition by the Secretary of State for Scotland in respect of Area 3. The first burden listed again referred to the route indicated by the brown tint:

> There is reserved to the proprietor or proprietors of the area of ground including Ravenstone Castle known as 'Lot Number 1' and other users thereof in terms of the Disposition in Entry 2 a servitude right of access along the route tinted brown on the Title Plan …

In the sheriff's view, these entries demonstrated the existence of the necessary servitude in the defenders' favour. Accordingly, interdict had to be refused.

This conclusion, however, seems open to question, for two reasons. First, the argument appears to rest mainly on the third entry in the burdens section. This reserved a servitude in favour not only of the proprietors of Ravenstone Castle (which did not, of course, include the defenders) but also of the 'other users thereof'. And 'other users thereof' was taken to mean other users *of the road*. As the Secretary of State, as owner of all five areas by virtue of the 1966 disposition, had had a right to use the road, and as the defenders were successors of the Secretary of State in respect of Areas 1 and 2, it was said to follow that the defenders fell within the servitude in the third entry. That view can be challenged. A reading at least as plausible as the one adopted by the sheriff is to say that 'other users thereof' refers, not to other users of the road, but to other users of the dominant tenement, ie Ravenstone Castle. On this view, the servitude was to be exercised not only by the proprietors of the Castle but also by other people who were using the Castle. This reading would confer no rights on the defenders.

But, secondly, even if the reading adopted by the sheriff was correct, it could confer a servitude only if the entry was an accurate transcription of the deed in question. There is an important difference here between entries in the A and B sections of a title sheet, and entries in the C and D sections. Entries in the former, under s 3(1)(a) of the Land Registration (Scotland) Act 1979, attracted 'the Midas touch'. They became valid (albeit in some circumstances potentially rectifiable) simply by being made. But entries under the latter (the D section) were Midas-free. If they were wrong, they remained wrong, and acquired no validity merely by being mentioned on the Register. The point was emphasised in the present case by the fact that the disposition in question had been registered in the Register of Sasines (in 1981) and not in the Land Register. Was the third entry in the D section right or wrong? The answer is that we do not know, for the disposition was not produced to the court. The most that can be said is that, insofar as the entry was intended as a summary rather than a full transcription of the disposition, it would carry the benefit of the presumption in s 6(2) of the 1979 Act that the summary was accurate; but such a presumption could of course be rebutted.

(13) Reid v Aberdeen Cafe Co Ltd
2015 GWD 12-205, Sh Ct

A servitude granted in 1822 conferred a right of access to 'disponees and tenants, but to no other persons'. It was held that the right could not be used by the public at large to access the dominant proprietor's café. See **Commentary** p 178.

(14) Gardner v Kerr
27 July 2015, Airdrie Sheriff Court

In 1948 James Gardner acquired a farm extending to 186.77 acres and known as Blacktongue Farm, Greengairs, Lanarkshire. Forty years later, in 1988, James Gardner disponed what he still owned of the Farm – which was most of it – to eight relatives, one of whom was John James Gardner. In 2003 the eight relatives disponed the farmhouse and some surrounding land to a Mr and Mrs Miller but retained the rest of the Farm. The disposition was executed and, it may be, delivered on 18 July 2003 but was not recorded until 12 March 2004. The subjects conveyed were described as forming part and portion of the farm and lands of Blacktongue extending to 186.77 acres or thereby. The disposition included the following reservation:

> There is reserved to us and our successors as proprietors of the remainder of Blacktongue ... heritable and irredeemable servitude right of access and egress over Blacktongue Farm Road for all purposes.

The effect of this reservation was to create an access servitude over Blacktongue Farm Road in favour of such parts of the Farm as the eight relatives did not convey in the disposition. That was not in dispute. But the position was complicated by the fact that, at around the same time as the disposition was granted, John James Gardner and his wife became owners of The Paddock, an area which had originally formed part of Blacktongue Farm but which had been split off 25 years earlier, in 1978. The disposition in favour of the Gardners was recorded on 10 November 2003, although entry had been taken (and the disposition presumably delivered) on 20 June 2003.

In this action, John James Gardner and his wife sought a declarator that, as owners of The Paddock, they had a servitude right of access along Blacktongue Farm Road. The defenders were the current owners of the farmhouse and road. The pursuers' argument was simple. (i) The 2003 disposition by the relatives reserved a servitude over the road 'to us and our successors as proprietors of the remainder of Blacktongue'. (ii) The first pursuer (John James Gardner) was one of the eight relatives. (iii) The first pursuer was also, at the material time, an owner of The Paddock, and The Paddock was historically part of Blacktongue. (iv) Hence the servitude reserved in the 2003 disposition was reserved in favour of The Paddock (among other properties).

This argument was rejected by the sheriff (Frank Pieri) at debate and the action was dismissed. There were three main grounds of rejection. First, on a proper construction, the reservation was in favour of the eight relatives as a group and not as individuals, with the result that the dominant tenement was, and was only, the parts of the Farm which the eight continued to own as a group. 'What the deed is concerned with is land owned by the disponers collectively as a group and not land owned by each disponer as an individual' (para 35).

Secondly, while the first pursuer was one of the eight, the second pursuer (his wife) was not. Yet The Paddock was owned by both pursuers. On the pursuers' interpretation, therefore, only the share of the first pursuer in The Paddock could qualify as a dominant tenement. But that was impossible, for a mere *pro indiviso* share cannot be a dominant tenement. It 'cannot be reconciled with the principle that servitudes go with the land and are not personal' (para 38).

Thirdly, the servitude was 'reserved' from the disposition. But this word had a special meaning (paras 40–41):

> It is inherent in the concept of reserving something that you possess it. Reserving means holding back something you have. The group of eight granters of the March 2004 Disposition had a right of access over Blacktongue Farm Road as it was part of the land they owned. When they disponed land including the road they were therefore clearly able to reserve a right of access over it. The title to The Paddock on the other hand contains no right of access over Blacktongue Farm Road ... [The first pursuer] therefore cannot have been reserving a right of access along Blacktongue Farm Road in relation to The Paddock and the March 2004 Disposition cannot be construed to include The Paddock as part of the benefited land. Reserving something and granting something new are certainly not the same thing. For the Disposition registered in March 2004 to have benefited The Paddock with the right of access along Blacktongue Farm Road it would have had to have granted such a right. It did not.

The first two grounds of rejection are plainly sound and were sufficient to dispose of the case. In relation to the third ground we would merely remark that to reserve a servitude – to hold back something which the granters had – is not of itself incompatible with reserving it in favour of an area of land owned by a third party.

One other issue was raised in the case but did not in the end have to be determined. Even if the pursuers' interpretation had won acceptance, there was a further difficulty in their way. Although the pursuers took entry to The Paddock on 20 June 2003 the disposition in their favour was not recorded until 10 November 2003. The effective date for the creation of the servitude, however, was 18 July 2003, the day on which the disposition of the farmhouse was executed by the eight relatives and, it may be, delivered. (It was not recorded until 12 March 2004.) This is because, as the law then was, servitudes were created by deed followed by possession and without the need for registration. (Since 28 November 2004 registration has been required: see Title Conditions (Scotland) Act 2003 s 75.) That meant that, as at the date when the servitude was created, the first pursuer was not yet owner of The Paddock. This was not necessarily fatal to the pursuers' case. The decision of the House of Lords in *North British Railway Co Ltd v Park Yard Co Ltd* (1898) 25 R (HL) 47 is authority for the view that a servitude can sometimes be created in favour of a property which the dominant proprietor is yet to acquire. But that would require evidence that it was within the contemplation of the eight granters of the disposition that The Paddock would be acquired and become part of the land to benefit from the servitude. Had the sheriff otherwise found in favour of the pursuers, he indicated that he would have allowed a proof before answer on the matter.

(15) Fowlie v Watson
9 July 2013, Peterhead Sheriff Court

The pursuer and the defender were owners of neighbouring farms in Aberdeenshire known, respectively, as Upper Cabra Farm and Gaval Farm. In this action the pursuer sought declarator that his farm, Upper Cabra, was not subject to a servitude right to use the water supply in favour of Gaval Farm. He also sought interdict against the defender from encroaching on his land and in particular from laying a new pipeline. The defence was that a servitude had been constituted (i) expressly or (ii) by implication or (iii) by positive prescription. After a proof the sheriff rejected all three defences and granted decree in favour of the pursuer.

The argument in respect of (i) centred on a disposition of Gaval Farm from 1926 which granted a servitude right to water from Upper Cabra Farm as 'at present so used'. But the two farms were united under the same ownership only two years later and remained in the same ownership until 1971, so that any servitude would have been extinguished by confusion. And even if this had not been so, the water supply used in 1926 was different from the one now claimed by the defender.

The argument in respect of (ii) turned on the disposition, recorded on 19 March 1971, by which Upper Cabra Farm was split off from Gaval Farm. No express servitude was reserved in the disposition, but it was argued that a servitude must be implied. The sheriff (Peter Grant-Hutchison) rejected this argument. The test for implied reservation of a servitude was one of necessity. As Gaval Farm had other possible sources of water, that test was not met. Indeed the sheriff doubted whether, even if this had been a case of implied grant rather than implied reservation, the less exacting test for implied grant (necessary for the convenient and comfortable enjoyment of the property) could have been met.

The argument in respect of (iii) was based on the long use of water from Upper Cabra Farm. This had begun immediately in 1971, on separation of the farms, and the water supply was certainly still being used more than 20 years later – indeed much more recently than that. Nonetheless, this argument too was rejected by the sheriff, for three reasons.

First, the evidence did not suggest use for a *continuous* period of 20 years. In particular, the pursuer withdrew the water supply in January 1991 – just short of 20 years after the separation of 19 March 1971 – when the pursuer ceased to use the water supply himself.

Secondly, the defender's possession was not peaceable, especially in the early 1990s. In particular, there had been a lot of trouble over the electric pump which was used for the supply to Gaval Farm. This was switched off when the pursuer changed his own water supply, but the following year the defender switched it back on again. The pursuer switched it off, and attempted to disable it, first by locking the door to the shed in which the pump was contained, then by removing the fuse, and then by removing the wires. In each case the defender restored the pump. When, finally, the pursuer removed the pump altogether, the defender installed his own pump. None of this could be said to be peaceable possession. As the sheriff put it (transcript p 46), 'The defender cannot establish an adverse right against the pursuer when he is only securing a water supply by stealth or intimidation'.

Thirdly, the defender's possession was not as of right. The sheriff set out the applicable law as follows (transcript pp 44–45):

> In terms of 'right' I was asked to consider the *ratio decidendi* of McInroy v Duke of Athole (1891) 18 R (HL) 36 for the proposition that in order to found a prescriptive right of servitude the acts of possession must be of such as to indicate unequivocally to the proprietor of the servient tenement the fact that a right is asserted and the nature of that right. I accept that proposition. It receives support from such authorities as *McGregor v Crieff Co-operative Society Ltd* 1915 SC (HL) 93 and although not authoritative the highly persuasive more recent decision in *Middletweed Ltd v Murray* 1989 SLT 11 to the effect that whoever seeks to rely on continuous use for a 20 year period has the onus of proof, and 'the law does not readily make any presumption against the alleged servient proprietor'.

The sheriff then set about applying the law to the facts. On the pursuer's side, he found that the defender's possession was explicable by tolerance. On the defender's side he found little evidence of assertion of a right. It was true that the defender had carried out some repairs. But this was best characterised as 'a favour requested of the defender'. The sheriff continued (transcript p 45):

> The defender's actings were generally not consistent with using said water supply as of right. If the defender was using the water supply as of right then it would be reasonable for him to engage with British Gas whose actings in laying pipes may have been expected to and in fact did interfere with the supply of water. What is most telling against the defender is that in June 1990 when the pursuer told the defender that the water supply was going to be switched off the defender did nothing. The supply was switched off in January 1991. The defender did not do anything lawfully to assert his purported right.

Perhaps the defender would indeed have been wise to protest. At the same time, there would have been a risk that his bluff was called and his title challenged. For (using the handy terminology found in English cases such as *R (Newhaven Port & Properties Ltd) v East Sussex County Council*, below) there is a distinction between possession 'by right' and possession 'as of right'. In order to establish a servitude by prescription, a person must possess for 20 years, not 'by right' (ie by virtue of an enforceable right, whether personal or real), but 'as of right' (ie *as if* he already has the right he is seeking to acquire). A person who possesses 'as of right' has no right at all until the end of the prescriptive period, and so is not in a position to enforce a right against anyone. The question of whether or not to 'engage with British Gas' was thus a difficult one. And it may be unfair to place much weight on the defender's failure to do so.

(16) R (Newhaven Port & Properties Ltd) v East Sussex County Council [2015] UKSC 7, [2015] AC 1547

This decision of the Supreme Court in an English appeal contains an extensive discussion of the position in Scots law in relation to 'statutory incompatibility' and the prescriptive acquisition of servitudes and public rights of way.

The claimant in the case was the owner and operator of Newhaven Port, which included an area of land known as West Beach. When the claimant fenced the Beach in 2006 so as to prevent public access, East Sussex County Council applied to have the Beach registered as a town or village green under s 15 of the Commons Act 2006. In order to qualify as a village green under the Act it was necessary to show that 'a significant number of the inhabitants of any locality, or of any neighbourhood within a locality, indulged as of right in lawful sports and pastimes on the land for a period of at least 20 years'. The application for registration was successful. The claimant sought judicial review.

A key issue was statutory incompatibility. One effect of registration under the 2006 Act was to create criminal offences in respect of damage to the registered site or interruption to its use and enjoyment. But this was incompatible with the statutory regime applying to the claimant in its operation of the harbour. Did such statutory incompatibility prevent the acquisition of the status of village green? In considering this question, the Supreme Court considered the position in Scotland in relation to the analogous question of the acquisition of servitudes and public rights of way by prescription (paras 81–90). The judgment in question was given by Lords Neuberger and Hodge, and it may be assumed that Lord Hodge was responsible for the discussion of Scots law.

In two cases from the beginning of the twentieth century, the First Division had denied such acquisition in the face of statutory incompatibility. See *Ellice's Trs v Commissioners of the Caledonian Canal* (1904) 6 F 325 and *Magistrates of Edinburgh v North British Railway Co* (1904) 6 F 620. The reasoning, however, was rather opaque. On the one hand, the court was influenced by the rule that a statutory body has no power to alienate lands which it had acquired for a statutory purpose or to grant any right over such land which was inconsistent with its use for a statutory purpose. But on the other hand, the court expressly rejected the idea that a prescriptive right derived from the implied consent of the owner of the land. This made it difficult to know whether the principle of statutory incompatibility survived, or was inconsistent with, the Prescription and Limitation (Scotland) Act 1973, especially as it took no account of nonage or other incapacity on the part of the landowner. Modern textbooks are divided in their views. Compare, for example, R R M Paisley and D J Cusine, *Servitudes and Public Rights of Way* (1998) para 4-02 (in favour of survival) with D Johnston, *Prescription and Limitation* (2nd edn, 2012) para 19-27 (against survival).

The Supreme Court declined to take sides (para 90): 'It is not necessary in this appeal, which concerns English law, to express any view on whether in Scots law the doctrine of statutory incompatibility has survived the enactment of the 1973 Act. It suffices to note that it is a matter of controversy.' So far as English law was concerned, the court concluded that s 15 of the Commons Act 2006 did not apply to land acquired by a statutory undertaker and held for statutory purposes which, as in the present case, were inconsistent with its registration as a town or village green. The judicial review was accordingly successful.

REAL BURDENS

(17) Marriott v Greenbelt Group Ltd
2 December 2015, Lands Tr

This was a challenge to the validity of a real burden which required the homeowners on a housing estate to pay for the cost of maintenance of amenity areas which were owned, not by them, but by a third party (Greenbelt). The challenge succeeded on the ground that the scope of the burden could only be determined by reference to a document extraneous to the deed of conditions (the grant of planning consent), and that the area to be maintained was in any event indeterminate. See **Commentary** p 138.

[Another aspect of this case is digested at (9) above.]

VARIATION ETC OF TITLE CONDITIONS
BY LANDS TRIBUNAL

(18) Ferguson v Gunby
2015 SLT (Lands Tr) 195

The applicants owned a bungalow in a 1970s housing estate in Balmullo, Fife. They had planning permission to build a two-storey extension, but this was contrary to a deed of conditions which, in clause 1, prohibited alterations to the external appearance and also any building on the garden. The applicants sought variation of clause 1 to the extent required to build the extension. Their application was opposed by the owners of two houses on the opposite side of the road and further up the hill. Their main ground of objection was that the extension would interfere with their views.

The Tribunal granted the application. It could not be said that the purpose of the burden (Title Conditions (Scotland) Act 2003 s 100 factor (f)) was to protect views because many houses on the estate had no views to protect. Overall, it was clear 'that the burden outweighs the benefit' (para 33). In relation to the former (factor (c)) (para 31):

> we are of the opinion that prohibition of the works, or limiting the height of the extension would significantly diminish the opportunity for the Fergusons to develop their property as they would wish. They would not be able to take full advantage of their possibilities as have many others on the estate, including the objectors. That is a serious impediment to the enjoyment of their property. As indicated in both *Franklin v Lawson* 2013 SLT (Lands Tr) 81 [*Conveyancing 2013* Case 16)] and *MacKay v McGowan* 2015 SLT (Lands Tr) 6 [*Conveyancing 2014* Case (12)], 'enjoyment' includes the right to enjoy the full potential of property. The increase in the accommodation would add value to the house. As it seems to us, the proposed extension accords very well with the nature of the site and existing house. It takes full advantage of the character of the plot.

As for the latter (factor (b)), 'there will be some diminution in the impression of openness which existed by virtue of the elevation of the respondents' sites' but the impact will not be 'very great' (para 29). Further, 'we do not consider that someone arriving fresh on the scene with the development completed would find the revised outlook at all objectionable. It would be normal for an estate of this character' (para 29).

A surprising feature of the decision is the role accorded to interest to enforce. As is well known, for a person to enforce a real burden it is necessary to show both title and interest to do so, and interest is defined in s 8 of the Title Conditions (Scotland) Act 2003 as meaning 'material detriment' to the value or enjoyment of the benefited property. Plainly, interest in this sense will sometimes be relevant in respect of factor (b) because a burden which cannot be enforced confers no benefit: see *Conveyancing 2012* pp 122–23. In *Ferguson v Gunby*, however, the Tribunal used interest to enforce as a threshold requirement for respondents, so that a respondent who failed to show interest would be unable to oppose the application. There is no warrant for this approach in the legislation, which requires of respondents only that they can show title to enforce: see Title Conditions (Scotland) Act 2003 s 95(a). The Scottish Law Commission, which was responsible for the provision, was clear that interest is not required: see *Discussion Paper No 106 on Real Burdens* (1998) para 6.57 and *Report No 181 on Real Burdens* (2000) para 6.52 n 103. And to require interest is contrary to the position adopted in a recent decision of the Tribunal itself, *Whitelaw v Acheson*, 29 February 2012. In that case the Tribunal said that (at para 4):

> Although we heard some discussion of the question of interest to enforce the existing conditions, we are satisfied that we should proceed on the basis that the respondents have undisputed title and, as proprietors of the adjacent residential subjects, have a proper interest to oppose any change to the existing conditions. We are not persuaded that their interest falls to be measured by reference to the degree of interest necessary to enforce a condition in respect of any alleged breach in terms of section 8(3). That would require assessment of the particular facts and circumstances bearing on the breach. The question of materiality cannot arise except in such a context. We consider that it begs the question to consider the interest of the respondents only in terms of the proposed change. They plainly have an interest to maintain the existing condition.

As it happens, the Tribunal in *Ferguson v Gunby* considered that the threshold had been reached. But it warned that 'we should be inclined to view the interest of properties on the estate more distant than number 28 as failing this test' (para 14). With respect, that is the wrong approach.

(19) Sinton v Lloyd
11 June 2014, Lands Tr

The application concerned a 28-metre garden at the rear of a house on the north side of Great King Street in Edinburgh's New Town. The applicants, who owned the ground and basement flat at 70 Great King Street, had obtained planning permission and listed building consent to erect a mews house at the end of their garden, access to be from South West Cumberland Street Lane. This, however, was contrary to a condition in an instrument of sasine of 1813 (following on from a feu charter granted by the Governors of Heriot's Hospital in the same year). The condition read:

> That the ground marked stable ground shall be applied to no other purpose than for stables and coaches or washing houses or other offices for the use of the occupiers of the front tenements.

The applicants sought the variation or discharge of this condition so as to allow the building work to proceed. The application was opposed by their immediate neighbours, who had earlier opposed the application for planning permission. The neighbours were willing to accept a mews house but only if it did not exceed 6 metres in depth. The applicants' house was to be 10 metres – a depth which, the neighbours said, would have a significant impact on their privacy, outlook and light.

The Tribunal concluded that the burden on the applicants (factor (c)) outweighed any benefit which the condition provided to their neighbours (factor (b)). If the condition was to be left in place, the applicants would be prevented from making use of a development site which might be worth £200,000. If the condition was to be discharged, the impact on the neighbours, while not negligible, would be 'decidedly limited' (para 25). But in any case the purpose of the condition (factor (f)) was to prevent separate occupation of the house and the 'offices' and not to restrict the size of what was built. Others of the factors in s 100 of the Title Conditions (Scotland) Act 2003 supported the applicants' position. There had been significant changes in the neighbourhood since 1813, with quite a number of mews houses being built in South West Cumberland Street Lane (factor (a)). Planning permission had been granted (factor (g)), although this involved a review of general environmental factors rather than the amenity of individual neighbours. Next, the condition was unusually old (factor (e)); indeed we would add that it was in the very first wave of real burdens in Scotland. However, 'given the status of the New Town as a World Heritage Site we would nevertheless be cautious before dismissing a condition on the basis of age alone, absent other relevant factors' (para 29). Finally (factor (j)), it was not possible to be sure what area was affected by the condition, given that the original plan had not been preserved. All in all, the Tribunal concluded that these various factors 'weigh decisively' in favour of granting the application (para 39). In view of the condition's uncertain scope, it was decided to grant a complete discharge rather than a variation.

In the absence of expert evidence as to loss of value to the neighbours' property, the Tribunal declined to award compensation under s 90(7)(a). Indeed the applicants' architect suggested that the construction of a mews house on number 70 might actually increase the value of the property next-door by setting a precedent which would unlock its development value.

(20) Yule v Tobert
2015 GWD 39-620 (merits), 4 December 2015 (expenses), Lands Tr

This was, as the Tribunal said (para 39), 'an unusual case'. The person proposing change was not the applicant, but the respondent. Instead of planning permission being granted for the change, it was refused, although only after the Lands Tribunal hearing had taken place. And the application was for the imposition of a use condition on a servitude – the first of its kind to be heard by the Lands Tribunal.

At the back of the terraced houses on the south side of South Street in St Andrews lie the 'Land Riggs', a group of some half dozen long and narrow gardens running for about 100 metres as far as Queen's Terrace. At the foot of the rigg attached to number 44 South Street is a cottage, and in 1984 the cottage was sold separately from the house. In the disposition there was reserved to the owners of number 44 a servitude of pedestrian and vehicular access. The access ran from a public lane through a double gate to a small courtyard belonging to the cottage and then through another double gate which led, at right angles, into number 44. In this application, the owners of the cottage sought to vary the servitude so as to restrict it to access for residential purposes. The application was opposed by the owner of number 44 (ie the dominant owner).

The immediate *casus belli* was a new building which the respondent had built in the rigg close to the cottage and which was used as a nursery school. For the pupils and their parents, access was on foot only, by a different gate, but the respondent intended that the teachers should park on number 44, taking access by means of the servitude. Hence the application.

The building of the school was, the Tribunal thought, a major change of circumstances (factor (a)). And although the servitude gave significant benefit to the respondent (factor (b)), the Tribunal accepted that this was outweighed by the potential burden to the applicants from the increased noise and loss of privacy which would result from parking by teachers (factor (c)). As the Tribunal explained (para 46):

> The access is through what would otherwise be a private back area of the cottage. It is in fact now the main entrance to the cottage. Any vehicle taking access requires to go through two sets of double gates. The angles of the gates are at right angles to each other and, given that there is relatively little room, are not particularly easy to negotiate. The discreet parking area for No 44 is also fairly tight for the purpose of three vehicles and a certain amount of manoeuvring would be inevitable. Both sets of gates require to be pinned back in order to leave them open for the driver to drive through. There is noisy gravel …

Providing parking for the teachers would make things worse (para 47):

> We think it is inevitable that there would be an intensification of use. All else being equal, the addition of new floorspace and the introduction of staff working on the benefited subjects is, objectively, likely to produce a greater trip generation. We accept the argument that, theoretically, the house could have at any one time a large number of residential occupants each using a car which could generate more trips than the school use. However, adding the school use, objectively speaking, is only likely to lead to an intensification of use.

All in all, the Tribunal would have been disposed to grant the application. But there was a problem. The original grant of planning permission to the respondent had contained a condition which prevented parking on number 44 by teachers. As the Tribunal case was in progress, the respondent was seeking to have this condition varied, but without success. An appeal to Scottish Ministers was unsuccessful. Thus, there was no prospect, now or in the foreseeable future, that teachers would use number 44 for parking. The application was thus aimed at an eventuality that could not occur. 'In effect the applicants are asking us to vary a title condition because the vicissitudes of the planning system might mean the respondent could come back another day with another application and another intrusive development which might affect them' (para 51). That was not sufficient reason for granting it. As the threatened increase in parking was no longer a live issue, nothing had really changed since the servitude was first created. In those circumstances, the application must fail.

No expenses were awarded. Strictly speaking, the respondent had been successful; but if the planning decision had gone the other way, it would have been the applicants who would have prevailed.

(21) United Investment Co Ltd v Charlie Reid Travel Ltd
2016 GWD 1-13, Lands Tr

The applicant had planning permission for a major redevelopment of its property in a run-down area in Kirkcaldy. The redevelopment included a convenience store and a care home. A vehicular right of access in favour of a neighbouring shop stood in the way. The purpose of this application was to have the servitude varied or discharged. The application was opposed by the owner of the shop.

The Tribunal concluded, without much difficulty, that the servitude should be varied or discharged. On the one hand (factor (c)) it was preventing a major and desirable development. On the other hand (factor (b)), its use by the owner of the shop – as a possible alternative fire escape to the rear from the first floor of the shop, and as an occasional means of delivering goods – was modest. Indeed it was even argued for the applicants that the servitude had been extinguished by non-use for 20 years, although this was not an issue that the Tribunal had jurisdiction to determine. While, however, the application was to be granted, the Tribunal delayed issuing the order so that the parties could try to reach agreement about (i) possible compensation, and (ii) an access for the shop for the purposes of carrying out inspection of and maintenance to the shop's gable wall.

(22) MacKay v McGowan
29 April 2015, Lands Tr

When this application was considered on its merits, the applicant had substantial, but not complete, success: see 2015 SLT (Lands Tr) 6 (*Conveyancing 2014* Case (12)). Nonetheless, the respondent argued strongly against an award of expenses. The Tribunal rejected that argument. 'Many of the points imply that the respondent is of the view that it is unfair upon the owner of benefited property to be expected to engage in a process concerning variation or discharge of title conditions. This is a perilous view, given the existence of section 103' (para 6), which provides that in awarding expenses the Tribunal 'shall have regard, in particular, to the extent to which the application, or any opposition to the application, is successful'. The Tribunal awarded expenses to the applicant but with a 10% reduction in acknowledgement of the applicant's incomplete success.

(23) Grant v National Trust for Scotland
5 May 2015, Lands Tr

The applicants, having had substantial, but not complete, success on the merits (see decision of 8 August 2014, summarised in *Conveyancing 2014* Case (14)), moved for expenses. The respondent sought to have the expenses reduced. Having regard to (i) the applicants' incomplete success, (ii) the fact that the application was not accompanied by a conceptual proposal until late in the case, and (iii) the respondent's statutory duty to promote the preservation of places of historic or national interest, which meant that it was not in the same position as a normal landowner, the Tribunal decided to modify the expenses to 70% on the sheriff court scale. On the other hand, the Tribunal awarded an additional fee of 20% in view of the novelty of the question as well as the complexity of the evidence. This was in terms of head (i) of the Act of Sederunt (Fees of Solicitors in the Sheriff Court) (Amendment and Further Provisions) 1993, SI 1993/3080. The Tribunal rejected a claim for a further fee under other heads.

TENEMENTS

(24) Cumbernauld Housing Partnership Ltd v Davies
[2015] CSIH 22, 2015 SC 532, 2015 SCLR 459

A factor sought to recover unpaid maintenance costs from the owner of a tenement flat. The owner defended on the basis (i) that the pursuer had failed to establish that the work claimed for had been carried out and paid for, and (ii) that, as the five-year prescription applied, some of the sums claimed for had prescribed. The defender failed on (i) but succeeded on (ii). See **Commentary** p 189. See also Gordon Junor, 'Recovering costs of tenemental works: section 12 of the 2004 Act and prescription' (2015) 83 *Scottish Law Gazette* 22.

(25) Mitchell v Reilly
11 July 2006, Glasgow Sheriff Court

The owner of one flat in a four-flatted block challenged the actions of another owner in carrying out alterations to the common property, including the installation of CCTV. See **Commentary** p 187.

PROPERTY FACTORS

(26) Grant & Wilson Property Management Ltd v Egbuka
2015 SLT (Sh Ct) 193, 2015 Hous LR 30

One of the purposes of the Property Factors (Scotland) Act 2011 was to set up a procedure for dispute resolution: see *Conveyancing 2011* pp 115–16. The rules can be found in part 2 of the Act. Homeowners who consider that a factor has failed to comply either with a contractual obligation or with the Code of Conduct can apply to the homeowner housing panel. Assuming certain conditions are satisfied, the panel must refer matters on to a homeowner housing committee. If the applicant's case is judged to have been made out, the committee issues a 'property factor enforcement order'. This cannot be enforced directly by the homeowner, but failure to comply is both a criminal offence and also a ground for the factor being removed from the Register of Property Factors. Full details can be found in the Homeowner Housing Panel (Applications and Decisions) (Scotland) Regulations 2012, SSI 2012/180. The 'overriding objective' of the Regulations is, as reg 3 explains, 'to enable the panel and any committee to deal with the proceedings justly', by which is meant:

(a) dealing with the proceedings in ways which are proportionate to the complexity of the issues and to the resources of the parties;
(b) seeking informality and flexibility in the proceedings;
(c) ensuring, so far as practicable, that the parties are on an equal footing procedurally and are able to participate fully in the proceedings, including assisting any party in the presentation of the party's case without advocating the course they should take;
(d) using the special expertise of the panel and the committees effectively; and
(e) avoiding delay, so far as compatible with the proper consideration of the issues.

Since the Act came into force, a significant number of decisions have been made by homeowner housing committees, and these can be found at https://hohp. scotland.gov.uk.

By s 22 of the Act an appeal from the panel or committee may be made on a point of law to the sheriff. This is done by summary application. The sheriff's decision is final and there is no further right of appeal.

This case is the first to be reported involving an appeal to the sheriff. Having affirmed the committee's decision (subject to raising concerns in two respects), the court turned its attention to the question of expenses. No provision as to expenses was made by the Act. But, as the procedure was essentially administrative in nature, the usual rule for such cases – no expenses due or by – should apply. This corresponded to the rule which applied in respect of the initial hearing itself. And, as the sheriff (A E Swanson) noted (para 21), there were strong policy reasons for this approach:

> The Act is designed to improve services and maintain standards to his benefit. If the homeowner is unsuccessful that will be because of a failure on the panel's part to reasonably exercise its discretion. To penalise such a homeowner in expenses seems unjust. Such a homeowner has sought to use the 'flexible' dispute resolution system under the Act to arbitrate on a dispute about the standard of service from his property factors; a system he is encouraged to use on the basis that there is no risk of cost to him. The nature and scope of the legislation does not sit well with a penalty in expenses being imposed at the stage of appeal to the sheriff.

COMPETITION OF TITLE

(27) Chalmers v Chalmers
[2015] CSIH 75, 2015 SLT 793, 2015 Hous LR 82

At first instance, the Court of Session declined, on the grounds of personal bar, to order the reduction of a forged disposition: see [2014] CSOH 161, 2014 GWD

38-699, *Conveyancing 2014* Case (22). The Inner House has now reversed: see
Commentary p 200.

(28) Douglas & Angus Estates v McAllister
[2015] CSIH 2, 2015 SC 411

The pursuers raised an action of declarator and removing against the defender
in respect of land known as Muirfoot Toll, Rigside, Lanarkshire, of which the
defender was in occupation. The defender queried the pursuers' title to the
property and averred (without providing any more detail) that it was believed
to belong to the local authority.

The title of the first pursuer was a disposition of a one half *pro indiviso* share
in Muirfoot Toll granted in 2009. The title of the second pursuer was a disposition
of 1993 (recorded GRS) which disponed the subjects conveyed in an earlier
disposition dated January 1933, but not recorded until June 1934, but under a large
number of exceptions none of which, it eventually appeared, included Muirfoot
Toll. The 1933/34 disposition conveyed numerous different areas of land by the
sort of general name in which conveyancers delight: for example, the twenty
merk land of old extent of Pittinane; the fifty shilling lands of Crawford; the
eight pound land of old extent of Grange, commonly called Inglisberry Grange;
and the lands of Ponfeich. It was the last of these within which Muirfoot Toll
was said to lie.

The question to be determined was whether the pursuers had done enough
to establish their title. It was held that they had. The starting point was *Mather
v Alexander* 1926 SC 139 which was 'authority for the proposition that, where
a defender has no competing title to proffer, it is sufficient for the pursuer to
produce an *ex facie* valid conveyance in his favour. That is what the pursuers
have done in this case' (para 23). The Lord Justice-Clerk (Carloway) continued
(paras 26 and 27):

> Exactly what may be regarded as an *ex facie* valid title in a pursuer's favour may
> depend upon its particular terms. In the present case, for example, the second pursuer
> maintains that his title depends upon the disposition in his favour dated 1993.
> That disposition specifically conveys part of the estate disponed in 1933, under the
> exception of certain subjects designated in a schedule. If it were clear, upon looking
> at the 1933 deed, that the land at Muirfoot Toll could not have been carried in the
> 1933 deed, because, for example, it related only to land in a different county, the *ex
> facie* validity of the title relative to the land in question may have been challengeable.
> … As matters stand, but no doubt subject to review in a competition with a third
> party should further dispositions be located, and using a necessary double negative
> in the circumstances, it cannot be said that the 1933 disposition did not carry the
> Muirfoot Tollhouse land.

The pursuers would only be put to a proof of title if the defender proffered a
competing title. That title need not be his: see *Lock v Taylor* 1976 SLT 238. In the
present case the defender had done no more than to suggest, without giving
any details, that title to Muirfoot Toll might be held by the local authority. That
was insufficient.

LAND REGISTRATION

(29) Rivendale v Clark
[2015] CSIH 27, 2015 SC 558

This was an appeal against a refusal to rectify the Register which (as is typical) was in substance a dispute between neighbours at Baluachrach, Tarbert, Argyll. The problem arose out of overlapping Sasine titles. A successor of the disponee of the second of the titles to be granted – which was thus *a non domino* in respect of the area of overlap – was the first to apply for first registration in the Land Register. The title plan issued by the Keeper included the overlap area. A successor of the disponee of the first of the titles then applied for rectification of the Register to the effect of removing the overlap area.

The main defence was that the registered proprietor was in possession, thus preventing rectification by virtue of s 9(3)(a) of the Land Registration (Scotland) Act 1979. In the event, the Lands Tribunal found that the registered proprietor (the respondent) was in possession of some but not all of the area to which the inaccuracy related. Accordingly, rectification was allowed in respect of the part which was not possessed. See *Rivendale v Keeper of the Registers of Scotland*, 30 October 2013 (*Conveyancing 2013* Case (35)).

The applicant appealed, arguing that the evidence was insufficient to amount to possession by the registered proprietor. The Inner House summarised the arguments as follows (para 29):

> First, it was said that the culverting of the burn, which lay outside the disputed area on the side away from South Cottage, could not be used as an adminicle of evidence of possession. Furthermore, the culverting work was carried out by contractors, not by the respondent herself. Secondly, it was said that personal use by the respondent herself was insufficient to amount to possession of the disputed area; her evidence was that she occasionally strimmed the grass in the disputed area and walked her dog along it. Thirdly, it was submitted that the respondent's authorisation of use of the disputed area by others, as by widening and improving the track and removing a gate, could not constitute possession by her, as they lacked the necessary corpus for possession. Fourthly, .. it was said that use of the area of roadway as an access track was insufficient because that was equally consistent with a servitude right of access and ownership. It therefore could not amount to an act of possession as owner.

In rejecting these arguments the Inner House provided helpful guidance as to the meaning of 'possession' in the context of s 9(3)(a) of the 1979 Act. It was observed that possession includes civil possession (though that terminology was not used). The guidance is worth quoting in full (paras 30–32):

> In our opinion these submissions are unfounded. First, the fact that individual acts, such as strimming or walking a dog, may not by themselves be enough for possession is immaterial; the critical question is the total picture, and these individual acts are merely adminicles of the evidence that builds up that total picture. The same is true of the culverting of the burn. While the burn was to one side of the disputed area, the tribunal held that the work was related to the surfacing of the track. That means

in our opinion that it too may be regarded as an adminicle of evidence of possession. Similarly, we consider that the respondent's permitting the widening and surfacing of the track itself evidenced possession, as did the respondent's arranging for the removal of the gate put up by the appellant; the critical point there is that the removal of the gate was not challenged by the appellant.

Secondly, the fact that a particular act such as the use of a roadway is consistent with both exercise of a servitude right of access and possession as owner is immaterial. It is not essential that possession be unequivocally referable to ownership and nothing else. Once again, the total picture is important. Consequently if an act can reasonably be construed as involving possession *qua* owner, it may be taken into account with the various other adminicles of evidence to the same effect. Ultimately all of the individual pieces of evidence must be taken together to discover whether they yield a reasonable inference that the possession was referable to ownership. That in our opinion is what the tribunal did in the present case.

Thirdly, possession for the purposes of sec 9(3) of the 1979 Act may in our opinion be exercised through contractors. The purpose underlying sec 9(3) is to confer protection from rectification on a registered proprietor who is in possession of a particular area of land. The assumption is that in other cases a financial indemnity will suffice to compensate him for the loss of his rights, but where there is possession of the land financial compensation will not be enough (see *Kaur v Singh (No 1)* 1999 SC 180, 194A–B). In this context we do not consider it necessary that the acts of possession should be the personal acts of the individual or other legal person who claims to be a proprietor in possession. Indeed, in the case of a corporate owner this would not be possible, as a corporation must inevitably act through agents. The same is true of other types of proprietor; an example is a case where a house is held by testamentary trustees for behoof of the testator's widow in liferent and children in fee. In such a case it appears to us that possession by the widow and liferentrix must be treated as possession by the owners, the trustees. Otherwise the underlying purpose of sec 9(3) could not apply to such a case. Consequently we consider that the acts of servicing the track and removing the gate may be regarded as evidence of possession, even though they were carried out by contractors.

The appellant also had a second argument. The protection conferred on a proprietor in possession under s 9(3)(a) was only available where the rectification would cause 'prejudice'. But, said the appellant, the respondent had led no evidence as to prejudice. The obvious reply to this point is that rectification, where (as here) it would lead to a loss of property, is in its nature prejudicial. That, on the whole, was the line taken by the Inner House (para 35):

Section 9(3) of the 1979 Act requires prejudice, but it is not stated that the prejudice must be material. Thus in *Tesco Stores Ltd v Keeper of the Registers* 2001 SLT (Lands Tr) 23, 37H–I, the Lands Tribunal stated that 'an effect which produces loss of heritable rights can be described as being to the prejudice of the proprietor of those rights at least when these rights have some identified value'. We agree with that view, which was referred to by Lord Osborne in *Safeway Stores plc v Tesco Stores Ltd* 2004 SC 29 (para 59). In respect of the triangular area, if the solum did not belong to the respondent, it would be competent for the appellant to remove that area of track, which would substantially impair its utility as a means of access. It is also quite possible that loss of that area might lead to a dispute with the owners of the two plots to the north where houses have been built. In all the circumstances we consider that the evidence accepted by the tribunal was sufficient for it to draw the inference that prejudice had been demonstrated by the loss of the triangular area.

[Another aspect of this case is digested at (84) below.]

(30) Wight v Keeper of the Registers of Scotland
2015 SLT (Lands Tr) 195, 2015 Hous LR 93

The Sasine titles of neighbouring properties each included a certain area of land. When the title of the first of the properties entered the Land Register, in 1984, the disputed area was included in the title plan. The other property, a farm, remained, and remains still, on the Register of Sasines. Oddly, the fact that the two titles overlapped did not come to light until 2013. The owners of the Sasine land, two men by the name of Wight, applied to the Keeper for rectification, but the application was rejected. The Wights then appealed to the Lands Tribunal. The appeal was opposed by the owner of the registered property, Amanda Beach, but in the event Ms Beach did not appear at the appeal hearing.

Although the appeal was thus unopposed, the Tribunal nonetheless decided to hear evidence because of the unusual fact that the disputed area had been in a registered title, unchallenged, for over 30 years (para 3). Having heard the evidence, the Tribunal was satisfied that the Wights had been in possession of the area ever since the disposition in their favour was recorded in 1965. From this it followed (i) that their title to the area was fortified by positive prescription; (ii) that the area was not, therefore, within the title of the other property immediately prior to its first registration in 1984; (iii) that the registered title to that property was therefore inaccurate in including the area; and (iv) that, as Ms Beach was not in possession, there was nothing to stop the Register from being rectified against her. The appeal was therefore allowed.

The case also raised an important transitional issue. The Land Registration etc (Scotland) Act 2012 came into force on 8 December 2014 (the 'designated day'). Both the Keeper's refusal of the application for rectification and the lodging of the appeal, under s 25 of the Land Registration (Scotland) Act 1979, had occurred before that date, but the hearing itself took place after the designated day, on 30 June 2015. Two questions arose. First, was the appeal still competent, even although the 1979 Act had been repealed? And if so then, secondly, what law was to apply – the 1979 Act or the 2012 Act?

On the first question, the Tribunal decided that the appeal remained competent. There was an express provision in the 2012 Act (sch 4 para 14) that applications for rectification under the 1979 Act fell if they had not been determined by the Keeper by the designated day. But the present application *had* been determined by that day. As to appeals from such a decision, the 2012 Act was unfortunately silent. Yet, said the Tribunal, there were two reasons for supposing that such an appeal remained competent. One was that the successor provision in the 2012 Act, s 103, was restricted to appeals 'against any decision of the Keeper *under this Act*' and so could not be used for appeals against decisions made under the 1979 Act. Unless, therefore, appeals under s 25 of the 1979 Act remained competent, there would be no appeal mechanism at all, and the Keeper's decision would be unchallengeable.

Secondly, s 16(1) of the Interpretation Act 1978 preserved the appellants' right of appeal despite the repeal of the 1979 Act. Section 16(1) provides that:

> Without prejudice to section 15, where an Act repeals an enactment, the repeal does not, unless the contrary intention appears, –
> (a) revive anything not in force or existing at the time at which the repeal takes effect;
> (b) affect the previous operation of the enactment repealed or anything duly done or suffered under that enactment;
> (c) affect any right, privilege, obligation or liability acquired, accrued or incurred under that enactment;
> (d) affect any penalty, forfeiture or punishment incurred in respect of any offence committed against that enactment;
> (e) affect any investigation, legal proceeding or remedy in respect of any such right, privilege, obligation, liability, penalty, forfeiture or punishment;
> and any such investigation, legal proceeding or remedy may be instituted, continued or enforced, and any such penalty, forfeiture or punishment may be imposed, as if the repealing Act had not been passed.

Both of the Tribunal's reasons are cogent. In relation to s 16(1) it is easy to argue (i) that as at the time of the repeal, the appellants already had an accrued right to appeal (within para (c)), and (ii) that accordingly the 'legal proceeding' of the appeal hearing (para (e)) should go ahead. We would add that, while s 16 applies to Acts of the Scottish Parliament (see s 23A), there are now equivalent provisions – ss 15 and 16 – in the Interpretation and Legislative Reform (Scotland) Act 2010 which are even more helpful to the Tribunal's argument. These, however, are confined to the case where an Act of the Scottish Parliament, and not an Act of the UK Parliament such as the 1979 Act, has been repealed.

On the second question (whether the appeal should apply the 1979 Act or the 2012 Act), the Tribunal was firmly of the view that it should apply the 1979 Act. The relevant provisions of the 2012 Act are paras 17–24 of sch 4. These provide for inaccuracies on the basis of their status immediately before the designated day. If an inaccuracy could have been rectified at that time, then, on the designated day, parties were given such rights as if the power to rectify had in fact been exercised (para 17). Conversely, if an inaccuracy could not have been rectified (typically because to do so would have been to the prejudice of a proprietor in possession), then it ceased to be an inaccuracy on the designated day (para 22). To assist in the determination of the state of possession, para 18 provides that 'the person registered as proprietor of the land is to be presumed to be in possession unless the contrary is shown'. These provisions, said the Tribunal, did not apply to appeals (such as this one) which were taken under the 1979 Act. On the contrary, they were 'only intended to apply to applications or referrals regarding rectification made after the coming into force of the 2012 Act, ie applications etc coming under the provisions of the 2012 Act itself'.

We doubt, however, that the position is so simple. Insofar as the purpose of an appeal is to determine whether the Keeper, in a decision issued before the designated day, decided a point correctly, then it is true that that determination must, like the original decision, be made under the 1979 Act. But that would only fix the parties' rights at the date of the Keeper's decision. It would not, by itself, fix their rights as of today.

In *Wight*, however, the Tribunal sought to fix the parties' rights as of today. Its order, issued on 23 July 2015, was:

> We therefore order that the triangular area be removed from the interested party's title LAN 5785. The correct boundary between the parties' subjects should be the existing old fence.

23 July 2015 was after the designated day, and on the designated day the rights of the parties, like it or not, changed as a result of paras 17–24 of sch 4 to the 2012 Act (described above). Of course, the repeal of the 1979 Act did not, of itself, alter the parties' rights: s 16(1) of the Interpretation Act 1978 saw to that. But, equally, there was nothing to prevent paras 17–24 of sch 4 to the 2012 Act from applying to the inaccuracy on the Register – as it applied to all other inaccuracies on the Register on the designated day. By the time, therefore, that the Tribunal issued its order, the rights of the parties had *already* changed. And, on the basis of the Tribunal's evaluation of the state of possession (and hence of the prospects for rectification immediately before the designated day), the effect of para 17 of sch 4 would have been to restore ownership to the Wights, as at the appointed day.

It would remain true that the Register was inaccurate, although the inaccuracy was now 'actual' rather than 'bijural' (ie the Register showed Ms Beach as owner when the owner was actually the Wights). And, following the Tribunal's determination, the inaccuracy would be 'manifest' and hence one which the Keeper was bound to rectify under s 80 of the 2012 Act. In the end, therefore, there would be no difference in result between a finding under the 1979 Act and one under the 2012 Act. The path, in both cases, would lead to rectification.

But this might not always be so. Sometimes the evidence of possession might be much more contested and uncertain than in the present case. If so, the presumption of possession by the registered proprietor introduced by sch 4 para 18 might turn out to be crucial in the weighing of evidence.

Behind this detailed analysis lies a broader point. On the designated day all existing inaccuracies on the Register were affected by the provisions in sch 4 paras 17–24 of the 2012 Act. All were treated in the same way. That is, of course, as it should be. And this uniformity of treatment is unaffected by whether the procedure adopted for determining the parties' rights is an appeal originating under the 2012 Act or under the 1979 Act.

(31) Campbell-Gray v Keeper of the Registers of Scotland
2015 SLT (Lands Tr) 147 (merits), 31 March 2015 (expenses), Lands Tr

The appellant, who held on a Sasine title, appealed against the Keeper's refusal to rectify the Register to the effect of excluding the verge of a road from a

neighbouring registered title. The appellant's case was that the verge was part
of her property.

After hearing evidence, the Tribunal decided that the verge was not part
of the appellant's property and hence that there was no inaccuracy on the
Register. Even if there had been an inaccuracy, however, the Tribunal thought
that the neighbours might have been able to establish that they were proprietors
in possession despite an almost complete absence of possessory acts. The
Tribunal gave some weight to an application to BT for a wayleave payment
in respect of an existing telegraph pole. It was true that Lord Hamilton in
Safeway Stores plc v Tesco Stores Ltd 2004 SC 29, para 82 had emphasised the
importance of physical acts of possession. 'However, we think there can be civil
possession, and an application for payment … is an assertion of ownership'
(para 62).

Absent from the Tribunal's consideration – why we do not know – was any
consideration of acts of possession on the part of the *appellant*, which appear to
have been much more numerous than those of the registered proprietor.

The appellant was found liable for expenses, even although rectification was
conceded in relation to one of the areas. This was because the entire three-day
hearing was taken up with a consideration of matters on which the appellant
was unsuccessful.

[Another aspect of this case is digested at (83) below.]

(32) Balfour v Keeper of the Registers of Scotland
2015 SLT (Lands Tr) 185

In 2007 solicitors acting for James Brydie persuaded the Keeper to register an
a non domino disposition of a strip of ground in Arncroach, Fife. Despite title
research, it had not been possible to trace the owner; and the ground, it was
said, had previously belonged to Mr Brydie's family but had been erroneously
conveyed. The Keeper excluded indemnity in the usual way.

In 2012 Isobel Balfour and Edna Myles applied for registration in respect of
the same strip of ground on the basis that they had a *habile* Sasine title which had
been fortified by prescription. (Whether that title was itself originally granted *a
non domino* we do not know.) The Keeper accepted the application but excluded
indemnity. This followed the Keeper's then practice – now forbidden by s 12(2)
of the Land Registration etc (Scotland) Act 2012 – of allowing the same property
to appear in two title sheets.

Ms Balfour and Ms Myles applied for rectification of the Register to the
effect of having Mr Brydie's title sheet cancelled; but as Mr Brydie contested
the question of possession, the Keeper refused the application. Ms Balfour and
Ms Myles appealed. Initially, Mr Brydie maintained his resistance but, a few
days before the hearing, he conceded the rectification. The only remaining issue
was expenses. The appellants sought expenses against both the Keeper and Mr
Brydie.

The applicants' case for expenses being awarded against the Keeper was (i)
that the Keeper should not have accepted Mr Brydie's application for registration,

and (ii) that the Keeper should have accepted their application for rectification. The Tribunal rejected both grounds. In respect of (i) the Keeper had been entitled, in the light of the evidence produced, to accept the application. In respect of (ii), the Keeper's hands were tied once it became evident that Mr Brydie contested the issue of possession (para 10):

> The real complaint relates to the fact that the Keeper did not rectify in favour of the appellants in the s 9 application. We do not think it has been argued, let alone decided, that the Keeper has, as it were, a duty in expenses to 'get it right' in a rectification application. That would seem to be a bold proposition. The question is perhaps more whether the Keeper has a duty to take an obvious and clear cut decision so as to avoid the necessity of the s 25 appeal. This is potentially a point of some importance, and we were not addressed with argument on the matter. As it is, it is unnecessary for us to decide it as we do not think there are grounds upon which to criticise the Keeper's actions at the s 9 stage. The appellants' argument implies that the Keeper was, in effect, bound to rectify the register because of what may have appeared a strong case in terms of the numerous affidavits and other documents produced for the appellants. But as appears from a letter from the Keeper to the appellants' solicitor of 18 March 2013, the interested party [Mr Brydie] had responded and contested the issue of possession. There was accordingly an issue of fact between the parties. To resolve it would have meant taking a view on credibility and reliability of factual evidence for one or other of the parties. The Keeper's office is not geared up to determine disputes such as the factual dispute which had emerged. It follows there is no question of abrogation of responsibility. Accordingly we refuse the appellants' motion for expenses against the Keeper.

We would add that the position is much the same under the 2012 Act where, in determining whether there is a 'manifest' inaccuracy on the Register which, in terms of s 80, would require to be rectified, the Keeper is not in a position to adjudicate on disputed questions of fact.

Having refused expenses against the Keeper, the Tribunal awarded expenses against Mr Brydie on the familiar basis that expenses follow success. The Tribunal took the view that it did not have power to award expenses in respect of the pre-Tribunal stage, ie the application for rectification. It might be added that under the 2012 Act s 84(1)(a) a party who succeeds in an application for rectification can recover extra-judicial legal expenses from the Keeper.

(33) East Lothian Council v Keeper of the Registers of Scotland
2016 GWD 4-91, Lands Tr

Tourist Services (Edinburgh) Ltd was the registered owner of a plot of ground at the rear of premises in Haddington owned by East Lothian Council. The Council applied for rectification of the Register on the basis that the Council was the 'true' owner of the plot. The Keeper refused the application and the Council appealed to the Lands Tribunal. At first Tourist Services maintained its opposition but ultimately it withdrew its representations. The application was dealt with by written submissions.

The Council's title turned on a disposition from 1960 which conveyed

ALL and WHOLE the subjects comprising the house, shop and back shop known as 7 Brown Street, Haddington, together with the plot of ground at the rear thereof and at the rear of the property known as 6 Brown Street, Haddington.

The plot in dispute was the plot at the rear of 6 (now 10/11) Brown Street. The plot was part of a car park, and it was accepted that the Council had been in possession since the 1960 disposition.

The Tribunal found (i) that the 1960 disposition was *habile* for the purposes of acquiring the plot by prescription; (ii) that as the Council had been in possession, it was indeed the 'true' owner of the property; (iii) that the disposition which led to the first registration of the plot in favour of a predecessor of Tourist Services was *a non domino*; (iv) that the Register was accordingly inaccurate; and (v) that as Tourist Services, though proprietor, was not in possession, the Register should be rectified in the manner requested by the Council.

(34) McKenna v Keeper of the Registers of Scotland
21 August 2015, Lands Tr

The application was in respect of the upper floor of a two-storey building in Perkhill Road, Lumphanan, Aberdeenshire. An earlier application in respect of the same building had concerned the ownership and possession of a garden shed: see *Nicol v Keeper of the Registers of Scotland* 2013 SLT (Lands Tr) 56 (*Conveyancing 2013* Case (34)). One of the applicant's aims was to reopen that decision, but the Tribunal properly pointed out that this could only be done by an appeal to the Court of Session (para 21).

The present application arose out of a conveyancing and registration mishap. A Mrs Pauline Robertson had a registered title to the upper flat together with some adjacent land. In 2010 she sold the flat, but not the adjacent ground, to Mrs Irene McKenna. By mistake, Mrs McKenna's solicitors applied for registration using a form 2 rather than a form 3. Whether for that or some other reason (some of the details of what happened are unknown to us), Mrs McKenna was registered on 8 July 2010 as owner of both the flat and the ground. The mistake was noticed when the land certificate was sent to Mrs McKenna's solicitors. They contacted the Keeper and entered into discussion as to remedial proceedings. Mrs McKenna had meanwhile died, on 18 August 2010.

The Keeper proposed a two-stage correction process. First, Mrs Robertson would be restored as owner. Then the disposition would be re-registered as a transfer of part, resulting in the opening of a new title sheet for the flat. We assume that this rather convoluted method was suggested in order to retain the original title sheet and title number for Mrs Robertson's parent title (now to be reduced to the adjacent ground). The first stage was carried out at once, on or before 8 September 2010. Because of the death, however, the second stage required the execution of a new disposition in favour of Mrs McKenna's executors. This was done on 28 October 2010 but, for reasons which are unexplained (but seem to have been to do with a disagreement with the appellant), the disposition was not submitted for registration (now with a form 3) until 18 March 2013. It was registered on 20 March 2013, a new title sheet being opened for the upper flat and showing the executors as owner.

The current applicant was the daughter, but not an executor, of Mrs McKenna. The application was determined by written submission, and the applicant's 'various writings' were described by the Tribunal as 'diffuse and quite difficult to follow' (para 10). A fundamental difficulty was her title to bring the application. She was not the registered proprietor of the upper flat; nor was she one of her mother's executors (who were the registered proprietors); nor was she acting with the agreement of the executors.

One of her arguments was that there was included in the sale to Mrs McKenna, and hence should have been included in the title sheet, a certain area of ground. But insofar as the argument had merit, this was concerned with whether the disposition had properly implemented the missives and so was not a matter for the Tribunal. The Tribunal was satisfied that the entry on the Register gave proper effect to the disposition.

The applicant's main point concerned the process for correction of the error in the Register and the long period – from 8 September 2010 to 20 March 2013 – during which ownership of the flat was again in the name of Mrs Robertson. The applicant asked the Keeper to rectify the title sheet 'to the state that it was in, on the day my late mother purchased the property on 2 July 2010'. The Keeper refused to do so and the present application was by way of an appeal against that decision. The Tribunal refused the appeal. Quite apart from the problem of the applicant's standing, to 'return the register to the state it was in briefly with effect from 8 July until early September 2010 would mean that the register would be palpably inaccurate as to true ownership. It would show the deceased owning property which had not been conveyed to her' (para 19).

One issue which arose was whether the Keeper had been entitled to rectify the Register against Mrs McKenna. The applicant's argument appears to have been that Mrs McKenna was a proprietor in possession, and hence that rectification should not have been possible. The Tribunal in response doubted whether Mrs McKenna could properly be said to have been in possession; but even if she was, the failure of her solicitors to use the correct application form might have amounted to carelessness, thus allowing rectification under s 9(3)(a)(iii) of the Land Registration (Scotland) 1979.

In its analysis of possession, the Tribunal said this (para 25):

> As explained by Lord Hamilton in *Safeway Stores v Tesco Stores* 2004 SC 29 at paragraphs 77–78, 'possession' in the statutory context suggests a 'proprietor' who has, on the faith of the register, had use and enjoyment of the property. There has to be 'an act of mind' involving 'holding it as his own property'. As the deceased's agents immediately recognised that the title was erroneous and set about remedying it we cannot see how the deceased or anyone deriving possession through her could have had 'faith' in the register or held an intention to hold the property as their own. . . . At this stage it is not necessary to get into the vexed topic of whether any possession requires to be in 'good faith reliance' of the register; it is enough for us to find that there could not have been reliance at all.

In this passage, the Tribunal (following Lord Hamilton in *Safeway Stores*) suggests two requirements for possession under s 9(3)(a) of the 1979 Act, namely that a person (i) must hold the property as his or her own, and (ii) must do so 'on the faith of the register' or, as the Tribunal proceeds to gloss it, in 'reliance' on the register. The first of these we may accept at once as being simply a normal requirement of possession. The second is potentially more troublesome. Unlike in the case of positive prescription where, in terms of s 1(1) of the Prescription and Limitation (Scotland) Act 1973, the possession is required to be 'founded on' the registration of a deed, there is no requirement, in s 9(3)(a) of the 1979 Act, that the possession must be on the faith of or in reliance on the Register. All that s 9(3)(a) requires is that the proprietor possess. No doubt in practice that possession will almost always be in the knowledge of a registered title, although it is possible to think of cases where this would not be true. But knowledge is not the same as 'reliance' or acting on the 'faith of the register'.

(35) Sebry v Companies House
[2015] EWHC 115 (QB), [2015] 4 All ER 681

Though neither Scottish nor about conveyancing, this case merits mention. A company called Taylor and Son Ltd went into liquidation. The Registrar of Companies entered that fact in the Companies Register but in doing so made a small mistake: the entry stated that it was Taylor and Sons Ltd – a different and, despite the likeness of the names, unconnected company – that had gone into liquidation. The mistake was due to the failure of the winding-up order to state the company's registration number. The mistake was picked up and rectified within a few hours. But the damage had been done. Word had gone out that Taylor and Sons Ltd was in liquidation, with consequences for that company's business standing. Companies House was sued for damages, the claimant in the action being the company's assignee. It was held that the Registrar owed a duty of care and that accordingly the claim was competent.

The reason we mention this case is that it could be relevant to the question of whether the Keeper might be liable to pay compensation for errors, over and above the express provisions about compensation to be found in the Land Registration etc (Scotland) Act 2012.

BARONY TITLES

(36) Sturzenegger Ptr (No 2)
2015 SLT (Lyon Ct) 2

The petition in this case (decided in 2010 but not reported until 2015) is best introduced by the opening words of the judgment of the Lord Lyon (W D H Sellar):

> This is a petition of date 10 February 2006 brought by Willi Ernst Sturzenegger of Arran, designing himself as 'Feudal Earl of Arran', in which he seeks official

recognition 'in the name, style and dignity of Willi Ernst Sturzenegger of Arran, Feudal Earl of Arran' with appropriate heraldic additaments. On the face of it this is a surprising proposition. The style has the appearance of a peerage title, yet the style being sought is not the recognised peerage title of Earl of Arran which is currently held, as a subsidiary title, by the Duke of Hamilton. It also has the appearance of being a feudal title, yet the last remnants of feudal tenure in Scotland were brought to an end by the Abolition of Feudal Tenure Act 2000 which came into force on 28 November 2004.

What the petition sought was official recognition of the title, as opposed to the informal right which anyone has to use any name he or she cares.

In refusing the petition, the Lord Lyon gave a full and learned account of the history of barony titles, a subject which, as he pointed out, was well documented (paras 13–17). But there was no such clarity or historical continuity in respect of territorial or feudal earldoms (as opposed to modern personal earldoms) (para 35):

> On the contrary there is a clear break between the type of territorial earldoms which existed before the evolution of a personal peerage, and the later erection of lands into what has been termed a 'territorial earldom'. I therefore do not accept that it follows from the recognition of a feudal baron, or one possessed of the dignity of a former feudal barony, as 'Baron of X', that the person in possession of a 'territorial earldom' stemming from the erection by the Crown of lands into a free earldom, should be recognised as an 'Earl' or 'Countess', 'feudal' or otherwise.

Such a view was unsupported either by authority (save some recent Lyon cases which were not fully argued) or by example.

(37) Menking Ptr
2015 SLT (Lyon Ct) 21

When the feudal system was abolished as at Martinmas 2004, what remained of barony titles – which was essentially the right to be called 'baron' and to matriculate arms accordingly – was detached from the land and became a free-floating incorporeal heritable right. See Abolition of Feudal Tenure etc (Scotland) Act 2000 s 63 and, for analysis, K G C Reid, *The Abolition of Feudal Tenure in Scotland* (2003) paras 14.2–14.5. One immediate consequence was that it ceased to be competent to register deeds of transfer in the Land or Sasine Register. But as barony titles were and remain valuable, the decision was made to set up an unofficial Register of Scottish Baronies under the direction of Alistair Rennie, who had recently retired as Deputy Keeper of the Registers. This is run from Mr Rennie's home, the (entirely appropriate) address of which is 98 Barons Hill Avenue, Linlithgow, West Lothian EH49 7JG. In the decade or so since feudal abolition, the Register of Scottish Baronies has come to be well regarded. So it was that in *Menking Ptr* the Lord Lyon (J J Morrow) gave the following endorsement (para 5):

The Scottish Barony Register is the only register for the Lord Lyon to have reference to in these matters, albeit a non-statutory register. The present practice was established by previous Lord Lyons. The practice is that 'a person of skill' who is at present the custodian of the register (Mr Alistair Rennie) provides a report based on an examination of a prescriptive progress of title that the owner is entitled to the dignity. This system has in practice operated efficiently and effectively in relation to baronies. I am content to follow this practice as long as the present custodian is 'a person of skill'. I noted that the register is a 'Barony Register' and, as such, is protecting the dignity and legal entity of barony in Scots law.

The case itself concerned a petition 'to be officially recognised in the name George David Menking, Lord of the Garioch with a grant of arms suitable and according to the law of arms, to himself and his descendants, together with all the additaments appropriate to the dignity of lord in the baronage of Scotland'. The petition was granted. The petitioner had established his title through an assignation registered in the Barony Register, and the petitioner's regality title was simply a form of barony title.

COMMUNITY RIGHT TO BUY

(38) West Register (Property Investments) Ltd v Lord Advocate
11 March 2015, Selkirk Sheriff Court

Section 37 of the Land Reform (Scotland) Act 2003 provides for the creation of a 'community interest in land', this 'interest' being registered – no surprises here – in the Register of Community Interests in Land. The process begins with an application by the community body to the Scottish Ministers, who, if they approve, proceed to carry out the registration. The effect of registration is to limit the owner's power of sale and to give the community body a type of pre-emption right.

Section 61 of the 2003 Act provides for appeals, and the owner of the land, West Register (Property Investments) Ltd, appealed. Though called an 'appeal', the procedure takes the form of a summary application to the sheriff, with the person 'appealing' being identified as the pursuer rather than appellant, and the Lord Advocate (representing the Scottish Ministers) being identified as defender rather than respondent. Such cases are heard in the sheriff court. Sheriff Peter Paterson noted (para 6):

> What s 61 … does not do is provide any guidance as to the correct approach to the appeal process. Is the sheriff to approach the appeal in the manner akin to judicial review, hear evidence if there is a dispute as to fact, or consider the merits of the application? Fortunately in this case both parties were in agreement that I was to approach my task in the manner of a judicial review. In my opinion the parties are correct in this view.

In the present case an interest was registered against Halmyre Steading, Halmyre Mains, Peeblesshire, a property extending to 3.35 acres. The community body in whose favour registration was made was called Halmyre Community Company. The owner, West Register (Property Investments) Ltd, appealed.

Section 38(1)(b) of the 2003 Act makes it a requirement that, among other things:

  (i) a significant number of the members of the community ... have a substantial connection with the land; or
 (ii) the land is sufficiently near to land with which those members of that community have a substantial connection and that its acquisition by the community body is compatible with furthering the achievement of sustainable development;

In their original decision the Scottish Ministers had founded on (i), concluding that: 'As the land is wholly located within the defined community, Ministers consider that the criterion in s 38(1)(b)(i) of the Act (that a significant number of members of the community defined under s 34(1)(a) ... have a substantial connection with the land) has been met' (para 10).

Though the pursuer presented a number of arguments, the core of his case, as summarised by the sheriff, was as follows (para 10):

The pursuer's contention is that the Scottish Ministers have simply failed to apply any of the criteria set out in s 38(1)(b)(i). The pursuer's position is that on the face of the decision there is no evidence that the ... Ministers have considered any part of the legislation. The ... Ministers' position was essentially that the residence in the defined community established the connection. The ... Ministers submitted that in dealing with this question in the way it did the ... Ministers were following established practice and if the pursuer was correct it would make registration very difficult if not impossible.

The sheriff agreed with the pursuer (paras 11, 12 and 13):

I fail to see how mere residence can establish a substantial connection. This is particularly so in the context of this registration as the community is spread over a large area and the land in question is composed of disused farm buildings. A connection suggests some form of interaction between the member of the community and the land. It may amount to no more than passing through the land or perhaps even just looking at it. Residence is a passive act. Given the size and nature of the land it is quite possible that a resident may not even know of the land's existence. If they do not know of its existence, in my opinion it is not possible for a connection to exist. The mere fact that someone lives in the community carries with it no automatic implication of a connection, in the sense of an interaction between the resident and the land.

  If however residence is enough to establish a connection for the ... Ministers' approach to be correct as a matter of law the residence would have to establish not only a connection but a substantial connection. But if that is correct the qualification that the connection has to be substantial is unnecessary, because the same fact, residence, establishes both ...

  [T]he error in the ... Ministers' reasoning become even clearer when consideration is given to the opening words of s 38(1)(b)(i), 'a significant number'. If the ... Ministers are correct in their approach to 'substantial connection' it means that all members of the community have a substantial interest. Therefore if the ... Ministers' approach is correct then the words 'a significant number' are redundant. To favour an interpretation of a statutory provision that rendered part of the provision redundant would be contrary to the principles of statutory interpretation.

This was evidently an important case, and it is unfortunate that it is unreported, does not appear on the Scottish Courts website, and is not in databases such as Westlaw. The defender's position, that 'if the pursuer was correct it would make registration very difficult if not impossible', is noteworthy. The Community Empowerment (Scotland) Act 2015 has now amended s 38 in a number of ways, including the repeal of the word 'substantial': see ss 41, 144(2), and sch 5. (For more about this Act, see p 75 below.) This may or may not fully deal with the issues raised in the present case.

RESIDENTIAL RIGHT TO BUY

(39) Boyle v South Lanarkshire Council
2015 SLT (Lands Tr) 189, 2015 Hous LR 99 (merits)
2015 SLT (Lands Tr) 205 (expenses)

In this and the next two cases the basic issue for determination by the Lands Tribunal was not whether there was a right to buy (that was a matter of concession), but the amount of the discount, in each case the tenant arguing for the 'old' discount level whilst the landlord argued for the new, and lower, discount under the 'modernised' right to buy. In all three cases the Tribunal found in favour of the landlord.

In the present case the applicant sought to buy her council property at 44 Ansdell Avenue, Blantyre. The Council offered her a discount based on the 'modernised' right-to-buy regime (Housing (Scotland) Act 2001 s 49) since her tenancy had begun in 2013. She applied to the Tribunal under s 65(2) of the Housing (Scotland) Act 1987, asserting that, as a council tenant since 1990, she was entitled to discount at the old and higher level as provided for by the 1987 Act s 62 in its original form.

It was held, after consideration of the Housing (Scotland) Act 2001 (Scottish Secure Tenancy etc) Order 2002, SSI 2002/318, that the discount offered by the Council was correct. The terms of the legislation, whereby the crucial issue (subject to certain qualifications) is when the *current* tenancy began, were unambiguous.

(40) Ireland v Dundee City Council
2015 GWD 40-635, Lands Tr

This case has some similarity with the previous one. A public-sector tenant moved to another property, and his daughter became tenant instead. When she applied to buy the property (4 Crombie Terrace, Dundee), the question was whether she could benefit from the 'old' discount level to which her father would have been entitled. It was held that, since her tenancy had begun under the 'modernised' right-to-buy regime, she could claim discount only at the lower level.

The Tribunal criticised the Council for the poor drafting of its housing documentation and also for its poor record-keeping.

(41) Mark v City of Edinburgh Council
2015 SLT (Lands Tr) 157

This case was similar to those above, though the tenant's argument was different. The tenant exercised his right to buy a property at 46/3 Dumbryden Gardens, Edinburgh. The housing authority offered a discount on the basis of the 'modernised' right to buy but the tenant sought the higher discount calculated at the old rate. The case was argued on the basis that the housing authority had not properly explained to the tenant, at the time when he gave up a previous tenancy, that the tenancy of the new property would be subject to the lower discount rate if he ever wished to exercise his right to buy. He argued that if that had been properly explained to him he would not have moved into the new property.

It was held that the task of the Tribunal was simply to determine the correct rate of discount, and that the discount offered by the housing authority had been correctly calculated in terms of the legislation, and that accordingly the tenant's argument could not succeed. 'Mr Mark's complaint', observed the Tribunal at para 35, 'if factually well founded, is a serious one, but it is not one for which the tribunal is empowered to provide a remedy.' On this latter issue, see also the next case.

(42) Lee v Highland Council
2015 GWD 38-601, Lands Tr

A public-sector tenant applied to buy her property at 59 Dunain Road, Inverness. The application was refused because the area had been designated a 'pressured area' (as to which see Housing (Scotland) Act 1987 s 61B and also *Conveyancing 2010* pp 52–53), and in such areas the right to buy is suspended. The tenant then applied to the Lands Tribunal. There were various grounds, only two of which seem worth mentioning. One was that the refusal letter was not sufficiently clearly a 'refusal' as required by s 68 of the Act. This was the letter:

> Dear Ms Lee,
>
> PURCHASE OF COUNCIL HOUSE
>
> I refer to your recent enquiry regarding the purchase of your council house.
>
> With effect from 13 October 2010, the Highland Council's housing stock was designated as a 'Pressured Area' as defined in the Housing (Scotland) Act 2001. What this means is that tenants who began their current tenancy on or after 30 September 2002 have had their 'Right to Buy' suspended. I note from our records that you commenced your current tenancy on 17 February 2003 and therefore your right to buy has been suspended.
>
> I am sorry that this news will come as a disappointment to you …

Perhaps unsurprisingly, the Tribunal took the view that, whilst the word 'refuse' was not used, the letter was a refusal.

The other ground was that the Council had failed in certain information duties, the main one being that contained in s 23(5) of the Housing (Scotland) Act 2001: 'Where the tenant's right under [Part III of the 1987 Act] to purchase the house is affected by any amendment to that Part or the exercise of any power conferred by that Part, the landlord must inform the tenant of that fact and of the extent to which the tenant's right to purchase is affected.' Where, if anywhere, this argument might have brought the applicant we do not know. The Tribunal declined to consider it (para 23):

> We do not propose to resolve this point since the respondents rested their position upon the fact that the Tribunal does not have jurisdiction to deal with claims based upon any failure to provide information under s 23. This is what we said in *Boyle* [Case (39) above]. We are aware of no provision from which jurisdiction could be inferred.

On this latter point, see also the preceding case.

LEASES

(43) Tenzin v Russell
[2015] CSIH 8A, 2015 Hous LR 11

The Tenancy Deposit Schemes (Scotland) Regulations 2011, SSI 2011/176, have generated numerous actions launched by tenants of residential property where the landlord has failed to comply with the Regulations. The incentive to the tenant is that the court can order the landlord to pay the tenant up to three times the amount of the tenancy deposit. In the present case, involving property at 4/6 Admiralty Street, Edinburgh, the sheriff awarded the maximum. The landlord appealed to the sheriff principal, without success: see 2014 Hous LR 17 (*Conveyancing 2014* Case (51)). The landlord then appealed to the Inner House. There were two grounds of appeal. One was that the amount awarded was excessive. The other was technical: the tenant, a party litigant, had had a declaratory crave, but had had no crave for decerniture for payment.

It was held that both grounds of appeal failed. As to the amount awarded, the Inner House stressed 'the limited role of an appellate court in considering the exercise of a discretion held by the court below' (para 11). As to the second ground of appeal, 'the sheriff was well entitled in the exercise of his discretion to allow the application to be amended' (para 9).

(44) Jenson v Fappiano
2015 GWD 4-89, Sh Ct

The landlord of residential property at 9/9 Hopetoun Crescent, Edinburgh failed to pay the deposit into an approved scheme. The tenant, after having been evicted for non-payment of rent, sought payment from the landlord under the Tenancy

Deposit Schemes (Scotland) Regulations 2011. He claimed the maximum amount, which is to say thrice the deposit. The case is of interest because the sheriff (Tom Welsh QC) attempts to give some basis for quantifying the award, the legislation being silent on the subject. The sheriff observed (para 15) that 'the quantification of sanction is not measured by loss or prejudice suffered by the tenant, nor, may I say, should it be measured only by the length of the Lord Chancellor's foot, ie subjectively. There must be an objective basis and rationale to the sanction.' He took the view (para 17) that 'the wider financial dispute between these parties' was not relevant, for 'they each have adequate remedies for any damages they can prove arising from breach of contract'. He noted (para 18) that this was not a case of 'repeated and flagrant non-participation in, or non-compliance with the regulations, by a large professional commercial letting undertaking'. The landlord had also eventually, albeit belatedly, paid the money into an approved scheme. Taking these various factors into account, the sheriff concluded (para 18) that it would be 'fair, proportionate and just' to set the award at one third of the amount of the deposit (ie one ninth of the possible maximum).

(45) Kirk v Singh
2015 SLT (Sh Ct) 111

The facts of this case were somewhat similar to those in *Jenson v Fappiano* (above). The deposit had been £380, and the award made by the sheriff (George Jamieson) was £500. He expressly approved the overall approach adopted by Sheriff Walsh in *Jenson*. One factor present in this case that was not present in *Jenson* was that the landlord had acted through an agent (para 10):

> The defender, a registered landlord, acted through his agent. Although that ignorance is no excuse, it is a factor to be taken into account in the exercise of my discretion. Furthermore, the tenancy has now ended. The deposit was returned to the pursuer at the end of the tenancy.

(46) Omale v Barcenas
2015 GWD 8-157, Sh Ct

There was a tenancy of residential property at 24 Caledonian Road, Corpach, Fort William. The deposit was £500, which the landlord did not pay into an approved scheme. After the end of the tenancy the tenant asked for return of the deposit. The landlord refused, alleging damage to the property. The tenant sued for the £500, less £84 of unpaid rent. Decree in favour of the pursuer was granted, with expenses. 'It would be contrary to public policy,' observed the sheriff (R Davidson) at para 11, 'to entertain the defender's assertions of the pursuer's breach of the tenancy agreement when he has unlawfully failed to place the deposit into the hands of the Tenancy Deposit Scheme administrator'. In other words, where a landlord has been in breach of the Tenancy Deposit Schemes (Scotland) Regulations 2011, the deposit must be returned without deduction. The sheriff added that (para 13):

The present claim should not be in court. It should have been adjudicated upon, free of charge and any award of expenses, by an adjudicator appointed in relation to an approved Tenancy Deposit Scheme. That would have happened but for the defender's unlawful action in retaining the deposit which he knew or ought to have known should have been deposited with the administrator of such a scheme.

It will be noted that in this case the former tenant did not seek an actual award under the Regulations.

(47) Cordiner v Al-Shaibany
2015 SLT (Sh Ct) 189

This case involved the question of what counts as a 'deposit' for the purposes of the Tenancy Deposit Schemes (Scotland) Regulations 2011. There was a tenancy of a flat at 2 Lawrence Street, Broughty Ferry, Dundee. The tenancy agreement required payment of two months' rent in advance. The landlord did not pay this money into an approved scheme, and the tenant later sought an award, on the basis that the landlord had contravened the Regulations. The landlord denied that the money was a 'deposit'. Section 120 of the Housing (Scotland) Act 2006 says that 'a tenancy deposit is a sum of money held as security for (a) the performance of any of the occupant's obligations arising under or in connection with a tenancy or an occupancy arrangement, or (b) the discharge of any of the occupant's liabilities which so arise'.

It was held (by Sheriff L A Drummond, para 13) that 'these payments were payments of rent and not payments held as security for the performance of any of the tenant's obligations'. An English case, *Johnson v Old* [2013] EWCA Civ 415, [2013] HLR 26, was cited with approval.

(48) Malin v Crown Aerosols UK Ltd
[2015] CSOH 58, 2015 GWD 17-290

A large site (4.4 acres) at Houstoun Industrial Estate, Livingston, West Lothian had been leased out in 1977 for a term of 90 years (with an option to the tenant to extend to 180 years). The tenant wished to demolish a derelict building. It asserted that in terms of the lease it had the right so to do. The landlords (who were individuals) asserted that demolition was forbidden by the lease, except with their consent. They raised the present action to interdict the tenant from demolishing the building.

Various provisions of the lease were invoked by the parties, in particular the provision in clause sixth whereby the tenant was to 'maintain in good order and when necessary to re-erect' the buildings on site. The Lord Ordinary (Lord Tyre) adopted an interpretation that was midway between the opposing views. He did not agree with the landlords that 'necessary' should be understood to refer only to 'a destructive event external to the parties, such as fire or explosion' (para 6). He approached the provisions of the lease from the standpoint of commercial common sense, stressing in particular that this was a lease of a large site that was for a very long term. He remarked (para 15):

I accept the tenant's alternative submission that there may be circumstances where re-erection of a building is 'necessary' even though an existing building is still standing on the site. These might include (i) where the existing building is obsolete and unsuitable for any reasonable use, regardless of cost of repair; or (ii) where the cost of repair is excessive in relation to what it would cost to demolish and rebuild premises similar to the existing building. In each of these cases (and I note that the tenant offers to prove in the present case that both of those descriptions apply), I consider that it is in accordance with commercial common sense to describe re-erection as 'necessary'. It must follow, as a matter of practicality, that demolition of the existing obsolete and/or uneconomic building is also 'necessary' in order to allow re-erection to proceed.

Nevertheless he held that the demolition, and the plans for rebuilding, would require the landlords' consent on a 'not to be unreasonably withheld' basis. He concluded (para 17) that 'it is not appropriate at this stage either to grant decree for interdict as concluded for or to dismiss the action. If parties are not agreed on whether demolition of the existing building and erection of a new building is "necessary", then proof may be required'.

(49) Marks and Spencer plc v BNP Paribas Securities Services Trust Co (Jersey) Ltd
[2015] UKSC 72, [2015] 3 WLR 1843

The claimant in this English case was the tenant of a sub-underlease of four floors of a building in Paddington, London. Each floor was held on a separate sub-underlease, but the parties were the same, and the contractual terms were substantially the same. Rent was payable 'yearly and proportionately for any part of a year by equal quarterly instalments in advance' on the English quarter days (Lady Day, Midsummer, Michaelmas and Christmas). There was a break clause allowing the tenant to terminate the leases on 24 January 2012 by giving the landlord six months' notice, provided that, on the break date, the tenant paid break premiums equivalent to a year's rent, and also subject to the condition that no rent arrears existed.

In July 2011 the tenant served break notices. In December 2011 it paid a quarter's rent (for each sub-underlease) and also, soon thereafter, it paid the break premiums. The report reveals that the break premium was £919,800 plus VAT for one of the floors: presumably there were comparable figures for the other three.

There was no dispute that the four leases were all validly terminated with effect from 24 January 2012. But the question arose whether the landlord was entitled to retain the whole of the rent for the quarter that ran from Christmas 2011 to Lady Day (25 March) 2012. The tenant demanded that part of the rent paid in December 2011 should be returned, on the basis of an apportionment, the two relevant periods being from 25 December 2011 to 24 January 2012 (for which rent was undeniably due) and from the latter date to 25 March 2012 (for which period no rent was due, in the opinion of the tenant). When the landlord declined to return any of the rent, the tenant sued. The tenant was successful at first instance: see [2013] EWHC 1279 (Ch). The Court of Appeal, however, found in favour of the landlord: see [2014] EWCA Civ 603. The case then went to the Supreme Court.

'It is rightly accepted on behalf of the claimant', noted Lord Neuberger at para 14, 'that there is no provision in the lease which expressly obliges the landlords to pay the apportioned sum to the tenant. Accordingly, it follows that in order to succeed the claimant has to establish that such an obligation must be implied into the lease.' The court reviewed the law of implied terms, and this case may now come to be regarded, for the time being at least, as the leading case on that subject. It is not possible here to set out the court's approach in detail, but in a nutshell it adopted a strict approach to the argument based on an implied term, and thus was disapproving of the more liberal approach that had been attracting some support in recent years. No implied term was found to exist with the result that the tenant's claim failed.

There are heretics who question whether there is really a distinction between the law of interpretation on the one hand and the law of implied terms on the other. The Supreme Court re-asserted the difference. As Lord Neuberger said (para 26): 'construing the words used and implying additional words are different processes governed by different rules'. Whether the heretics will be silenced may be doubted.

Whilst not binding in Scotland, the decision will be strongly persuasive here, given the similarity of the law in this area. As with *Arnold v Britton* [2015] UKSC 36, [2015] AC 1619 (Case (50) below), the Supreme Court is adopting a tough-minded approach to commercial contracts, including commercial leases. Bleeding-heart sympathy is, for the time being, out of fashion.

The Supreme Court took the view that the Apportionment Act 1870 was not applicable, and said that a court should not readily upset the long-settled interpretation of a statute, especially when that interpretation had the sanction of judicial authority: see paras 45, 57, 75). That may seem common sense. Why then in *Royal Bank of Scotland plc v Wilson* [2010] UKSC 50, 2011 SC (UKSC) 66 (*Conveyancing 2010*, Case (66)) did the Supreme Court upset the accepted interpretation of the enforcement rules for standard securities contained in the Conveyancing and Feudal Reform (Scotland) Act 1970, an interpretation that was not only of long standing but also had the sanction of Inner House authority?

It might be added that the Apportionment Act seems nowadays not to be discussed in Scotland in relation to leases. The most recent discussion seems to have been in J Rankine, *The Law of Leases in Scotland* (3rd edn 1916) chapter XV.

(50) Arnold v Britton
[2015] UKSC 36, [2015] AC 1619

Between 1977 and 1991, 21 chalets at Oxwich Leisure Park, Oxwich, Gower, Swansea were let out on 99-year leases. The leases provided that there would be an annual service charge payable to the landlord, which would be £90 in the first year and which would increase by 10% every year. Other properties on the estate (which had been leased before 1977) had less burdensome annual service charge provisions. As time went on the charge to the 21 lessees became increasingly burdensome, and the tenants eventually litigated, hoping to have their leases interpreted to mean that the escalator sum meant only a maximum, the actual sum payable to be ascertained in terms of proportionality.

Cases about the interpretation of contracts never end, and the approach that courts will take in individual cases is not always predictable, albeit that the verbal formulations of the rules may not vary much. Here the court came to the conclusion that the natural meaning of the words – which was the interpretation favoured by the landlord – prevailed. Two passages from the main opinion, that of Lord Neuberger, are worth quotation. The first, from para 15:

> The meaning has to be assessed in the light of (i) the natural and ordinary meaning of the clause, (ii) any other relevant provision of the lease, (iii) the overall purpose of the clause and the lease, (iv) the facts and circumstances known or assumed by the parties at the time that the document was executed, and (v) commercial common sense, but (vi) disregarding subjective evidence of any party's intentions.

And at para 20:

> While commercial common sense is a very important factor to take into account when interpreting a contract, a court should be very slow to reject the natural meaning of a provision as correct simply because it appears to be a very imprudent term for one of the parties to have agreed, even ignoring the benefit of wisdom of hindsight. The purpose of interpretation is to identify what the parties have agreed, not what the court thinks that they should have agreed. Experience shows that it is by no means unknown for people to enter into arrangements which are ill-advised, even ignoring the benefit of wisdom of hindsight, and it is not the function of a court when interpreting an agreement to relieve a party from the consequences of his imprudence or poor advice. Accordingly, when interpreting a contract a judge should avoid re-writing it in an attempt to assist an unwise party or to penalise an astute party.

Since the lessees were individuals, it might be wondered whether consumer protection legislation was applicable: see in particular Directive 93/13/EEC, transposed in the UK originally by the Unfair Terms in Consumer Contracts Regulations 1994, SI, 1994/3159, later by the Unfair Terms in Consumer Contracts Regulations 1999, SI 1999/2083, and now by part 2 of the Consumer Rights Act 2015. It is well settled that this area of law can apply to contracts relating to land: see eg *Marriott v Greenbelt Group Ltd*, 2 December 2015, Lands Tribunal (Case (9) above). That question did not, however, arise, because at the dates when these leases came into being the legislation was not yet in force. Whether or not the rules just mentioned might apply to new leases to individuals, *Arnold* will still be relevant to commercial leases where the protective rules are not applicable. As noted in connection with the previous case, the Supreme Court is at present adopting a tough-minded approach to commercial contracts.

Being an English case, *Arnold* is not binding in Scots law, but given that the approach to the interpretation of contracts, including leases, is similar on the two sides of the border, this decision will be highly persuasive here, and indeed signs of its influence are apparent in the next case.

(51) @Sipp (Pension Trustees) Ltd v Insight Travel Services Ltd
[2015] CSIH 91, 2016 SLT 131

A lease of Gareloch House, Port Glasgow came to an end in 2012. The landlord raised the present action as to the tenant's repairing obligations, concluding for the sum of £1,051,086.25 in terms of a schedule of dilapidations. The issues were summarised at first instance ([2014] CSOH 137, 2014 Hous LR 54, *Conveyancing 2014* Case (42)) by the Lord Ordinary (Lord Tyre) thus (paras 2 and 3):

> The first issue is whether, on a proper construction of the lease, the defender's obligation at termination is limited to putting the premises into the condition in which they were accepted by it at the commencement of the lease. The second issue is whether, on a proper construction of the lease, the pursuer is entitled to payment of a sum equal to the cost of putting the premises into the relevant state of repair, regardless of whether it actually intends to carry out any such work.

The Lord Ordinary found in favour of the tenant on both issues. As to the second, he considered *Grove Investments Ltd v Cape Building Products Ltd* [2014] CSIH 43, 2014 Hous LR 35 (*Conveyancing 2014* Case (41)) to be indistinguishable.

The landlord reclaimed, successfully. On the first issue, the Inner House (Lord Menzies, Lady Smith, Lady Clark of Calton) took the view (para 20) that:

> The balance of authority (*Credit Suisse v Beegas Nominees Ltd* [[1994] 4 All ER 803], as followed in *Taylor Woodrow Properties Ltd v Strathclyde Regional Council* [unreported, Lord Penrose, 15 December 1995]; *Lowe v Quayle Munro Ltd* 1997 SC 346; *L Batley Pet Products Limited v North Lanarkshire Council* [[2014] SC (UKSC) 174]) supports the conclusion that an obligation to keep subjects in good and substantial repair carries an obligation to put them into that state of repair.

On the second issue, the court commented, at para 30:

> The *Grove Investments* case was materially different. It concerned a clause which provided for parties to 'make a financial settlement' according to the 'value' of the Schedule of Dilapidations and that led the court to conclude that 'value' was to be ascertained by principles analogous to those which would apply to a claim for damages. The tenant's obligation to pay did not, in that case, depend on the landlord making an election and serving a notice. By contrast, the clause in the present case concerned not a claim for damages but for a contractual debt comparable to that which was claimed by the landlord in *Jervis v Harris* [1996] Ch 195 where Millet LJ, as he then was, drew that distinction in relation to a claim arising from a tenant's failure to fulfil a repairing obligation. There was no room for the importation of concepts applicable to damages claims and none for construing a clause conferring an express contractual entitlement as though it was a claim for damages. It was also significant that the landlord's right to payment under clause 7 depended on his making an election and serving a notice at termination; that accorded with the right to a contractual payment.

The influence of the decision of the Supreme Court in *Arnold v Britton* [2015] UKSC 36, [2015] AC 1619 (Case (50) above) is evident.

(52) Mapeley Acquisition Co (3) Ltd (in receivership)
v City of Edinburgh Council
[2015] CSOH 29, 2015 GWD 13-234

This was a dilapidations claim for £8,062,006.91, in relation to a lease of Chesser House, 500 Gorgie Road, Edinburgh. Some degree of dilapidation was admitted by the tenant. There were two matters in dispute as to the interpretation of the lease. In the words of the Lord Ordinary (Lord Doherty) at paras 3–4:

> The first issue is whether ... clause 3.37.2 entitles the landlord to payment of a sum equal to the cost of putting the premises into the relevant state of repair, regardless of whether it actually intends to carry out any such work. The second issue is whether clause 3.37.1.1 obliges the tenant to replace at expiry or termination of the lease all items of plant and equipment which were on the premises at the date of entry, whatever the condition of those items at expiry or termination; or whether the tenant's obligation is restricted to replacing, at expiry or termination, such items as are missing, broken, worn, damaged or destroyed.

It was held that the tenant's interpretation of the lease was to be preferred on both issues. It may be noted that the case was decided before the Inner House decision in @Sipp (Pension Trustees) Ltd v Insight Travel Services Ltd [2015] CSIH 91 (Case (51) above) appeared.

(53) PDPF GP Ltd v Santander UK plc
[2015] CSOH 40, 2015 Hous LR 45

This case concerned a 15-year lease, running from 1998 to 2013, of an office building at South Gyle Business Park, Edinburgh. Two weeks before the ish the landlord served a dilapidations notice and, when the tenant did not do the work, claimed £753,471.24 by way of the estimated cost. The defence was that the landlord had not given sufficient notice, for it would not have been possible to carry out the works in just two weeks. The defender argued that accordingly it was not bound to pay anything. This argument was rejected by the Lord Ordinary (Lord Woolman). The obligation to maintain was an ongoing one and did not require notice to activate it.

(54) BNP Paribas Securities Services Trust Co (Jersey) Ltd
v Mothercare (UK) Ltd
[2015] CSOH 47, 2015 Hous LR 42

This case concerned a dilapidations claim for property at 123 Sauchiehall Street, Glasgow. The lease had begun in 1986, and expired in 2013. The landlords were, intriguingly, 'BNP Paribas Securities Services Trust Company (Jersey) Ltd and BNP Paribas Securities Services Trust Company Ltd as trustees of Threadneedle Property Unit Trust'.

After the action had begun, the parties agreed to a remit to a chartered surveyor. The current stage of the case concerned objections raised by the defender to the surveyor's draft report. The court dismissed the defender's objections. The case was fact-specific, but it may be noted that the court cited with approval the approach to such disputes that was laid down by Lord Hodge in *BAM Buchanan Ltd v Arcadia Group Ltd* [2013] CSOH 107A, 2013 Hous LR 42 (*Conveyancing 2013* Case (41)).

(55) Beatsons Building Supplies Ltd v Trustees of the Alex F Noble & Son Ltd Executive Benefits Scheme
2015 GWD 15-271, Sh Ct

The Loon Burn, a tributary of the North Esk in Midlothian, is a bonnie burn. But not all of it is bonnie, and indeed not all of it is visible, for a stretch is nowadays buried, culverted in a steel pipe, 2 metres in diameter, under the Eastfield Industrial Estate, Penicuik. Perhaps the bonnie burn resented the indignity, for the culvert deteriorated, causing problems to the concrete yard above.

Who was to pay for the repair work? The issue was whether property which had been leased included the culvert. If it did, responsibility, under the lease, lay with the tenant. The sheriff (N A Ross) held that 'the default common law position means that the lease of the premises carries with it all rights *a coelo usque ad centrum*' (para 43) and that, accordingly, the culvert was presumptively part of the leased property. The valiant attempts of counsel for the tenant did not succeed in persuading the sheriff that the lease should be read as departing from that default position.

(56) Gyle Shopping Centre General Partners Ltd v Marks and Spencer plc
[2015] CSOH 14, 2015 GWD 6-127

This case was a further stage of the Great Primark Crisis at Edinburgh's Gyle Centre. The owner (the pursuer) wished to lease part of the centre's vast car-park to Primark. At the first stage, Marks and Spencer plc succeeded in blocking this on the ground that the car-park was included, to the extent of a *pro indiviso* share, in its long lease: see [2014] CSOH 59, 2014 GWD 18-352 and [2014] CSOH 122, 2015 SCLR 171 (*Conveyancing 2014* Case (34)). In this second stage, the owner tried a new approach. Clause 24 of the lease authorised the owner to carry out 'works' provided that the consent of the tenants was obtained, such consent not to be unreasonably withheld. After a careful consideration of the lease as a whole, the Lord Ordinary (Lord Tyre) concluded that clause 24 was to be read as capable of authorising the owner to develop a new store in part of the car-parking area. That still left open the factual question of whether the refusal of consent by the defender had been reasonable: the Lord Ordinary concluded that it had not been reasonable.

An issue not explored in the case is how the new development might alter the real right of Marks and Spencer plc in the affected part of the car park, and how any such alteration would be given effect to in the Land Register.

(57) Homebase Ltd v Grantchester Developments (Falkirk) Ltd
[2015] CSOH 49, 2015 Hous LR 38

This case, and the next, concern that familiar term of commercial leases, that the lease is not assignable except with the landlord's consent, and that consent is not to be 'unreasonably withheld'. The issue of what counts as reasonable or unreasonable in this context is the subject of a substantial volume of case law on both sides of the border.

There was a lease of a shop at Central Retail Park, Grahams Road, Falkirk, running from 1995 to 2020. The tenant wished to assign, and the proposed assignee was of good financial standing. But the landlord understood that there was to be a reverse grassum (reverse premium), and before making a decision as to consent it asked for details about this reverse grassum. The tenant declined to supply the information and, after a period of deadlock, the tenant raised this action, seeking declarator that the landlord was refusing consent unreasonably. The tenant's position was that the landlord's legitimate interest was (para 7):

> limited to the proposed assignee being of sound financial standing and demonstrably capable of fulfilling the tenant's obligations in terms of the lease. If the proposed assignee satisfied those requirements, it was unreasonable for the landlord to withhold consent. The issue of whether a rent subsidy or reverse premium was to be payable by the tenant to the proposed assignee was a collateral matter falling outside the considerations specified as relevant by clause 5.11.2. Failure to provide information relating to such matters could not therefore be a ground upon which consent could reasonably be withheld.

The Lord Ordinary (Lord Tyre) did not agree (para 11): 'In my opinion the landlord's request for this information is reasonable, entitling it to withhold consent unless and until the information is supplied. There are ample judicial dicta recognising that the payment of a rent subsidy or reverse premium may affect the rental value of the property.' He cited such cases as *Burgerking Ltd v Rachel Charitable Trust* [2006] CSOH 13, 2006 SLT 224 (*Conveyancing 2006* Case (57)), and *Norwich Union Life Insurance Society v Shopmoor* [1999] 1 WLR 531.

(58) Homebase Ltd v Hammersons (Kirkcaldy) Ltd
[2015] CSOH 50

The facts of this case were substantially the same as those of the previous case. The Lord Ordinary (Lord Tyre) issued a short opinion adopting what he had said in that case.

(59) STV Central Ltd v Semple Fraser LLP
[2015] CSIH 35, 2015 SLT 313

Since rent review clauses were introduced in the 1960s, they have proved all too easy to get wrong. Here the pursuer took a 20-year lease of premises at Pacific

Quay, Glasgow. The rent was composed of two elements, namely (i) the basic rent plus (ii) an 'enhanced rent', the latter being agreed on because the landlord had had to spend a substantial amount of money making the premises meet the high-tech requirements of the pursuer. The enhanced rent was to be increased annually so as to track the Retail Prices Index. The wording was:

> subject to review and compounded (upwards only) at each successive anniversary ('the Relevant Date') of the Date of Entry, according to the formula $R = 1 \times A/B$ where R is the Enhanced Rent payable from and after the Relevant Date, 1 is the Enhanced Rent payable prior to the Relevant Date, A is the RPI for the date two months before the Relevant Date … and B is the RPI for the date two months before the Date of Entry.

The meaning of this formula may not be apparent at first glance. But careful scrutiny shows it to be absurd. We quote the Lord Ordinary (Lord Woolman) (though we have not checked his calculation): 'If … the retail prices index increased at the rate of 3 per cent each year, STV would have been liable to pay an annual rent of £100 million in 2025' (see [2014] CSOH 82, para 4).

Possibly this would have been a suitable case for a rectification action, but 'on the advice of senior counsel, it decided against raising an action for rectification' (para 4). Eventually, agreement was reached between landlord and tenant for a replacement formula, the details of which are unknown. But at all events the tenant ended up with financial loss and sued the law firm that had acted for it, Semple Fraser, in professional negligence. The defender admitted liability and the claim was settled at an undisclosed sum. The defender then sought recovery from the firm of surveyors, CBRE Ltd, that had been involved, basing its recovery claim on s 3(2) of the Law Reform (Contributory Negligence) (Scotland) Act 1940, the factual basis of the claim being that the firm of surveyors had had some involvement with the terms of the rent review clause. The law firm framed its claim both in contract and in the law of voluntary assumption of responsibility.

At first instance it was held that its written pleadings failed to establish a relevant claim, and the action was dismissed: see [2014] CSOH 82, 2014 GWD 16-299 (*Conveyancing 2014* Case (61)). The pursuer reclaimed and, by a majority (Lady Clark dissenting), the reclaiming motion was allowed. Accordingly the case could now proceed to a proof.

(60) West Dunbartonshire Council v William Thompson and Son (Dumbarton) Ltd
[2015] CSIH 93, 2016 SLT 125

In 1971 a 60-year lease was entered into for premises at Birch Road, Broadmeadow Industrial Estate, Dumbarton. In 2011 the landlord served a rent review notice on the tenant, who was designed in the notice as 'Wm Thompson & Sons Ltd'. In fact its name was 'William Thompson and Son (Dumbarton) Limited'. The question was whether the notice was valid, given that the name in the notice did not match the name of the tenant. It will be observed that there were five discrepancies: (i) 'Wm' instead of 'William'; (ii) '&' instead of 'and'; (iii) 'Sons' instead of 'Son'; (iv) the omission of '(Dumbarton)'; and (v) 'Ltd' instead of 'Limited'. The sheriff held that the notice was invalid, and on appeal the Inner House agreed.

It was noted that in the authorities there were *obiter dicta* to the effect that minor spelling errors might not matter. The court declined (para 29) to comment on those *dicta*, but held that the cumulative effect of the errors was fatal to the validity of the notice.

We would suggest that the fifth of the discrepancies does not signify: 'Ltd' is, in our view, not an error but a permissible abbreviation of 'Limited'; cf the Company and Business Names (Miscellaneous Provisions) Regulations 2009, SI 2009/1085, sch 2 para 1(a).

(61) Akram v Ahmad
2015 GWD 6-128, Sh Ct

The 'Madras Cottage Takeaway' at 10A Lochend Road South, Edinburgh, was held on a 25-year lease, beginning in 2003. The owners and pursuers (Javaid Akram and Arshad Anwar Javaid) sought to irritate the lease because of non-payment of rent. The tenant (the defender) denied that any arrears existed. The difficulty was that all rent payments had been in cash (although the lease provided for payment by bank transfer) and so no banking records were available as evidence. Nor was it the practice of the landlords to offer, or of the tenant to ask for, receipts. The question of whether rental payments were up to date thus came down to the credibility of the witnesses, a matter made more difficult because evidence had to be given through interpreters. The outcome of the proof was that the pursuers' evidence was preferred, and accordingly the sheriff (Tom Welsh QC) pronounced decree of irritancy.

(62) Dem-Master Demolition Ltd v Healthcare Environmental Services Ltd
[2015] CSOH 154, 2015 GWD 38-604

An industrial unit (Unit 3, Centrelink 5, Calderhead Road, Shotts) was leased for five years from 1 January 2010. The tenant did not remove at 1 January 2015, on the basis that the lease was continuing by tacit relocation. The landlord then served a notice of irritancy on the ground of failure to maintain the property, and raised the present action of declarator and removing, and with pecuniary conclusions, including a conclusion for violent profits. The cost of restoring the property, averred the landlord, would be £2,081,350.74 (a curiously high figure given that the annual rent was only £82,000). The lease provided that:

> The Tenants accept the Premises as being in such condition as shown on the attached Photographic Schedule and in all respects fit for the Tenants' purposes and shall at their sole expense and, to the reasonable satisfaction of the Landlords, repair and maintain and renew (and, if necessary for the purposes of maintenance and repair, to

replace and rebuild) and decorate and keep the Premises and all permitted additions and new buildings, if any, in like condition as is evidenced on the said Photographic Schedule.

The parties were in disagreement as to whether the property had in fact deteriorated during the period of the lease, and moreover were in disagreement as to the proper interpretation of the quoted provision. Both the factual question as to whether there had been any deterioration (which the tenant denied), and the question of interpretation, were bedevilled by the fact that neither the landlord's nor the tenant's copy actually contained any 'photographic schedule'. Indeed, it rather seemed that no such schedule had ever existed.

The Lord Ordinary (Lord Doherty) commented (para 14) that 'I am not currently in a position to determine the proper construction of the repairing provision. ... That exercise cannot be conducted in a vacuum, without knowledge of all the material circumstances surrounding the execution of the lease.' At this stage of the proceedings he was not able to make any decision as to violent profits, but he took the opportunity to survey the authorities, and the survey is a valuable one.

(63) Inverclyde Council v McCloskey
2015 SLT (Sh Ct) 57, 2015 Hous LR 14

Section 4 of the Law Reform (Miscellaneous Provisions) (Scotland) Act 1985 says that a landlord who wishes to irritate for non-payment of rent must first serve an ultimatum notice. The statute is not wholly clear as to the form of notice, and over the years there have been a number of cases on the point, cases in which the tenant has challenged the validity of the ultimatum notice on the ground that it was disconform to the requirements of the 1985 Act, such challenges in some cases failing and in others succeeding. In *Conveyancing 2011* pp 103 ff we gave an extended account of the authorities, together with some practical suggestions. One of the cases reviewed there was *Scott v Muir* 2012 SLT (Sh Ct) 179 (*Conveyancing 2011* Case (60)), where Mhairi Stephen, sheriff principal of Lothian and Borders, said (para 43): 'For the notice to be effective it should specify the periods from which the rent arrears arise.' In the present case D L Murray, sheriff principal of North Strathclyde, disagreed (para 74):

I depart from her view in relation to her decision that the periods from which the rent arrears had arisen also require to be stated in the notice. I find no basis for this in terms of the statute or in the Scottish Law Commission report. I take the terms of the statute as being clear. While I can see that there would be merit in providing more explanation in the notice as to the basis for the calculation of the sum due I do not consider that to be required by the statute.

There is thus a conflict of authority. Until it is resolved, the position is that the decision of Sheriff Principal Stephen is binding in Lothian and Borders, that of Sheriff Principal Murray is binding in North Strathclyde, while in other sheriffdoms the position is open.

(64) River Clyde Homes Ltd v Woods
2015 Hous LR 33 (relevancy), 2015 GWD 33-542 (proof), Sh Ct

Can the ECHR be invoked to prevent an owner taking back possession of rented property, where, under general law, the right to take back possession exists? The answer is: sometimes yes. Article 8 (right to respect for private and family life) can apply where both (i) the tenancy is residential and (ii) the landlord is a public-sector entity.

In this case the pursuer sought to take back possession under s 36 of the Housing (Scotland) Act 2001. The tenant pled that the landlord's action was disproportionate and thus contrary to her Article 8 rights. At the first stage it was held that her averments were relevant and at the second stage they were, after proof, upheld.

(65) Van Lynden v Gilchrist
[2015] CSOH 147, 2015 SLT 864

A sublease conferred an option on the subtenant to remove a holiday chalet at the end of the sublease. Removal was resisted by the owner of the land, who claimed that the chalet had become hers by accession. It was held that the subtenant was entitled to remove the chalet. See **Commentary** p 163.

(66) ELB Securities Ltd v Love
[2015] CSIH 67, 2015 SLT 721, 2015 Hous LR 88

When a company is struck off the Companies Register, it ceases to exist. It dies. Its juristic personality is extinguished. And that, usually, is that. But the Companies Act 2006 (ss 1024–1034) says that a dead company can, by legal magic, be brought back to life, and when this is done 'the general effect of an order by the court for restoration to the register is that the company is deemed to have continued in existence as if it had not been dissolved or struck off the register' (s 1032(1), and see also s 1028). Retrospectivity, however, is never free from problems, because it seeks to change the past: a company ceased to exist, but also did not cease to exist.

Prestwick Hotels Ltd held a lease of the fifth floor at 166 Buchanan Street, Glasgow. The company was dissolved on 13 June 2013. On 3 October 2013 it was revived. So what happened to the lease?

In the normal case, by the time that a company is dissolved it no longer has any assets. But if for any reason a company is dissolved still holding assets, those assets pass to the Crown. This is the general rule of common law for any dissolved juristic person, but for companies there is an express statutory rule: Companies Act 2006 s 1012. Section 1013 then says that the Crown (represented by the Queen's and Lord Treasurer's Remembrancer) can disclaim such property. Section 1014 further provides that 'where notice of disclaimer is executed … as respects any property, that property is deemed not to have vested in the Crown under s 1012' (more retrospectivity).

In the present case, the Crown, acting through the QLTR, disclaimed the lease on 15 July 2013. So the sequence of events was: (i) dissolution on 13 June, with the lease immediately vesting in the Crown; (ii) Crown disclaimer on 15 July, with the lease immediately un-vesting in the Crown, or, rather, being deemed never to have vested in the first place; (iii) company restored to existence on 3 October, or, rather, being deemed never to have ceased to exist.

The landlord, ELB Securities Ltd, did not wish the revived company to continue as tenant, and the issue for the court was whether the revived company could or could not insist on doing so. At first instance the sheriff found in favour of the tenant. The landlord appealed to Sheriff Principal C A L Scott, who found in favour of the landlord: see 2014 GWD 28-562 (*Conveyancing 2014* Case (38)). The tenant appealed to the Inner House, which has refused the appeal. In doing so, it followed the reasoning of the sheriff principal.

There were two strands in particular to that reasoning. In the first place, s 1020 of the Companies Act 2006 says that 'the Crown's disclaimer operates to determine, as from the date of the disclaimer, the rights, interests and liabilities of the company, and the property of the company, in or in respect of the property disclaimed'. So, although the company was deemed never to have ceased to exist (s 1032), that fact did not rescue the lease which, since 15 July, had been dead beyond rescue.

The second strand to the sheriff principal's reasoning, also adopted by the Inner House, was that if the tenant's view of the law were correct, the results would be unworkable from a practical standpoint, because the period during which a dissolved company can be revived is (subject to certain qualifications) six years. If a lease could come back into existence at any time for six years, the title to the property would be blighted for that period. 'The construction contended for by the defenders would lead to uncertainty and confusion' (para 28).

(67) McManus v City Link Development Co Ltd
[2015] CSOH 178, 2016 GWD 6-126

Two tenants of housing association property in Motherwell raised an action for damages on the basis that their health had suffered because the properties they lived in had been built on ex-industrial land that had not, they claimed, been properly dealt with when the housing estate had been developed in the 1990s. They alleged that noxious fumes were emitted from the soil. They brought in three defenders, namely (i) the company that had developed the site, (ii) the company that had advised on the environmental aspects of the soil before the development took place, and (iii) the landlord, Lanarkshire Housing Association Ltd. The local authority was also initially a fourth defender, but had dropped out of the picture early on.

This stage of the case was about relevancy. No proof of the pursuers' averments had yet taken place, and it seems that all the defenders denied the pursuers' averments about health problems caused by noxious fumes.

The case against the first two defenders was primarily a delictual one, though with a claim based on alleged breach of environmental legislation added. The latter was unsuccessful. The delictual claim was dismissed against the first defender, but not against the second. The case may therefore now go to proof against the second defender.

The case against the third defender, the pursuers' landlord, was not delictual but contractual, based on the law of landlord and tenant, that law being primarily a matter of common law, though with an overlay of terms imposed by the housing legislation. It was held that the obligations of the landlord concern the *fabric* of the building that is let. Since there was no suggestion that there were any such problems, the pursuers' case against the third defender was held irrelevant.

The case is a remarkably long one, and contains extensive and valuable discussion of the authorities.

STANDARD SECURITIES

(68) Swift Advances plc v Martin
[2015] CSIH 65, 2015 Hous LR 50

A heritable creditor sought to enforce. The defence to the action was that the debtor-protection rules had not been sufficiently complied with by the pursuer. The case is of particular interest in that it was a situation of negative equity, and a central issue was how that fact might affect the rules. The Inner House, affirming the sheriff principal, who had in turn affirmed the sheriff, granted decree in favour of the pursuer. See **Commentary** p 197.

(69) Westfoot Investments Ltd v European Property Holdings Inc
2015 SLT (Sh Ct) 201, 2015 Hous LR 57

A heritable creditor sought to enforce. The defence to the action was that the debtor-protection rules had not been sufficiently complied with by the pursuer. This defence was rejected and decree granted.

The property in question was residential, but the interest of the owner, a Panamanian investment company, was commercial. The sheriff stated that, in his view, the debtor-protection rules do not apply in cases of this sort. See **Commentary** p 193.

(70) Glasgow City Council v Chaudhry
2015 SLT (Sh Ct) 107

Section 12(3A) of the Bankruptcy (Scotland) Act 1985 provided (until recently) that a sequestration petition is to be refused if the debtor 'gives or shows that there is sufficient security for the payment of' the petitioner's debt. In this case the debtor resisted a sequestration petition on the ground that the debt was secured by a standard security that her brother-in-law had granted over his property. But the courts have tended to interpret s 12(3A) and its predecessors very restrictively, and in this case the sheriff principal (C A L Scott) adhered to the traditional approach and granted the petition for sequestration. The decision is, however, now of only historical interest because the quoted provision has been repealed by the Bankruptcy and Debt Advice (Scotland) Act 2014 sch 4.

Given the hurdles that exist currently where a creditor seeks to enforce a debt secured by standard security over residential property, the alternative of enforcement via sequestration has some attractions.

(71) Alexander v West Bromwich Mortgage Co Ltd
[2015] EWHC 135 (Comm), [2015] 2 All ER (Comm) 224

In this English case, Mr Alexander borrowed money from the defendant, secured by a mortgage. The loan offer said that the loan term was 25 years, and the interest rate would be 1.99 percentage points over Bank of England base rate. Despite this the lender upped the interest rate to 3.99 percentage points over Bank of England base rate and asserted the right to demand repayment in full at any time on one month's notice. Mr Alexander raised an action for declaration (ie declarator) of the terms of the loan. Remarkably, he lost. See **Commentary** p 154.

SOLICITORS AND SURVEYORS

(72) Greig v Davidson
[2015] CSOH 44, 2015 SCLR 722

This strange case has been engaging the courts for some years. It has had two phases. In the first, a seller sued Mr Greig for breach of missives. Mr Greig's defence was that he had not instructed acceptance and so was not bound. That defence failed – see *Lorimer Homes Pittodrie Ltd v Greig* 2011 GWD 33-697 (*Conveyancing 2011* Case (5)) – and as a result, Mr Greig ended up paying damages of £125,000. In the second phase, Mr Greig raised the present action against the partners of the firm that had acted for him, a firm called KWAD, seeking to recoup his loss, namely £125,000 plus expenses, the sum sued for being £192,972.42 with interest.

The present stage of the second action is concerned with pleading points, the outcome of which was that proof before answer was allowed. In the action the pursuer pled, in the alternative, that he had not instructed acceptance, and, *esto* he had instructed acceptance, then (in the words of the Lord Ordinary, summarising the pursuer's pleadings) 'the defenders were in breach of their professional duties of care to the pursuer with the result that they negligently concluded missives in terms that were not agreeable to the pursuer'. Much of the debate was whether it was permissible for the pursuer to plead this *esto* case.

An issue not discussed, at least at this stage of the case, was that if the pursuer was successful on the first and primary branch of his pleadings (namely that he had not instructed acceptance), that would be contrary to the decision in the previous case that he *had* instructed acceptance. We will not explore this issue except to note that the doctrine of *res judicata* applies only between the same parties or parties in the same interest, which was not the situation here.

The background facts of this case, outlined in our 2011 volume (see above), were decidedly odd. Between Mr Greig and KWAD there was an intermediary, Mr Ingram, or perhaps Mr Ingram's firm with the odd name of PurpleSky.com LLP (but everything about this case is odd). This intermediary (whether Mr Ingram personally, or the LLP) received commission from Mr Greig of £15,000, for reasons which are unclear. The relationship of Mr Ingram to KWAD is likewise unclear: he may have been an 'employee' or a 'consultant'. The Lord Ordinary (Lord Stewart) was baffled: 'a mysterious business all round'. We are equally baffled. This must be the way they do conveyancing on Pluto.

(73) Dunvale Investments Ltd v Burness Paull & Williamsons LLP
[2015] CSOH 32, 2015 SCLR 567

The pursuer, a company, was a property developer that made extensive use of loan finance from a bank. Its banking arrangements were complex, but one element was that it was contractually obliged not to breach certain loan-to-value ratios. When, as a result of declining property values, such a breach took place, the company had, at the bank's insistence, to enter into a 'forward starting hedging agreement'. The net cost to the company of doing this was the remarkable sum of £2,716,842. In the present action the company sued its (former) law firm for that sum, arguing that this expense was incurred only because of the firm's negligence. Quantum was not in dispute, but the defender denied liability. It was held by the Lord Ordinary (Lord Tyre) that the defender had indeed been negligent, and decree for £2,716,842 was granted.

The core of the case was that the loan-to-value covenant was based on the value of properties over which the bank held heritable securities. The company had one property that was not subject to such a security, and if a security had been granted the effect would have been to remedy the breach. The defender's negligence lay in not having drawn this to the pursuer's attention. We quote the Lord Ordinary (para 55):

> What went wrong was that the defenders failed, during the period between execution of the RCF 2 agreement providing for security to be taken over the Osborne Street site and the drawdown of the £3.5 million facility, to alert Mr Wheatley [the company's manager and sole shareholder] to the adverse effect on the loan-to-value percentage of drawdown without additional security. I further conclude that that failure constituted a breach of the defenders' duty owed to the pursuer to carry out their instructions to the *Hunter v Hanley* standard.

(74) Gordon's Trs v Campbell Riddle Breeze Paterson LLP
[2015] CSOH 31, 2015 GWD 12-216

The pursuers were owners of three fields in Killearn, Stirlingshire, all let to the same tenant. They instructed their solicitors to serve notices to quit. The three notices were served on 8 November 2004, to take effect on 10 November 2005. The tenant did not remove, and the pursuers raised an action, in the Land Court, for removing. The action failed. The reason was that the notices had been fatally defective. They had designed the tenant as 'the Firm of Messrs A & J C Craig and John C Craig, sole proprietor of and trustee for said Firm'. Although at one stage the field had indeed been let to the firm of Messrs A & J C Craig, that had been long ago, and the current tenant was John Campbell Craig as an individual. We pause to note that it is a familiar fact that there cannot be a partnership with only one partner, so the designation just quoted perhaps should have rung an alarm bell.

The owners now sought damages from their law agents for professional negligence. The defence was negative prescription. The present action had been raised on 17 May 2012. The issue boiled down to whether the five-year period had begun to run in November 2008, when the Land Court had issued its ruling, in which case the present action had been raised timeously, or whether the period had begun to run in November 2004, when the invalid notices were served, or perhaps November 2005, in either of which cases the action had been raised too late. The Lord Ordinary (Lord Jones) held that any claim that the pursuers may have had had been extinguished by negative prescription.

(75) Gilchrist v McClure Naismith LLP
[2015] CSOH 134, 2015 GWD 33-533

Mr and Mrs Gilchrist, on the one hand, and Mr Barr, on the other, joined forces to buy and let out property at Riverside Business Park, Irvine, Ayrshire. The arrangement, described as a joint venture, involved various company vehicles. The relationship eventually broke down, and the Gilchrists took the advice of the defender as to what to do. One aspect of the advice given was to transfer the property, which was held by a company, Hawkhill Estates Ltd, which, we understand, was controlled by the Gilchrists, to another company, seemingly also controlled by them. In response, Mr Barr (or possibly one of his companies) raised an action against Hawkhill, arguing that the transfer was in breach of Hawkhill's fiduciary duties. In an unreported decision in 2011, Lord Hodge granted summary decree against Hawkhill.

In the present action the Gilchrists sought damages for allegedly negligent advice. This phase of the action was concerned with the pursuers' pleadings, especially the way that the alleged loss was quantified.

The specific facts of the case (which were of considerable complexity) cannot be fully reconstructed from the information available to us. The case is a reminder that if property is owned by one party but subject to obligations to deal with the property for, or partly for, the benefit of another party, the result may be to set up fiduciary duties between those parties.

(76) Bank of Ireland (UK) plc v Knight Frank LLP
[2015] CSOH 157, 2015 GWD 40-627

This was an action for damages for negligence in carrying out a valuation for lending purposes. The defender had provided the pursuer with a valuation of the property (at Haddockston, by Kilmacolm, Renfrewshire) of not less than £4.25 million. The bank made a loan which the borrower failed to repay. In this action the bank said that the property had in fact been worth only £170,000. We would guess that the bank had enforced its security, the sale price being the latter figure, but this and other background matters are unclear.

The case as reported concerned jurisdiction. The defender argued that the contract between itself and the bank was to be governed by English law and was subject to the exclusive jurisdiction of the English courts. Whilst the defender's standard terms did so provide, the question was whether those standard terms had in fact been incorporated into the contract. The Lord Ordinary (Lord Woolman) held that they had, and accordingly held that the action fell to be dismissed for want of jurisdiction.

(77) Sneddon v Scottish Legal Complaints Commission
[2015] CSIH 62, 2015 GWD 26-458

In a residential conveyancing transaction, the buyers noticed, just before settlement, that there had been minor storm damage to the roof of the property they were buying (in Falkirk, Stirlingshire). The transaction was settled on the basis of a £1,000 retention. A dispute then ensued between the buyers and the sellers about the roof problem. The buyers made a complaint about the way that their law agents had handled the matter, and a finding of inadequate professional service was made by the Scottish Legal Complaints Commission. Against this decision an appeal was made to the Inner House. The significance of the case lies mainly in what was said by the appellate court about retentions on settlement, a matter on which there is surprisingly little authority. We venture to say that henceforth no conveyancer should settle on the basis of retention without an awareness of this decision. See **Commentary** p 133.

(78) Schubert Murphy v The Law Society
[2014] EWHC 4561 (QB), [2015] PNLR 15

In this English case, Mr Kristofi engaged Messrs Schubert Murphy to act for him in buying a house. The transaction went through. But after moving in it emerged that the seller's law firm was a fake law firm and that it had vanished with the money. Mr Kristofi was compensated by his own law firm, who in turn were reimbursed by their insurer. The insurer then claimed against the Law Society (the claim being in the name of Messrs Schubert Murphy, on the subrogation principle). The basis of the claim was that the fake law firm had been listed as a genuine law firm on the Law Society's website. See **Commentary** p 172.

SPECIAL DESTINATIONS

(79) Hamilton v Campbell Smith WS
2015 GWD 10-174, Sh Ct

This was not a conveyancing case as such, but is a cautionary tale as to the perils of survivorship clauses. AN (the report does not give names) owned a property in Dalkeith, Midlothian. She disponed it, for love, favour and affection, to herself and to KH, equally between them, and to the survivor of them. Later she decided that she wanted JH to inherit her share. She consulted the defenders in this action, and they drew up a will for her which bequeathed to JH her 'whole right, title and interest' in the property. AN then died.

Who inherited the half share? Was it JH, *qua* legatee? Or was it KH, *qua* substitute in the destination? The answer was the latter. Whilst AN had (given the specific facts of the case) the *power* to evacuate the destination, she had not validly *exercised* that power, for the *mortis causa* evacuation of a special destination requires a special clause, as laid down by s 30 of the Succession (Scotland) Act 1964.

JH was not happy. She took the view that she had lost the half-share of the property through the negligence of the law firm that drew up AN's will. In this action she sued for damages. This stage of the case was concerned with the question of whether the pursuer's pleadings were satisfactory in terms of relevancy and specification. The sheriff (P A Arthurson) decided on a proof before answer.

We would mention that the parallel situation has arisen in England and Wales, where the Court of Appeal has held that in such cases there can be liability: *Carr-Glynn v Frearsons* [1998] 4 All ER 225.

BOUNDARIES, ENCROACHMENT AND PRESCRIPTION

(80) Munro v Finlayson
2015 SLT (Sh Ct) 123

The defenders constructed a driveway and yard on a small part of the pursuer's property. Ten years passed after which the pursuer sought an order ordaining the defenders to remove from the ground and an interdict against them from entering it. He did not seek removal of the driveway and yard. At first instance the sheriff exercised the court's equitable power to decline to order the defenders to remove. The sheriff principal reversed on appeal. See **Commentary** p 160.

(81) McLellan v J & D Pierce
[2015] CSIH 80, 2015 GWD 37-594

A new building by the defenders encroached to the extent of 4 to 6 metres on the pursuers' land. The sheriff ordered its removal. The defenders had known that they were encroaching, and so there was no basis for the court to exercise its equitable power to refuse removal. This finding was not challenged on appeal to the Inner House. See **Commentary** p 159.

(82) Jones v Muir
2015 GWD 11-183, Sh Ct

By agreement, the pursuers built a bungalow at their own expense on the defenders' land on the basis that they would be able to live in it for the rest of their lives. (The defenders were the daughter and son-in-law of the pursuers.) When the parties fell out, and the pursuers left the house, the pursuers claimed the value of the bungalow on the basis of unjustified enrichment. The claim was rejected. See **Commentary** p 161.

(83) Campbell-Gray v Keeper of the Registers of Scotland
2015 SLT (Lands Tr) 147

In 1980 land was split off from the Fanans Estate at Taynuilt in Argyll. This was done by two separate dispositions. At some places the boundary was a private road over which the disponee was granted a servitude of access. Much later, a dispute arose as to whether certain verges of the road were included in the disposition or whether, on the contrary, they continued to be owned by the estate. The verges were quite substantial, extending to several metres. They were grassy, with some trees. In places there was a ditch.

In the dispositions, the description comprised three elements, namely (i) a verbal description, (ii) a plan, and (iii) measurements.

The verbal description stated the subjects to be bounded by the access road, and it is settled law that a feature by which land is said to be bound is itself excluded from the subjects. The access road was thus excluded. The question to be determined, therefore, was whether 'the access road' included the ditch. The Tribunal decided that it did. Case law, admittedly, was equivocal. In *Butt v Galloway Motor Co Ltd* 1996 SC 261 the boundary feature of a 'driveway' was held not to include an adjacent hedge, but the hedge had not, on the facts, been integral to the driveway. The Roads (Scotland) Act 1984 s 151 (and predecessor legislation) defined 'road' to include the verge. Furthermore (para 45):

> In a case like the present we do not think the estate owners should be lightly taken to have conveyed to a third party the verges of roads being maintained and operated by them. The tarmac carriageway is narrow, being approximately 2.6–2.8 metres wide. It is not wide enough for two vehicles to pass. One of the verges contains a fairly deep ditch which is evidently of considerable utility as a ditch. We heard evidence of vehicles being accidently driven into the ditch on two occasions. If an adjacent owner were to be taken to have acquired the verge and were to appropriate it say by placing a fence hard against the tarmac there would be even less passing room. Pedestrians would have no place of refuge. The opportunity for widening the hard surface would be lost. Roadside maintenance would become more difficult. Similarly we infer the estate would not wish unnecessarily to lose control of the drainage system at the side of the road.

The interpretation of 'access road' as including the verges was, the Tribunal decided, consistent with the other two descriptive elements, ie the plan and the measurements. It was clear, therefore, that the verge was excluded from the 1980 dispositions.

Might title nonetheless have been acquired by positive prescription? For that, both title and possession were needed. It was, of course, perfectly possible for the dispositions to be *habile* for the purposes of prescription even if, on a natural interpretation, they did not include the verge. This was because the test was different. In this context, the Tribunal quoted a well-known passage by Lord Justice-Clerk Moncreiff in *Auld v Hay* (1880) 7 R 663, 668–69 which had been relied on by counsel:

> [T]he effect of forty years' possession on a habile title is not, in any accurate sense, to construe the title. Its effect is to establish the right. It is of no consequence what the true construction of the title may be, as long as it is susceptible of a construction consistent with the prescriptive possession, and when that has run, it is the possession, not the words of the charter, which establishes the right.

The Tribunal, however, found this an unappealing prospect (para 52):

> Such an approach would require us, in effect, to take a different and somewhat unattractive interpretation of the words of the deed, which would have the effect of creating an inconsistency with both the plan and the measurements. We would then require to ignore the plan and measurements but nevertheless conclude that the deeds are habile to allow prescriptive possession.

This result could be avoided, the Tribunal thought, because, taken together, the three descriptive elements amounted to a bounding description from which the verge was excluded, and hence the title was not *habile* for the purposes of prescription. We would add that if only one of three descriptive elements (in this case, the verbal description) could possibly be read as including the verge, that is most unlikely to amount to a *habile* title: see *Conveyancing 2012* pp 151–55.

Even if a *habile* title could be established, however, the Tribunal doubted whether sufficient possession had taken place. It is true that there had been regular cutting of the grass and so on by the would-be owner. But that owner had undisputed servitudes over the road, and therefore the verge, for access and drainage, and the possession could equally be attributed to the servitudes. As a result, '[w]e are not satisfied that the respective owners of Fanans could reasonably have been aware that the various appellant's activities were unequivocally referable to an assertion of ownership rather than the exercise of servitude rights' (para 54). Indeed the fact that the owners generally lived abroad made things worse.

[Another aspect of this case is digested at (31) above.]

(84) Rivendale v Clark
[2015] CSIH 27, 2015 SC 558

In 1950 a landowner sold two cottages in Baluachrach, south of Tarbert in Argyll. Unhappily, the plan which showed South Cottage was attached to the disposition of West Cottage, and the plan for West Cottage was attached to the disposition of South Cottage. It was to be a full decade before the error was noticed and the necessary corrective conveyancing carried out. The corrective disposition of South Cottage – now with the right plan – described the property as follows (our lettering):

> All and Whole [A] that area of ground at Baluachrach, near Tarbert, in the Parish of South Knapdale and County of Argyll [B] as occupied and possessed by the said Catherine McQuilken the former tenant thereof, [C] which subjects hereby disponed are delineated in red and coloured pink on the plan annexed and subscribed by me as relative hereto (a duplicate of which plan shall be recorded along with these presents in the Division of the General Register of Sasines applicable to the County of Argyll) but which plan, though believed to be correct, is not guaranteed …

Later the question to be determined was whether this description was *habile* for the purposes of acquiring, by positive prescription, a track which lay outside the lines depicted on the plan.

The relevant law is not in doubt. A description is sufficient for the purposes of prescription if it is capable of being read as including the target property even if that is not its natural or most plausible interpretation. On the other hand, a description which clearly excludes the property will not do.

The description in the disposition comprised three distinct elements. Element [A] was so general as to be capable of encompassing any property at all at Baluachrach. Element [B] depended on extrinsic evidence of possession and so was, presumably, irrelevant for the purposes of prescription. The difficulty arose with element [C], the plan. On the one hand, the track lay outside the boundary lines. On the other hand, the plan was only 'believed to be correct' and was 'not guaranteed'. Were these expressions of doubt sufficient to overcome the awkward fact that the track lay beyond the boundaries?

At first instance, the Lands Tribunal thought that, while the matter was not 'altogether easy', the correct answer was 'no'. See *Rivendale v Keeper of the Registers of Scotland*, 30 October 2013, para 48. In our commentary on that decision (*Conveyancing 2013* pp 44–46) we suggested that the answer 'yes' might also have been a possibility:

> If the plan had been declared 'demonstrative not taxative', as is so often the case, we would have tended to agree with the Tribunal's view, because even a demonstrative plan is intended as an accurate description of the subjects conveyed (albeit one which must give way to the verbal description in the event that there is a discrepancy). But the present wording goes further than this. The plan is only 'believed to be correct' and 'not guaranteed', and something which is 'believed to be correct' may also be incorrect. In this very possibility of error – however slight it may be – lies the possibility that the track might, after all, be included within the subjects; and if it might lie within the subjects, then the description could perhaps be regarded as habile for the purposes of prescription.

When the decision was appealed to the Inner House, this passage was used in argument by the appellant.

The Inner House, however, refused the appeal. In the court's view, the plan could not be set aside merely because of the absence of a guarantee (para 23):

> The reference to the plan is followed by the statement that, although believed to be correct, it was not guaranteed. The lack of a guarantee serves the obvious purpose of excluding warrandice in respect of the precise boundaries shown on the plan.

That in our opinion is all that it is intended to achieve. … It is no doubt true that if a plan is only 'believed to be correct' it may be incorrect, as Profs Gretton and Reid indicate (*Conveyancing 2013* p 46). Nevertheless this consideration is in our opinion outweighed by the factors discussed in the last paragraph.

Those factors were (para 22):

> First, the general rule is that so far as possible the full wording of a clause in a disposition should be given effect, and the reference to the plan is an integral part of the description of the subjects in the dispositive clause. Secondly, the plan in question was professionally prepared, and for that reason it appears to be intended to fulfil a significant role in the disposition. Thirdly, and most importantly, without the plan the disposition was completely imprecise as to the subjects conveyed, and the obvious purpose of incorporating a plan was to denote the extent of those subjects. The reference would have no point otherwise. The dispositive clause must in our opinion be construed in the light of that clear objective.

This is certainly a defensible approach although not, we think, the only one that was possible. We would make only one comment. In a later passage (para 24) the court commented that its interpretation was supported by the background circumstances that surrounded the grant of the disposition, and in particular the fact that, as the disponer did not reserve a servitude over the track, it must be assumed that he intended to exclude the track from the grant. That may well be true; yet it is an inquiry of a quite different kind. There is an important distinction between (a) the interpretation of a description, and (b) whether a description is *habile* for the purposes of prescription: see, for example, *Campbell-Gray v Keeper of the Registers of Scotland* 2015 SLT (Lands Tr) 147 (Case (85) above). In the first case the question is: what does the description mean, and hence what land does the deed convey? In the second case the question is: is it possible to interpret the description in a manner which supports the possession taken even if that interpretation is not the most natural and plausible? For the first inquiry, extrinsic evidence (such as background circumstances) is relevant; for the second, it is forbidden. The Inner House does not seem to have kept these two inquiries sufficiently apart, an impression reinforced by the fact that two of the cases relied on – *Currie v Campbell's Trs* (1886) 16 R 237 and *Reid v Haldane's Trs* (1891) 18 R 744 – are concerned with the first inquiry and not with the second.

[Another aspect of this case is digested at (29) above.]

INSOLVENCY

(85) Brown v Stonegale Ltd
[2015] CSIH 12, 2015 SCLR 619

This case – a set of three actions to reduce gratuitous alienations – will chiefly be of interest to insolvency lawyers, but will nevertheless have some interest for conveyancers.

The Pelosi family had numerous properties in the Glasgow area, letting them out. There were six commercial properties in the portfolio, all let out to a vehicle-hire business. There were also 120 residential properties ('unfit for human habitation' – see [2013] CSOH 189 para 2). The family acted through a variety of companies, including Oceancrown Ltd, Ambercrest Ltd, Ambercroft Ltd, Lakecrown Ltd, Loanwell Ltd, Questway Ltd, Strathcroft Ltd and Stonegale Ltd.

Most or all of the properties had standard securities over them, initially in favour of Anglo Irish Bank (which collapsed in 2009) and later, following the assignations of the securities, by Hadrian Sàrl (a Luxembourg bank in the Banco de España group). The total lending involved was about £17 million. Most of the companies had joint and several liability (or solidary liability, to use an academic term).

Following the economic downturn, the companies were in financial difficulties and were all, other than Stonegale, eventually placed in administration. The present case was an action (or strictly speaking three actions) by the administrators to reduce, as gratuitous alienations, the dispositions (granted in 2010) of four of the properties, namely 110 Glasgow Road, 210 Glasgow Road, 260 Glasgow Road, all in Rutherglen, and 64 Roslea Drive, Glasgow. (It appears that there may have been other, connected actions, possibly concerning other properties, but if so we have no specific information about them.) The three properties in Glasgow Road, Rutherglen were disponed to Stonegale Ltd, and 64 Roslea Drive, Glasgow was disponed to N R Pelosi personally (and was soon sold on, to a Mr Lazari).

As well as the four properties just mentioned, the Pelosis sold a fifth property (also in Glasgow Road, Rutherglen, namely No 278) to a public-sector company, Clyde Gateway, for about £2.4 million. This was a price much higher than valuation. 'The reason for the difference between that valuation and the sum paid by Clyde Gateway was not explored at the proof. Either the valuation was unduly low, or, for whatever reason, Clyde Gateway, which is a publicly funded organisation involved in the regeneration of the east end of Glasgow in connection with the Commonwealth Games, paid well over the market price': [2013] CSOH 189 para 10.

The family saw the sales as an opportunity to get value out of the hands of the companies that were in financial difficulty and into the hands of Stonegale Ltd. They adopted a circuitous route to achieve this aim, disguising what they were doing. They told the bank that all five properties were being sold, and said that £2.4 million was the collective price for all. A letter to the bank's law firm from the Pelosi family's law firm set forth the following prices: 278 Glasgow Road (£762,000); 210 Glasgow Road (£934,000); 260 Glasgow Road (£450,000); and 110 Glasgow Road (£200,000). It is unclear whether this letter mentioned the fifth property, 64 Roslea Drive, Glasgow, which was being disponed to R N Pelosi, but it seems likely that it did so, for the bank's law firm proceeded to include that property in the list that it sent to the bank, the 'price' at which it was being 'sold' being stated as £68,000. The bank was asked for discharges of the standard securities on the basis that it would be paid the sale proceeds of the properties. It granted the discharges. As Lord Brodie was later to comment ([2015] CSIH 12 para 11), 'Had AIB known that a sum in excess of £2.4 million was being paid for 278 Glasgow Road, it would not have discharged the securities over the other properties unless both the true purchase price of 278 Glasgow Road and the value of the other properties was paid to AIB'.

To help conceal what was happening, the only actual sale (278 Glasgow Road) was done as a back-to-back transaction, with the property being 'sold' to another Pelosi company, Strathcroft Ltd at a 'price' coinciding with valuation (£762,000), and then immediately resold to the real buyer, Clyde Gateway. The securities were thus cleared off not only the property that was actually being sold (278 Glasgow Road, to Clyde Gateway) but also off the four properties that were not being sold, but rather disponed gratuitously and kept in the family.

In the action the defender produced a document (the details of which are unclear) which was said to show that the transfers had in fact been made for value. The Lord Ordinary rejected this document as a fabrication. He also rejected the argument made for the defender (para 28) that 'the alienating company received a value for that disposal – here in the form of the commensurate reduction in their indebtedness to the bank. There was no detriment to the general body of their creditors.' See [2013] CSOH 189, 2014 GWD 2-27 (*Conveyancing 2013* Case (71)).

The defender reclaimed, unsuccessfully. The opinion of the Inner House confirmed the approach taken by the Lord Ordinary. The properties had been transferred gratuitously to keep them out of the hands of the creditors, which the law does not allow. 'The transactions under consideration were devices for the diversion of assets from creditors, facilitated by a misrepresentation to the banker of the companies which were involved' (para 32).

The state of knowledge of the Pelosi family's law firm, at the time that it wrote to the bank's law firm (see above), is a most interesting question, but was not a point at issue in this litigation. Reconstruction of that state of knowledge might not be easy, especially given that the relevant staff member said that he kept no file notes of his telephone conversations: see [2013] CSOH 189 para 13.

An appeal has been lodged with the Supreme Court.

(86) 3052775 Nova Scotia Ltd v Henderson
[2015] CSOH 126, 2015 SLT 691

This is yet another phase in one of the longest, most expensive and most chaotic litigations in Scottish legal history. An account of the conveyancing history, and of the litigation history up to 2014, can be found in *Conveyancing 2014* pp 200–05, and to save innocent trees from being felled we will not repeat it here.

In summary, Letham Grange Development Co Ltd ('LGDC') bought Letham Grange in Angus in 1994, the price being about £2 million, and in 2001 sold it to 3052775 Nova Scotia Ltd ('NSL') for a sum stated in both the missives and disposition (dated February 2001) to be £248,100. In 2003 NSL granted a standard security to Foxworth Investments Ltd ('Foxworth').

At first sight three wholly separate companies were involved: LGDC, NSL and Foxworth. In reality they were all companies that belonged to a single family, the Liu family, and all were in practice controlled by a single member of that family, a man who used a variety of names, including 'Dong Guang Liu', 'Tong Kuang Liu', 'Peter Liu', 'Toh Ko Liu' and 'J Michael Colby'. Some of the documents in the case were written from Mr Liu to himself, using different names for himself as sender and as recipient.

LGDC went into liquidation in December 2002. It had been in financial difficulties for some time, and it does not seem to have been in dispute that it was already absolutely insolvent in February 2001, when the disposition to NSL was granted. Unsurprisingly, LGDC's liquidator raised an action to have the LGDC/NSL disposition reduced as a gratuitous alienation. This action, which went all the way to the House of Lords, was successful.

The action was only against the LGDC/NSL disposition, not against the NSL/ Foxworth standard security. That was the subject of a separate action, which was fought all the way to the Supreme Court. In it Foxworth was successful, on the ground that the LGDC/NSL disposition had *not* been voidable. This was the stage that matters had reached last year: *Liquidator of Letham Grange Development Co Ltd v Foxworth Investments Ltd* [2014] UKSC 41, 2014 SC (UKSC) 203 (*Conveyancing 2014* Case (70)).

Now yet another action has been launched, in which NSL seeks to obtain a decree of reduction of the decree of reduction. The present stage of the action was about relevancy, and involved much examination of the authorities as to the circumstances in which a decree can be reduced. It was held (by Lord Jones) that the action was relevantly pled. What will happen next in this bizarre and disastrous dispute?

(87) Fortune's Tr v Medwin Investments Ltd
[2015] CSOH 139, 2015 GWD 34-552

Mr Fortune was sequestrated in December 2010, owning numerous properties. The trustee in sequestration did not sell these properties. In March and April 2014 Mr Fortune (i) granted standard securities over four of these properties to Medwin Investments Ltd, (ii) granted dispositions of another three to the same company, and (iii) granted dispositions of another five properties to Cooper Watson Ltd. All these deeds were registered in the Land Register. Both companies were aware of Mr Fortune's sequestration.

The trustee in sequestration then raised two actions, one against Medwin Investments Ltd and the other against Cooper Watson Ltd, seeking reduction of these various deeds. Difficult issues concerning the interface of bankruptcy law and conveyancing law were involved. It was held by the Lord Ordinary (Lord Jones) that all the deeds fell to be reduced. See **Commentary** p 180.

(88) Fortune's Tr v Cooper Watson Ltd
[2015] CSOH 140, 2015 GWD 34-553

See the previous case. Whilst these were formally separate actions, the facts were substantially the same, and the opinion issued was in substantially the same terms in both cases. See **Commentary** p 180.

CRIMINAL PROPERTY LAW

(89) Trustunion LLC, Noters
[2015] CSOH 38, 2015 GWD 13-223

This was a petition for the recall of a restraint order in relation to a house at 34 Kenilworth Road, Bridge of Allan, Stirlingshire. The property was owned by a US company, Trustunion LLC (in some documentation spelt Trust Union LLC), whereas the offender was someone else, Michael Voudouri. The case is thus an illustration of how broad the criminal confiscation scheme is. The property owner's sole shareholder was a relative of the offender, and the money to buy the house had come, via a circuitous route, from the offender.

The petition was unsuccessful. For Mr Voudouri's £3,041,114.07 scam, see such cases as *Voudouri v HM Advocate* 2003 SCCR 448, and *Voudouri v HM Advocate* 2008 JC 431. Matters have been rumbling on for about fifteen years, for reasons of which we are unaware. This would seem to explain why the applicable legislation has been the Proceeds of Crime (Scotland) Act 1995 rather than the Proceeds of Crime Act 2002.

(90) Islington Council v Panayi
16 October 2015, Blackfriars Crown Court

This English case does not appear in the law reports or on databases such as Westlaw, but it is interesting as an illustration of the way that criminal property law is expanding its range. A landlord rented out a basement room in breach of planning law. The council served an enforcement notice, which he ignored. He was fined £2,000 with costs of £15,900. The rent he had received for the property was confiscated under the Proceeds of Crime Act 2002, the confiscation order being for £70,000.

Full details of the case are not available, but general accounts can be found in the mainstream media (eg the *Guardian* on 22 October 2015: www.theguardian. com/society/2015/oct/22/landlord-andrew-panayi-back-70000-rent-substandard-flat) and also on the Islington Council website: www.islington.gov.uk/islington/ news-events/news-releases/2015/10/Pages/PR6218.aspx.

MISCELLANEOUS

(91) Royal Bank of Scotland plc v Carlyle
[2015] UKHL 13, 2015 SC (UKSC) 93, 2015 SLT 206

The defender was a property developer, using loan finance from the bank on a project-by-project basis. In the summer of 2007 RBS advanced two loans, of £845,000 and £560,000, to help him buy land. He needed more than this to carry through the development, and expected to obtain a further loan during 2008. But RBS refused to lend more. Soon thereafter RBS sued for repayment of the existing loans. The defence was that the RBS had, through conversations between its staff and the developer, committed itself to make available the further funding necessary to carry through the development. The developer counterclaimed for damages of £1.5 million for breach of that commitment.

At first instance the Lord Ordinary found in favour of the developer: see [2010] CSOH 3, 2010 GWD 13-235 (*Conveyancing 2010* Case (67)). The RBS reclaimed, successfully see [2013] CSIH 75, 2014 SC 188 (*Conveyancing 2013* Case (75)). The developer in turn appealed, and the Supreme Court has now reversed the decision of the Inner House and reinstated the decision taken at first instance. See **Commentary** p 151.

(92) Macallans v W Burrell Homes Ltd
2015 SLT (Sh Ct) 243

The pursuers sold heritable property for their clients, W Burrell Homes Ltd. That company had two directors, who were also two equal shareholders, and they were at loggerheads as to what should happen to the free proceeds of sale. Unable to get instructions from the company, the pursuers eventually raised this action of multiplepoinding. There were three defenders: the company, plus the two directors/shareholders. One of the latter opposed the action on the ground that there existed no double distress, double distress being a prerequisite for an action of this sort. The free proceeds, he argued, were payable to the company itself, so that there existed no problem to be resolved. This was clearly a strong argument. Nevertheless in the end the sheriff (Stuart Reid) took the view that the traditional requirement for double distress had been considerably relaxed in modern case law and that he was prepared to allow the action to proceed.

(93) Dickens v Anderson
[2015] CSOH 161, 2016 GWD 3-63

Paul Dickens was a landlord. He owned several properties, and also had substantial borrowings secured against the properties. On the whole he seems to have acted in his own name, but in at least one case he acted through a company of which he was the sole owner, New Alba (Redwood House) Ltd. When that company went into liquidation, in 2006, its liquidator, K V Anderson, sued Mr Dickens for money he owed to the company. The action was successful, and in 2008 decree was granted against the pursuer for £280,750 plus expenses and interest: see *Anderson v Dickens* [2008] CSOH 134, 2009 SCLR 609, a case of some interest from the standpoint of insolvency law. Lacking available funds to pay this sum, Mr Dickens explored the possibility of selling one or more properties, or borrowing against the security of one or more properties.

These possibilities did not materialise. What happened thereafter to the £280,750 (plus) debt does not appear in the judgment, but in this action Mr Dickens sued his former company and its liquidator for £2 million in damages for allegedly having reneged on a promise to restrict an inhibition that had been taken out against him. The unrestricted inhibition, Mr Dickens argued, had prevented him from obtaining secured finance from Barclays Bank plc. How that failure is supposed to have caused £2 million of loss does not appear from the judgment, which was concerned solely with two factual matters: (i) whether the liquidator had in fact undertaken to restrict the inhibition, and (ii) whether the continued subsistence of the inhibition had been the reason that Barclays had declined to lend. Mr Dickens needed to prove both points. He failed to prove either.

As for (i), the alleged promise had been given orally. An undertaking to discharge or restrict an inhibition probably does not have to be in writing (though this issue seems not to have been explored in the litigation) but, obviously, proving an oral undertaking about an inhibition would never be straightforward. As to (ii), the evidence showed that the refusal to lend had been made for other reasons.

The judgment of the Lord Ordinary (Lord Tyre) ends with sharp criticism of Barclays Bank (para 39): 'I cannot conclude this opinion without expressing the court's displeasure at the attitude adopted by Barclays Bank in response to requests by the defenders' agents ... for co-operation in providing evidence'.

(94) Jack v Jack
[2015] CSOH 91, 2015 Fam LR 95

Whether property is partnership property, or, on the other hand, the property of one of the partners, is an issue that crops up quite often and can cause much difficulty. The terms of the title are not conclusive.

The present action was a divorce action. Title to the farm at Torebanehill, West Lothian, was in the name of the husband, following a disposition to him by his father. The disposition bore to be gratuitous, containing the usual 'love, favour and affection' clause. The land had never been included as an asset in the partnership accounts. As against that, it was accepted that (paras13 and 14):

> the partnership used the lands and buildings at Torbanehill Farm, that the partnership insured the land and the buildings, that repairs, works and other costs relative to the farm have been paid by the firm, that VAT has been paid and reclaimed by the farming partnership, that wayleaves and payments for communication masts situated on the farm premises were claimed by and paid to the farming partnership and that Single Farm subsidy was claimed in respect of Torbanehill... There was no contract of lease between the partnership and the heritable proprietor.

The wife, who was in partnership with her husband, argued that the farm was partnership property. The Lord Ordinary (Lord Brailsford) held that the farm belonged to Mr Jack as an individual and was not partnership property. In coming to this conclusion the terms of the disposition were stressed.

The case is not free from difficulty. Though the question of what is partnership property is governed by ss 20 ff of the Partnership Act 1890, those provisions were not cited in the case. Nor was the standard text on the subject cited, ie J Bennett Miller, *The Law of Partnership in Scotland* (2nd edn, 1994, ed by G Brough). Nor was the case law on the law of partnership property. What appears to lie at the core of the decision, namely the intention of the father at the time of the disposition, seems to us to be of limited relevance. The fact that the husband's father gave the land to the husband as an individual seems not conclusive of the point at issue between husband and wife. The question to be answered was whether the land, though acquired by the husband as an individual, had become a partnership asset.

We understand that there is a reclaiming motion.

PART II

STATUTORY DEVELOPMENTS

STATUTORY DEVELOPMENTS

Legal Writings (Counterparts and Delivery) (Scotland) Act 2015 (asp 4)

This important Act makes clear that execution in counterpart (ie where different parties sign different copies of the same document) is competent (s 1). It also removes the doubts raised by *Park Ptrs (No 2)* [2009] CSOH 122, 2009 SLT 871 (*Conveyancing 2009* 85–89) by providing that 'traditional' (ie paper) documents can be delivered by a PDF attached to an e-mail, by fax, or by other electronic means (s 4). See **Commentary** pp 125 and 167. The Act came into force on 1 July 2015: see the **Legal Writings (Counterparts and Delivery) (Scotland) Act 2015 (Commencement) Order 2015, SSI 2015/242**.

Community Empowerment (Scotland) Act 2015 (asp 6)

As its name suggests, this Act is intended to empower communities and community bodies in a number of ways. In particular, provision is made for community bodies to acquire heritable property. There are three different aspects.

In the first place, with effect from 15 April 2016 the community right to buy contained in part 2 of the Land Reform (Scotland) Act 2003 is extended from rural areas to the whole of Scotland (s 36, amending s 33 of the 2003 Act).

Secondly, and unlike the community right to buy (which requires a willing seller), community bodies will be able to buy certain land and buildings (but not a person's home) even if the owner does not wish to sell. This controversial power of (non-consensual) appropriation is contained in a new part 3A (comprising ss 97A–97Z), inserted into the Land Reform (Scotland) Act 2003 (by s 74 of the 2015 Act), although no commencement order has yet been made. The power applies to land which, in the opinion of the Scottish Ministers, is wholly or mainly abandoned or neglected or 'the use or management of the land is such that it results in or causes harm, directly or indirectly, to the environmental wellbeing of a relevant community' (s 97C). Much will depend on how these criteria are interpreted. The procedure involves an application to Ministers, the application being registered in a new register which, assuming an amendment made by the Land Reform (Scotland) Bill s 44A (for that Bill, see p 85 below) comes into effect, will be called the Register of Applications by Community Bodies to Buy Land (ss 97F, 97G). Ministers cannot approve an application unless satisfied that the acquisition is in the public interest and compatible with furthering the achievement of sustainable development, and that the achievement of sustainable development would be unlikely to be furthered by the existing owner (s 97H(1)). There is a right of appeal to the sheriff (s 97V). Market value is payable, calculated by a valuer in accordance with s 97S and subject to a right of appeal to the Lands Tribunal (s 97W). Provision is made for mediation (s 97Z1), and this is extended to the rights to buy set out in parts 2 and 3 of the 2003 Act. The Scottish Government produces an annual survey of vacant and derelict land: see p 114 below for the most recent survey.

Thirdly, the new legislation is not limited to heritable property in private hands. Heritable property held by public bodies may also be affected. Once part 5 of the new Act is in force, community bodies will be able to request a whole range of other public bodies to sell or lease heritable property to them (s 79). These bodies, listed in sch 3, include local authorities, the Scottish Government, the Scottish Courts and Tribunal Service, the Scottish Police Authority, Scottish Natural Heritage, and Scottish Water.

In considering such an 'asset transfer request', the public body is required to assess the community body's proposals against the current use or any other proposal, and must agree to the request unless there are reasonable grounds for refusal (s 82). Among the factors that it must take into account are whether agreeing to the request would promote economic development, regeneration, public health, social wellbeing or environmental wellbeing, and whether it would be likely to reduce inequalities of outcome which result from socio-economic disadvantage. During the period when a request is under consideration, the public body must not sell, lease or otherwise dispose of the land (s 84(2)). There is a right of appeal against refusal of the request, or the imposition of conditions, to the Scottish Ministers (s 85). In order to assist community bodies, and in the interests of transparency more generally, each schedule 3 body must establish, maintain and publicise – including on a website – a 'Register of Land' which, to the best of the body's knowledge and belief, lists all land owned or leased by the authority (s 94). A diagram summarising the procedure can be found at www.gov.scot/Resource/0048/00489822.pdf.

The opportunity is also taken to reform and simplify the rules for the community right to buy contained in part 2 of the Land Reform (Scotland) Act 2003 (ss 37–61). The changes, which come into force on 15 April 2016 (see **Community Empowerment (Scotland) Act 2015 (Commencement No 3 and Savings) Order 2015, SSI 2015/399**), include:

- making it easier for communities to define their 'community' in ways other than by postcode (2003 Act s 34(5) amended by 2015 Act s 37(7));
- extending the legal entities that can use the community right to buy provisions to include Scottish charitable incorporated organisations (SCIOs) and community benefit societies, and allowing for other legal entities to be added by subordinate legislation (2003 Act s 34(1A), (1B), (4A) inserted by 2015 Act s 37(4), (6));
- altering the rules for late applications, including replacing the 'good reasons' test with one which sets out clear requirements to be met by

community bodies when submitting a late application (2003 Act s 39 amended by 2015 Act s 42);

- in relation to the ballot required after the right to buy has been triggered, providing for the Scottish Ministers to arrange for this to be conducted by an independent third party, and for Ministers to meet the cost, making the community right to buy process easier for community bodies (2003 Act s 51A inserted by 2015 Act s 49);

- extending the period available to complete the right to buy from six to eight months (2003 Act s 56(3)(a), amended by 2015 Act s 54(a));

- making the valuation process more robust by allowing for counter-representations between the landowner and the community body (2003 Act s 60(1A) inserted by 2015 Act s 56(a));

- giving Ministers discretion to recover the cost of the independent valuation from the landowner where the landowner has withdrawn the land from sale after the valuer has been appointed, thus deterring landowners from allowing the process to proceed where the land is not genuinely being offered for sale (2003 Act s 60A inserted by 2015 Act s 57).

Further provision is made by the **Community Right to Buy (Scotland) Regulations 2015, SSI 2015/400.** This includes a new application form for registering a community interest in land. Again the commencement date is 15 April 2016 (reg 1(3)). Some drafting mistakes were pointed out by the Scottish Parliament's Delegated Powers and Law Reform Committee (www.scottish. parliament.uk/parliamentarybusiness/CurrentCommittees/94751.aspx) and corrected by the **Community Right to Buy (Scotland) Amendment Regulations 2016, SSI 2016/4**. A research report on the impact of the community right to buy was published in October 2015; further details are given at p 115 below.

Modifications are also made to the rules for the crofting community right to buy contained in part 3 of the Land Reform (Scotland) Act 2003 (ss 62–73), although no commencement order has yet been made.

Further provisions in the Act concern common-good property, a matter of increasing public interest and concern. Every local authority must compile a 'Common Good Register', ie a register of all property which is held as part of the common good, and to make this available for public inspection free of charge, including on a website (s 102). In addition, before taking any decision to dispose or change the use of common-good property, a local authority must publish details of its proposal, notify community councils and any community body with an interest in the property, and consider representations (s 104). These provisions are not yet in force.

Finally, part 9 of the Act (ss 107–138) will, when it comes into force, replace the existing legislation on allotments, mainly contained in the Allotments (Scotland) Act 1892 (as amended), with up-to-date (and generally simpler) provisions. Part 9 places a duty on local authorities to hold and maintain waiting lists for allotments (s 111), and to take reasonable steps to provide more allotments if the waiting list exceeds certain trigger points (s 112). It also prevents local authorities from disposing of or changing the use of an allotment site without the consent of the Scottish Ministers, thereby providing a level of protection to allotment sites (s 117). In future, local authorities will have to publish an annual allotments report and a food-growing strategy, setting out land that has been identified for allotments or other community growing in the local authority's area, and how it will meet demand (ss 119–121). This builds on the Scottish Government's *National Food and Drink Policy – Recipe for Success* (2009) and on the deliberations of the Grow Your Own Working Group.

The Act is discussed by Malcolm Combe in an article published at (2015) 60 *Journal of the Law Society of Scotland* August/40.

Consumer Rights Act 2015 (c 15)

The Consumer Rights Act 2015 brings together in a single piece of legislation a number of different provisions concerned with consumer protection. The only part of potential relevance to conveyancers is part 2 (ss 61–76) which replaces and substantially re-enacts the Unfair Terms in Consumer Contracts Regulations 1999, SI 1999/2083.

Part 2 came into force on 1 October 2015: see **Consumer Rights Act 2015 (Commencement No 3, Transitional Provisions, Savings and Consequential Amendments) Order 2015, SI 2015/1630**, art 3. It provides (in s 62(1)) that 'an unfair term of a consumer contract is not binding on the consumer'. A 'consumer contract' is 'a contract between a trader and a consumer' (s 61(1)) and so includes, for example, builders' missives or leases by business organisations (including local authorities) (s 2(2), (7)) to individuals who are not acting in a business capacity. A term is 'unfair' 'if, contrary to the requirement of good faith, it causes a significant imbalance in the parties' rights and obligations under the contract to the detriment of the consumer' (s 62(4)). A non-exhaustive list of terms that may be regarded as unfair is set out in part 1 of schedule 2.

Finance Act 2015 (c 11) and Finance (No 2) Act 2015 (c 33)

For the changes introduced by these Acts, so far as relevant to land, see **Commentary** p 210.

Mortgage Credit Directive

The Mortgage Credit Directive 2014/17/EU was in part a response to the outbreak of hazardous lending and in part an attempt to create a single market in secured lending. There is a strong consumer focus. So for example lenders will have to provide a European Standardised Information Sheet (ESIS) which will allow consumers to shop around for the best loan. To alert consumers to potential rate variations, the ESIS will include worst-case scenarios as far as variable-interest and foreign-currency loans are concerned. The Directive is transposed partly by the **Mortgage Credit Directive Order 2015, SI 2015/910** (as amended by the **Mortgage Credit Directive (Amendment) Order 2015/1557**) and partly by new Financial Conduct Authority (FCA) rules. Both come into force on 21 March 2016 (art 1(5)(c)). We will pass over the word 'mortgage' in silence.

Much of the Mortgage Credit Directive Order consists of amendments to existing legislation, both primary and secondary, but an extended part 3 brings the providers of consumer buy-to-let mortgages under the supervision of the FCA.

For many lenders operating in the residential sector, the significant aspects of transposition are largely found in new FCA rules, notably in additions to the FCA's Mortgage and Home Finance: Conduct of Business (MCOB) Rules. These transpose in particular article 14 (pre-contractual information) of the Directive. As from 21 March 2016 lenders will have to provide an adequate explanation of the proposed 'mortgage contract' and any ancillary services, and the explanation must include the pre-contract information, the essential features of the product, and the potential impact on the consumer (including the consequence of default) (MCOB 4.A2). The new rules require lenders to issue a European Standardised Information Sheet (ESIS), a mandatory product-disclosure document that is replacing the Key Facts Illustration (KFI) and must be used by 21 March 2019 at the latest (MCOB 5A).

So far as conveyancers are concerned, the most significant change is the requirement on lenders, from 21 March 2016, to make a binding 'mortgage' offer and to give the borrower at least seven days to reflect on it. During the reflection period, the offer is binding on the lender, but the borrower can accept the offer at any time. This is provided for in MCOB 6A. The key parts of that rule are as follows:

MCOB 6A.3.1 [R]
(1) If a firm offers to enter into an MCD [Mortgage Credit Directive] regulated mortgage contract with a consumer, it must provide the consumer with a binding offer set out in an offer document.
(2) The firm may also provide an ESIS.
(3) The firm's offer in the offer document must be on the basis of the information in the ESIS relevant to that offer.
(4) When an MCD mortgage lender provides the consumer with a binding offer, that offer must be accompanied by an ESIS where the characteristics of the offer are different from the information contained in the ESIS previously provided.

MCOB 6A.3.3 [G]
(1) MCOB 6A.3.1 does not prevent a binding offer from being subject to lawful conditions, including conditions which make the binding offer subject to one or more of the matters listed below:
  (a) there being no material change to the facts and circumstances relating to the binding offer which occurs after the date on which the binding offer is made;
  (b) the fact that the consumer has not knowingly provided incomplete or inaccurate information for the purpose of the assessment of affordability,

and has not knowingly falsified or withheld the information provided for the purpose of that assessment.

(2) The material changes referred to in (1)(a) include a material change:
  (a) affecting the condition, value or title to the property;
  (b) in the borrower's circumstances (such as loss of employment or further secured borrowing taken out after the borrower's application for an MCD regulated mortgage contract) which is likely to have a material impact upon the borrower's ability to afford the loan.
(3) However, the lender cannot use conditions in binding offers as a means of avoiding the requirement to undertake a proper affordability assessment under MCOB 11 before the binding offer is made.

MCOB 6A.3.4 [R]

(1) Where an MCD mortgage lender provides the consumer with a binding offer, it must give the consumer a reflection period of at least seven days.
(2) The MCD mortgage lender must ensure that, during the reflection period:
  (a) the offer remains binding on the MCD mortgage lender;
  (b) the consumer may accept the offer at any time.

MCOB 6A.3.5 [G]

The purpose of the reflection period is to provide the consumer with sufficient time to compare offers, assess their implications and make an informed decision.

MCOB 6A.3.6 [R]

A firm must provide the consumer with a copy of the draft agreement for the MCD regulated mortgage contract at the beginning of the reflection period.

One immediate result of these new rules is a change in the CML *Lenders' Handbook*. There is to be a new version of rule 10.2 which allows conveyancers to accept the mortgage offer on the borrower's behalf by submitting a certificate of title to the lender. This allows the lender, in cases where the lender does not require the borrower formally to accept the mortgage offer, to have evidence of the acceptance by virtue of the certificate of title. It also indicates that the borrower has brought the reflection period to an end. The new rule 10.2 is as follows:

10.2 We shall treat the submission by you of the certificate of title as confirmation that the borrower has chosen to proceed with our mortgage offer and as a request for us to release the mortgage advance to you. Check part 2 to see if the mortgage advance will be paid electronically or by cheque and the minimum number of days notice we require.

The Land Register: fees and completion

The **Registers of Scotland (Voluntary Registration, Amendment of Fees, etc) Order 2015, SSI 2015/265,** makes a number of changes designed to help meet the target of completing the Land Register by 2024. As of 1 April 2016 the Keeper loses her discretion to refuse applications for voluntary registration; this is done by repealing s 27(3)(b) of the Land Registration etc (Scotland) Act 2012 (art 2).

Also with effect from 1 April 2016 standard securities cease to be registrable in the Register of Sasines (art 3). If, therefore, a standard security is granted over Sasine land, registration of the security will necessitate first registration of the plot of land itself. This will involve voluntary registration, because automatic plot registration ('APR') does not generally apply to standard securities. (The exception is standard securities granted over unregistered subordinate real rights, notably Sasine long leases.) An owner who wishes to grant a standard security must therefore apply for voluntary registration either before or at the time the security is presented for registration. The second will usually be the more attractive option because, in another change made by the 2015 Order (art 4(5)), no additional fee is charged for a voluntary registration which accompanies the registration of a standard security.

A number of other changes were made to the existing structure of fees set out in the Registers of Scotland (Fees) Order 2014, SSI 2014/188, with effect from 30 June 2015 (art 4). These include a 25% reduction in the fees for voluntary registration, and a fixed fee of £60 for each affected title sheet in respect of dispositions which aim merely to evacuate survivorship destinations.

The **Lands Tribunal for Scotland Amendment (Fees) Rules 2015, SSI 2015/199,** sets a fee of £45 for applications to place, renew, restrict or recall caveats under ss 67(2), 69(1), 70(1) and 71(1) of the Land Registration etc (Scotland) Act 2012.

Further developments affecting the Land Register can be found at p 93 below.

Private rented housing panel

The private rented housing panel hears applications from tenants in the private rented sector in circumstances where the landlord has failed to comply with a request to carry out repairs: see Housing (Scotland) Act 2006 s 23 and, for a discussion, *Conveyancing 2005* p 27. The **Private Rented Housing Panel (Tenant and Third Party Applications) (Scotland) Regulations 2015, SSI 2015/369,** make new provision as to applications. These include applications by local authorities and other authorised third parties under ss 25–27 of the Housing (Scotland) Act 2014, provisions which were brought into force on 1 December 2015 by the **Housing (Scotland) Act 2014 (Commencement No 3 and Transitional Provision) Order 2015, SSI 2015/272.**

Section 35 of the Private Rented Housing (Scotland) Act 2011 was brought into force on 22 September and 1 December 2015 by the **Private Rented Housing (Scotland) Act 2011 (Commencement No 7) Order 2015, SSI 2015/326.** This inserts new ss 28A–28C into the Housing (Scotland) Act 2006 to the effect of allowing private-sector landlords who are having trouble gaining access to the property in order to check on its state of repair or to carry out work to seek the assistance of the private rented housing panel rather than having to apply to the court or wait until the end of the lease. Provision about applications is made by the **Private Rented Housing Panel (Landlord Applications) (Scotland) Regulations 2015, SSI 2015/403.**

Fees for registration as a property factor

Anyone who practises as a property factor must apply for and be accepted for registration in the Register of Property Factors: see Property Factors (Scotland) Act 2011 ss 1–12, discussed in *Conveyancing 2011* pp 113–14. Registration lasts for three years but can be renewed. The **Property Factors (Registration) (Scotland) Amendment Regulations 2015, SSI 2015/217,** increases the registration fees from £100 to £200 (where the factor acts in relation to 100 or fewer properties) and from £370 to £750 (where the factor acts in relation to more than 100 properties). The new fees came into force on 1 July 2015.

PART III
OTHER MATERIAL

OTHER MATERIAL

Land Reform (Scotland) Bill

The work of the LRRG

The origins of the Land Reform (Scotland) Bill, currently before the Scottish Parliament, lie in the independent Land Reform Review Group ('LRRG') set up by the Scottish Government in July 2012 and chaired by Dr Alison Elliot. (For background, see *Conveyancing 2012* pp 94–96 as well as the LRRG's website: www. scotland.gov.uk/About/Review/land-reform.) An initial call for evidence resulted in almost 500 responses, ranging from a couple of paragraphs to 266 pages from Scottish Land and Estates(www.scotland.gov.uk/Publications/2013/07/2790, and, for an analysis, www.scotland.gov.uk/Publications/2013/05/4519). An interim report was published by the LRRG in May 2013 (www.gov.scot/ Resource/0042/00426905.PDF) and was widely castigated by the land-reform lobby for what was seen as a lack of ambition. A year later that criticism was met to some degree by the LRRG's final report, *The Land of Scotland and the Common Good* (www.scotland.gov.uk/Resource/0045/00451087.pdf), which was published in May 2014: see *Conveyancing 2014* pp 98–102.

As the title chosen for the final report indicated, the idea underlying the LRRG's work was that of the 'common good'. This was said to describe 'a comprehensive and complex concept which brings into its embrace questions of social justice, human rights, democracy, citizenship, stewardship and economic development' (p 235). The LRRG continued (p 236):

> Land is a resource not just for the present generation, but also generations to come. It is also home to other species. Care of the land therefore calls for a strong sense of stewardship. Finally, successful economic development is also a critical element of the common good: the way in which land is used to generate economic activity and sustainable livelihoods is, and will be, crucial to an economically successful Scotland. The Review Group therefore regards the common good as the general outcome which informs and drives land reform. It has guided decisions about which recommendations the Group should support, without the suggestion that any single action will realize the common good.

Among the 62 recommendations was a call for more statistical information as to patterns of land ownership, and for a speeding-up of the task of getting land on to the Land Register. The Crown Estate Commissioners should cease to operate in Scotland, and Crown rights should be pared back. Community control over land and buildings should be encouraged and extended. The law of riparian rights should be reformed to reflect the public interest. So should the law of common good in the narrow, technical sense of that expression. Crofting law should be modernised and simplified. The exemption from non-domestic rates for agricultural, forestry and other land-based businesses should be reconsidered. The idea of a land value tax should be explored. In the interests of transparency, non-EU companies should be barred from acquiring land in Scotland, though it was accepted that the gains from such a measure would be modest. There was a proposal to empower local authorities to make a 'compulsory sale order' over vacant or derelict land. Particularly controversial was the suggestion that there should be an upper ceiling on the amount of land which could be owned by any one person. Finally, the report argued that, rather than proceeding by piecemeal reform, the Government should devise a 'National Land Policy', with a permanent 'Scottish Land and Property Commission' to 'provide a single, overall and integrated focus on the different aspects of Scotland's system of land ownership, including land information, property law, land use, fiscal measures and land markets' (p 238).

The Scottish Government's response

In welcoming the LRRG report the Scottish Government announced an immediate 10-year target for completion of the Land Register, a policy which went much further than the LRRG's recommendation. Further, some of the LRRG's concerns about community involvement were met by the Community Empowerment (Scotland) Act 2015 (see p 75 above). Beyond that, the Government proceeded to consult on some, but by no means all, of the LRRG's recommendations. *A Consultation on the Future of Land Reform in Scotland* (www.scotland.gov.uk/Publications/2014/12/9659) was published on 2 December 2014, with responses invited by 10 February 2015. The ministerial preface gave as the aspiration 'a fairer and more equitable distribution of land in Scotland where communities and individuals can own and use land to realise their potential. Scotland's land must be an asset that benefits the many, not the few.' 1,269 responses to the consultation were received, mainly (82%) from individuals. A summary of the responses was published in May 2015: see www.gov.scot/Publications/2015/05/4885; the responses themselves can be found at www.gov.scot/Topics/Environment/land-reform/consultation.

The Land Reform Bill

A Bill based on the consultation document and hence, indirectly, on parts of the LRRG report was introduced to the Scottish Parliament on 22 June 2015. The Bill also included provisions on agricultural holdings which derived from the recommendations of a separate Agricultural Holdings Legislation Review (www.gov.scot/Resource/0046/00468852.pdf). The Stage 1 proceedings were conducted by the Rural Affairs, Climate Change and Environment Committee. Six mornings were set aside for oral evidence, and in addition the Committee received 200 written submissions (available at www.scottish.parliament. uk/parliamentarybusiness/CurrentCommittees/91072.aspx). Stage 1 was successfully completed on 16 December 2015 and Stage 2 on 10 February 2016. It is assumed that the final stage will be completed before the pre-election dissolution of Parliament on 24 March 2016. The Bill itself is in ten main parts.

Parts 1 and 2: the Scottish Land Commission

Part 1 would require the Government to issue and keep under review a 'land rights and responsibilities statement', being a statement of its objectives for land reform (s 1). Part 2 establishes a Scottish Land Commission, to comprise five ordinary Commissioners and a sixth 'Tenant Farming Commissioner' (s 2). The functions of the Commission would be, 'on any matter relating to land in Scotland (a) to review the impact and effectiveness of any law or policy, (b) to recommend changes to any law or policy, (c) to gather evidence, (d) to carry out research, (e) to prepare reports, and (f) to provide information and guidance' (s 20(1)).

Part 3: information about control of land

Part 3 presupposes that the people of Scotland have the right to know who owns, controls and benefits from land – a presupposition which, critics would say, does not leave much room for privacy. In the form in which the Bill was introduced, part 3 attracted sharp criticism for not doing enough to increase transparency: see Rural Affairs, Climate Change and Environment Committee, *Stage 1 Report on the Land Reform (Scotland) Bill* (www.scottish.parliament.uk/parliamentarybusiness/ CurrentCommittees/94538.aspx) paras 177–221.

There are only two sections. Section 35 sets up a system whereby certain people with a suitable interest ('requesters') would be able to request from a 'request authority' information on persons 'in control of land' – as opposed to information on who owns land (which can already be obtained from the Land or Sasine Registers). Widely criticised as ineffective, this provision is to be dropped. During Stage 2, the Minister for Environment, Climate Change and Land Reform (Dr Aileen McLeod) announced that she would bring forward amendments at Stage 3 to replace s 35 with new provisions to establish a public register of persons with a controlling interest in landowners (*Official Report*, Rural Affairs, Climate Change and Environment Committee, cols 61–2 (20 January 2016)):

> We believe that, in principle, it is possible to increase the transparency of land ownership in Scotland through requiring the public disclosure of information about persons who control land. I would therefore like to reconfirm to the committee that the Government will lodge amendments at stage 3 in the form of a power to make regulations to provide for the creation of a public register that will contain the information that is required to provide greater transparency on who controls the land in Scotland. As the committee is aware, providing greater transparency of land ownership gives rise to many complex legal issues that we have been trying to work our way through, most notably the right to free movement of capital under EU law – which has been mentioned already – and the interaction with rights that are protected under the ECHR.

There are also considerable practical difficulties to overcome in ensuring that we provide a robust and viable solution that will provide the greater transparency of land ownership that we all seek to achieve. We are confident that we can map out the overall scope of a requirement to provide such information in a public register that will allow us to produce a regulation-making power at stage 3. Some issues that we are looking at include what information should be disclosed and in what circumstances disclosure should be required; how any requirement to provide the information would interact with registration law and our commitment to complete the land register; how the information should be obtained and kept up to date; fees and charges; what provisions would be necessary to protect the legitimate interests of individuals in maintaining their privacy; whether there should be any exceptions on de minimis grounds—for example, flats and houses owned by private individuals; how requirements to disclose and update information could be enforced; and how we could ensure that landowners could not avoid the disclosure requirements.

As part of all that, we will consult key stakeholders. Given the significance and importance of the proposed regulations and the details of the proposed register, it is important that the Government consults widely on them. This policy development and consultation cannot be carried out within the timetable for the bill, given that we have only a number of weeks between now and March. Therefore, introducing a regulation-making power will allow further policy work to be undertaken on the issues that I have outlined and further consultation to be carried out so that we can introduce detailed regulations at the earliest opportunity in the next session of Parliament.

As a holding measure, a backbench amendment (no 30) was passed without Government opposition at Stage 2 to require information as to the control of certain classes of landowner to be included on the Land Register itself. It is assumed that this provision will be removed at Stage 3.

Section 36 adds a new s 48A to the Land Registration etc (Scotland) Act 2012. This would allow the Keeper to request information from those who own land or are applying for registration as to the category of person or body into which a proprietor falls. No penalty is imposed for failure to comply with the Keeper's request.

Part 4: engaging communities in decisions relating to land

The very short part 4 would require the Government to issue guidance to those who own and control land as to the need to engage local communities in respect of decisions which might affect them. No sanction is provided for ignoring the guidance, although the *Policy Memorandum* which accompanied the introduction of the Bill suggests that this might be taken into account where an application is made to buy the land under part 5 (para 166).

Part 5: right to buy land to further sustainable development

Rights of community organisations to buy land have been a feature of land reform legislation ever since the Land Reform (Scotland) Act 2003. To the community right to buy and the crofting community right to buy introduced by that Act, the Community Empowerment (Scotland) Act 2015 has recently added the community right to buy 'abandoned, neglected or detrimental' land (see p 75 above). Part 5 of the Land Reform Bill would add a right to buy land to further sustainable development. The Government's target is to have 1 million acres of land in community ownership by 2020 (see eg *Stage 1 Report* para 248).

The procedure proposed in part 5 is familiar from earlier models. Like the crofting community right to buy and the right to buy 'abandoned, neglected or detrimental' land (but unlike the community right to buy), the new part 5 right would not require a willing seller. It would apply to most types of land though there would be some exceptions including an individual's home (s 39). The right could only be exercised by community bodies (which must be a company limited by guarantee, a Scottish charitable incorporated organisation, or a community benefit society) or by a person nominated by such a body (s 45(1)). An application to buy would be made to the Scottish Ministers, having first been approved by the community by means of a ballot (ss 47(3)(h), 48) and registered in a new register maintained by the Keeper, the Register of Applications by Community Bodies to Buy Land (s 44). In reaching a decision, the Scottish Ministers would have a broad duty to consult (s 46). The substantive criteria for accepting an application have been criticised by some as over-strict (see eg *Stage 1 Report* paras 247 and 258), and were obviously designed partly with article 1 Protocol 1 of the European Convention on Human Rights in mind. The question of whether part 5 is ECHR-compatible is explored by Douglas Maxwell in 'Human rights and land reform' (2016) 61 *Journal of the Law Society of Scotland* Jan/22, but without reaching any firm conclusion.

In terms of the criteria (set out in s 47(2)), an application is not to be accepted unless the Scottish Ministers are satisfied that –

(a) the transfer of land is likely to further the achievement of sustainable development in relation to the land,

(b) the transfer of land is in the public interest,

(c) the transfer of land –
   (i) is likely to result in significant benefit to the relevant community (see subsection (9)) to which the application relates, and
   (ii) is the only practicable way of achieving that significant benefit, and

(d) not granting consent to the transfer of land is likely to result in significant harm to that community.

There is no definition of 'sustainable development' (which some have criticised) but para 143 of the *Policy Memorandum*, drawing on the work of the Labour Government's Land Reform Policy Group in 1998, states that:

Sustainable development is defined as development that is planned with appropriate regard for its longer term consequences, and is geared towards assisting social and economic advancement that can lead to further opportunities and a higher quality of life for people whilst protecting the environment. Sustainable development requires an integrated approach to social, economic and environmental outcomes. Sustainable communities are more self-reliant, with increasing economic independence and a better quality of life, while conserving or enhancing their environment. Contrasted with unsustainable communities, where populations are declining, local economic and social activity is inhibited and the natural heritage is damaged.

Provision is made for valuation of the land being bought (s 56), and for the making of Government grants towards the purchase (s 59). There would be a right of appeal to the sheriff court (s 60) or, in respect of the valuation, to the Lands Tribunal (s 61).

Parts 6–10

The remainder of the Bill is of less interest to conveyancers other than those involved in agricultural leases (an area of law which we do not seek to cover in this series). The provision in part 6 to end the exemption of shootings and deer forests from non-domestic rates (an exemption which dates from 1995) is highly controversial and was not supported by the *Stage 1 Report* in the absence of 'a thorough, robust and evidence-based analysis of the potential impacts of ending the … exemption (including what impact imposing the exemption had in 1995)' (para 310).

Prompted by the difficulties encountered in building Portobello High School on common-good ground – difficulties which in the end required to be solved by a special Act of Parliament (see *Conveyancing 2014* p 71) – part 7 amends s 75 of the Local Government (Scotland) Act 1973. At present s 75(2) provides that where a local authority wants to dispose of 'land forming part of the common good with respect to which a question arises as to the right of the authority to alienate', the local authority can do so with the authorisation of a court. But, as the Inner House pointed out in *Portobello Park Action Group Association v City of Edinburgh Council* [2012] CSIH 69, 2013 SC 184 (discussed in *Conveyancing 2012* pp 172–75), there is no equivalent mechanism where a local authority wishes to keep the land but appropriate it for a different purpose. The effect of the amendment is to allow a court to give consent to such appropriation.

Part 8 is about deer management, a topic that is proving to be controversial: see *Part 1 Report* paras 353–391.

The LRRG concluded that, in general, the provisions on access rights in part 1 of the Land Reform (Scotland) Act 2003 were working well and that only minor amendments were needed. Part 9 introduces some amendments. A new subsection (7A) is added to s 28 (s 73). The effect is that where a declarator is sought as to whether a person has exercised access rights responsibly, the application must be served on the person in question. The other amendments are all to the provisions on core paths (s 72). A replacement s 20(1) makes clear (as the current version does not) that local authorities are free to review their existing core paths plan when they consider it appropriate to so do (and must do so if so required by Ministers). New provision is made for consultation on any amendments which result from the review.

Part 10 contains far-ranging and controversial provisions in relation to agricultural holdings. See *Stage 1 Report* paras 400–561.

Private Housing (Tenancies) (Scotland) Bill

The private rented sector ('PRS') in Scotland has more than doubled in size in the past decade and now covers 13% of homes. This increase in size has been matched by an increase in attention by government and parliament. Developments in the last few years have included (i) HMO regulation (2000), (ii) landlord registration (2006), (iii) a new repairing standard, to be enforced in a new private rented housing panel (2007), (iv) tenancy deposit schemes (2012), (v) tenant information packs (2013), (vi) a much-enhanced jurisdiction for the private rented housing panel (2014), and (vii) a registration system for letting agents (2014). Now there is a new Bill in the Scottish Parliament, the Private Housing (Tenancies) (Scotland) Bill which, if enacted, will introduce a new and mandatory PRS tenancy known as a 'private residential tenancy'. This will replace the assured and short assured tenancies which, since 1989, have been the only form of PRS tenancy available for ordinary houses.

The Bill follows on from *A Place to Stay, A Place to Call Home: A Strategy for the Private Rented Sector in Scotland* (www.scotland.gov.uk/Publications/2013/05/5877), published in 2013 (see *Conveyancing 2013* pp 89–90), and from the work of the Government's PRS Tenancy Review Group, which reported in May 2014 (www.scotland.gov.uk/Topics/Built-Environment/Housing/privaterent/government/Tenancy-Review/report). The Bill was the subject of two consultation documents by the Scottish Government, one in October 2014 (www.gov.scot/Publications/2014/10/9702) and the other in March 2015 (www.gov.scot/Publications/2015/03/6142). There were 2,500 responses to the first consultation and 7,689 to the second, although most of the latter were in support of one of four organised campaigns. The responses are summarised at www.gov.scot/Publications/2015/03/1968 and www.gov.scot/Publications/2015/08/3653. The Bill itself was introduced to Parliament on 7 October 2015 and completed Stage 2 on 10 February 2016. As this is a Government Bill, it may be assumed that it will complete its parliamentary stages before the pre-election dissolution of Parliament on 24 March 2016.

Once the Bill is enacted and in force, the only permitted PRS tenancy will be the new 'private residential tenancy' (ss 1, 2), and it will no longer be competent to enter into assured or short assured tenancies (sch 5 paras 1, 2, amending the Housing (Scotland) Act 1988). In most cases existing tenancies will be unaffected.

A key feature of short assured tenancies, which make up 94% of all PRS tenancies, is that the landlord is entitled to remove the tenant at the contractual ish. This will no longer be the case with private residential tenancies (s 35). Instead, tenants will have security of tenure and can only be removed if either they agree or if the landlord is able to establish, to the satisfaction of the First-Tier Tribunal (subsuming the private rented housing panel with effect, probably, from 1 September 2016), that one of the sixteen grounds for eviction set out in schedule 3 has been satisfied (ss 40 and 41). The grounds are:

1. landlord intends to sell;
2. property to be sold by lender;
3. landlord intends to refurbish;

4. landlord or family member intends to live in property;
5. landlord intends to use for non-residential purpose;
6. property required for religious purpose;
7. tenant no longer an employee;
8. tenant no longer in need of supported accommodation;
9. tenant no longer a student;
10. tenant not occupying let property;
11. breach of tenancy agreement;
12. rent arrears of three consecutive months;
13. criminal behaviour
14. anti-social behaviour
15. association with person who has relevant conviction or engaged in anti-social behaviour
16. landlord has ceased to be registered
17. HMO licence has been revoked
18. overcrowding statutory notice.

Some of these grounds are at the discretion of the Tribunal in whole or in part while others are mandatory. Landlords will also be able to bring a lease to an end during the contractual period ('initial period', defined in s 51), but only on certain grounds (s 43). As always, termination requires to be preceded by what is now called a 'notice to leave'.

An element of rent control is a feature of the present law in respect that the private rented housing panel has power to fix a market rent, in certain circumstances, for both assured and short assured tenancies: see Housing (Scotland) Act 1988 ss 24 and 34. Equivalent provision is made in the Bill in respect of the new private residential tenancy. While landlords are able to increase the rent, they cannot do so more than once a year (s 17). Tenants must be sent a rent-increase notice. If they are unhappy with the new rent they can request a rent officer at Rent Service Scotland (www.gov.scot/Topics/Built-Environment/Housing/privaterent/advice) to set an open market rent using the assumptions laid down in s 27 (s 20). There is a right of appeal to the First-Tier Tribunal (ss 24, 25). If the present law and practice are any guide, referrals to a rent officer are likely to be uncommon.

A (controversial) novelty in the Bill is the special provision made for 'rent pressure zones'. On application by a local authority, the Scottish Ministers can designate an area as a rent pressure zone for a period of up to five years (ss 30, 32). This is for areas where rent levels are rising excessively. Following such designation, Scottish Ministers can then cap rent increases according to a formula which includes the consumer prices index. Information on recent rent levels can be found in *Private Sector Rent Statistics, Scotland, 2010 to 2015* (www.gov.scot/Publications/2015/11/3376) published on 10 November 2015. This shows a 13.7% cumulative increase in average rents from 2010 to 2015 for 2-bedroom properties at the Scotland level – which is 2% above CPI – although there is considerable regional variation.

As under the present law, landlords in private residential tenancies must provide their tenants with a written tenancy agreement and certain other information (ss 8–11). In order to assist with this, the Bill's *Policy Memorandum* para 41 explains that:

> the Scottish Government will develop a model tenancy agreement which will contain mandatory and discretionary clauses and a statutory guidance note that would summarise the meaning of the clauses in plain language. The mandatory content of the model tenancy agreement will be set out in forthcoming subordinate legislation. This is to allow stakeholders to be consulted about the content of the model agreement during the legislation's development to help ensure it would be fit for purpose.

The legislative basis of the mandatory clauses is ss 5 and 6. These must include the clauses set out in schedule 2, which deal with receipts for rent paid in cash, rent increases, notification as to adult residents (other than the tenant), restrictions of subletting, and rights of access for repairs and inspection.

Consultation on a code of practice and training requirements for letting agents

Part 4 of the Housing (Scotland) Act 2014 makes provision for a registration system for the 750 or so letting agents for private-sector residential tenancies: see *Conveyancing 2014* p 70. There is also to be a Code of Practice and a training requirement. The Scottish Government has been consulting on both of those: see www.gov.scot/Publications/2015/08/6563. The draft Code of Practice covers matters such as: (i) standards of practice (eg 'You must be honest and fair in your dealings with landlords, tenants and applicants'); (ii) engaging landlord clients and the need for a contract written in plain language; (iii) the letting of property (eg 'Your advertising and marketing must be clear, accurate and not knowingly or negligently misleading'); (iv) maintenance and management (eg 'You must put in place appropriate written procedures and processes for tenants and landlords to notify you of any repairs and maintenance required'); and (v) ending the tenancy (eg 'Where a landlord wishes to retain part or all of the tenancy deposit, you must, where negotiating on their behalf, take reasonable steps to come to an agreement with the tenant'). The consultation closed on 15 November 2015.

Registers of Scotland

Application rejection guidance

On 30 January 2015 the RoS customer ezine gave the following guidance on the most common reasons for the rejection of applications:

> *Company/non-natural person designation.* Section 113(1) of the Land Registration etc (Scotland) Act 2012 requires additional information to be entered in the title sheet for a non-natural person designation. A larger than expected number of applications failed to include this information and had to be rejected. We have reviewed our policy and internal guidance for staff to see whether we could do anything more to help applicants. Application guidance has been updated to provide greater clarity on the information the Keeper will accept as sufficient [as to which see *Conveyancing 2014* p 152].

Application form errors. Insufficient company/non-natural person designation information has been the most common rejection reason since 8 December 2014. Please remember to provide all of the information that is required. Other than that, the most common rejection reasons have been for administrative errors related to forms (eg form not signed or 1979 Act forms submitted). This replicates the most common rejection reasons under the 1979 Act. If you have had applications rejected for these types of errors, our advice is that you review your processes.

Servitudes. When submitting for registration a 'deed over an unregistered plot', you should confirm if the plot of land to which the application relates is the benefited subjects in relation to any servitude, even where that is also set out in the deed submitted for registration. Part B of application form contains a question relating to servitudes, and the details of any prior deeds in which servitude rights were constituted must be listed at this part the form.

Dual registration. You should be aware that the RoS eform automatically calculates the fee that is payable for the deed being registered, based on the information entered in the 'application details' part of the application form. Where the application requires dual registration in the Land Register to create real burdens or servitudes, only a single application form is required in order to give effect to the deed against both properties. However, you should ensure that the additional title number(s) are provided in the form. The full registration fee should be met by the lead agent, since they will be submitting the application form. Where dual registration is required in respect of an application to register a 'deed over part of a registered plot', the title number of the part being transferred will not yet be known. Applicants using the eform to dual register such deeds should enter the parent title number twice to ensure the additional £60 fee is calculated.

Advance notice over part. The main rejection reason in relation to advance notices over part is that the Keeper is not provided with sufficient information to delineate the property on the cadastral map either because: (1) the property cannot be identified on the Ordnance Survey map, and (2) use of a location plan. If you are intending to submit an advance notice over part, please refer to the *General Guidance: Advance Notices - Guidance for plans and descriptions for advance notices for deeds affecting part of a registered plot* (v.01 17/12/14).

Tenements. The requirements for tenement mapping have been further clarified, in particular the requirement to define the tenement steading when submitting an application to register an individual flat. Where the Keeper already holds an acceptable extent for the tenement steading, the application can proceed based on that extent, for example where there is a previous registration of a flat within that tenement, and the extent of the tenement steading is already delineated on the cadastral map. [See further under Mapping below.]

An updated version of the *General Guidance: Application Forms* – the fourth so far – was issued on 8 June 2015.

Rejection rates

At the end of February 2015, RoS reported as follows:

Since the designated day in December, we have seen a steady decline in the number of applications that have needed to be returned. We invested significant resource in the lead up to the designated day to minimise the issues that changing our and your practices would entail. This activity, coupled with changes post-designated day, saw the rejection figures drop to 6% by the end of last week. If this trend continues, rejection rates will soon be at or below pre-2012 Act levels. It's in our joint interests to reduce this figure further and we will continue to work with our customers to achieve this.

A snapshot from one day of rejections last week showed that the main reasons for rejected applications at intake were as follows:

Application form not signed/completed 31
Error in deed or no deed provided 20
Incorrect fee (where payment is by cheque) 5
No SDLT certificate 4
No or wrong plan 4

We also carry out a more comprehensive examination of FR and TP applications post the date the application enters the application record in order to establish any obvious issues with the deeds presented for registration. The main issues we encounter concern the plotting of the subjects on to the cadastral map; either the subjects conflict with a title that is already on the cadastral map, or we simply cannot plot the subjects on to it based on the current deed plan and/or conveyancing description. An appropriate plans report will highlight if there is a problem with respect to either of these issues. In terms of what to do should a report disclose either of these matters, please see our guidance.

Report on reports

At the end of February RoS reported as follows:

Since the start of the year, 100% of legal reports have been completed within 24 hours. Over 90% of plans reports have been completed within the same time frame, with almost all of the remainder having been done first thing the following day. This is in spite of the demand for plans reports doubling, and the turnaround time reducing from 72 hours to 24.

Defects in plans will fall foul of the one-shot rule, so do make sure you get the appropriate plans report prior to application for registration, and action any results of the report before you apply. Our reports service identifies potential issues before registration, helping reduce the likelihood of rejection when the registration application is submitted. As a result, none of the applications that originated from one of our reports should, if appropriate steps are taken, result in rejection.

We have heard it said, however, that plans reports do not infallibly detect overlaps; yet the application for registration will still be rejected on the ground of the overlap.

E-mail communications

In the initial weeks of the new Act, a standard complaint about e-mails from RoS was the absence of the property address from the headings: see *Conveyancing*

2014 pp 156–57. This was altered with effect from 2 April 2015. Notification e-mails now show the address of the property in the subject line of the e-mail, and additional key information has been added to the body of the e-mail.

Mapping

On 18 March 2015 RoS issued the following statement about mapping:

Mapping requirements under the 2012 Act

The 2012 Act places mapping at the heart of the Land Register. The focal point for that is the new cadastral map. The cadastral map, is, in essence, a map showing all registered property in Scotland.

  Plans and maps have always presented challenges for registration. Under the Land Registration (Scotland) Act 1979, the main reason for a first registration application being stood over pending further dialogue with the submitting agent, or for being cancelled was due to difficulties identifying the subjects and plotting them on to the Land Register map.

  One of the emerging areas of challenge for first registration applications is around meeting the mapping requirements of the 2012 Act, with the result that some applications are having to be rejected. There are two main requirements under the 2012 Act in so far as the cadastral map is concerned:

  (i) the deed being registered must be capable of enabling the Keeper to plot the subjects on to the cadastral map; and

  (ii) the property extent being registered must not overlap with an existing registered title.

In the event that either requirement is not met, the Keeper must reject the application. Crucially, those requirements must be met at the date the application is submitted.

  The most effective way of ensuring those requirements are met is to obtain a plans report. However, it does appear that for certain first registration transactions – such as those for no consideration which prior to the designated day would have been recorded in the Sasine Register – a plans report is not always being obtained. There is, of course, no legal requirement for a plans report to be obtained and, in relation to suitability of a deed plan for registration, we have published deed plan criteria on our website aimed specifically at aiding solicitors in determining whether or not a deed plan is likely to be acceptable. That can aid with requirement (i) above. The risk still remains that there may be an overlap with an existing registered title and for that reason we would always recommend that a level-one plans report is obtained.

  It is equally crucial that action is taken on the output of a plans report. If the report discloses that the subjects cannot be mapped, a fresh plan should be obtained. Similarly if – as sometimes happens – a new plan has been drawn up to support the subsequent application and that plan forms the basis of the report request, it is crucial that the new plan is included as a deed plan to the deed inducing registration. We have examples where a report is requested based on a new plan, but the application is submitted along with the original aged conveyancing plan only. If we cannot identify the subjects from that deed, the application will fall to be rejected.

  If an overlap is disclosed, the deed as it stands will not be acceptable for registration; during a three-week sampling period we had to reject 30 applications because of an overlap. Of those 30, we are aware of a plans report being obtained in 17 instances, all of which highlighted the overlap. Faced with an overlap, there are two broad courses of action that can be taken in order to meet the requirements of the 2012 Act:

(i) prepare a fresh deed plan excluding the area of overlap; or

(ii) seek to have the neighbouring title rectified to remove the area of overlap.

Please note that, where the neighbouring title was registered under the 1979 Act framework, the transitional provisions in schedule 4 of the 2012 Act will be relevant. Where the 1979 Act title was inaccurate immediately before the designated day (8 December 2014), one must assess whether the Keeper was able to rectify under the 1979 Act rectification provisions. Broadly, assuming consent of the neighbour to rectification was not in place immediately before the designated day, there is no exclusion of indemnity in the 1979 Act title and there was no aspect of fraud or carelessness in the application for that title, then possession of the area in question will be the determining factor. Under the transitional provisions in the 2012 Act, the date for determining possession is immediately before the designated day (ie possession as on 7 December 2014). The 2012 Act also introduces a presumption whereby the person registered as proprietor of the land is to be presumed to be in possession unless the contrary is shown. So the onus is firmly on the person challenging to demonstrate that the registered proprietor was not in possession. If they cannot demonstrate that, then the inaccuracy is washed out and the remedy – if there is a remedy – lies in compensation and that will be a matter of fact and circumstance.

When submitting your application for registration, please remember to submit the extent deeds and any relevant burden deeds or deeds containing rights. It is equally important to note that if a right or encumbrance has to be shown on the cadastral map, then the Keeper needs to be able to identify that as well.

Tenements

When the subjects are a flat, the Keeper will typically, under section 16 of the Act, represent the building and all the registered flats as a single cadastral unit. This is generally referred to as the tenement steading approach and it will be used for all flatted or sub-divided buildings where it is suitable to do so. In the same way as any other registration, the Keeper must be able to identify the extent of the area to be mapped (the tenement steading) on the cadastral map – a plans report will disclose if a tenement steading cadastral unit already exists. If the Keeper does not have an extent for the tenement steading cadastral unit defined on the cadastral map, then this must be provided in the application. If the extent of the tenement steading is not defined in the deeds, then a plan showing the tenement steading must be prepared and submitted with the application. The tenement steading should be drawn to include the tenement building itself and all the pertinents to that building and the flats within it.

Voluntary registration and certified plans

On 29 May 2015 RoS issued the following guidance about the use of certified plans in applications for voluntary registration:

In relation to an application for voluntary registration, it is a condition of registration at s 28(1)(a) that 'there is submitted with the application a plan or description of the plot sufficient to enable the Keeper to delineate the plot's boundaries in the cadastral map'. Similarly, there are conditions of registration relating to registrable encumbrances affecting a lesser area within the plot being registered. Usually, the prior titles referred to will contain a suitable description and/or a plan allowing registration to proceed.

In limited cases, a plan which is not annexed to a deed will be submitted to fulfil the relevant conditions of registration relating to the boundaries of a plot.

It is the Keeper's policy that certified plans may be used in two situations:

1. to confirm the extent of the subjects to be registered, or the area to which encumbrances relate, where this is not clear from the deeds supporting an application for voluntary registration; or
2. where the application for registration includes a request for the inclusion of a servitude created by prescription.

Key requirements of certified plans:

(a) the plan must accompany the application; and
(b) the plan should be referred to in the application form (for example in the Further Information field); and
(c) it should be clear that the plan submitted is the plan referred to in the application form; and
(d) the plan must be of sufficient quality to fulfil the Keeper's deed plan criteria; and
(e) the purpose of the reference(s) on the plan should be clear from the information provided either in the form, from a legend on the plan or in any docket on the plan. For example, whether the plan (or a particular reference on it) discloses the extent of the plot for which registration is sought or the route of a prescriptive servitude right of way, or the areas affected by a specific burdens in previously recorded deeds; and
(f) the plan should be annexed to the application form.

The plan does not require to be 'certified'. For example, any docket on the plan does not require to state 'I/We certify….' Nor is it necessary that the plan be signed by either the applicant or by their agent submitting the application. It is recommended that the docket used on the plan take a form similar to one of the following:

• This is the plan of plot [*address or general description*] for which registration is sought, referred to in the application for voluntary registration by [*applicant's name*].
• This is the plan referred to in the application for voluntary registration by [*insert name of applicant or applicants*]. The boundaries of the plot [*describe nature of plot where separate tenement such as eg 'salmon fishing rights'*] for which registration is sought are [*edged red*].
• This is the plan of the route of the right of access for vehicular and pedestrian purposes created by prescription, referred to in the application for voluntary registration by [*applicant's name*] of [*description of plot transferred*].

Before submitting the application for registration, the parties must have satisfied themselves that the information provided in the plan is supported by the title deeds and, where appropriate, prescriptive possession. The applicant and their agent are certifying that the information is correct, and accordingly it is not acceptable to qualify the certification (for example, by suggesting that the plan is merely indicative or demonstrative).

Extension to period during which deeds without title number will be accepted

Following discussion with the Law Society of Scotland, the Keeper has amended her policy in respect of deeds submitted for registration but which do not bear the title number of the registered plot to which they relate. While a deed should, wherever possible, narrate the title number, the Keeper will accept a deed that does not do so provided that (i) the deed contains an otherwise sufficient description of the subjects or the security being discharged, and (ii) it is executed before (or up to 28 days after) the title number is known. This will assist solicitors particularly when obtaining discharges in respect of first registrations.

E-forms and downloading drafts

A save and share functionality for drafts has been made available on the RoS e-forms service via a 'save and exit' button. This includes advance notices, thus meeting a shortcoming that was much criticised: see *Conveyancing 2014* p 149. A 'download draft' button has also been added to each of the pages in the application form. Draft versions of advance notices or e-forms cannot, however, be submitted for registration. Once users are content that the form contains the required information, they must continue to use the 'finish and download PDF' button to apply for registration.

Consultation on completion of the Register

In July 2014 Registers of Scotland launched a public consultation on *Completion of the Land Register*. There were 47 responses, including seventeen from local authorities but only four from firms of solicitors. The responses and all other papers on this topic can be found at www.ros.gov.uk/consultations/completion-of-the-land-register. A paper summarising the responses and giving the RoS reaction was issued by RoS in February 2015 (https://www.ros.gov.uk/__data/assets/pdf_file/0015/11670/LR-completion-consultation-report-v-0-9.pdf).

Since then, some of the proposals have been implemented by the Registers of Scotland (Voluntary Registration, Amendment of Fees, etc) Order 2015, SSI 2015/265. Thus, the Register of Sasines is to be closed to standard securities with effect from 1 April 2016. This means that the registration of a security will have to be preceded by voluntary registration of the plot of land. No fee will be charged for the voluntary registration. RoS estimates that this will lead to the registration of around 5% of remaining titles between now and 2024 (para 13). For FAQs on standard securities, see www.ros.gov.uk/about-us/land-register-completion/closure-of-the-grs-to-securities-guidance.

In addition, to encourage 'ordinary' voluntary registrations, the fee is to be reduced by 25% (the original proposal having been a mere 10% reduction). A number of respondents had suggested that voluntary registration should be free or at least that applicants with large landholdings or complex titles should be able to agree a fee based either on a fixed fee or on actual staff costs (para 27). RoS have welcomed these suggestions and indicated that 'we will work with stakeholders to explore the feasibility of these options' (para 34).

There is power under s 48(3) of the Land Registration etc (Scotland) Act 2012 to close the Register of Sasines to other deeds, such as deeds of conditions or deeds of servitudes. Following the consultation, however, RoS have indicated that there are no plans to use this power for the present (para 24):

The closure of the Sasine Register to deeds other than standard securities would not introduce a requirement for proprietors to apply for voluntary registration. Instead, the Keeper would require to make up a title sheet for any land affected by a deed presented for registration. This would inevitably result in a piecemeal approach to increasing coverage that would cut across the Keeper's intention to promote voluntary registration of the whole of a proprietor's land and to undertake a structured programme of Keeper-induced registration (KIR). We note that there is no clear consensus amongst respondents to the consultation as to whether particular deed types (other than standard securities) should trigger registration in the Land Register. We do not therefore propose closing the Sasine Register to other deeds at this stage. We will, however, return to this issue and consult further with stakeholders in due course.

As well as the target of 2024 for completion of the Register, there is a separate target of 2019 for moving all public land on to the Register. RoS envisages that this will largely be achieved by voluntary registration rather than by KIR. In responding to the consultation, however, some local authorities were hesitant as to the prospects of achieving this (para 48):

Local authority respondents raised several specific concerns about the expectation of registration of all public land within five years. Most local authority respondents suggested that they would be unable to provide the financial or staff resource needed from existing budgets, and several stated that they would be unlikely to submit applications for voluntary registration ... South Lanarkshire Council asserted: 'We are unable to see how voluntary registration would serve the functions of the Council and accordingly consider that undertaking this exercise would be challengeable as *ultra vires*.'

Finally, mention should be made of the informative and candid chapter on the topic by John King, the Business Development Director at RoS, which appears at pp 317–44 of Frankie McCarthy, James Chalmers, and Stephen Bogle (eds), *Essays in Conveyancing and Property Law in Honour of Professor Robert Rennie* (2015; available to download free of charge at www.openbookpublishers.com/product/343/essays-in-conveyancing-and-property-law-in-honour-of-professor-robert-rennie).

Consultation on KIR

Following on from the consultation just mentioned, RoS launched a separate consultation on Keeper-induced registration (KIR) in October 2015: www.ros.gov.uk/consultations/keeper-induced-registration. The current plan is to use KIR for the 58% of unregistered titles which lie within research areas. These areas comprise housing estates and other developments which are subject to uniform burdens. In relation to such areas KIR is relatively straightforward because, in preparation for registration counties first becoming operational under the 1979 Act, RoS had already examined the titles and identified common burdens. The plan is to work through the research areas one by one, and to alert conveyancers and the general public to which areas are next by means of a timeline on the RoS website (paras 14, 15, and 51). The extent to which KIR will be used beyond the research areas remains unclear. Pilot studies conducted by RoS have been discouraging, even where the co-operation of the owner was sought. The consultation closed on 8 January 2016. The first property to be registered under KIR was the National Trust for Scotland's Georgian House in Edinburgh's Charlotte Square. St Kilda followed shortly afterwards.

The designated day – one year on

The Keeper issued a message to mark the first anniversary of the designated day on 8 December 2015: see (2015) 60 *Journal of the Law Society of Scotland* Dec/9. The following is an extract:

> It's one year since the Land Registration etc (Scotland) Act 2012 introduced a different legal framework for land registration. Twelve months on, most of the changes are familiar to all. Those involved in conveyancing have adapted well and some 460,000 applications (including advance notices) have been presented for registration.
>
> The 1979 Act is largely becoming a thing of the past. As expected, we received a significant influx of applications in advance of the designated day, leaving us with 41,000 applications to process under the old legislation. Virtually all of those applications have been completed, with only 55 left, which are held up because we are in dialogue with the submitting agent.
>
> Dealings of whole have never been quicker or simpler, both for the applicant and for RoS. Seventy per cent of applications were completed in under five days, reflecting the fact that solicitors generally no longer need to submit supporting documentation other than the deed inducing registration. Transfers of part have the potential to be just as straightforward, especially with our development plan approval (DPA) service, which ensures any title and extent issues are resolved prior to sales of individual plots. The mapping requirements under the 2012 Act have encouraged developers to use DPA and we now have 249 developments throughout Scotland using this service. Find out more on our dedicated DPA service page.
>
> First registrations present different challenges, reflecting the fact that conveyancing is less straightforward for properties held on titles recorded in the Sasine Register. To assist in the preparation of these applications, we've launched a plan assistance service, which translates old descriptions to the ordnance survey map, and we'll soon be introducing a new application checking service. This service will offer a preregistration check of your potential application to ensure it can meet the conditions of registration. Find out more at ros.gov.uk/services.

No manual amendments to advance notices in the Register of Sasines

On 9 March 2015 RoS announced that:

> Manual amendments to advance notice of first registration are not acceptable for recording in the Sasine Register for the following reasons:
>
> • An advance notice which is recorded in Sasines is not simply a notice (which it is in the Land Register) but a writ which requires to be stamped and recorded like any other. In accordance with the Requirements of Writing (Scotland) Act 1995, if any other deed had manual amendments which appear to have been made after it was signed, those amendments would be narrated in the testing clause. However, an advance notice is not subject to the 1995 Act.

- The information inserted for the advance notice is saved on the system in case a discharge is required by the applicant. Obviously, manual amendments are not saved on the system so if a discharge were created, it would contain the inputted information which is not the same as the information contained on the amended notice. If such a discharge were recorded, it would not have the desired effect of discharging the advance notice as the information would not match.
- As it takes very little time to prepare a replacement advance notice, RoS would not usually accept an advance notice which has been manually amended. However, if the applicant confirmed that they had satisfied him or herself that a manually amended notice were valid and had the intended effect and insisted that it be recorded, then RoS would do so.

RoS General Guidance

The indispensable series of RoS 'General Guidance' on 2012 Act topics has been extended and updated in the course of 2015: see www.ros.gov.uk/about-us/2012-act/general-guidance. General Guidance is provided for the first time on land and buildings transaction tax and on the Long Leases (Scotland) Act 2012; and there is updated Guidance on application forms, the one-shot rule, fees, reports, inaccuracy and rectification, prescriptive claimants, leases and automatic plot registration, title conditions, and encumbrances and off-register rights.

Updates

No less indispensable is RoS's longstanding 'Update' series: see www.ros.gov.uk/about-us/what-we-do/our-business/publications/registers-updates. Two new Updates were issued in 2015, numbers 44 and 45. Both are considered below.

Aronson and postponed standard securities: the RoS response

RoS *Update 44* is concerned with the aftermath of the decision in *Aronson v Keeper of the Registers of Scotland* [2014] CSOH 176, 2015 SLT 122. The issue goes back to the decision of the Supreme Court in *Royal Bank of Scotland plc v Wilson* [2010] UKSC 50, 2011 SC (UKSC) 66 which overturned 40 years of consistent interpretation as to how standard securities can be enforced: see *Conveyancing 2010* pp 129–49. The title litigated in *Aronson* was one of a fairly limited number of titles that were affected in a certain specific way by *Wilson*. The titles in question all involved a sale by a heritable creditor where there existed postponed securities. More narrowly, they concerned cases where the sale figure was not enough to pay off the postponed creditors. The general law is well known: such securities are discharged by the sale, and the creditors are simply ordinary unsecured creditors for any sums they may still be owed: see s 26(1) of the Conveyancing and Feudal Reform (Scotland) Act 1970. Accordingly, the Keeper deletes such securities from the title sheet and the buyer obtains an unencumbered title.

This is what happened in all cases before *Wilson*, because the Keeper did not know that there was anything wrong with the method of enforcement then commonly used. And in cases since *Wilson*, there has not normally been a problem, because heritable creditors have generally made sure that they enforced in the new approved manner. But there were some cases that were unlucky in their timing: they were enforced before *Wilson* but the buyer applied to the Keeper for registration after *Wilson*. In those cases, what the Keeper did was to register the buyer, but to leave on the title sheet the postponed securities, on the ground that it was not certain that the sale, having been done in a manner that was disconform to the *Wilson* decision, might be subject to challenge. That practice was challenged in *Aronson* and held to be unsound. Section 26 was found to apply, with the result that the Register was inaccurate in continuing to show the postponed securities. See *Conveyancing 2014* pp 44–47.

Update 44 sets out the Keeper's response to the decision:

> The Keeper has decided not to appeal the decision and to rectify both the Aronson title and titles in all similar cases. There are estimated to be around 130 similarly affected titles, all historic as lenders have changed their practices in response to the *Wilson* decision.
>
> The Keeper will take steps to remove the standard securities from those affected titles. The B Section of the affected title sheets will continue to show that indemnity is excluded in respect of loss which may arise as a result of the failure to comply with the statutory procedures. The Keeper understands that in many cases title insurance has been taken out in respect of that risk.
>
> There is no need for an application for rectification to be made, as under section 80 of the 2012 Act the Keeper is under a duty to rectify manifest inaccuracies where what is needed to do so is also manifest. The Keeper intends to remove all affected standard securities as soon as possible and will give notice under section 80(4)(b) of such rectifications to persons who appear to be materially affected by them, namely, the registered proprietor, the creditor whose securities have been removed and those whose securities remain but are ranked differently. The Keeper will also send a copy of the updated C section to creditors and a plain copy of the whole title sheet to registered proprietors.

Conversion of ultra-long leases into ownership

RoS *Update 45* concerns the registration implications of the automatic conversion into ownership, on 28 November 2015, of all ultra-long leases, ie leases granted for more than 175 years and which had an unexpired duration of either 100 years (private dwellinghouses) or 175 years (other cases). Conversion was by virtue of the Long Leases (Scotland) Act 2012. For details, see *Conveyancing 2012* pp 132–37.

One result of conversion is that the Land Register is now inaccurate in showing as lease title sheets what are now title sheets for plots of land. There will also be inaccuracy in respect of the burdens. In theory, it is for the Keeper to make the necessary corrections herself, for s 80 of the Land Registration etc (Scotland) Act 2012 requires the Keeper to rectify manifest inaccuracies. But in practice, as *Update 45* explains, rectification is likely to come about mainly on the initiative of the affected parties. We quote the key passages in full:

Updating the Land Register

Where conversion has occurred for a lease with a lease title sheet, that title sheet will be rendered inaccurate in disclosing that the right is that of a tenant and not an owner and it may also be inaccurate in disclosing certain lease conditions as subsisting.

Similarly, a plot title sheet affected by a converted lease will be rendered inaccurate as the land is no longer owned by the registered proprietor.

A request for the Land Register to be updated to give effect to conversion can be made either –

• by submitting a request for rectification; or
• by certifying that conversion has occurred in an application for registration of a deed, for example in the Additional Information field on the application form.

The request or application should also make clear which leasehold conditions disclosed in the lease title sheet have been rendered extinct, though the Keeper would seek to give effect to the extinction of the obligation to pay rent when updating a lease title sheet. Where an update is made to the lease title sheet to show that it is now a plot title sheet and the right of the former owner was registered, a corresponding amendment will be made to the former owner's plot title sheet or it will be closed if necessary.

There is no fee for rectification. By virtue of section 85(1) of the 2012 Act, no entitlement to compensation arises on rectification of such inaccuracies since they arise otherwise than as a result of an entry or change in an entry in the Land Register made by the Keeper.

Applications for registration relating to a converted lease

Applications for first registration

After conversion has occurred, the ownership right of a former tenant necessarily will be transmitted by disposition. The provisions of the Long Leases Act also operate to convert certain qualifying conditions set out in the lease, or other deeds pertaining to the lease, into real burdens such as facility and service burdens. Certain lease conditions which affected or benefited the tenant's right prior to conversion will also become servitudes burdening or benefiting the land. Further, notices or agreements may have been recorded to convert certain leasehold conditions into real burdens or reservations of sporting rights in the lease into separate tenements.

Heritable securities and proper liferents that affected the land prior to conversion will be extinguished on the appointed day. However, other encumbrances affecting the land such as existing real burdens or servitudes, or those which affected the lease (for example a heritable security over the lease or a non-qualifying long sublease) are unaffected.

The applicant will need to consider how the conversion affects the particular lease and then provide the Keeper with details of any encumbrances and rights that require to be entered in the title sheet, as part of their application for registration of a disposition or application for voluntary registration. Where a servitude right or encumbrance requires to be delineated on the cadastral map, the application must include a plan or sufficient description of the extent.

Applications affecting a lease title sheet

After conversion has occurred, the ownership right of a former tenant necessarily will be transmitted by disposition. Where parties submit an application for registration of a deed after the appointed day without the lease title sheet having previously been rectified, their application for registration affecting that title sheet should confirm that the right of the tenant has converted to ownership. A disposition or other deed affecting the converted lease submitted for registration after the appointed day can properly refer to the title number of the lease title sheet. The application should also specify which, if any, of the leasehold conditions disclosed on the lease title sheet the applicant considers were extinguished on conversion. In general the Keeper's staff will not proactively consider whether a particular lease has converted when processing an application which otherwise meets the conditions of registration.

A shorter version of the above can be found in RoS's *General Guidance: Long Leases (Scotland) Act 2012*, which was issued on 27 November 2015.

The 2012 Act made provision for the registration by the (soon to be ex-) landlord of a whole suite of notices on various matters such as the conversion of leasehold conditions to real burdens by nomination of a benefited property or the conversion of reserved sporting rights into separate tenements. Full details can be found in *Conveyancing 2013* pp 139–50. In almost every case the notice had to be registered, at latest, by the appointed day for conversion (ie 28 November 2015). RoS have kindly supplied us with figures for the number of notices registered. The total was a mere ten notices, comprising (i) four notices seeking exemption from conversion (2012 Act s 63); (ii) one agreement seeking exemption from conversion (s 64); (iii) three notices of conversion of leasehold conditions by nomination of a benefited property (s 14); and two notices of conversion of leasehold conditions into personal pre-emption burdens or personal redemption burdens (s 23).

Significant changes to Law Society's Property Law *Guidance*

The Law Society's Property Law Committee has reviewed and updated its *Guidance* in Section F Division C of the Society's *Rules and Guidance*: www.lawscot. org.uk/rules-and-guidance/table-of-contents/. New topics covered include (i) where lenders wish to remit funds directly to the *seller's* solicitor, and (ii) where lenders wish a repairs grant to be discharged.

Letters of obligation and the Master Policy

The Law Society *Guidance* Section F Division C (www.lawscot.org.uk/rules-and-guidance/table-of-contents/) states in relation to letters of obligation:

> (c) How will the Master Policy cover for letters of obligation be affected after the designated day?
>
> For the rest of the insurance year Nov 2014 to Oct 2015, there will be no change to the Master Policy regarding the grant of letters of obligation. Once practice develops under the 2012 Act, the position may be reviewed at renewal of the Master Policy in 2015.

The Law Society reports (*Professional Practice Update*, November 2015) that Marsh have confirmed that the above position regarding the Master Policy will continue after October 2015 for the time being in respect of letters of obligation in the classic form.

ScotLIS

The Keeper is leading a task force to develop an online system that will allow users to find out comprehensive information about any piece of land or property in Scotland with a single inquiry. See www.ros.gov.uk/about-us/scotlis. This could include information such as school catchment areas, mining reports, flood risks and crime statistics. The online service is called ScotLIS (Scotland's Land and Information System) and the target date for getting it up and running is October 2017. For further details, see Stewart Brymer, 'Land information: a one-stop shop' (2015) 60 *Journal of the Law Society of Scotland* April/36.

10-year property-market report

RoS have issued a 10-year property-market report: see www.ros.gov.uk/__data/assets/pdf_file/0008/3977/RoS10yearreport2004-2014.pdf.
      Key findings include:

- Nationally, average residential house prices grew steadily between 2005–06 and 2007–08, with fairly stable prices between 2007–08 and 2013–14, and then an increase in 2014–15.
- The average prices of all residential property types increased significantly since 2005–06, with terraced properties showing the biggest increase in price across the decade. Flatted dwellings represented the largest share of the market, making up 41.2% of all residential sales in the last 10 years.
- Over the decade, sales volumes decreased by 35.1%, from 142,933 in 2005–06 to 92,798 in 2014–15. Volumes in 2014–15 were the highest since 2007–08 and were up by 6.2% when compared to 2013–14. Volumes for 2014–15 still remained 38.7% below the 10 year high achieved in 2006–07.
- The number of sales being registered with a mortgage in 2014–15 fell by 45% when compared with 2005–06, and rose by 9.5% when compared with 2013–14. Cash sales now equate to 35.6% of the market, as compared to 17.6% in 2005–06.

Standard securities: restrictions on the right to redeem after 20 years

Section 11 of the Land Tenure Reform (Scotland) Act 1974 gives borrowers the right to redeem a standard security over a private dwelling house after it has been in force for 20 years. Its purpose – rather oddly, to modern eyes – was to prevent the use of 'sales', in which the 'price' was repayable over a very long period and secured by a standard security, as a substitute for the leases of more than 20 years which, for dwellinghouses, were banned by s 8 of the Act. (See J M Halliday, *Conveyancing Law and Practice* vol 2 (2nd edn, 1997) paras 55–65.) If that particular device was ever known in practice it is unknown now. On the other hand, the 20-year rule has caused difficulty, especially in respect of the stipulation in subsection (5) that the amount due on redemption cannot be larger than, in essence, the amount originally advanced plus interest. This does not fit in well with certain types of financing arrangements that now exist such as shared equity loan and equity release schemes.

      With this in mind, an exemption was added to s 11 by s 93 of the Housing (Scotland) Act 2014 in respect of 'a heritable security which is in security of a debt of a description specified in an order made by the Scottish Ministers'. Since the provision was passed, the Scottish Government has consulted on a proposal to apply the exemption to the following Government schemes: the

Help to Buy (Scotland) Scheme; Homestake; New Supply Shared Equity Scheme; Open Market Shared Equity Scheme (for which see www.scotland.gov.uk/Publications/2014/04/7891); and the Help to Adapt Scheme. See www.scotland.gov.uk/Resource/0046/00461603.pdf. Consultation responses were published on 23 February 2015 (www.gov.scot/Publications/2015/02/2800) and further action is awaited.

CML *Lenders' Handbook*

In consultation with the Law Society, some changes have been made to the CML *Lenders' Handbook for Scotland* with effect from 8 June 2015. The changes respond to the introduction of the Land Registration etc (Scotland) Act 2012 and of land and buildings transaction tax. Most are minor. The affected clauses are 5.5.1, 10.4, 14.1, 14.2 and 15.1. For discussion, see the notes by Ken Swinton (2015) 83 *Scottish Law Gazette* 20 and by Alison MacKay (2015) 60 *Journal of the Law Society of Scotland* June/33. The main re-drafting occurs in clause 14.1, which now reads:

14.1 Application to Registers

14.1.1   You must forthwith after settlement record/register our standard security in the Register of Sasines or Land Register of Scotland as appropriate. Before making your application for recording/registration you must place on your file certified copies of the disposition or other conveyance in favour of the borrower, our standard security and any discharge from a previous heritable creditor.

14.1.2   Where the application for registration of our standard security is to be made to the Land Register of Scotland, we require you, where in your professional judgement it is appropriate:

- to apply for an advance notice under the Land Registration etc (Scotland) Act 2012 in respect of our standard security;
- to have seen a Legal Report which discloses such advance notice and no other competing advance notice; and
- to submit the application for registration within the protected period afforded by that advance notice.

For the avoidance of doubt these requirements and expectations in no way detract from our requirement to have a fully enforceable first ranking standard security over the property (see paragraph 5.8.1).

14.1.3   Where our standard security is recorded in the Register of Sasines you must check that the deeds appear to have been properly recorded and that the completed Searches disclose the relevant deeds, with no adverse entry.

14.1.4   Where our standard security is registered in the Land Register of Scotland before 8 December 2014, following registration you must check the Land and Charge Certificates for accuracy where we require paper Certificates to be issued (see part 2). For such of those pre-8 December 2014 cases where we do not require paper Certificates, and for all cases where the application for registration is accepted by the Land Register of Scotland on or after 8 December 2014, you must check that the Title Sheet has been updated accurately. In the latter case we may require either that you instruct the Registers of Scotland on your application form to send us direct notification to our designated email address that registration of our standard security has been completed, or that you send us a paper or electronic copy of the updated Title Sheet which shows the registration of our standard security (see part 2).

The equivocal terms of clause 14.1.2 in relation to advance notices will be noted. A prospective change to the *Lenders' Handbook* is mentioned at p 80 above.

Consumer protections in conveyancing cases

The report of an investigation undertaken on behalf of the Law Society by Sheriff Principal Edward Bowen QC on *Consumer Protections in Conveyancing Cases* was published in February 2015 (www.lawscot.org.uk/media/439009/Law-Society-report-Consumer-Protections-in-Conveyancing-Cases.pdf). Sheriff Principal Bowen investigated two highly unfortunate cases in which, over a period of many years, purchasers of residential property were left without a satisfactory title and at the mercy of litigation. The first, concerning property in Queens Gardens, Aberdeen, involved the fraudulent alteration of a disposition which may have been carried out by a solicitor (but not the solicitor who acted for the purchaser). The second concerned the unfortunately-named Happy Valley housing estate in Blackburn, West Lothian where, it turned out, a small number of houses were built partly on land not belonging to the builder and where the builder subsequently became insolvent. The first, but not the second, has resulted in reported litigation: *Pocock's Tr v Skene Investments (Aberdeen) Ltd* [2011] CSOH 144, 2011 GWD 30-654 (discussed in *Conveyancing 2011* pp 126–29).

The task of Sheriff Principal Bowen was not, of course, to solve the cases themselves but to see what, from the Law Society's point of view, could be learned from them. As the first case appeared to involve solicitor's fraud, it was likely to fall within the ambit of the Guarantee Fund. The second looked like a case of solicitor's negligence – and hence involved a claim on the Master Policy – although it remained uncertain whether the negligence was on the part of the solicitor who acted for the seller or the solicitor who acted for the purchaser, or indeed both (or neither).

From all of this the sheriff principal proposed a number of conclusions and recommendations. In the first place, taking the Guarantee Fund and the Master Policy together, there was 'no general problem of cases falling between the two schemes' (para 3).

Secondly, '[t]here is no justification for any conclusion, or indeed perception, that the Guarantee Fund does not meet, or for that matter contrives to avoid, claims which fall within the ambit of its provisions' (para 4).

Nonetheless, thirdly, the Aberdeen case suggests that that ambit might be too narrow. The Guarantee Fund is established and governed by s 43 of the Solicitors (Scotland) Act 1980. As amended, the first four subsections read as follows:

(1) There shall be a fund to be called 'The Scottish Solicitors Guarantee Fund' (in this Act referred to as 'the Guarantee Fund'), which shall be vested in the Society and shall be under the control and management of the Council.

(2) Subject to the provisions of this section and of Schedule 3 the Guarantee Fund shall be held by the Society for the purpose of making grants in order to compensate

persons who in the opinion of the Council suffer pecuniary loss by reason of dishonesty on the part of –

(a)   any solicitor, registered foreign lawyer or registered European lawyer in practice in the United Kingdom, or any employee of such a solicitor, registered foreign lawyer or registered European lawyer in connection with the practice of the solicitor, registered foreign lawyer or registered European lawyer, whether or not he had a practising certificate in force when the act of dishonesty was committed, and notwithstanding that subsequent to the commission of that act he may have died or had his name removed from or struck off the roll or may have ceased to practise or been suspended from practice;

(aa) any conveyancing or executry practitioner or an employee of the practitioner in connection with the practitioner's practice as such, even if subsequent to the act concerned the practitioner has ceased to provide conveyancing or executry services;

(b)   any incorporated practice or any director, member, manager, secretary or other employee of an incorporated practice, notwithstanding that subsequent to the commission of that act it may have ceased to be recognised under section 34(1A) or have been wound up; or

(c)   any licensed legal services provider or person within it in connection with its provision of legal services (with the same meaning as for Part 2 of the 2010 Act), even if—

   (i)   the Society is not its approved regulator, or

   (ii)   subsequent to the act concerned it has ceased to operate.

(3)   No grant may be made under this section –

(a)   in respect of a loss made good otherwise;

(b)   in respect of a loss which in the opinion of the Council has arisen while the solicitor was suspended from practice;

(c)   to a solicitor or his representatives in respect of a loss suffered by him or them in connection with his practice as a solicitor by reason of dishonesty on the part of a partner or employee of his;

(ca) to a conveyancing or executry practitioner in respect of a loss suffered by reason of dishonesty on the part of a partner or employee of the practitioner in connection with the practitioner's practice as such;

(cc) to an incorporated practice or any director or member thereof in respect of a loss suffered by it or him by reason of dishonesty on the part of any director, member, manager, secretary or other employee of the incorporated practice in connection with the practice;

(cd) to a licensed provider or any investor or person who owns, manages or controls or is within the licensed provider in respect of a loss suffered by it or any such person in connection with the licensed provider's provision of legal services by reason of dishonesty on the part of any such persons;

(e)   in respect of any default of a registered European lawyer, or any of his employees or partners, where such act or default takes place outside Scotland, unless the Council is satisfied that the act or default is closely connected with the registered European lawyer's practice in Scotland;

(f)   in respect of any act or default of a registered foreign lawyer, or any of his employees or partners, where such act or default takes place outside Scotland, unless the Council is satisfied that the act or default is closely connected with the registered foreign lawyer's practice, or any of his partners' practice, in Scotland; or

(g) in respect of any act or default of any member, director, manager, secretary or other employee of an incorporated practice which is a multi-national practice, where such act or default takes place outside Scotland, unless the Council is satisfied that the act or default is closely connected with the incorporated practice's practice in Scotland.

(4) The decision of the Council with respect to any application for a grant shall be final.

Payment under the Fund is made where someone suffers 'pecuniary loss by reason of dishonesty' on the part of a solicitor, and most claims concern misappropriation by a solicitor or a solicitor's employee. The Aberdeen fraud (if proved) would clearly be a case of 'dishonesty'. A difficulty, however, was the last resort provision in s 43(3)(a) which requires other remedies to have been exhausted. 'The need to do so has protracted the situation as well as creating the perception of members of the legal profession pointing the finger of blame at each other with no one prepared to take ultimate responsibility' (para 12). There should perhaps be a discretion, as in England and Wales, 'to make grants before requiring the applicant to resort to other means of recovery' (para 15).

Fourthly, the term 'Guarantee Fund' is something of a misnomer. 'Compensation Fund', the name in England and Wales, might be more appropriate (para 18).

Finally, in view of the difficulty in determining whether solicitors were negligent in the 'Happy Valley' case, 'more needs to be done to clarify and define what the ordinary house purchaser should expect of his solicitor in relation to confirming that the boundary of lands being acquired matches that owned by the seller' (para 39).

Following on from Sheriff Principal Bowen's report, and from an independent review by KPMG, the Law Society launched a consultation on the Guarantee Fund – re-named as of 1 November 2015 as the 'Client Protection Fund' – in August 2015. Questions under consideration included who should pay into the Fund, who should be able to make a claim, and whether there should be new rules on capital adequacy and whistleblowing. The consultation closed on 9 October 2015 and the results are awaited. An article on the issue by James O'Reilly appeared at p 5 of the *Journal of the Law Society of Scotland* for September 2015.

The Scottish New Build Standard Clauses

Standard clauses for new-build sales have been prepared by a working party representing both builders' solicitors and solicitors who act for purchasers. The members were Ross MacKay, Paul Carnan and Alan Minty. This important initiative follows the success of the Scottish Standard Clauses which were prepared for 'ordinary' residential sales. The Scottish New Build Standard Clauses, together with a Client Guide and a Practitioners' Guide, are available at www.lawscot.org.uk/rules-and-guidance/section-f-guidance-relating-to-

particular-types-of-work/division-c-conveyancing/advice-and-information/
scottish-new-build-standard-clauses/.

The Practitioners' Guide gives some of the background:

> The Scottish New Build Standard Clauses 2015 Edition is a new creation. It can be
> used throughout Scotland and it is intended in the long run to replace many styles
> of Builders'
>   Missives particularly styles of small and medium sized builders and developers.
> The larger Builders may wish to use their own styles and have the negotiating position
> to insist. However it is hoped that when larger Builders see the advantages in theory
> or practice they may be persuaded to use or to a large extent use and refer to these
> Standard Clauses … Adoption of the Standard Clauses allows the Builder to claim
> that it is trying to be 'consumer friendly' by following the recommendations of the
> Consumer Code for Home Builders and it is not trying to catch people out in the
> small print nor is it imposing more onerous terms on their purchasing customers
> just for the sake of it or the sake of their own style. The clauses are an attempt at a
> reasonable balance of rights and does recognise certain clauses that were perceived
> non-negotiable.

Where builders use their own style, the Clauses provide a yardstick against
which the style can be judged, as well as a source of wording for the qualified
acceptance. Indeed the Clauses represent the kind of compromise which might
emerge from negotiation:

> The Working Party worked from the premise that many individual firms attempted
> to amend the style Builders' missives based on a 'wish list' of best possible outcomes
> but the reality is that counter qualified acceptances by Builders or outright rejection
> of amendments to the Builders' style cut these down to size and there then emerged
> a wording that most people will 'settle for'.

New PSG styles for residential conveyancing

The admirable Property Standardisation Group has co-operated with the Law
Society to produce a suite of styles for residential conveyancing. These became
available in December 2015 (www.psglegal.co.uk/). The styles cover ordinary
dispositions as well as dispositions creating title conditions (including reciprocal
conditions), and include variants for (i) dispositions of registered land (whole),
(ii) dispositions of registered land (part), (iii) dispositions of unregistered land
(whole), and (iv) dispositions of unregistered land (part). Further styles cover
discharges of standard securities, deeds of restriction, affidavits in respect
of possession for the purposes of prescriptive acquisition of ownership or
servitudes, and a letter to factors on the sale of a property.

Exploring the barriers to community land-based activities

On behalf of the Scottish Government the James Hutton Institute has been
carrying out a study of the 'barriers to community land-based activities' (http://
www.hutton.ac.uk/news/understanding-barriers-community-land-based-

activities-scotland.) The study was published on 25 September 2015 (www. gov.scot/Publications/2015/09/5827) together with a separate summary of the research findings (www.gov.scot/Publications/2015/09/5913). The latter begins by explaining the project's aim:

> There are many different community activities that require rights to land and each community will have its own particular priorities. Such activities range from housing developments to community gardens, renewable energy installations to local paths. Each type of activity will, in turn, require different property rights. While the land reform debate has to date been dominated by the advantages and disadvantages of (outright) community land ownership, this project considers barriers associated with the distribution of all types of property rights and responsibilities between land owners and communities.
>
> The project aims to develop a classification scheme of barriers to community land-based activities and uses this scheme to examine the nature and significance of each type of barrier for different types of community activities, types of land owners and geographical contexts (eg urban versus rural areas). Where possible, the project also highlights the types of strategies that have been used to resolve conflicts between land owners and communities when they arise.

The following classification scheme of ownership barriers was adopted:

Categories of barriers	Sub-categories	Underlying cause
Deficiencies in ownership rights	A. Ownership unknown or unclear	A.1 Information on title deeds is incomplete, missing or difficult to access A.2 Ownership in dispute A.3 Owner lacks legal capacity (including executors/administrators)
	B. Ownership rights divided	B.1 Land held in Trust [functionality of Trust] B.2 Land subject to leases or licences [or subordinate real rights] B.3 Land subject to mortgages or other securities B.4 Land subject to restrictive Title conditions/real burdens B.5 Land subject to servitudes or rights of way B.6 Land subject to options or conditional contracts
Landowner behaviour	C. Assembly of ownership required	C.1 Ransom strips C.2 Multiple ownership

Categories of barriers	Sub-categories	Underlying cause
	D. Unacceptable terms	D.1 Restrictive terms of conditions of sale/ transfer of lesser rights
		D.2 Different valuations
	E. Owner unwilling to sell or lease land	E.1 Retention for continued current use (includes for occupation/investment/ making available to others on non-profit basis)
		E.2 Retention for control or protection/ conservation
		E.3 Retention for subsequent own development
		E.4 Retention for subsequent sale (due to indecision, postponement, uncertainty or speculation)
External factors affecting communities	F. Structural barriers facing communities	F.1 Inability to raise funding
		F.2 Regulations and limitations to advisory support
		F.3 Lack of legitimacy
Internal factors affecting communities	G. Community constraints and decisions	G.1 Potential liabilities of ownership disproportionate to community benefits
		G.2 Differing community aspirations
		G.3 Lack of community capacity
		G.4 Lack of willingness to engage with landowner

The research then goes on to consider the effect of these barriers on different types of community activities and as between rural and urban areas.

Statutory guidance to local authorities on 'missing shares' in tenement repairs

By s 4A of the Tenements (Scotland) Act 2004, which was added by s 85 of the Housing (Scotland) Act 2014, local authorities are able to pay the share of an owner who is unable or willing to pay for tenement maintenance, and then to recover the cost from that owner. See *Conveyancing 2014* p 76. The provision came into force on 1 April 2015: see Housing (Scotland) Act 2014 (Commencement No 2) Order 2015, SSI 2015/122, art 2. The Scottish Government has now issued guidance to local authorities on how this power is to be exercised: see *Implementing the Housing (Scotland) Act 2006, Parts 1 and 2: Advisory and Statutory Guidance for Local*

Authorities: Volume 3: Maintenance (www.gov.scot/Publications/2015/07/7697) ch 6. Of particular interest is the following:

> 6.9. Local authorities may want to provide advice and guidance about the missing share powers in this chapter. However, it is for owners to make decisions about maintenance and apportion costs under the tenement management scheme and the local authority's role may be limited to responding to proactive requests from owners to pay 'missing share'. It is at the local authority's discretion whether a missing share should be paid in any circumstances. The local authority should consider how a policy on missing shares fits into its scheme of assistance (see volume 4 of this guidance).
>
> 6.10. Local authorities may be faced with cases where a majority of owners in a building may agree that repair or maintenance work is needed to common parts, and those owners are willing to meet the cost of the work, but a minority of owners refuse to cooperate and effectively prevent the work from going ahead. The missing share power helps the local authority to intervene by targeting enforcement against the non-cooperating owners. It allows local authorities to support owners who recognise and value regular maintenance to look after their property.
>
> 6.13. Under the tenement management scheme decisions can be made by a majority of owners. The majority decision is binding on all owners. Any owner can enforce a majority decision against any other owner. The local authority may want to consider whether owners should take their own enforcement action against a non-cooperating owner rather than pay a missing share. The local authority can provide advice to owners on their right to recover under the Tenements (Scotland) Act 2004. However, in some cases the uncertainty of recovery and the scale of costs may make it difficult for the other owners to carry out work that they have agreed to do.
>
> 6.14. Before intervening, the local authority should ensure that the process for a decision under the tenement management scheme has been properly made in accordance with Schedule 1 of the Tenements (Scotland) Act 2004. In particular, they should be satisfied that a majority has been correctly calculated, that all owners had proper notice of the meeting or consultation that the decision is based on, and that dissenting owners have had due opportunity to exercise their right to apply to the Sheriff.

A willingness on the part of local authorities to use this power could make a considerable difference to the prospects of carrying out repairs to tenements. And the potential financial exposure is far less than where the local authority has itself to carry out the repairs by virtue of a statutory notice.

Scottish Vacant and Derelict Land Survey 2014

The Scottish Government, through its 'Communities Analytical Services', conducts an annual survey of vacant and derelict land based on returns from local authorities. For this purpose 'vacant' land is land which is unused for the purposes for which it is held and is viewed as an appropriate site for development; the land must either have had prior development on it or preparatory work has taken place in anticipation of future development. 'Derelict' land (and buildings) is land which has been so damaged by development that it is incapable of development for beneficial use without rehabilitation. The annual surveys may be watched with greater attention following the introduction of a community right to buy 'abandoned, neglected or detrimental land' by s 74 of the Community Empowerment (Scotland) Act 2015 (as to which see p 75 above).

Key findings from the 2014 survey (www.gov.scot/Publications/2015/02/8577) include (pp 7–8):

- The total amount of derelict and urban vacant land in Scotland decreased by 129 hectares or 1.2 per cent from the previous year, to 10,874 hectares in 2014.
- The local authority with the highest amount of recorded derelict and urban vacant land is Highland, containing 1,373 hectares (13% of the Scotland total). North Ayrshire has the second highest amount with 1,341 hectares (12%), North Lanarkshire is third with 1,297 hectares (12%), followed by Glasgow City with 1,171 hectares (11%).
- 28.9% of Scotland's population are estimated to live within 500 metres of a derelict site in 2014.
- For those sites where the previous use is known, 24% of derelict land recorded in 2014 had been previously used for defence (1,964 hectares), 23% for mineral activity (1,851 hectares), and a further 21% for manufacturing (1,747 hectares). The most common previous use for urban vacant land, where previous use is known, was agriculture (20%, or 403 hectares) and the second most common previous use was residential development (19%, or 384 hectares).
- 3,355 hectares (35%) of derelict and urban vacant land in 2014 was reported to be developable in the short term, with an expectation of development within five years. A total of 900 hectares (9%) of derelict and urban vacant land is seen by local authorities as being uneconomic to develop and/or is viewed as suitable to reclaim for a 'soft' end use (ie non-built use).
- The most common new use for derelict land was residential, with 30% (60 hectares) of the derelict land that was brought back into use since the previous survey reclaimed for this purpose. The second most common new use was for agriculture, accounting for 19% (38 hectares). For urban vacant land the most common new use was residential, with 54% (63 hectares) of the land reclaimed for this purpose.
- Of the 319 hectares of land reused in 2014, a total of 103 hectares involved some form of public funding, either a full or partial contribution.
- Since its inception in 2005/06, the Scottish Government's Vacant and Derelict Land Fund has contributed (either fully or partially) to the reuse of 328 hectares (in total) of previously vacant and derelict land across Dundee City, Glasgow City, Highland, North Lanarkshire and South Lanarkshire.

Impact evaluation of the community right to buy

An *Impact Evaluation of the Community Right to Buy* was carried out by Ipsos MORI in collaboration with Scotland's Rural College and published by the Scottish Government on 12 October 2015: see www.gov.scot/Publications/2015/10/8581 and, for the research findings, www.gov.scot/Publications/2015/10/9555. The community right to buy was introduced by part 2 of the Land Reform (Scotland) Act 2003, and the research covers its first decade of operation (ie 2004–2014). The main findings of the research were (p 1):

- As of late November 2014, 206 community bodies had been approved by Ministers as a company limited by guarantee for the purposes of land acquisition.
- However, the number of community bodies completing a purchase was much lower. At the time of the evaluation, there had been 174 applications made by 94 community bodies to register an interest in land and 22 purchases of land or assets had been made.
- Around half of those registering did not have the opportunity to purchase land as it had not come up for sale. Among community bodies where the land had come up for sale, around half were successful in purchasing (either wholly or partially, and within or outwith the CRtB legislation).
- In general, the positive outcomes that were anticipated from the CRtB such as an increase in knowledge and skills, community cohesion, motivation to develop initiatives, and involvement in land decisions have been delivered but to varying extents and in relation to various stages of the process.
- The extent to which positive outcomes had been achieved in the case studies varied in relation to a number of factors, including community capacity, stage of the process reached, and (where land and assets had been acquired) the scale and income generating potential of the asset. A fuller range of outcomes such as income and employment development and greater influence on land assets was evident in cases where land and assets had been acquired.

The full research report runs to 78 pages and contains much of interest.

Land reform – from the House of Commons

The wide-ranging Land Reform (Scotland) Bill, currently before the Scottish Parliament, seeks to implement some of the recommendations of the independent Land Reform Review Group ('LRRG') which was set up by the Scottish Government in July 2012: see p 85 above. But from the summer of 2013 until shortly before the general election on 7 May 2015, the Scottish Affairs Committee of the House of Commons was conducting an inquiry of its own into land reform: see www.parliament.uk/scotaffcom. An initial briefing paper was commissioned from James Hunter, Peter Peacock, Andy Wightman, and Michael Foxley. The paper, *432:50 – Towards a comprehensive land reform agenda for Scotland*, questioned the level of public subsidy available to private landowners (eg by fiscal arrangements, agricultural support, and forestry grants), criticised the devices used by such owners to avoid tax, and called for more community ownership (including of land and foreshore currently in public ownership), for the introduction of an absolute right to buy for agricultural tenants, and for the replacing of council tax and rates by a land value tax. The Committee took written and oral evidence from a range of sources and, on 18 March 2014, issued an interim report (www.publications.parliament.uk/pa/cm201314/cmselect/cmscotaf/877/877.pdf): see *Conveyancing 2014* pp 102–04.

The Committee's final report was published shortly before the UK general election, on 24 March 2015: see www.publications.parliament.uk/pa/cm201415/cmselect/cmscotaf/274/274.pdf. In the light of the earlier rhetoric, the report is notably brief and unambitious. Its main focus is on taxation. The report questions the rationale for and the value of the conditional exemption tax incentive scheme and of agricultural property relief. It expresses surprise that there are no firm data on the effect of tax reliefs on the value of land. More generally, the report emphasises that (para 14):

> Tax reliefs represent a cost to the public due to the tax income forgone. It should be a guiding principle that both new and existing tax reliefs should only be offered where there is a clear justification. The case for many tax reliefs is still to be proven. The incoming Government should ensure that those tax reliefs where a clear and proven benefit cannot be demonstrated are abolished.

For a discussion of the report, see Ross Simpson, 'Unfinished business' (2015) 60 *Journal of the Law Society of Scotland* May/36.

Housing Statistics 2014–15

Key findings of the annual survey of housing show a continuing increase in new houses, a 20% rise in the exercise of the right to buy ahead of its abolition on 1 August 2016, and a 4% increase in HMO licences (which now stand at 14,908). Full details can be found in *Housing Statistics for Scotland 2015: Key Trends* (www.gov.scot/Publications/2015/09/5480). We quote the 'Key Findings for 2014–15':

Housing supply (private and public sector)
- *New housing supply*: New housing supply (new build, refurbishment and conversions) increased by 6% between 2013–14 and 2014–15, from 16,110 to 17,149 units, mainly driven by an 11% rise in private led new build completions.
- *New house building*: In 2014–15, 16,281 new homes were completed in Scotland, an increase of 9% on the 14,890 completions in the previous year, the highest number of completions since 2010–11. During the same time-period the number of homes started rose by 3%, from 15,577 to 16,028, the highest number of starts since 2008–09.
- *Affordable housing*: In 2014–15, there were 7,069 units completed through all Affordable Housing Supply Programme (AHSP) activity – this figure is up 1% on the previous year.

Local authority housing
- *Local authority housing stock*: At 31 March 2015, there were 317,005 local authority dwellings in Scotland, a decrease of 567 (0.2%) homes from the previous year.
- *Sales of local authority dwellings*: Sales of public authority dwellings (including local authorities with total stock transfers) rose by 20% in 2014–15, from 1,527 to 1,835. This is the second consecutive annual increase after years of declining numbers of sales. The increases are likely to be due to the announcement in 2013 that right to buy was to be ended for all tenants.
- *Right to buy entitlement*: Just over two-thirds (67% or 236,594) of tenancies provided by local authorities (or the relevant housing association following a stock transfer) had some right to buy entitlement on 31 March 2015, down from 76% the previous year.

- *Vacant stock*: At 31 March 2015, local authorities reported 6,515 units of vacant stock, of which 40% consisted of normal letting stock. This represents 1% of all normal letting stock, and is down from 6,556 the previous year.
- *Lettings*: During 2014–15 there were 27,006 permanent lettings made, a decrease of 6% compared to 28,679 lettings in the previous year. Lets to homeless households represented 38% of all lets made by local authorities in 2014–15, a total of 10,390 lettings to homeless households, which is a decrease of 2% on the 10,656 lettings in 2013–14.
- *Evictions*: Eviction actions against local authority tenants resulted in 1,215 evictions or abandoned dwellings in 2014–15 (694 evictions, 521 abandoned dwellings). This is up by 32%, or 294 actions evictions or abandonments, on the 921 in 2013–14.
- *Housing lists*: Household applications held on local authority or common housing register lists decreased by 4% to 173,587 in March 2015, the seventh consecutive annual decrease.

Local authority housing assistance and licensing

- *Scheme of assistance*: In 2014–15, 9,226 scheme of assistance grants were paid to householders, totalling £29.5 million. The majority of these were for disabled adaptions, 6,487 grants totalling £22.3 million.
- *Houses in multiple occupation*: In 2014–15, 8,679 applications were received in respect of the mandatory licensing scheme for houses in multiple occupation. At 31st March 2015 there were 14,908 licences in force, representing an increase of 4% over the previous year.

Books

Craig Anderson, *Possession of Corporeal Moveables* (Studies in Scots Law vol 3: Edinburgh Legal Education Trust 2015; ISBN 9780955633270)

Frankie McCarthy, James Chalmers and Stephen Bogle (eds), *Essays in Conveyancing and Property Law in Honour of Professor Robert Rennie* (Open Book Publishers 2015; ISBN 9781783741472; available to download free of charge at www.openbookpublishers.com/product/343/essays-in-conveyancing-and-property-law-in-honour-of-professor-robert-rennie)

Kenneth G C Reid, *Requirements of Writing (Scotland) Act 1995*, 2nd edn (W Green 2015; ISBN 9780414039490)

Kenneth G C Reid and George L Gretton, *Conveyancing 2014* (Avizandum Publishing Ltd 2015; ISBN 9781904968580)

Robert Rennie et al, *Leases* (W Green 2015; ISBN 9780414018617)

Jill Robbie, *Private Water Rights* (Studies in Scots Law vol 4: Edinburgh Legal Education Trust 2015; ISBN 9780955633287)

Articles

James Aitken, 'Property taxation update' (2015) 136 *Greens Property Law Bulletin* 5

Craig Anderson, 'Extinction of leases *confusione*' 2015 *Juridical Review* 185

Mike Blair, 'Ancillary rights as real rights' (2015) 60 *Journal of the Law Society of Scotland* October/32 (considering ancillary rights in leases)

Heather Bruce, '21st Century letting vehicles: the journey' (2015) 135 *Greens Property Law Bulletin* 5

Stewart Brymer, 'A register of home reports' (2015) 134 *Greens Property Law Bulletin* 3

Stewart Brymer, 'Development plan approval' (2015) 136 *Greens Property Law Bulletin* 4

Stewart Brymer, 'Digital dealing room: a room with a view?' (2015) 138 *Greens Property Law Bulletin* 1

Stewart Brymer, 'Electronic discharges' (2015) 139 *Greens Property Law Bulletin* 4

Stewart Brymer, 'Land information: a one-stop shop' (2015) 60 *Journal of the Law Society of Scotland* April/36

Stewart Brymer, 'Minerals and examination of title' (2015) 137 *Greens Property Law Bulletin* 3

Stewart Brymer, 'Standardisation in conveyancing' (2015) 135 *Greens Property Law Bulletin* 3

Daniel J Carr, 'Is there an equitable exception to reduction for forgery?' (2015) 19 *Edinburgh Law Review* 273 (considering *Chalmers v Chalmers* [2014] CSOH, 2015 SCLR 299)

Malcolm Combe, 'Digesting the Community Empowerment Act' (2015) 60 *Journal of the Law Society of Scotland*/August 40

Andy Duncan, 'Execution in counterpart – dragging Scots law into the 21st century' (2015) 137 *Greens Property Law Bulletin* 5

Andy Duncan, 'Souvenir plots – fresh air in a can?' (2015) 139 *Greens Property Law Bulletin* 1

Jonathan Edwards, 'Tools for today's titles' (2015) 60 *Journal of the Law Society of Scotland* April/12 (providing a 'toolkit' in respect of the Land Registration etc (Scotland) Act 2012; a response by John King of RoS appears at May/6))

Matthew Farrell and Stephen Goldie, 'Dilapidations: reinstating the law' (2015) 60 *Journal of the Law Society of Scotland* Jan/36 (considering *Grove Investments Ltd v Cape Building Products Ltd* [2014] CSIH 43, 2014 Hous LR 35 and *@Sipp (Pension Trustees) Ltd v Insight Travel Services Ltd* [2014] CSOH 137, 2014 Hous LR 54)

David Findlay, 'Perils of the owner-occupied croft' (2015) 60 *Journal of the Law Society of Scotland* June/34 (considering the interaction of s 19D(6) of the Crofters (Scotland) Act 1993 with the legislation on land registration)

George L Gretton, 'Aronson v Keeper of the Registers of Scotland [2014] CSOH 176, 2015 SLT 122' 2015 SLT (News) 33

David Haughey, 'Transmission of lease conditions in Scots law – a doctrinal-historical analysis' (2015) 19 *Edinburgh Law Review* 333

Martin Hogg, 'Promises to lend, collateral warranties, and red herrings' (2015) 19 *Edinburgh Law Review* 384 (considering *Royal Bank of Scotland plc v Carlyle* [2015] UKSC 13, 2015 SC (UKSC) 93)

Michael Hughes, 'The curious case of division and sale with a sist' 2015 SLT (News) 61

Gordon Junor, 'Financing council house purchasers: *Khosprowpour v MacKay*' (2015) 83 *Scottish Law Gazette* 8

Gordon Junor, 'Gordon's Trustees v Campbell Riddle Breeze Paterson LLP' 2015 SLT (News) 71

Gordon Junor, 'Homebase Ltd v Granchester Developments (Falkirk) Ltd [2015] CSOH 49' 2015 SLT (News) 79

Gordon Junor, 'Interpreting commercial leases and common sense' (2015) 83 *Scottish Law Gazette* 30 (considering *Mapeley Acquisition Co (3) Ltd (in receivership) v City of Edinburgh Council* [2015] CSOH 29, 2015 GWD 13-234)

Gordon Junor, 'No collaterals at all!: *Royal Bank of Scotland v Carlyle*' (2015) 83 *Scottish Law Gazette* 47

Gordon Junor, 'No panacea for debtors: *Swift Advances v Martin*' (2015) 138 *Greens Property Law Bulletin* 5

Gordon Junor, 'Non-supersession clauses – the continuing story' (2015) 83 *Scottish Law Gazette* 53

Gordon Junor, 'NRAM plc v Steel [2014] CSOH 172' 2015 SLT (News) 58

Gordon Junor, 'Recovering costs of tenemental works: section 12 of the 2004 Act and prescription' (2015) 83 *Scottish Law Gazette* 22

Gordon Junor, 'Retentions and remedies' (2015) 83 *Scottish Law Gazette* 55 (considering *Sneddon v Scottish Legal Complaints Commission* [2015] CSIH 62, 2015 GWD 26-458)

Gordon Junor, 'Tenzin v Russell [2015] CSIH 8A' 2015 SLT (News) 51

Gordon Junor, 'The fraudulent client – agent liability affirmed' (2014) 82 *Scottish Law Gazette* 91 (considering *Frank Houlgate Investment Co Ltd v Biggart Baillie LLP* [2014] CSIH 79, 2015 SC 187)

Gordon Junor, 'The limits of appeal – again!: *Foxworth Investments v Henderson*' (2014) 82 *Scottish Law Gazette* 87

Deborah Lovell, 'Land, leases and LBTT' (2015) 60 *Journal of the Law Society of Scotland* Sept/32

Laura Macgregor, 'Crossing the line between business common sense and perceived fairness in contractual interpretation' (2015) 19 *Edinburgh Law Review* 378 (considering *Grove Investments Ltd v Cape Building Products Ltd* [2014] CSIH 43, 2014 Hous LR 35)

Laura Macgregor, 'Moors the pity: the case of missing grouse': *Cramaso LLP v Ogilvie Grant, Earl of Seafield and others*' (2015) 19 *Edinburgh Law Review* 112

Alison Mackay, 'CML Handbook: the new deal' (2015) 60 *Journal of the Law Society of Scotland* June/33

Alison Mackay, 'LBTT: what does it mean in practice?' (2015) 60 *Journal of the Law Society of Scotland* May/40

Cat MacLean and Liina Tulk, 'Broken promises' (2015) 60 *Journal of the Law Society of Scotland* May/18 (considering *Royal Bank of Scotland v Carlyle* [2015] UKSC 13, 2015 SC (UKSC) 93)

Eilidh Ross MacLellan, 'Crofting law update for 2015' (2015) 136 *Greens Property Law Bulletin* 1

Hector MacQueen and Charles Garland, 'Signatures in Scots law: form, effect, and burden of proof' 2015 *Juridical Review* 107

Hector MacQueen, Charles Garland and Lauren Smith, 'The Legal Writings (Counterparts and Delivery) (Scotland) Act 2015' 2015 SLT (News) 111

Peter Nicholson, 'Take care with Lender Exchange' (2015) 60 *Journal of the Law Society of Scotland* Feb/36

Jill Robbie and Malcolm Combe, 'A square foot of old Scotland: ownership of souvenir plots' (2015) 19 *Edinburgh Law Review* 393

Frances Rooney and Chris Kerr, 'Advance notices and letters of obligation' (2015) 60 *Journal of the Law Society of Scotland* Dec/34

Frances Rooney and John King, 'Plans reports: yes or no?' (2015) 60 *Journal of the Law Society of Scotland* July/10

Frances Rooney and Kaira Massie, 'Application forms: should the seller adjust?' (2015) 60 *Journal of the Law Society of Scotland* May/10

Frances Rooney, Kaira Massie and Chris Kerr, 'Examination question: how should solicitors answer the application form question about limitation on examination of title?' (2015) 60 *Journal of the Law Society of Scotland* Aug/9

Frances Rooney, Kaira Massie and Chris Kerr, 'How far can we rely on the Register?' (2015) 60 *Journal of the Law Society of Scotland* Nov/35

Frances Rooney, Kaira Massie and Chris Kerr, 'Land registration and leases' (www. bit.ly/1No6HH3)

Frances Rooney, Kaira Massie and Chris Kerr, 'Questions of form' (2015) 60 *Journal of the Law Society of Scotland* Sept/18 (considering completion of the application form for land registration)

Ross Simpson, 'Unfinished business' (2015) 60 *Journal of the Law Society of Scotland* May/36 (considering the final report on land reform by the Scottish Affairs Committee of the House of Commons)

Ann Stewart, 'Are you ready for counterpart signing?' (2015) 60 *Journal of the Law Society of Scotland* July/33.

Ken Swinton, 'Amendments to CML Handbook for Scottish Solicitors' (2015) 83 *Scottish Law Gazette* 20

✢ PART IV ✢
COMMENTARY

COMMENTARY

EXECUTION IN COUNTERPART

Originating in a report by the Scottish Law Commission,[1] the Legal Writings (Counterparts and Delivery) (Scotland) Act 2015 is the first piece of legislation to have been passed under a new procedure in the Scottish Parliament which is designed to increase the throughput of law reform measures. Both the initiative and the Act are to be welcomed. Although only seven sections long, the Act is of considerable importance for conveyancers. As its name suggests, it provides for execution in counterpart and also for electronic delivery of documents. The topics are related, because one of the main uses of electronic delivery will be in respect of documents executed in counterpart. But they are also distinct topics, and they will be dealt with separately here, beginning with execution in counterpart.[2] The Act came into force on 1 July 2015.[3]

The basics

Introduction

Execution in counterpart has been used in England for many years, although on the basis of practice rather than statute. One purpose of the new Act is to remove doubts as to the validity of such execution in Scotland,[4] and hence to allow Scotland, so to speak, to catch up with England.

The device seeks to address the difficulty of executing deeds and documents with multiple parties. For if the same physical document has to be sent round ten different people, it may be a long time before execution is complete, a problem which is compounded if some of the parties are abroad and if there is more than

---

1 Scottish Law Commission, *Report No 231 on Formation of Contract: Execution in Counterpart* (2013; available at www.scotlawcom.gov.uk). A valuable analysis of the Act, bringing out some of the practical implications, has been provided by the team at the Scottish Law Commission which was responsible for the Report: see H MacQueen, C Garland and L Smith, 'The Legal Writings (Counterparts and Delivery) (Scotland) Act 2015' 2015 SLT (News) 111.
2 For electronic delivery, see p 167 below.
3 Legal Writings (Counterparts and Delivery) (Scotland) Act 2015 (Commencement) Order 2015, SSI 2015/242. The Act is not retrospective.
4 It can be argued that counterpart execution was *already* competent in Scotland: see *Smith v Duke of Gordon* (1701) Mor 16987, and the discussion in Scottish Law Commission, *Report No 231* paras 2.2–2.10.

one document to be signed.[1] Of course, the problem is avoided if the document is prepared in good time, as typically with conveyancing deeds. Other possible solutions are to collect everyone together for a signing session or use signing mandates or powers of attorney. But with commercial contracts, multiple signatures are often required in respect of documents which are finalised at the last minute,[2] and it is here that execution in counterpart will be of particular use. The idea is that, instead of ten people taking turns to execute a single document, ten people execute ten separate versions ('counterparts') of the same document. Once the ten counterparts are collated, there is then deemed to be one single document, albeit in ten separate parts.[3]

Execution in counterpart is likely to be used mainly for bilateral documents, especially commercial contracts. But it can also be used for unilateral documents such as dispositions and standard securities, and it may be attractive to do so where there are large numbers of granters.

The Act is not confined to 'traditional' (ie paper) documents but applies also to the electronic documents which, since 2014, have had equal status with paper documents.[4] But as electronic documents can be sent instantly by e-mail to whomever needs to sign, wherever in the world they happen to be, there is unlikely to be any advantage in using counterpart execution, and in practice it is likely to be confined to paper documents.[5]

Practicalities

The practicalities are straightforward. A copy of the document – the 'counterpart' – is sent to each of the signatories. This is most conveniently done by e-mail, and the copy printed out in full (as it must be).[6] It is then signed in the usual way (although we will have more to say about this later on). The Act then requires that the executed counterpart be delivered either to each of the other signatories or – a much more attractive option in practice – to a person nominated to take delivery of the counterparts, who is typically the solicitor acting for one of the

---

1 MacQueen, Garland and Smith 2015 SLT (News) 111: 'The basic problem which is solved through execution in counterpart in its modern form is that of completing the multi-party, multi-document and quite often multi-jurisdictional transaction. Such transactions arise in a wide variety of commercial settings: for example, mergers and acquisitions, commercial property, banking, joint ventures, university spin outs, share purchases, secured transactions, fund financing, and oil and gas and other energy related contexts. Often in these situations it is necessary to ensure that all the documents are executed more or less at the same time and together, usually to ensure the release of transaction finance at a particular moment.'

2 Typically, such contracts do not *require* to be in writing, and the use of writing is simply a matter of agreement, in the interests of recording accurately what has been agreed.

3 Legal Writings (Counterparts and Delivery) (Scotland) Act 2015 s 1(2)–(4).

4 Requirements of Writing (Scotland) Act 1995 part 3. For discussion, see *Conveyancing 2014* pp 140–46.

5 A point noted in Scottish Law Commission, *Report No 231* para 2.14.

6 A document that has been only partly printed would be neither an electronic nor a paper document but some unknown hybrid: see MacQueen, Garland and Smith 2015 SLT (News) 111, 117. As, however, the unsigned sheets of the counterpart, not being needed for the assembled document (see below), can be binned afterwards, one may suspect that they may never be printed off in the first place. And whilst in principle that (ie not printing off, as opposed to printing off and immediately binning) will subvert the execution, who is likely to find out?

parties.[1] Delivery can, and usually will, be electronic,[2] although delivery of the physical document is likely to follow.[3] On receipt, nominees are required to hold and preserve the counterparts for the benefit of the parties, although this duty can be contracted out of.[4] In practice, they are likely to co-ordinate the whole process and make sure that all copies are returned by the required date. In the case of unilateral deeds (ie where granters and grantees are separate and distinct persons, with only the former signing), delivery will also have to be made to the grantees, a requirement of the existing law.[5]

The practice of holding deeds as undelivered is expressly recognised by the Act.[6] This allows the counterparts to be collected in by the nominee and then, on an agreed (and pre-arranged) day, to be treated as delivered. The document is then 'live'.[7] There is support among law firms for mentioning the delivery date in the document itself, either at the top, in English fashion, or in the testing clause. For the former, the following wording has been suggested: 'The date of delivery of this Agreement is [ ]', or: 'This Agreement is delivered on []'; for the latter: 'IN WITNESS WHEREOF this Agreement between A, B, C, D and E is [executed in counterpart] by the parties as undernoted, with a delivery date of [ ]'.[8] If the date is unknown before execution, it can be added later; as it is simply for information, and without substantive effect, it does not matter that, being added after execution, it would not be covered by the signatures.

Statement that the document has been executed in counterpart?

Although there is no obligation to do so, there is something to be said for mentioning in the document that it is executed in counterpart. This can be done in the testing clause, as in the style just given, or alternatively a separate clause can be used in the body of the document. The latter can also be used to set out the procedure to be followed by the parties, as in the following style:[9]

---

1 LW(CD)(S)A 2015 ss 1(6), (7), 2. If, rather than being a solicitor, the nominee is one of the parties to the deed, he cannot deliver to himself and so must presumably deliver his counterpart to each of the other parties: see Scottish Law Commission, *Report 231* paras 2.58, 2.59. For a discussion of some of the practicalities of using nominees, see MacQueen, Garland and Smith 2015 SLT (News) 111, 112.

2 LW(CD)(S)A 2015 s 4. See pp 167–69 below.

3 The copy delivered by electronic means is not to be treated as being the original document: see LW(CD)(S)A 2015 s 4(6).

4 LW(CD)(S)A 2015 s 2(3), (4). Non-compliance does not affect the validity of the delivery: s 2(5). In an article which summarises a consensus reached among a number of law firms on some practical issues, it is suggested that the solicitor should usually be relieved of the duty of holding and preservation, thus reducing his role to 'an administrative one only'. See Ann Stewart, 'Are you ready for counterpart signing?' (2015) 60 *Journal of the Law Society of Scotland* July/33.

5 Scottish Law Commission, *Report No 231* para 2.46. This is one of the further steps which is contemplated by LW(CD)(S)A 2015 s 1(5)(b). Bilateral contracts do not require delivery: see eg J Erskine, *An Institute of the Law of Scotland* (1773; reprinted Edinburgh Legal Education Trust, 2014) III.2.44.

6 LW(CD)(S)A 2015 s 1(9).

7 LW(CD)(S)A 2015 s 1(5).

8 Stewart (2015) 60 *Journal of the Law Society of Scotland* July/33, 34.

9 Again this comes from Stewart (2015) 60 *Journal of the Law Society of Scotland* July/33, 34.

Counterparts and delivery

[ ].1. This Agreement may be executed in any number of counterparts [and by each of the parties on separate counterparts].

[ ].2. Where executed in counterparts:

[ ].2.1 this Agreement will not take effect until each of the counterparts has been delivered;

[ ].2.2 each counterpart will be held as undelivered until the parties agree a date on which the counterparts are to be treated as delivered;

[ ].2.3 the date of delivery may be inserted [in the testing clause in the blank provided for the delivery date]/[on page 1 in the blank provided for the delivery date]/[in Clause [ ] in the blank provided for the delivery date] of this Agreement.

For deeds which are to be presented for registration, and in the absence of a statement in the deed itself, the Keeper asks that the fact of execution in counterpart be disclosed in the 'additional information' part of the application form.[1]

Execution by companies and other juristic persons

Different parties can sign different counterparts. But can different signatories 'within' the same party do likewise?[2] The issue arises in the context of companies and other juristic persons. So if, for example, a document is to be signed on behalf of Counterpart (Scotland) Limited by two of its directors, is it competent for each director to sign a different counterpart? The answer is unclear. On one view there is nothing in s 1(2) of the Act – the key provision – to prevent this practice from taking place. On another view, a potential difficulty is caused by the fact that s 1 turns on the distinction between different 'parties' whereas the directors of a company belong to the same party. The safe course is for the directors to sign the same counterpart.

A cautious view would extend this practice even to trustees. Admittedly, the argument here is less strong, because a trust, unlike a company, is not a separate legal person, and the juridical act represented by the document is performed by the trustees and not by the trust. Nonetheless it is possible to argue that the trustees as a body constitute a single 'party', as demonstrated by the fact that a single trustee could be authorised by a majority to sign for all, and that accordingly all must sign the same counterpart.

Last-minute alterations

Sometimes a document needs to be altered at the last minute because, for example, a mistake is found or the parties have had a change of mind, or because negotiations have continued to the bitter end. What then? Does the whole execution process need to begin again? In principle the answer must be yes, for

---

1 Registers of Scotland, *Legal Writings (Counterparts and Delivery) (Scotland) Act 2015* (https://www.ros.gov.uk/services/registration/legal-updates/legal-writings-act-2015). The Keeper adds, however, that applications will not be rejected because of a failure to do so.

2 This is sometimes referred to as 'counterparts within counterparts'.

parties are only bound by the version of a document that they have signed. As the Requirements of Writing Act makes clear, granters are unaffected by post-subscription alterations unless the alteration is signed.[1]

If re-signing is an unattractive prospect, a possible way round it has been suggested:[2]

> There … seems to be no reason in principle why a person cannot be authorised to attach a signature page pre-signed by another person to a document so as to bind the latter to that document. The authority to do so will have to be capable of proof, so should ideally be in writing; and its scope should be clear. But the basic legitimacy of providing such authority seems generally indisputable. The major significance of this is likely to be the situation where an execution process has begun, with some subscriptions already applied and counterparts delivered, when it is discovered that the document text needs correction. Those who have already subscribed can be informed of the change to be made and requested to authorise the attachment of their already delivered subscriptions to the revised document.

The idea seems to be that parties execute signature pages rather than particular documents, so that, with appropriate authorisation, the signature page can then be attached first to one version of a document and later, if need be, to another. But is such a thing really possible? No legislation or case law can be prayed in aid. The argument, rather, is one of principle, or at least of analogy:[3]

> If a person can be authorised to sign in his or her own name so as to bind another person to a document, there seems no reason in principle why a person cannot be authorised to attach a signature page pre-signed by another person to a document so as to bind the latter to that document. The authority to do so will have to be capable of proof, so should ideally be in writing; and its scope should be clear. But the legitimacy of providing such authority seems indisputable.

That may be a correct statement of the law. But we do not think that it is 'indisputable', except where formal writing is not needed anyway and parties are free to do as they like.[4] The starting point is of course beyond dispute: a party can certainly authorise another to sign on his or her behalf, for example by way of a power of attorney or signing mandate. But signing a document on behalf of a person is one thing; attaching a person's floating signature to a document is something different. For a document to be validly executed under the Requirements of Writing Act, it must be 'subscribed by the granter'.[5] In the first case (power of attorney), the document is subscribed by the agent on behalf

---

1 Requirements of Writing (Scotland) Act 1995 s 5(1).
2 MacQueen, Garland and Smith 2015 SLT (News) 111, 115–16. See also Legal Writings (Counterparts and Delivery) (Scotland) Bill: Policy Memorandum (2014) para 19.
3 H MacQueen and C Garland, 'Signatures in Scots law: form, effect and burden of proof' 2015 *Juridical Review* 107, 116.
4 The Scottish Law Commission is properly cautious on this point, saying that execution carried out in this way is valid 'on one view': see *Report No 231* para 3.13.
5 Requirements of Writing (Scotland) Act 1995 s 2(1).

of the granter in a manner which the Act expressly permits.[1] In the second case (floating signature), it is not clear that the document is subscribed at all. It is not subscribed by the agent; nor, at least in the normal sense of the word, is it subscribed by the granter. What the granter subscribes (or rather, signs) is not the physical document itself but a separate sheet of paper which is either entirely blank or, at best, contains a signing block, and which is not (at that stage) connected to any particular document. Whether that is sufficient compliance with the Act seems open to question. Parties faced with last-minute alterations would be better advised, and no more inconvenienced, to have the deed re-executed by an agent under a pre-prepared power of attorney rather than take the risk of a floating signature.[2]

Assembly, probativity, registration

Assembly: types (1) and (2) documents

If ten counterparts are signed, which one counts as the document? The answer given by the Act is that they all count, but only when taken together: on execution, 'the counterparts are to be treated as a single document', and that single document is made up of 'all the counterparts in their entirety'.[3] There is also a much briefer alternative to this 'type (1) document', which is especially useful if a deed requires to be registered. As well as *all* of the counterparts, the single document can also be constituted by 'one of the counterparts in its entirety, collated with the page or pages on which the … other counterparts have been subscribed'.[4] So for a 'type (2) document' it is simply a matter of tacking the originals of nine signature pages on to the original of the remaining counterpart. Admittedly, a deed made up in this form will look a bit odd. As well as one complete version, there will be nine further pages, each with the final few lines of the deed plus a signature. But such a deed is nonetheless perfectly valid and, provided at least one of the signatures is in probative form (ie with a witness or equivalent), it could be registered in the Land or Sasine Register or in the Books of Council and Session.[5]

In order to avoid possible oddness in the appearance of type (2) documents, it has been suggested that only the counterpart which is to be used as the principal should be signed on the last page, with the others being signed on an additional signing page (typically in a signing block). When put together, such a deed would then look relatively normal, for there would be one signature at the end of the document proper, followed by nine signing pages each bearing a single signature. Now, certainly such a document would be probative, that is to say, would *appear* to have been validly executed;[6] for s 7(3) of the Requirements

---

1 RW(S)A 1995 s 12(2).
2 See also the discussion of the issue in Scottish Parliament: Delegated Powers and Law Reform Committee, *Stage 1 Report* (2014) paras 130–140.
3 LW(CD)(S)A s 1(3), (4)(a).
4 LW(CD)(S)A s 1(4)(b).
5 RW(S)A 1995 ss 6, 9G.
6 Whether or not beauty is skin-deep, probativity is. Probativity is about appearance.

of Writing Act allows signatures to be made on empty pages provided 'at least one granter signs at the end of the last page'. But whether it is *actually* validly executed is perhaps less certain.

The argument for validity of the execution may be something like the following.[1] (i) In terms of the Act, 'A document is executed in counterpart if it is executed in two or more duplicate, interchangeable parts'.[2] (ii) 'It' in the sentence just quoted refers to the document rather than the counterpart, ie it is the *document* which must be executed (albeit in parts), not the counterpart. (iii) The document, the Act further provides, can comprise 'one of the counterparts in its entirety, collated with the … pages on which the … other counterparts have been subscribed'.[3] (iv) As, therefore, the nine signing pages are to be treated as a part of the tenth counterpart, there is no need for them to be signed on the last page of the counterpart from which they are drawn; such counterparts are not independent documents.

This argument may well be correct. Importantly, it seems to have the support of the Scottish Law Commission, which was the originator of the legislation.[4] Yet it faces the difficulty that, in terms of the Act, the counterparts are said to be treated as a single document only *after* execution, not before.[5] That suggests that each counterpart must be separately and validly executed before the single document can come into being; and if that is correct, each must be signed at the end of the last page and not on a separate and otherwise blank page. The Requirements of Writing Act so requires.[6]

We reach no concluded view. The new legislation can, we think, be read in more than one way. The attraction for practitioners in being able to sign detached signing pages is obvious. It would allow a document to be sent out for signing with pre-printed signature blocks, all but one of which would occur after the last page of the document proper. The attraction may prove irresistible. If it does, we must hope that, in the event of a challenge, the courts take the same view as the Scottish Law Commission.

Assembly: plans and other annexations

The signature at the end of the document may not be the only signature that exists. Where the land to which a document relates is described in a plan or other annexation to the document, s 8(2) of the Requirements of Writing Act provides that the annexation must itself be signed and, in the case of a plan or other visual representation, that it be signed on every page. Does that mean that any signed annexation page (or pages) must also be included in a type (2) document – so that an assembled document which was executed in ten counterparts would need

---

1 We have not, however, seen it set out anywhere.
2 LW(CD)(S)A 2015 s 1(2)(a).
3 LW(CD)(S)A 2015 s 1(4)(b).
4 Scottish Law Commission, *Report No 231* paras 3.28–3.33.
5 LW(CD)(S)A 2015 s 1(3): 'On *such* execution, the counterparts are to be treated as a single document'. MacQueen, Garland and Smith 2015 SLT (News) 111 gloss s 1(3) as follows: 'If this [subscription and delivery of the counterpart] is successfully accomplished, the counterparts are to be treated as a single document'.
6 Requirements of Writing (Scotland) Act 1995 s 7(1), (3).

to comprise (i) one counterpart in its entirety, (ii) nine signature pages, and (iii) nine signed annexation pages?

The answer, unfortunately, is unclear. There is a certain tension between s 8(2) of the 1995 Act and s 1(4)(b) of the 2015 Act. The former requires that plans and other annexations be 'signed'; the latter provides that a type (2) document comprises 'one of the counterparts in its entirety, collated with the page or pages on which the other counterpart has, or other counterparts have, been *subscribed*'. On a literal reading of s 1(4)(b), therefore, it would not seem necessary to include in a type (2) document any annexation page which had merely been signed. Of course, in practice plans and other annexations are usually signed at the foot and, hence, are subscribed. But even where this is not the case it would seem prudent, when assembling a type (2) document, to include any signed plan or annexation page. The Keeper has gone so far as to say that subscription must now always be used for plans and other annexations to documents executed in counterpart, but this view has no basis in the legislation.[1]

Probativity

As already mentioned, type (2) documents will look odd, and indeed odder still if, in a spirit of caution, the final lines of text are repeated in each of the signing pages. There may be a worry that the whole looks too odd to count as probative. We do not share this worry.[2] A document signed and assembled in this way is fully compliant with the 2015 Act.[3] What seems a novelty at the moment will, it may be expected, soon become a commonplace. But if reassurance is sought, it can be provided by indicating in the document, in the manner already suggested, that it is signed in counterpart. There can then be no doubt that it meets the standard for probativity by *appearing* to have been validly executed.[4]

Registration

The Keeper has issued the following guidance in relation to the registration of deeds executed in counterpart:[5]

---

1   Registers of Scotland, *Legal Writings (Counterparts and Delivery) (Scotland) Act 2015* (https://www.ros.gov.uk/services/registration/legal-updates/legal-writings-act-2015). As an alternative, the Keeper suggests that the plan (or other annexation) could be signed by everyone in advance, so that a type (2) document could then comprise (i) a complete counterpart, (ii) nine signature pages, and (iii) the signed plan (or other annexation) from the complete counterpart. We have doubts as to whether this can be right. LW(CD)(S)A 2015 s 1(2) requires that each counterpart be executed, which would mean that the signatory would also have to sign any plan (or other annexation) attached to the counterpart.
2   That is also the view of the Scottish Law Commission: see *Report No 231* paras 3.16–3.3.19.
3   It is equally compliant with the 2015 Act, and the 1995 Act, if the signature at the end of the principal counterpart post-dates that of some of the 'later' signatures in the signing pages. For each signature is independently valid, provided it has been placed at the end of the last page of each counterpart, and no reliance is being placed on s 7(3) of the 1995 Act. The worries expressed in Scottish Law Commission, *Report No 231* paras 3.20–3.22 seem, we would suggest, misplaced.
4   RW(S)A 1995 s 3(1).
5   Registers of Scotland, *Legal Writings (Counterparts and Delivery) (Scotland) Act 2015* (https://www.ros.gov.uk/services/registration/legal-updates/legal-writings-act-2015).

Land Register

The Land Register application form includes a declaration that the application complies with the general application conditions in section 22 of the Land Registration etc (Scotland) Act 2012. Accordingly, signing the declaration in the application form will serve as confirmation that a document executed in counterpart has been subscribed in accordance with the 1995 Act.

In addition, with both version [type] 1 and 2 single documents, the Keeper will accept the certification of the application form as confirmation that all the counterparts, whether submitted or not, are duplicate and interchangeable ...

Register of Sasines and Books of Council and Session

The Keeper will process applications for recording of documents executed in counterpart in line with existing practice in these registers. The deeds will be checked by staff in these registers to ensure that they are in self-proving form, but staff will not check multiple counterparts (if a version 1 single document as described above is submitted) in order to make sure that they are duplicate and interchangeable. The Keeper takes the view that it is an applicant's responsibility to ensure that documents executed in counterpart are indeed duplicate and interchangeable. Where a version 2 single document is submitted, the Keeper will accept the application without seeking additional confirmation as to the content of the other counterparts.

RETENTION AT SETTLEMENT: BEWARE!

Introduction

When a seller cannot comply with all obligations at the date of settlement, the transaction may nonetheless settle on the basis of a retention. This will often suit both the buyer (who wants the keys at the expected date) and the seller (who wants the money at the expected date, but who can survive if the money paid is a bit below the full sum). Of course, it is not the only solution that can be used. The buyer might decline to settle until the problem is resolved. Or it might be that a price reduction can be agreed, though this is not a common approach.

The risk structure for retention is different from the risk structure for price reduction. In the former, the seller must resolve the problem, regardless of whether the cost of so doing is higher or lower than the amount of the retention. So risk is with the seller. In the latter case, risk is with the buyer, because the problem must be resolved at the buyer's expense, regardless of whether the cost turns out to be higher or lower than the amount of the price reduction. It may be noted that retention keeps to the risk structure contemplated by the missives, at least if the missives are in standard terms. In advance, it may not be possible to say which approach will be better for the buyer, because the cost of sorting out the problem may well not be known with any accuracy at the time of settlement.

But whilst retention is commoner in practice than price reduction, it has its pitfalls, as *Sneddon v Scottish Legal Complaints Commission*[1] shows.

---

1 *Sneddon v Scottish Legal Complaints Commission* [2015] CSIH 62, 2015 GWD 26-458. The judgment of the Extra Division was given by Lady Smith.

What happened in *Sneddon*

Missives were concluded for a house in Falkirk at a price of £370,000. Settlement was due on 20 January 2012. A couple of weeks earlier the buyers noticed that a winter storm had caused minor roof damage. The missives were subject to the Combined Standard Clauses (2011 edn) which said:

> 18 RISK
>
> a. The Seller will maintain the Property in its present condition, fair wear and tear excepted, until the time at which settlement takes place.
>
> b. The risk of damage to or destruction of the Property howsoever caused will remain with the Seller until the time at which settlement takes place.

On 19 January, the day before settlement was due to take place, the buyers' agents wrote to the sellers' agents:[1]

> Our clients have contacted us to advise that they have been in contact with your clients by email. Apparently your clients were unaware of the storm damage to the roof. We understand that your clients are arranging for the roof to be repaired next week. In the circumstances we would propose to make a retention of £1,000 from the purchase price until the roof repairs are satisfactorily completed. Please take immediate instructions and revert to us by return fax with confirmation that this is acceptable.

This met with a reply by return:[2]

> Our clients are agreeable to a £1,000 retention in respect of roof repairs. As soon as the repairs have been carried out our clients wish immediate release of the retained funds.

The transaction settled as scheduled on the next day, with payment of the sum of £369,000. The buyers had put their agents in full funds, so that the £1,000 retention money was held by the buyers' law firm.[3] The buyers, however, were not happy. They complained about a variety of things that they considered wrong with the property. As to the roof problem, confusion reigned, with the two law firms receiving unclear or conflicting information about what work had or had not been done.

On 1 February the buyers' law firm wrote to the other side:[4]

> Our clients have also advised us that no repairs have yet been carried out to the roof. As you are aware your clients agreed with our clients that the roof repairs would be carried out last week. We therefore put your clients on notice that if your clients have not had the roof repairs carried out by Sunday 5th February, then our clients will instruct their own tradesmen to carry out the necessary repairs and use the retention of £1,000 to cover the costs therefor.

---

1 Paragraph 6.
2 Paragraph 7.
3 Formerly the practice was for the retention money to be put on deposit receipt in joint names. It seems that the banks no longer offer this service.
4 Paragraph 10.

The same day the sellers' law firm sent a reply:[1]

> We have received an email from our clients confirming that the roofer was to have
> visited the property last week. Our clients are seeking confirmation from the builder
> that they instructed as to whether or not this has been done and we shall revert to
> you on this matter in due course. In the meantime should your clients instruct their
> own tradesmen to carry out any work then this is strictly on the basis that our clients
> do not consent to the use of any of the retention monies.

The dispute rumbled on for some weeks. The buyers' law firm backed down
from its position that the retention money could be used for the repair. Eventually
the roof was repaired by a roofer engaged by the sellers, at their expense. What
the bill was we do not know, but we do know that at one stage the buyers obtained
their own estimate, which was for 'considerably less' than £1,000.[2] The report
does not say what happened to the £1,000, but we have been informed by the
buyers' law firm that it remains in their hands; furthermore, the missives had
the usual two-year supersession clause, a period that has expired, so that what
is to happen now to the £1,000 is not free from difficulty. We will, however, not
explore that issue here

The buyers made a complaint about their solicitors to the Scottish Legal
Complaints Commission:[3]

> The essence of that part of the complaint which is the subject of this appeal, as
> articulated by the clients, was that the first appellant [the solicitor] changed his advice
> – that initially, he told them that they would be able to use the retention money to
> instruct their own repairs but a week later he told them that they could not do so – the
> respondents [the SLCC], once they had considered that complaint in the context of
> the whole surrounding facts and circumstances, analysed matters differently. They
> concluded that what mattered was the cause of that complaint and it was that the
> solicitor failed, at the outset, to ensure that the terms of the retention were adequate.
> In that regard, they noted that the agreement about the retention was lacking in
> detail; for example, it failed to identify the extent of the repairs to be carried out,
> failed to state who was to be responsible for instructing the repairs, failed to provide
> a time limit and failed to state what was to happen if the parties disagreed about
> the standard of the repairs carried out. Nor did it provide for the client to uplift the
> retention monies and carry out the repairs themselves.

The SLCC 'concluded that the solicitor had provided an inadequate professional
service and determined that his firm should waive certain fees and pay
compensation'.[4] The solicitor appealed to the Inner House.

The appeal to the Inner House

The importance of the Inner House's decision, for conveyancers, lies in what
the court said about retentions, and the reason that it is important is that until

---

1 Paragraph 11.
2 Paragraph 15.
3 Paragraph 19.
4 Paragraph 1. The SLCC thus found against both the individual solicitor and his firm. Both were
  appellants in the case as reported.

now there has been, as far as we know, almost no authority in this area. The court began by looking at the guidance on retentions issued by the Law Society of Scotland:[1]

> Where a sum of money is to be retained at settlement of a conveyancing transaction, the conditions upon which it is retained should be set out in writing at settlement. The agreement should specify the time limit for implementation. Matters should not be left to recollection of telephone conversations which may become vague with the passage of time.
>
> If funds were retained pending fulfillment of certain conditions by the seller, they should be released when those conditions have been fulfilled in terms of the written agreement. The purchaser's solicitor does not need to seek instructions from his or her client at that stage.
>
> Solicitors are entitled to rely upon agreements reached with other solicitors at settlement which set out conditions on which funds will be released. If the client instructs the solicitor not to release funds there could be a conflict of interest between solicitor and client requiring the solicitor to withdraw from acting.
>
> It may be that the conditions for release of the funds have not been fulfilled by the seller. In these circumstances if the purchaser's solicitor produces vouching for the actual or estimated expenditure required to fulfil the conditions, the seller's agent does not require the seller's instructions to agree to the release of the funds as so vouched. Again solicitors are entitled to rely on the reciprocity of such agreements.

The court accepted this guidance. More than that, the court held that, unless otherwise agreed, retention money cannot be used to remedy the problem for which the money was retained:[2]

> The retention agreement was limited in effect and did not include any provision whereby his clients [the buyers] would, at any time, be entitled to use the retention money to carry out the repairs themselves. We do not consider that there was any room for the implication of such a provision whether at common law or on a consideration of the terms of this retention agreement.

The appeal was refused.

As far as we are aware, this is the only authority on this issue. Is it right? Given that this is Inner House authority, perhaps the question should not be asked. But it seems to us that there may be room for doubt. What if a seller does not do the work in question, and there is no agreement as to what is to happen to the retention money? Does the money sit there in the hands of the buyers' law firm, unavailable to either the sellers or the buyers, unless and until agreement is – if ever – reached? Suppose (unlike the actual case) that the retention money had not been in the hands of the buyers' law firm, but rather the buyers had simply paid over £369,000, rather than £370,000, to their law firm? In that case they would have had the £1,000 in their own hands, to spend on the roof, or on

---

1 See Law Society of Scotland, *Rules and Guidance* Section F Division C (www.lawscot.org.uk/rules-and-guidance/table-of-contents/).
2 Paragraph 35.

anything else that took their fancy. When could the sellers demand payment of the £1,000? Never? These, and similar, questions, seem hard to answer, at least on the approach taken by the Inner House.

The court had other criticisms:[1]

> The retention agreement did not include any provisions whereby failure on the part of the sellers could be pinpointed nor had the first appellant even attempted to have such provisions incorporated. What was meant by 'satisfactorily completed'? Who was to instruct the repairs, given that the date of entry was the following day? What about a time limit? None of these were addressed. The retention agreement did not include a time limit.

These comments are about 'inadequate professional service'.[2] But possibly they go further and indicate what is needed, as a matter of contract law, for a valid retention, though admittedly nothing is said expressly on this point. At all events, a critic might say that these comments go too far. 'Satisfactorily completed' – the expression used by the buyers' solicitors in their original letter – does not seem to us too vague. Provisions of that sort are part and parcel of the law: consider the 'satisfactory quality' of the law of sale of goods.[3] 'What about a time limit?' But it often happens in the law that, when no specific time limit is stated, a reasonable time is implied.

Be all that as it may, it is evidently wise, when arranging a retention, to agree these points of detail, though it may not always be easy to do so in the hectic scramble of daily practice, when the keys for the buyers or the money for the sellers must be obtained without any delay, and when it may also be reasonably hoped that the respective clients will not come to blows.

REAL BURDENS AND AMENITY AREAS

Three models for amenity areas

In arranging the ownership and maintenance of amenity areas in housing estates, two legal models predominate. By far the most common is for the amenity area to be conveyed to the homeowners as common property, accompanied, usually, by a maintenance real burden.[4] This we may refer to as the 'common-property model'. The main alternative, affecting around 20,000 homeowners, is for the amenity area to be held by a third party, such as a company nominated by the developer, or the local authority.[5] The third party manages and maintains the area, but the homeowners are subject to a real burden to pay the cost. Of the

---

1 Paragraph 36.
2 The case was not about professional negligence. As the court said (para 33), 'a service may be inadequate without being negligent and without having caused loss'.
3 Sale of Goods Act 1979 s 14(2).
4 Strictly, though, the real burden is not necessary, as *pro indiviso* owners are in any event bound as a matter of common law to pay for necessary maintenance.
5 Much useful information on this model is contained in Consumer Focus Scotland, *Consumer Experiences of Land-Owning Land Management Companies* (2011).

various operators of this 'owner-manager model' the most prominent is the Greenbelt Group which owns and manages land in a little under 200 housing estates.

From a legal point of view, neither model has proved straightforward. Each requires the developer both (i) to convey ownership of the amenity area (whether to the homeowners or a land maintenance company such as Greenbelt), and (ii) to impose a maintenance real burden on the homeowners. With the common-property model it is the first that has caused difficulty, for often the developer must begin selling houses – and hence conveying a share in the amenity areas – before the development is complete and so, it may be, before the boundaries of the amenity areas are finally determined. In the absence of proper identification, any purported conveyance of a share in the amenity areas will fail – a principle which was applied in a series of cases beginning with *PMP Plus Ltd v Keeper of the Registers of Scotland*.[1] In contrast, the owner-manager model has no difficulty with conveying the amenity areas, because this is not done until the development is complete, but is thought to encounter problems in respect of the maintenance real burden. We say 'is thought to' because, until now, the issue had not been tested in the courts. In *Marriott v Greenbelt Group Ltd*,[2] however, decided at the end of 2015, that issue was squarely before the Lands Tribunal, and the Tribunal's detailed Opinion has much to say, not only about the issue in question, but about the law of real burdens more generally.

Before looking at *Marriott v Greenbelt Group Ltd*, we should mention a third possible model for amenity areas which avoids the difficulties of the other two. Where a development is made subject to the (statutory) Development Management Scheme, title can be vested directly and conveniently in the owners' association, which is a body corporate, and provision can be made for common maintenance by means of a rule of the Scheme.[3] Like much else in the DMS, this provides a neat solution to a perplexing problem. So far, however, the take-up of the DMS has been smaller than it ought to be. On this subject developers and their advisers may need to think again.[4]

The owner-manager model: effective in theory

Introduction

Marriott v Greenbelt Group Ltd concerned a housing estate in Menstrie, Clackmannanshire, known as the Menstrie Mains Housing Development. The

---

1 2009 SLT (Lands Tr) 2, discussed in *Conveyancing 2008* pp 133–49. Significant later cases are: *Lundin Homes Ltd v Keeper of the Registers of Scotland* 2013 SLT (Lands Tr) 73, discussed in *Conveyancing 2013* pp 105–16; *Miller Homes Ltd v Keeper of the Registers of Scotland* 2014 SLT (Lands Tr) 79, discussed in *Conveyancing 2014* pp 134–39.

2 2 December 2015. Unusually, the case was heard by three members of the Lands Tribunal (Lord Minginish, R A Smith QC, and D J Gillespie FRICS), including both of the legal members.

3 For the Development Management Scheme, see G L Gretton and K G C Reid, *Conveyancing* (4th edn, 2011) pp 278–82.

4 A view also expressed, in reaction to *Marriott*, in Andrew Todd, 'The end of deeds of conditions?' (2016) 61 *Journal of the Law Society of Scotland* Jan/20.

developer was Bett Ltd.[1] At the time when the applicants, Mr and Mrs Marriott, bought their house, towards the end of 2004, some 70 houses had already been sold, but the site was still very much under construction. It might not therefore have been possible, at that stage, to identify the precise areas that were to be used for amenity and recreation. As, however, the owner-manager (and not the common-property) model was being employed, this was not an immediate concern. The ultimate aim was for the amenity areas (referred to in the deeds as 'open ground') to be conveyed to Greenbelt Group Ltd, and this was eventually done in three tranches between 2009 and 2015. Meanwhile, in terms of a deed of conditions an obligation was imposed on Mr and Mrs Marriott, and the other owners, to pay for the cost of maintenance as well as for insurance premiums and for 'reasonable estate management remuneration' for Greenbelt.[2] This obligation was to be enforceable by Greenbelt as (eventual) owner of the open ground. The open ground was to be set out as 'amenity woodlands, landscaped open spaces, play areas and others'.[3]

Exactly why Mr and Mrs Marriott were unhappy with these arrangements is not known. But unhappy they plainly were because they applied to the Lands Tribunal for a finding that the maintenance burden was invalid and unenforceable.[4] As senior counsel was instructed, it seems likely that this was a test case, in which Mr and Mrs Marriott represented a number of other proprietors. At the time of the application, the annual charge levied by Greenbelt was £150, which was said to be 'considerably more than a competitive cost'.[5]

The application was supported by a veritable onslaught of legal arguments, great and small. Two were of particular importance, and brief mention will also be made of the others.

The first argument: burden not praedial

In order for an obligation to be enforceable as a real burden, it must be praedial at both ends: that is to say, the obligation must 'relate in some way to the *burdened*

---

1 In the case the name takes three forms: 'Bett Homes Ltd', 'Bett Ltd' and 'Bett plc'. No company bearing any of these names could be found by us on the Companies House website. In what follows we use the form 'Bett Ltd'.
2 See p 147 below for the wording of the burden. Although the deed of conditions was registered on 6 November 2003, ie before the Title Conditions (Scotland) Act 2003 came into force (on 28 November 2004), s 17 of the Land Registration (Scotland) Act 1979 was expressly excluded, meaning that the burdens would only affect individual plots when the deed of conditions was incorporated into a disposition of the plot in question and the disposition was registered. Registration of the disposition in favour of Mr and Mrs Marriott took place on 16 June 2005. A transitional provision in the Title Conditions Act, s 6, allowed the continued use of pre-appointed day deeds of conditions in this way. The Tribunal decided, surely correctly (para 65), that 'the burden was created when the applicants took title to their property albeit it did not become effective (in the sense of being enforceable) until the respondents took title to theirs'. The Tribunal was also correct (paras 66–72) to see creation under s 6 as quite distinct from creation under s 4, so that for example the dual registration required by s 4 did not apply to creation under s 6. Each of the provisions is said to be 'without prejudice to' – as opposed to 'subject to' – the other.
3 See the preamble to the deed of conditions, quoted at para 5.
4 This was under the Tribunal's jurisdiction, new in 2004, to rule on the validity and enforceability of real burdens: see Title Conditions (Scotland) Act 2003 s 90(1)(a)(ii). Such applications are rare.
5 *Marriott v Greenbelt Group Ltd*, 2 December 2015, Lands Tribunal, para 23.

property'[1] and at the same time it must confer benefit on the *benefited* property. The relevant rules are set out in the first three subsections of s 3 of the Title Conditions (Scotland) Act 2003.[2] An obligation which binds or benefits only in a personal capacity and without any connection to land cannot be a real burden.[3]

On the facts of *Marriott v Greenbelt Group Ltd* the benefited property was the open land owned by Greenbelt, and the burdened properties were the individual houses one of which was owned by Mr and Mrs Marriott. That the obligation was praedial at the *benefited* end was reasonably clear.[4] Of course, Greenbelt was being paid as factor (in a broad sense)[5] rather than as owner, for the costs due under the burden were the costs of managing and maintaining the open ground. But Greenbelt was, separately, subject to a real burden, contained in the dispositions in its favour, to maintain the open ground,[6] and it was to meet the cost of this maintenance obligation – imposed on Greenbelt not personally but as owner of the open ground – that the burden on the homeowners was being exacted. The burden of meeting the cost could thus be said to benefit the benefited property (the open ground) rather than merely Greenbelt in a personal capacity.[7]

Much more difficult was the question of whether the obligation was praedial at the *burdened* end. Subsection (1) of s 3 provides that 'A real burden must relate in some way to the burdened property', to which subsection (2) adds that 'The relationship may be direct or indirect but shall not merely be that the obligated person is the owner of the burdened property'. But what, asked the applicants, was the relationship between (i) an obligation to pay for the maintenance of the open ground, and (ii) the burdened properties, ie the individual houses on the estate? The homeowners did not own the open ground. Nor, even, did they have a right to use it, other than the right of any member of the public, under s 1 of the Land Reform (Scotland) Act 2003, to exercise access rights in certain circumstances and subject to certain limitations. Could an obligation to maintain *someone else's* land really be said to relate, even indirectly, to the houses which the obligation sought to burden?

It is doubts as to how this question should be answered which have led to uncertainties as to the viability of the whole owner-manager model.[8] And indeed either answer – asserting a praedial link or denying one – seems eminently defensible. The case against a praedial link, which was set out above, is strong and

---

1 Title Conditions (Scotland) Act 2003 s 3(1).
2 Section 1(1) is also relevant although it does not really add anything to s 3(3). It was the former which was relied on by the Tribunal in *Marriott*: see paras 90 and 92.
3 For discussion, see Scottish Law Commission, *Report No 181 on Real Burdens* (2000, available at www.scotlawcom.gov.uk) paras 2.9–2.18.
4 Although the contrary position was strenuously argued: see *Marriott* para 19.
5 'Factor' means agent: a property factor is someone who acts for an owner in respect of the owner's property. In this sense the factor on a Highland estate and the factor for an urban tenement are both factors. Greenbelt was, therefore, not a factor in the strict sense.
6 We have not seen the three dispositions by Bett Ltd in favour of Greenbelt, but it appears that no rights to enforce the burden were conferred on the homeowners in the estate.
7 *Marriott* para 92.
8 It comes as a surprise, therefore, to see the second argument, discussed below, being described (at para 99) as 'the heart of the applicants' attack on the land-owning maintenance model'.

credible.[1] But it is no less possible to argue in favour of such a link. For even if the homeowners did not own the open ground, they – and their houses – benefited from the screening and the green lung which the open ground provided. And if they had no formal entitlement to use the ground, the fact was that the ground had been laid out precisely so that they *could* use it. Whatever the legal rights and wrongs of the matter, it was inconceivable that Greenbelt would try to stop them.

In *Marriott* a court, for the first time, had to choose between these competing arguments. Building on a hint given in a previous case,[2] the decision of the Lands Tribunal was firmly in favour of a praedial link:[3]

> [T]he only question is whether the real burden is related 'in some way' to the burdened property. In our view it is. The payment by the individual proprietors of the cost of upkeep of the open land leads to the open land being maintained, which preserves or enhances the amenity of the whole development and the value of the individual plots. ... The burden is related to the burdened property in that, taken together with the burden on the respondents to maintain the open land,[4] it benefits the burdened property in terms of preserving its amenity and value.

There was, however, a sting in the tail. The housing estate was large. So too was the open ground. 'There may', warned the Tribunal, 'be questions as to whether the maintenance of all parts of the open ground bears upon the amenity and value of the applicants' property. That is a matter which will require evidence'.[5] It is certainly possible to imagine cases where parts of the amenity ground are so distant from individual houses as to confer little benefit on these houses. Even so, it is to be hoped that the courts will usually view amenity ground as a single unit and not try to distinguish between parts which do, and parts which might not, confer benefit on individual houses. For to do otherwise would create huge complexity as well as create a shortfall in the maintenance contributions.

The second argument: burden creating a monopoly

The rule that real burdens must not create monopolies goes back to the start of the nineteenth century when the law was first being developed.[6] It is repeated by s 3(7) of the Title Conditions Act:

> Except in so far as expressly permitted by this Act, a real burden must not have the effect of creating a monopoly (as for example, by providing for a particular person to be or to appoint –

---

1 See also *Conveyancing 2008* p 144.
2 *Greenbelt Property Ltd v Riggens* 2010 GWD 28-586; see *Conveyancing 2010* pp 125–26.
3 Paragraphs 96 and 97.
4 It is unclear how much weight the Tribunal placed on the reciprocal burden on Greenbelt. It will be recalled that the burden, if enforceable by anyone, was enforceable by Bett Ltd and not by the homeowners on the estate.
5 Paragraph 98.
6 It appears in the authoritative set of rules for real burdens given by Lord Corehouse in *Tailors of Aberdeen v Coutts* (1840) 1 Rob 296, 307 (a real burden 'must not be contrary to public policy, for example by tending to impede the commerce of land, or create a monopoly').

(a) the manager of property; or
(b) the supplier of any services in relation to property).

In a broad sense, there was indeed something monopolistic about the arrangements with Greenbelt. Although not owned by the homeowners, the open ground was provided for their benefit. Yet while the homeowners had to pay for management and maintenance, they had no say in who was to provide the relevant services. On the contrary, Greenbelt could and in practice would provide the services itself, and could do so for the indefinite future. If the homeowners were dissatisfied with Greenbelt's performance, they had no power to seek a replacement. Greenbelt was owner, and that was that. At best they could challenge Greenbelt's performance by withholding payment of whatever charge was being levied.[1] But, whether successful in that or not, Greenbelt would remain in charge.[2]

It would all have been different if the common-property model, and not the owner-manager model, had been used for the open ground. Then any right of the developer to appoint the manager would have expired after five years; thereafter, control would vest in the owners themselves. The Title Conditions Act contains provisions to ensure that this is so.[3] Furthermore, any real burden which sought to provide otherwise would fall foul of s 3(7) of the Act (quoted above), and in particular of the illustrative example which that provision contains. But the owner-manager model works in a quite different way from the common-property model, and it tilts the balance of power decisively in the manager's favour.

And yet could s 3(7) not be made to apply to the maintenance burden in the applicants' title? The applicants argued strenuously that it could. In obliging the homeowners to pay Greenbelt for the costs of management and maintenance, the real burden created a monopoly in Greenbelt's favour. The burden could therefore be struck down under s 3(7). One Tribunal member was persuaded.[4] The majority of the Tribunal, however, rejected the argument.[5] In our view they were right to do so.

The difficulty with the applicants' argument is that the monopoly, if there was one, was not 'created', as s 3(7) requires, by the real burden. Rather it existed by virtue of Greenbelt's ownership of the open ground. In principle, an owner is always free to manage and maintain his own property; and if that is a monopoly, it is not a monopoly created by a real burden. As the majority of the Tribunal put it:[6]

[W]hat brings about the arguably objectionable result in the present case – that the proprietors have no control over who provides the services for which they, and they

---

1 *Marriott* para 155.
2 See the argument presented for the appellants in *Marriott* (paras 21–23), and the dissenting note by R A Smith QC (paras 114–24).
3 Title Conditions (Scotland) Act 2003 ss 28, 63, 64.
4 R A Smith QC: see paras 114–24.
5 Lord Minginish and D J Gillespie FRICS: see paras 100–113.
6 Paragraph 107.

only, pay – is not the real burden but the ownership model used for the maintenance of the amenity areas of this estate, whereby these areas are owned not by the proprietors in common but by a third party.

As for the real burden:[1]

> It is merely a burden for the payment of a share of the management operations relating to the open ground. That payment has, of course, to be made to the respondents as the providers of the management operations. It might be said to *reflect* a monopoly, that monopoly being the respondents' exclusive right to manage their own land, but it does not create one.

The matter can be tested by considering the position if the real burden had not existed. In such a case, the open ground would continue to confer benefit on homeowners such as Mr and Mrs Marriott – and Greenbelt would continue to have the exclusive right to manage the property. The 'monopoly', in other words, would continue to exist even in the absence of the burden.

Section 3(7), therefore, did not apply, any more than did the other provisions of the Title Conditions Act which are designed, in the context of the common-ownership model, to give homeowners control over the management of amenity ground.[2] The truth is that the Act is concerned with real burdens and not with a system of management which rests on a particular allocation of ownership. If such a system is to be controlled, it will have to be done in a different way, and perhaps by new legislation. Indeed a Government initiative in 2011 seemed to hold out the prospect of a legislative solution, but since then there has been silence.[3]

One other matter merits comment. Traditionally, the prohibition of monopolies was simply one aspect of a broader prohibition of burdens which were contrary to public policy. But in the Title Conditions Act the prohibition on grounds of public policy is placed in a separate subsection – subsection (6) of s 3 – from the prohibition of monopolies (which is in subsection (7)), leading to the suggestion, by one Tribunal member in *Marriott*,[4] that monopolies are disallowed even where they are fully compliant with public policy. Whatever the merits of that interpretation of s 3, it is contrary to the view of the Scottish Law Commission, expressed at the time that it was preparing the legislation. Thus in its explanatory note to the provisions which became subsections (6) and (7) of s 3, the Law Commission explained that the provisions implemented its recommendation 5.[5] And recommendation 5 made clear that the prohibition of monopolies was a facet of public policy:[6]

---

1 Paragraph 105.
2 Ie Title Conditions (Scotland) Act 2003 ss 28, 63, 64.
3 Scottish Government, *Maintenance of land on private housing estates* (2011, available at http://www. scotland.gov.uk/Publications/2011/03/04104005/0). For discussion, see *Conveyancing 2011* pp 117–18.
4 The suggestion appears in para 118 of the dissenting note by R A Smith QC.
5 Scottish Law Commission, *Report No 181 on Real Burdens* (2000) p 338.
6 *Report No 181* para 2.28.

A real burden should not be –
(a) illegal, or
(b) contrary to public policy, as for example in unreasonable restraint of trade, repugnant with ownership, or (subject to our other recommendations) requiring the employment of a particular person as manager or as the provider of other services.

Indeed, the Law Commission expressly contemplated the possibility that a monopoly might sometimes be justified, as for example in the case of a real burden to pay for a common heating system in a block of flats.[1]

The third argument: burden an 'unfair' term

Where a term in a contract concluded between a seller or supplier and a consumer is 'unfair', the term is not binding on the consumer. That is the rule contained in the Unfair Terms in Consumer Contracts Regulations 1999, which was in force at the time that Mr and Mrs Marriott were buying their house.[2] It is equally the rule in part 2 of the Consumer Rights Act 2015, which replaced the 1999 Regulations with effect from 1 October 2015.[3] Under the Regulations (and now the Act), a contractual term is unfair if (i) it has not been individually negotiated, (ii) it causes a significant imbalance in the parties' rights and obligations, to the consumer's detriment, and (iii) this is 'contrary to the requirement of good faith'.[4] A number of illustrative examples of unfair terms are given in a schedule.[5]

The contract entered into between Mr and Mrs Marriott and the developer, Bett Ltd, was a standard-form contract which was not, in practice, open to much in the way of negotiation.[6] And clause 9 of that contract was, according to the Marriotts, an 'unfair' term. The clause read:

> The title to be granted in favour of me may be granted subject to the terms of a Deed of Conditions appropriate to the Estate[7] may also contain further rights and obligations, including Factoring conditions, payment of a Factor's fee and other conditions relating to the subjects and others forming part of the Estate.

In the applicants' view, there was much in this clause that was 'unfair'.[8] It failed to disclose that the deed of conditions already existed and so was available for consultation; and it suggested, misleadingly, that the common-property model would be used for the amenity areas rather than the far less favourable

---

1 *Report No 181* para 2.23.
2 Unfair Terms in Consumer Contracts Regulations 1999, SI 1999/2083, reg 8(1).
3 Consumer Rights Act 2015 s 62(1).
4 Unfair Terms in Consumer Contracts Regulations 1999 reg 5(1); Consumer Rights Act 2015 s 62(4).
5 Unfair Terms in Consumer Contracts Regulations 1999 reg 5(5), sch 2; Consumer Rights Act 2015 s 63(1), sch 2.
6 That may change. In 2015 the Law Society produced a set of New Build Standard Clauses: see p 110 above.
7 At this point a word or words appear to be missing.
8 *Marriott* para 26.

owner-manager model. Both vouched for bad faith on the part of Bett Ltd. In addition, the clause allowed Greenbelt to control both the level of service and the price to be paid.

For reasons which need not be discussed, the Tribunal was not persuaded by this argument.[1] Of greater interest is why this argument was thought to be of relevance in the first place. The legislation on unfair terms is concerned only with the terms of *contracts*,[2] and a real burden is not a contract. Indeed the former rule by which a real burden was considered to be contractual as between the original parties to the disposition or other constitutive deed was expressly removed by the Title Conditions Act.[3] The legislation, cannot, therefore, be used for a direct attack on the terms of a real burden. What the applicants seem to have proposed is an indirect attack. They would begin by showing the 'unfairness' of clause 9 of the contract of sale. If this could be done, 'the fundamental unfairness of the contract between Bett Limited and the applicants carried over to the title condition with the respondents as successors to Bett Limited in the land'.[4] Why this should be so is unexplained, beyond the suggestion that 'unfairness' in the contract somehow made the real burden 'illegal' and hence invalid under s 3(6) of the Title Conditions Act.[5]

If that is the argument, it is, with respect, unsound. The legislation on unfair terms does not apply to real burdens. If a burden is thought to be unfair, the Title Conditions Act provides its own remedy in the form of an application to the Lands Tribunal for variation or discharge.[6] It is, perhaps, surprising that the Tribunal in *Marriott* should have expended so much energy on reviewing the possible unfairness of the contract of sale without, apparently, considering why or whether such possible unfairness might matter.

The fourth argument: burden a breach of competition law

A fourth argument for the appellants was that the arrangements with Greenbelt amounted to a breach of the 'Chapter II prohibition' set out in s 18 of the Competition Act 1998. This prohibits conduct 'which amounts to the abuse of a dominant position in a market … if it may affect trade within the United Kingdom'.

The Tribunal dismissed this argument due to lack of specification. Even if it was accepted that the relevant geographic market was (only) the housing estate, and the relevant product market the supply of management operations, with the result that Greenbelt was in a dominant position, there were insufficient averments that that dominant position was being abused. In the Tribunal's words:[7]

---

1 Paragraphs 143–160.
2 Unfair Terms in Consumer Contracts Regulations 1999 reg 4(1); Consumer Rights Act 2015 s 61(1).
3 Title Conditions (Scotland) Act 2003 s 61 provides that the constitutive deed ceases to bind as a contract 'when the deed has been duly registered and the real burden has become effective'.
4 *Marriott* para 26.
5 Paragraph 133.
6 Title Conditions (Scotland) Act 2003 part 9.
7 Paragraph 165.

It is not our practice to take a stringent view of written pleadings. However, it seems to us that the averments asserting that there is an 'abuse' are really no more than averments as to the rights of the respondents in terms of the deed of conditions. That is not instructing any more than that the respondents may be in a dominant position in the market. Nothing more is said in the pleadings; for example, that the respondents' charges are excessive or that the work carried out is of poor quality or unnecessary. We cannot imagine that an investigation by the Competition and Markets Authority under the 1998 Act would not look closely into such matters. Some sort of fair notice going beyond an ex parte statement at the bar is required as to allegations of abuse. The failure to give such notice strikes us as being fundamental.

Competition law has been lurking around the fringes of the law of real burdens for a number of years now, and it may be only a matter of time before a burden is struck down on this ground. But if this does occur, it will surely be in respect of a Chapter I and not a Chapter II prohibition.[1] For whereas Chapter I is directed at anti-competitive 'agreements', Chapter II is directed merely at the 'conduct' of particular persons ('undertakings') and says nothing about the validity of the agreement on which that conduct may be based.[2] So if Greenbelt was indeed abusing a dominant market position, the effect of the Chapter II provision would be to prohibit Greenbelt's abusive conduct. This would not invalidate the real burden itself, or prevent Greenbelt or some future owner of the open ground from providing management services which were not abusive.[3]

Further arguments

The remaining arguments for the applicants can be passed over quickly. It was argued that the burden was an illegal restraint of trade, that it was repugnant to ownership, and that it was illegal on various grounds. None of these arguments was strong and all were easily dismissed by the Tribunal.[4]

A green light for Greenbelt?

The decision in *Marriott* is a decision in favour of the owner-manager model. That such a model has certain disadvantages, especially in relation to homeowners' loss of control, the Tribunal readily accepted. At the same time, the Tribunal thought, certain advantages should not be overlooked:[5]

---

1 See *Conveyancing 2014* p 123. Chapter I is the UK equivalent of art 101 of the Treaty on the Functioning of the European Union ('TFEU') and Chapter II is the equivalent of art 102.
2 It is conceivable that an agreement of itself abuses a dominant position in a market, in which case it could amount to 'conduct' within s 18. *English Welsh and Scottish Railway Ltd v E.ON UK plc* [2007] EWHC 599 (Comm) is an example. But it could hardly be argued in *Marriott* that the real burden amounted to an abuse of a pre-existing dominant position.
3 Nonetheless, the applicants' argument was apparently that it was *the burden* which was in breach of the Chapter II prohibition, with the result that it was illegal and hence invalid under TC(S)A 2003 s 3(6): see *Marriott* para 27. The Tribunal did not comment on this aspect of the argument but seems to have accepted that an argument based on the Chapter II prohibition was potentially relevant.
4 *Marriott* paras 126–160.
5 Paragraph 139.

The model has corresponding advantages in the way of relieving the house owners of all the inconvenience of looking after the open ground themselves, including the holding of meetings, the appointment of factors or landscaping contractors, the monitoring of their performance and so on, with the risk of potentially damaging divisions among themselves to which these matters can give rise.

More importantly, there was nothing in the applicants' array of arguments which was fatal to the legal validity of the model. 'As an attack on the land-owning model *per se* it has failed'; there was no 'structural flaw' in the model.[1]

This might, therefore, have seemed like a green light for Greenbelt. But while Greenbelt won on the principle, they were to lose on the detail. The model was sound; the paperwork, it turned out, was not.

But ineffective in practice

The terms of the burden

The burden which was under challenge ran to some two pages. Its core terms, however, could be found from its opening words:

> 3.1 Whereas it is intended that GGC[2] will be taken bound in terms of the Disposition or Dispositions to be granted in their favour in respect of the Open Ground to carry out the Management Operations all Proprietors are hereby taken bound and obliged in all time coming to contribute to the whole costs of the Management Operations together with insurance premiums, reasonable estate management remuneration and charges incurred by GGC on a pro rata basis as aftermentioned and to pay and make over to GGC such annual sums (plus all Value Added Tax exigible thereon) as represent the pro rata share applicable from time to time to the relevant Plot of the total annual costs of effecting the Management Operations, insurance premiums, estate management remuneration and charges as aforesaid …

The 'Open Ground' was both the benefited property in the real burden and also the property in respect of which the 'Management Operations'[3] – the cost of which was to be met by the homeowners – were to be carried out. It was defined in the deed as 'the areas of amenity woodland, landscaped open spaces, play areas and others to be provided on the Whole Subjects in terms of the Planning Permission', while 'Planning Permission' was defined in turn as 'the planning

---

1 Paragraph 177.
2 Because of the discrepancy between this name and the name of the defender in the action, it should perhaps be explained that 'GDC' was defined in the deed to mean 'Greenbelt Group of Companies Ltd', and that that company later (in April 2003) changed its name to 'Greenbelt Group Ltd'. In short: GDC = Greenbelt Group of Companies Ltd = Greenbelt Group Ltd. As for Greenbelt Property Ltd, which appears in one decision (*Greenbelt Property Ltd v Riggens* 2010 GWD 28-586, *Conveyancing 2010* Case (24)), though it shares the same registered office, it is a separate company.
3 'Management Operations' were defined as 'all works and other matters comprised from time to time in the management, maintenance and, where necessary, renewal of the Open Ground in accordance with the Management and Maintenance Specification'. The latter was in turn defined as 'the management and maintenance specification annexed and executed as relative to this Deed as the said specification may be amended from time to time'. The terms of this 'specification' are not given in the Lands Tribunal's Opinion.

permission issued by the Scottish Ministers under Reference No.00/00129OUT on 7 Mar. 2002 together with any variation thereof or supplementary permission issued in respect thereof'.

The obligations were 'declared to be real reservations, burdens, conditions and land obligations affecting each and every Plot with the intent to confer upon GGC as proprietors of the Open Ground express right, title and interest *jus quaesitum tertio* to enforce performance of same against all Proprietors or any one or more of them'.[1]

The requirement of specificity

Real burdens must be expressed fully and clearly. Subject to the limited exception in s 5 of the Title Conditions (Scotland) Act 2003, which did not apply on the facts of *Marriott*,[2] s 4(2)(a) of the Act provides that the constitutive deed must set out 'the terms of the prospective real burden'. These statutory words seek to capture the rule of the common law that, as real burdens affect successors, and as successors may know nothing of the original circumstances of the deed, the burden must be set out in full within the four corners of the deed.[3] It comes as something of a surprise, therefore, to find Greenbelt seeking to argue that this rule was absent from the 2003 Act and so had ceased to be part of the law.

The argument was treated with greater seriousness by the Lands Tribunal than perhaps it deserved.[4] The Tribunal, too, was unable to find any provision in the Act which repeated the requirement of specificity, having looked – and looked in vain – at ss 2(5), 5(2) and 14. Nonetheless, applying the presumption that statute does not change the common law except by clear enactment, the Tribunal concluded that 'the rule that the extent of a real burden must be found within the four corners of the deed creating it remains part of our law'.[5] That conclusion was surely not in doubt.[6]

Application of the requirement to the terms

As just mentioned, an important aspect of the requirement of specificity is that it is not generally competent to seek the terms of real burdens from beyond the four corners of the deed. The leading case is the well-known decision in *Aberdeen*

---

1 The Tribunal's Opinion (paras 73–78) records some discussion as to whether the burden might be a community burden or a facility burden under s 56 or a manager burden under s 63. In fact it is none of those, though not, for the most part, for the reasons mentioned in the Opinion.
2 The exception allows limited types of extrinsic evidence (such as the valuation roll) to be used to specify the means of allocation of the liability for contributing to a maintenance or other cost.
3 See eg K G C Reid, *The Law of Property in Scotland* (1996) para 388.
4 *Marriott* paras 79–88.
5 Paragraph 88. It was applied by the Tribunal in a case from the previous year, *Sinton v Lloyd*, 11 June 2014 (Case (19) above).
6 So for example in its *Report No 181 on Real Burdens* para 3.25, the Scottish Law Commission emphasised that: 'In general, a real burden must not rely on material extrinsic to the deed. The rule is that the full terms of the burden must be discoverable from the words of the deed, and hence from the register itself.'

Varieties Ltd v James F Donald (Aberdeen Cinemas) Ltd[1] in which the Inner House struck down a burden on the ground that its scope was defined by reference to an Act of Parliament which, though in the public domain and so readily accessible, was not set out in full in the burden itself. But, well known as this decision is, the rule is sometimes overlooked in the excitement of drafting real burdens. We have seen many examples of otherwise blameless burdens which fail on this ground.[2]

When the real burden in *Marriott* is re-read with the requirement of specificity in mind, it is immediately obvious that the burden is invalid. The key term, for the identification both of the benefited property (now a statutory requirement under s 4(2)(c)(ii) of the Title Conditions Act) and of the property for whose maintenance liability is being imposed, is 'Open Ground'; and the definition of 'Open Ground' is periled on a document extrinsic to the deed itself, namely the planning permission, and any variation of that planning permission, obtained by the developers. As in the case of *Aberdeen Varieties* so now in *Marriott v Greenbelt Group Ltd*, the reference was held to be fatal to the burden.[3]

But that was not all. Even if the planning consent had been included as part of the deed, it would still not have been possible to identify with complete certainty the extent of the land which was to be maintained. This was because of the possibility, anticipated in the definitional scheme in the deed ('any variation thereof or supplementary permission issued in respect thereof'), that the planning permission, and hence the extent of the open ground, might later be varied. This, said the Tribunal, was a second reason why the burden could not succeed:[4]

> When the applicants registered their title the ultimate extent of the open ground was unknown. It was defined by reference to the planning permission for the development as that permission may be varied or supplemented. Even if resort to the planning permission was permissible, therefore, there was no means of knowing the extent of land for the maintenance of which they might end up having to pay a share … [A] burden of this kind is insufficiently specific. We agree, therefore, that the burden is bad for this reason also.

Practical implications

For Greenbelt properties

So far as concerns the particular housing estate litigated in *Marriott*, the effect of the decision is to relieve homeowners of any obligation to pay for the maintenance of the amenity area. The underlying obligation to maintain, however, remains with Greenbelt in terms of the original dispositions in its favour. Greenbelt must now shoulder this cost on its own.

---

1 1939 SC 788.
2 It is occasionally overlooked by the courts too: see *Heritage Fisheries Ltd v Duke of Roxburghe* 2000 SLT 800, discussed in *Conveyancing 1999* pp 57–59.
3 *Marriott* paras 166–175.
4 Paragraph 173. This is similar to, but distinct from, the argument that prevailed in *PMP Plus Ltd v Keeper of the Registers of Scotland* 2009 SLT (Lands Tr) 2: see *Marriott* para 171.

Greenbelt owns and operates around 200 other housing estates in Scotland, but we understand that the documentation used on those estates is different and so may not be subject to challenge on the grounds set out in *Marriott*.[1]

For the owner-manager model

For developers, an attraction of the owner-manager model was that it appeared to allow a decision as to the extent of the amenity areas to be postponed until the development was completed. This was because the amenity areas were disponed, later, to a third party and not, incrementally, to the individual homeowners. Now the Lands Tribunal in *Marriott* has found that view to be mistaken. If early identification of the amenity areas is not needed for the purpose of their conveyance, it will still be needed for the purpose of setting out the maintenance burden being imposed on the homeowners. It was the failure to identify the amenity ground that undermined the burden in *Marriott*.

Alive to the practical difficulty this might create for developers,[2] the Lands Tribunal in *Marriott* was prepared to venture a possible solution:[3]

> The requirement for such identification has the potential to cause difficulty more widely, given developers' need for flexibility. But it is possible to exaggerate that difficulty. In many small developments the developer will, we imagine, be sufficiently confident that things will go according to plan that the amenity areas can be identified precisely from the outset. In larger developments, involving more uncertainty, there will be, at the very least, an indicative layout plan from the outset which could be incorporated into the constitutive deed, the text of which could be worded to the effect that the area to be maintained will not exceed that shown on the plan. That *may* be sufficient to solve the problem but we express no concluded view.

We too would not care to express a concluded view on the matter. It is true that such an approach would set out the maximum area to be maintained, and hence the maximum liability which the burden could impose. But at the same time purchasers could not know, simply by looking at the deed, what their *actual* liability would be.

For the common-property model

Although *Marriott* is not a decision about the common-property model, it has implications for that model. But these relate, not to the current version of the model, but to how the model was sometimes run in the past, in the days before *PMP Plus*.[4]

Where the split-off conveyances in a development fall foul of *PMP Plus*, they do so because the description of the amenity areas is too imprecise to transmit ownership. The result, as we now know, is for the developer to be

---

1 See Wendy Quinn, 'Deeds of conditions: not dead yet' (2016) 61 *Journal of the Law Society of Scotland* Feb/20.
2 Paragraph 173.
3 Paragraph 177.
4 *PMP Plus Ltd v Keeper of the Registers of Scotland* 2009 SLT (Lands Tr) 2; see *Conveyancing 2008* pp 133–49.

left – unexpectedly – as owner of the amenity areas. In effect, the common-property model has mutated into something close to the owner-manager model. But what of the maintenance real burden imposed on the homeowners? Here the decision in *Marriott* seems directly applicable. Thus, while such a burden would, probably, not fail the praediality requirement,[1] it would normally fail the specificity requirement in respect that the areas to be maintained have not been sufficiently identified. This is good news for homeowners. As compensation for being deprived of a property right in the amenity ground, they are relieved of liability for its maintenance. The decision in *PMP Plus* has thus been balanced out, to some extent, by the decision in *Marriott*.

PROMISES, PROMISES: IS A BANK'S WORD ITS BOND?

Below we cover two cases – one Scottish, one English – in which a bank sought to repudiate what it had agreed with a customer, in both cases litigation being the result. The facts of the two cases were very different, but the basic issue was comparable. In one the bank lost and in the other it won. The first case went to the Supreme Court. The second was only a first-instance case but may be the more important.

Carlyle case: bank 0, customer 1

The first case is *Royal Bank of Scotland plc v Carlyle* which has progressed from the Outer House[2] to the Inner House[3] and from there to the Supreme Court.[4] It has been a slugfest, the pursuer winning at first instance, losing on appeal, and at last winning in the final round.

Mr Carlyle was a property developer. His usual practice was to buy a plot of land, build a house, and sell it, and then begin the whole process over again. Sometimes he lived for a while in a house he had built before selling it. Lacking capital, he used loan finance from RBS. Sometimes he operated by means of a company, Carlyco Ltd, of which he was the sole shareholder.

In 2007 Mr Carlyle had his eye on two plots (numbered 2 and 5) in Queen's Crescent, Gleneagles, Perthshire, which were being offered for sale by the Gleneagles Hotel. We quote the Lord Ordinary (Glennie):[5]

> The purchase price for Plot 5 was estimated at £1,250,000, with that for Plot 2 £975,000. The Build Cost in each case was £700,000. It was a feature of the purchase contracts envisaged for each site that there would be a buy-back clause. This was something which the vendors were insisting on, as was made clear in the brochure. The effect

---

1 We say 'probably' because (i) unlike in a genuine owner-manager model, there is no obligation on the developer to maintain the amenity areas, and (ii) the existence of such an obligation was one of the factors which persuaded the Lands Tribunal (at para 97) that the praedial requirement had been met in *Marriott*.
2 [2010] CSOH 3, 2010 GWD 13-235 (*Conveyancing 2010* Case (67)).
3 [2013] CSIH 75, 2014 SC 188 (*Conveyancing 2013* Case (75)).
4 [2015] UKHL 13, 2015 SC (UKSC) 93, 2015 SLT 206.
5 [2010] CSOH 3, para 7.

of the clause was that the purchaser of the plots would be tied to a target completion date of 31 March 2011. If he had not by that date completed the construction of the dwelling house on the site to such a stage that it was wind and watertight, with all external finishes and features and hard landscaping works completed, then the vendors would be entitled to require the purchaser to sell his interest in the property back to them at the original purchase price. The reason for this was that the Ryder Cup golf tournament was due to take place at Gleneagles later in 2011, and it was thought undesirable for there to be half-completed houses spoiling the outlook.

There was a meeting with bank officials. Mr Carlyle said in evidence:[1]

> I recall that at the meeting I clearly pointed out to them that there would be three stages for the provision of funding: (1) deposit funding; (2) land purchase; and (3) build costs. Even at that stage I stressed to them that it was a full development proposal and so if we went ahead with the deposit and the land purchase then the development funds really must follow because the land itself is no use to me. That is when I said 'so please do not give me the money for the land unless you give me the money for the build'.

Conversations continued over time, and according to Mr Carlyle's evidence the bank agreed to lend not only for the site acquisition but also for the development. During one telephone call the bank official in charge of dealing with Mr Carlyle's case said to him: 'You'll be pleased to know it's all approved; Edinburgh are going for it for both houses'.[2] In the summer of 2007 the bank made formal offers to lend on the security of the properties.[3] The sums offered were £845,000 and £560,000 and were for acquiring the plots: these sums did not include 'build costs'. Mr Carlyle accepted, and on that basis went ahead and bought the two plots. He believed that the 'build cost' lending would follow in due course.

At this point it should be mentioned that plot 5 was bought by Mr Carlyle in his own name and plot 2 was bought in the name of his company, and thus the borrowers were different in each case. The litigation that took place was between the bank and Mr Carlyle as an individual. What happened as to the company, and plot 2, we do not know.

Time went on, and Mr Carlyle began to press for the building funding. No progress was made and in August 2008 RBS told him that it had decided not to fund the development. Not only that, but it demanded immediate repayment of the existing loans, and when immediate payment was not made it at once raised an action, using both arrestment and inhibition.[4] In November 2009 Mr Carlyle

---

1　[2010] CSOH 3, para 8.
2　[2010] CSOH 3, para 15.
3　We note that in this offer from a Scottish bank to a Scottish borrower in respect of a Scottish project, the offer is for 'a mortgage'. The 'Scottish' banks ceased to be Scottish some time ago.
4　We presume that there were two actions, one against Mr Carlyle and one against his company, but we have no information about this. As already mentioned, the case that was fought up to the Supreme Court did not, as far as we can see, involve the company as a party. We would also mention that the action seems to have been an action for payment. Whether there were separate, or conjoined, proceedings for the enforcement of the heritable securities we do not know.

was sequestrated.[1] How he fought the case, given that he was sequestrated, is not known, but it sometimes happens that a trustee in sequestration will agree to the debtor litigating for himself in cases where the case is speculative rather than solid.

Mr Carlyle counterclaimed against the bank for £1.5 million by way of damages on account of the bank's failure to lend for the building costs, this sum being based chiefly on estimated lost profit.[2] In other words, his position was that if the bank had done what it had agreed to do, namely to advance the necessary building costs, the development would have gone ahead and would have been profitable.

There was a proof before answer, and the Lord Ordinary preferred Mr Carlyle's position: the bank had indeed committed itself, albeit orally, to an additional loan. The quantification of his loss was left to further procedure.[3] The basis of the decision was that the bank's undertaking to make the further advance had been a collateral warranty,

The pursuer appealed successfully to the Inner House. The Inner House, on reviewing the evidence, took the view that the conversations had indicated the bank's intentions but did not amount to a legally-binding commitment:[4]

> Without specification of the essential elements of that provision (including the maximum draw down, interest rates, time of draw down, method and time of repayment and securities), there could be no concluded agreement capable of enforcement. In this context, it is of some significance to note that the defender is a businessman, acting with advice from both an accountant and a solicitor. He has had a course of dealing with the pursuers and he is aware that, whatever oral discussions there may be between himself and the pursuers' local staff, no drawdown of funds (ie actual lending) would be permitted unless and until a written contract was entered into between the parties which set out, in detail, the parties' obligations in relation to the funds to be drawn down.

The bank's refusal to lend further sums 'may have been contrary to the spirit of the negotiations prior to the signing of the written agreements, but that spirit, or its moral content, cannot be taken as creating a legally binding voluntary obligation'.[5]

Mr Carlyle appealed to the Supreme Court, successfully: the decision was to 'remit the case to a commercial judge in the Court of Session to proceed accordingly', which presumably means to determine the quantum of damages. That may be a hurdle. In 2008 the property market was in serious difficulties, and if RBS had made the further loan, and Mr Carlyle had completed the development, one must wonder how much he would have been able to sell for. But on the pure legal point of whether the bank was liable, Mr Carlyle has won.

---

1 [2013] CSIH 75, para 8.
2 [2013] CSIH 75, para 5.
3 There are some obscurities about the procedure at first instance, about which the Inner House made some critical comments.
4 [2013] CSIH 75, para 58.
5 [2013] CSIH 75, para 63.

Why did the Supreme Court reverse the decision of the Inner House? In civil procedure the general principle is that appeals should be concerned with issues of law rather than issues of fact. Facts are to be determined by the court of first instance. Only in special circumstances should the appellate court intervene on matters of fact. But this general principle is not a precise one, and different judges tend to take slightly different views of it. In recent years there has been something of a conflict between the Inner House and the Supreme Court, with the former tending to take a more expansive view than the latter as to when the appellate court can disagree with the first-instance court as to issues of fact. As a result, there have been occasions when the Supreme Court has reversed the Inner House, reinstating the decision at first instance, not necessarily because the Supreme Court agreed with the first-instance decision, but because the Supreme Court considered that, on factual matters, appellate courts should take a back seat, intervening only if the first-instance decision was 'plainly wrong'.[1] Precisely this is what happened in Mr Carlyle's case. The Lord Ordinary had concluded, after hearing evidence, that there had been a binding obligation on the bank to make the further advance, and that decision had to be respected.[2]

On one issue, however, the Supreme Court did alter the first-instance decision, not as to the outcome, but as to the correct juridical pigeonhole to which the bank's obligation was to be allocated. The Lord Ordinary had said it was a collateral warranty. The Supreme Court disagreed. It was a promise.[3] A promise can be binding, as every law student knows by the end of first year, and there is no reason why promises to lend should be any less binding than other promises.

Alexander case: bank 1, customer 0

Introduction

The terms of offers to lend and of lenders' standard terms (referred to in the standard security, or, in England, the mortgage) are often in conflict. The offer sets out the terms that have in fact been agreed, while the standard terms may be quite different. The conflict tends to be sharpest in relation to the length of the loan and the interest rate. As to the former, the offer of loan will say, for example, '20 years' whereas the standard terms will often say 'repayable on demand'. As to the latter, the standard terms will often say, roughly speaking, that the lender can vary the interest rate at will, thus contradicting the loan offer, which says something different, namely what the parties have actually agreed.

---

1 See for instance *McGraddie v McGraddie* [2013] UKSC 58, 2014 SC (UKSC) 12 (*Conveyancing 2013* Case (32)), and *Henderson v Foxworth Investments Ltd* [2014] UKSC 41, 2014 SC (UKSC) 203 (*Conveyancing 2014* Case (70)), both conveyancing cases where the Supreme Court reinstated the Outer House decision. We lack expertise in civil procedure, but we think that the last word may not yet have been said as to whether the narrow approach of the Supreme Court or the broader approach of the Inner House is preferable. For the 'plainly wrong' formula see para 21 of the Supreme Court's decision in *Carlyle*.
2 There are actually some hints that the Supreme Court judges inclined to agree with the Inner House as to how the facts should have been interpreted. But they sternly resisted the temptation to disagree with the first-instance decision.
3 For further discussion, see Martin Hogg, 'Promises to lend, collateral warranties, and red herrings' (2015) 19 *Edinburgh Law Review* 384.

That this state of affairs has persisted for so long is strange. But getting financial institutions to depart from their practices is extraordinarily difficult, and in anything other than a major transaction almost impossible. The present case is the first that we know of in which the issue has been litigated, and the result seems to us disturbing.

Mr Alexander's buy-to-let tracker mortgage

In *Alexander v West Bromwich Mortgage Co Ltd*[1] Mr Alexander had a buy-to-let tracker mortgage. He took it out in the summer of 2008. It was for 25 years. For the first two years there was a fixed rate and thereafter it was to track the Bank of England base rate, plus 1.99%.

After two years the lender told Mr Alexander that the interest rate would not be 1.99% over base but 3.99% over base. And as for the term, it told him that it was not for 25 years but was repayable whenever it wanted the money back. Mr Alexander raised the present action for declarator[2] of the position as agreed.

This was a test case. We do not know the details, but the report discloses that Mr Alexander was 'representative of the Property 118 Action Group'. So it was not only Mr Alexander who was treated in this way by the lender.

What was agreed about the interest rate?

As just outlined, the formal offer of loan, which Mr Alexander accepted, said:[3]

6.29% fixed until 30.06.2010 … After 30 June 2010 your loan reverts to a variable rate which is the same as the Bank of England Base Rate, currently 5%, with a premium of 1.99%, until the term end …

The lender's Standard Conditions of Offer and Mortgage Conditions said:[4]

Interest is payable by you … at the rate or rates specified in your Offer of Loan Letter which, except during any period in which interest is expressed to be at a fixed rate, may be varied by the Company at any time for any of the following reasons:
- If there has been, or we reasonably expect there to be in the near future, a change in the Bank of England Base Rate or in interest levels generally;
- If investment interest rates have increased or decreased;
- To reflect market conditions generally;
- To take account of changes in the law, or any decisions, determinations, precedent, compelling guidance, regulations or instructions issued by a relevant governmental body, ombudsman, regulator or similar person or any code of practice with which we intended to comply;
- At the end of any period during which any fixed rate or concession or alternative rate (such as the Bank of England Base Rate) is in force;

1 [2015] EWHC 135 (Comm), [2015] 2 All ER (Comm) 224.
2 'Declaration' in English terminology.
3 Paragraph 3 of the judgment.
4 Paragraph 7.

- To reflect a change in the way the property is used or occupied;
- To make sure our business is carried out prudently, efficiently and competitively;
- To make sure we can meet our obligations to third parties.

If any of the above reasons is found to be invalid, we may still vary the interest rate for any of the remaining valid reasons.

What was agreed about the term of the loan?

The loan offer said that the term of the loan was 25 years, divided between 22 monthly payments at the initial fixed rate and 277 monthly payments at the tracker rate.[1] What did the lender's Standard Conditions of Offer and Mortgage Conditions say? The loan was repayable in full if:[2]

- we give you one month's notice requiring such repayment;
- any Payment remains unpaid for longer than one calendar month;
- you are in breach of any of the other obligations or conditions contained in these Mortgage Conditions;
- the Property becomes subject to a Compulsory Purchase Order;
- you are made bankrupt;
- you enter into an arrangement with or for the benefit of your creditors or propose to do so;
- you die or you become incapable of managing your affairs;
- you do anything which may damage or reduce the value of the property or you fail to perform any obligation (whether to pay money or otherwise) imposed upon you as the owner of the property;
- the Guarantor terminates or purports to terminate its obligations under the Mortgage Conditions or becomes insolvent or dies or becomes incapable of managing his affairs.

The conflict provision

Did either contain a provision saying which was to prevail in the event of inconsistency? Such a provision is not always to be found, but here there was such a provision:[3]

> These Mortgage Conditions incorporate any terms contained in the Offer of Loan. If there are any inconsistencies between the terms in the Mortgage Conditions and those contained in the Offer of Loan then the terms contained in the Offer of Loan will prevail.

By 'incorporate' what was meant was that the Conditions were to be *deemed* to incorporate the terms. A little oddly, the two sentences of the quoted passage would seem to be saying essentially the same thing.

---

1 The exact wording is not given in the judgment, but see paras 3 and 4.
2 Paragraph 35. Terms of this sort are almost universal, and they are puzzling. The first provision – that the loan is repayable almost on demand – would seem to make the others redundant. Conceivably the others are meant as back-up in case the first falls foul of consumer protection legislation. As against that, terms of this sort are used in non-consumer cases too.
3 Paragraph 6.

What did the court hold about the interest rate?

As to the question of the interest rate, the court said that there was no absolute inconsistency between the loan offer and the Mortgage Conditions. The former had the basic rule, and the latter had certain exceptions and qualifications which would apply in unusual circumstances. If this approach is right, it still leaves open the question of whether the interest that the lender chose to award itself, a rate far higher than had been agreed, did *in fact* 'reflect market conditions' etc. That factual question seems not to have been explored in the case. One wonders which side would have the burden of proof.

What did the court hold about the term of the loan?

More controversially, perhaps, the court took a similar approach to the question of the term. No doubt the offer of loan was for 25 years. Yet the offer also contemplated the possibility of earlier repayment;[1] and in any case 'a term of 25 years is a long time and it is unrealistic to suppose that during that period the lender had no right to terminate the mortgage'.[2] In the court's view, there was no absolute inconsistency in the documents so that, despite the terms of the loan offer, the lender could demand repayment on one month's notice.

Relationship of the two issues

Of the two issues, that about the term was the more important, in this sense, that even if an interest rate is contractually immutable, that means little if what is ostensibly a term loan is in substance not a term loan. If the debtor does not accept a higher interest rate, the lender can simply call up the loan.

Consumer-protection law?

What about consumer-protection legislation? This was a buy-to-let loan and, apparently, the lender took the approach outlined above only where customers had three or more buy-to-let loans 'and so were not regarded as "consumers"'.[3] The issue of consumer protection was not explored in the case. 'Consumer' is defined in the Consumer Rights Act 2015 as 'an individual acting for purposes that are wholly or mainly outside that individual's trade, business, craft or profession'.[4] Whether there is a financial-sector understanding as to which buy-to-let borrowers are and are not consumers, or whether the Financial Conduct Authority has rules or guidance on the issue, we have not been able to discover. Nothing is said about this in the case.[5]

In a case that was definitely a consumer case, what would the result have been? That would be a large subject which we will not enter into here, but will only say that it seems to us that there would indeed have been scope for

---

1　See in particular para 39.
2　Paragraph 40.
3　Paragraph 11.
4　Consumer Rights Act 2015 s 2.
5　The Mortgage Credit Directive Order, SI 2015/910, has provisions about buy-to-let loans and came fully into force on 21 March 2016: see p 78 above.

a challenge.[1] And of course documentation of the sort used in Mr Alexander's case is in widespread use in consumer lending for house purchase.

Reflections

We said earlier that we find the decision disturbing. By now it will be obvious why '25-year tracker mortgage at 1.99% over base' may be advertised in a bank's leaflets and its website, but in reality what that works out as may be 'repayable-on-demand loan at an interest rate of our choosing'. Clients who rely on their law agents to keep an eye on 'the legalities' should perhaps be warned.

Finally, we understand that the case is to go to the Court of Appeal.

BUILDING ON SOMEONE ELSE'S LAND

Introduction

It is rarely a good idea to build on someone else's land. Yet it occurs surprisingly often. Among the cases decided in 2015 are no fewer than four examples. The situation can come about in a number of ways. Sometimes it is because the boundaries between two properties are unclear, an ever-present danger in Sasine titles, especially in rural areas. Sometimes it is because the boundary fence is in the wrong place and so misleads. Sometimes again it is because the builder has not troubled to investigate the boundary line or, having investigated it, chooses to disregard it. Finally, building on another's land can come about because the other person consents to, or even encourages, the building project. In this last case, as we will see, it will usually be unwise to build without first obtaining a conveyance (or at least a lease) of the site.

Whatever the reasons, the actual building work tends to come in one of two forms. By far the more common is the minor encroachment: the building projects only to a small extent into the neighbour's property. But there can also be cases of major invasion, where all of the building is erected on the land of someone else. Both are illustrated in the case law from 2015 and both can give rise to serious legal difficulty. We consider each in turn.

Minor encroachment

'A proprietor is not allowed to encroach upon his neighbour's property even to the extent of driving a nail into it'.[2] The law, at least, is perfectly clear. But what is less clear is what should be done with encroachments if they occur. In theory, the neighbour is entitled to have the encroachment removed and the *status quo* restored. But in practice courts, in Scotland as elsewhere,[3] cannot always

---

1   The legislation on unfair terms in consumer contracts is now contained in the Consumer Rights Act 2015 (replacing the Unfair Terms in Consumer Contracts Regulations 1999, SI 1999/2083). See p 78 above.

2   *Leonard v Lindsay* (1886) 13 R 958, 964 per Lord Young. For encroachment in general, see K G C Reid, *The Law of Property in Scotland* (1996) paras 175–179.

3   For elsewhere, but with a particular focus on South Africa, see A J van der Walt, *The Law of Neighbours* (2010) ch 4.

bring themselves to order what may amount to the destruction of an expensive building merely because of some minor mistake as to the boundary line. There has been a growing tendency to award damages in place of removal, or even to award neither.

The leading modern case is *Anderson v Brattisanni's*, decided by the Inner House in 1978.[1] The defenders, who operated a fish-and-chip shop on the ground floor of a tenement, ran an external flue up the rear wall of the building. All the affected proprietors were consulted and offered no objection. The pursuer, a singular successor, raised an action seeking an order for the removal of the flue from his part of the wall. The court declined to order removal. This was in exercise of 'an equitable power in the court, in exceptional circumstances, to refuse enforcement of the proprietor's right'.[2] Three conditions were identified, all of which, it appears, must be met before the equitable power would be exercised:[3]

> [T]he court will have to be satisfied [1] that the encroachment was made in good faith in the belief that it was unobjectionable, [2] that it is inconsiderable and does not materially impair the proprietor in the enjoyment of his property, and [3] that its removal would cause to the encroacher a loss wholly disproportionate to the advantage which it would confer upon the proprietor.

The precise scope of the equitable power identified and applied in *Anderson v Brattisanni's* has been left unexplored in the almost 40 years since the case was decided. But famine has been followed by feast: in 2015 the court's power was considered in two separate cases.

One was straightforward. In *McLellan v J & D Pierce*[4] the pursuers were alerted to building works on the part of their neighbours which they suspected – and a surveyor's report confirmed – encroached to the extent of a few metres on to their property. Their solicitors wrote to the defenders asking them to stop work. The request was ignored. By this stage, a steel frame had already been erected, and the defenders now proceeded to roof it and then to complete the building.[5] The pursuers raised an action in which the second crave was:

> To grant an order requiring the defenders to reduce and demolish any buildings, erections or other constructions they have erected upon the pursuers' said properties all as shown delineated in red on the plans annexed as relative to the pursuers' land certificates … ; to reinstate the pursuers' lands to the condition they were in prior to said building works.

The defenders admitted the encroachment, but asked the court to exercise its equitable power to refuse an order for demolition. Unsurprisingly, the court refused. The defenders evidently failed the requirement of good faith, which was the first of the three requirements laid down in *Anderson v Brattisanni's*. Not only

---

1 1978 SLT (Notes) 42.
2 At p 43.
3 At p 43 (our numbering).
4 [2015] CSIH 80, 2015 GWD 37-594.
5 The defenders were equally cavalier in relation to planning consent and had to apply for retrospective consent after the building was completed.

had they continued with the work despite being warned of the encroachment, but they must be taken to have known the extent of their land all along because the titles of both parties were in the Land Register. Indeed it turned out that the defenders had attempted to buy from the pursuers back in 2006 the very land on which they had now encroached. The sheriff's decision was not challenged when the case came to be appealed, on other grounds, to the Inner House of the Court of Session.[1]

Munro v Finlayson[2] is a more difficult, and a more interesting, case. The encroachment was the construction of a driveway and yard on a small part of the pursuer's property. This had occurred a decade or so ago,[3] and apparently in good faith.[4] Unlike most encroachment cases, the pursuer was not seeking the removal of the works. On the contrary, he was content that the driveway should remain in place. What he sought was not the removal of the driveway, but the removal of the defenders from the driveway. Strictly, therefore, the case was concerned with trespass rather than with encroachment, although the lines between the two are blurred. As so often in encroachment cases, the encroachment in *Munro* was accompanied by trespass. What made the case unusual was that the pursuer did not seek the removal of the encroachment.

At first instance the sheriff chose to apply the equitable power as described in *Anderson v Brattisanni's*. No doubt the encroachment (and trespass) affected the rights of the pursuer. But this was nothing as compared to the loss to the defenders in the event that use of the driveway was denied. In the short term they would have to park on the other side of a busy trunk road. In the longer term they would have to spend considerable sums in creating a new driveway on their own property. That would be entirely disproportionate to the very marginal benefit, if any, to the pursuer.

The pursuer appealed to the sheriff principal.[5] The sheriff principal accepted that the court's equitable power could apply even where the pursuer's objection was not to an encroachment as such but to the defenders' continuing use of it. But the power was to be applied 'only sparingly and in exceptional circumstances'.[6] Three requirements had been laid down in *Anderson v Brattisanni's* (as already noted above). The sheriff had erred in his application of the second (that the encroachment was inconsiderable and did not materially impair the proprietor in the enjoyment of his property) in respect that he had looked to 'marginal benefit' rather than 'material impairment'.[7] On the evidence, it was clear that

---

1 The appeal failed. The main ground of appeal was that the sheriff's order, in response to crave 2, was insufficiently clear.
2 2015 SLT (Sh Ct) 123.
3 No argument, however, was made in respect of personal bar. The background to the original construction is unknown.
4 Thus satisfying the first of the three requirements laid down in *Anderson v Brattisanni's*.
5 Derek C W Pyle.
6 Paragraph 17. This paragraph contains a restatement of the principle in the form of a series of numbered points of which the most important is the last, which states that, in balancing the interests of the parties, 'future as well as past economic loss will be taken into account'.
7 Paragraph 22. In the sheriff's defence his remarks may have been directed at the third requirement rather than the second.

there *was* such material impairment of the pursuer's enjoyment. If the sheriff's decision was to stand, it would 'effectively prevent the pursuer from using the excepted land in any manner at all which would have the effect of impeding the defenders' right of access'.[1] Worse than that, it would involve 'the creation in anything other than name of an heritable and irredeemable servitude right of vehicular access over another's land. That, it seems to me, is a step too far in the context of a principle which should be applied only exceptionally and sparingly.'[2] The appeal was accordingly allowed, and the pursuer found entitled to exclude the defenders. In taking a narrow view of the court's equitable power the sheriff principal was doubtless influenced by the fact that the case was about the exclusion of people rather than the demolition of buildings.

Major encroachment

Some preliminaries

Minor encroachment is not the only possibility. Just occasionally, an entire building is built on land which belongs to someone else. Of course, such a thing can hardly happen by accident for, while encroachers might be unsure as to precise boundaries, they will at least know whether the site of a whole building is or is not theirs.[3] Furthermore, since whole buildings cannot be erected by stealth, the chances are that even the most negligent of owners will realise what is going on and either give his consent or consider the taking of preventative action. In other words, both parties – both builder and built-upon – will act, or omit to act, with their eyes open.

The response of property law is correspondingly uncompromising. Acceding to the land on which it is built, the building becomes the property of the owner of that land. And as the act of building does not confer a right of use any more than a right of ownership, the encroacher can use the building only if its owner is willing to let him. In such cases there is no scope for the kind of judicial discretion that is found in respect of minor encroachments. All of this leaves the encroacher at a serious disadvantage. If he is wise he will have some contractual arrangement in place with the owner of the land. If he is wiser still, he will have secured a transfer of the site. But if he has done neither, he is left at the mercy of the law of unjustified enrichment in his pursuit of a remedy.

From Barra to Sutton Coldfield

Insofar as there are typical examples of major encroachment, the new case of *Jones v Muir*[4] may perhaps be regarded as one. The scene is set by the sheriff principal:[5]

---

1 Paragraph 21.
2 Paragraph 20. It may be noted that since only ten years had passed, the possibility that a servitude might have been constituted by prescriptive usage (something that requires twenty years) did not arise.
3 However, a structure such as a wall might inadvertently be placed wholly within the boundary of neighbouring property.
4 2015 GWD 11-183.
5 Paragraph 1. The sheriff principal was Derek C W Pyle.

This unfortunate litigation involves a dispute between parents on the one part and their daughter and son-in-law on the other. It concerns an agreement reached among them for long term accommodation for the parents, doubtless in anticipation of their coming old age. In that spirit, the arrangements made did not have the legal clarity one would expect between parties unconnected to each other.

The daughter and son-in-law owned an acre of croft land in Barra, and lived in a bungalow on that land. With their agreement, the daughter's parents built a second house on the land at their own expense. The cost, around £60,000, represented most of their life savings. A transfer of property in the land seems never to have been on the cards, but the parents were to have a right and expectation of living in the house for the rest of their lives. In other words, the arrangement was in substance a liferent, or usufruct, in favour of the parents, with this vital distinction, that no real right of liferent or trust liferent was ever constituted.

Things did not work out as expected. Instead of living happily ever after, the family quarrelled and, only three months after the house's completion, the parents departed for Sutton Coldfield vowing never to return. In this action they sought to recover the open-market value of the house from the daughter and son-in-law on the grounds of unjustified enrichment.

By this stage both parties must have been ruing their failure to obtain legal advice and to draw up a contract in writing. For the parents, matters were particularly serious, for their life savings were tied up in a house which they did not own and which, for all practical purposes, they could not use. Yet if they succeeded in the action the result would hardly be fair to the other side. It is true that, in a sense, the daughter and son-in-law had been enriched. They now owned a house which, previously, they did not. But, as they already had a house, a second house was of no use to them unless they were willing to sell or let it to strangers, and that was something which they were not willing to contemplate.

To succeed in a claim for unjustified enrichment it is necessary to show (i) that the defenders have been enriched (ii) at the expense of the pursuers, and (iii) that the enrichment was unjustified.[1] In the present case, there was no difficulty as to (i) and (ii): the daughter and son-in-law had indeed been enriched, at least in a technical sense, and that enrichment was at the expense of the parents. The question to be determined was thus whether the enrichment was unjustified.

It was clear that there could be no recovery due to the mere fact of building. A person who builds a house knowing the land to be another's is assumed to have done so either for his own interests or as a donation.[2] Having acted with his eyes open he cannot now ask to be reimbursed. The law here is well settled.[3]

---

1 As the pursuers, indeed, so argued: see para 4.
2 The position is different where the building work was carried out in good faith, if indeed such a thing is possible: see R Evans-Jones, *Unjustified Enrichment, vol 2: Enrichment acquired in any other manner* (2013) paras 5.103–5.117.
3 This is enrichment by 'imposition' as opposed to enrichment by 'transfer' or by 'taking'. For a review of the authorities, see J Wolffe, 'Enrichment by improvements', in D Johnston and R Zimmermann (eds), *Unjustified Enrichment: Key Issues in Comparative Perspective* (2002) p 384 and especially pp 404–11; H L MacQueen, *Unjustified Enrichment* (3rd edn, 2013) pp 43–47.

In the present case, 'the pursuers built the bungalow because they wanted to live in it. That was an expression of their own interests'.[1]

The position might have been different if the money had been expended on the basis of some anticipated return which in the event did not occur. A claim would then arise on the basis of the *condictio causa data causa non secuta*.[2] A well-known example is *Shilliday v Smith*[3] in which the pursuer was able to recover money spent on improvements to a house in contemplation of a marriage to the defender (the house's owner), which did not take place. In the present case, however, the return *did* occur in the sense that the parents had an informal but apparently enforceable agreement which entitled them to live in the house.[4] No doubt that was an unattractive prospect even if – and here the evidence was disputed – the daughter and son-in-law were willing to have them back. But they had got what they bargained for, and if they chose not to take it up, that was a matter for them. What they could not do was abandon their contractual rights and recover in unjustified enrichment. The claim was accordingly rejected.

Holiday chalets and their removal

An altogether better attempt at preserving the position of those building on another's land can be found in the facts of *Van Lynden v Gilchrist*.[5] At issue was a holiday chalet, one of a number built on the Ballimore Estate, Otter Ferry, Argyll. The legal background was as follows. In 1969 the then estate owner granted a 31-year lease to a company. Among its terms was an obligation to build a number of holiday chalets. These were then to be sublet. The present dispute involved the sublease of chalet number 25, which was granted in 1970. This was to expire, with the head lease, on 1 March 2000. In terms of the sublease, the subtenant was to erect a chalet – referred to as a 'bungalow' – within a year. At the end of the sublease, he was then to have a range of options as to the chalet, which were set out in clause 15:

> On any termination of this sub-let otherwise than by the Sub-Tenant as aforesaid the Sub-Tenant shall be bound within one month from said termination to exercise one of the following three alternative options namely: — (Primo) to remove the said bungalow at his own expense, (Secundo) to call on the Company to purchase the said bungalow at a price of Three thousand five hundred pounds in which case the Company hereby binds and obliges itself so to purchase the said bungalow and to pay the price within one month or (Tertio) to call on the Company to act as his agent for the sale of the bungalow in which case the Company shall make reasonable endeavour

---

1 Paragraph 7.
2 This is enrichment by 'transfer': see generally R Evans-Jones, *Unjustified Enrichment, vol 1: Enrichment by Deliberate Conferral: Condictio* (2003) ch 4.
3 1998 SC 725.
4 Paragraph 6: 'The parties entered into a contract, the effect of which, whether they realised it or not, was that the bungalow would become the property of the defenders. The extent of the pursuers' rights under the contract was to occupy it for the remainder of their lives.' There is no indication from the report as to whether the contract was oral or in writing, whether it conferred entitlement to the formal grant of a liferent, and whether, if formality was required but was absent, there were sufficient actings for the operation of statutory personal bar (ie under s 1(3), (4) of the Requirements of Writing (Scotland) Act 1995).
5 [2015] CSOH 147, 2015 SLT 864.

to sell the said bungalow at the market price thereof to a purchaser acceptable as Sub-Tenant hereunder but the Sub-Tenant shall be bound to accept the terms of any such sale negotiated by the Company, and the Company shall be entitled to receive from the purchaser the price of the said bungalow and deduct therefrom a commission of eight per cent of the price thereafter within fourteen days accounting to the Sub-Tenant for the balance less any sums due hereunder by the Sub-Tenant.

The years passed and, when the subtenant died, the sublease was assigned to his son, Colin Gilchrist. Meanwhile the head lease also changed hands, coming ultimately to be held by Baron and Baroness van Lynden as trustees for the firm of Ballimore Farms. Finally, ownership of the estate also changed, the new owner being Baroness van Lynden.

On 1 March 2000 both the head lease and sublease came to an end, and a dispute arose as to the fate of the chalet. Mr Gilchrist wished to exercise his option under clause 15 of the sublease to remove the chalet – something which could, it seems, be done in sections and without the need for complete demolition. Baroness van Lynden resisted this claim, arguing that the chalet had acceded to the land and hence was her property. She raised an action against Mr Gilchrist in which she sought declarator that she was the chalet's owner, and interdict against dismantling or removing it. The action failed. According to the Lord Ordinary (Lord Philip), clause 15 conferred on the defender an option to remove the chalet which he was entitled to exercise. Insofar as the pursuer had property rights in the chalet, the terms of the head lease and sublease were such that she (and her predecessors) must be taken to have given them up.

At first sight, this victory for the defender looks like a triumph of good drafting, as well as an advertisement for the benefits of taking legal advice. Yet there are a number of things in the decision which seem open to question.

In the first place, it is unclear how a clause in a *sub*lease could bind the owner of the land. Such a clause was binding on the head landlord, of course; but while the pursuer, as well as being owner, was also one of the head landlords, this was merely as trustee for the firm of Ballimore Farms. The head lease, in other words, was held in a different (and trust) patrimony from the ownership of the land itself. And it was as owner, not as head landlord, that the pursuer was suing. As between subtenant and owner – between defender and pursuer – there was no privity of contract.[1] It appears, therefore, that the pursuer was not bound by clause 15 of the sublease.

Secondly, in the sublease the head landlord purported to create rights which it, the company, did not itself have. The only provision in the head lease about the fate of the chalet was that:

All buildings and works erected by the Tenants on the land shall be removed at the termination of this lease and the subjects of lease will be returned to the Proprietor in the condition in which they were received.

1 G C H Paton and J G S Cameron, *The Law of Landlord and Tenant in Scotland* (1967) p 168: 'There is no privity of contract between the principal landlord and the subtenant, and as a general rule no right of action lies between them arising out of the sublease as such.' See also A McAllister, *Scottish Law of Leases* (4th edn, 2013) para 7.34; R Rennie, *Leases* (2015) para 18-43.

But, as Lord Rutherfurd Clark put it in *Ferguson v Paul*,[1] a decision much relied on by the Lord Ordinary in *Van Lynden v Gilchrist*, 'an obligation to remove, if required by the landlord, does not … carry with it the implication that the tenant has a right to remove'.[2] And if the head landlord had no right to remove the chalet, it is unclear how he could create such a right in favour of the subtenant.

A complication – and this is the third point – was created by the involvement of successors. Even if it were to be accepted that the owner of Ballimore Estate was bound by clause 15 of the sublease, there was the difficulty that both owner and subtenant had changed. One way of dealing with the difficulty is to say that clause 15 was *inter naturalia* of the sublease and so binding on successors,[3] and that is certainly a possible view. The court, however, also saw merit in the application of the rule against offside goals:[4]

> I consider that there is force in counsel for the defender's argument based on *Stodart v Dalzell*.[5] His submission was that the defender's right of severance was capable of being made a real right and that the pursuer's knowledge of his right prior to her acquisition meant that it was valid against her. The right of severance was part and parcel of the right of property in the chalet conferred on Mr Gilchrist. That right of property has been made real by the defender's occupation of the chalet without challenge and he cannot now be denied the right of severance.

The idea of the defender having some kind of 'right of property' in the chalet is one to which we will need to return. For the moment it is only necessary to say that clause 15 did no more than give the pursuer an option, that the application of the offside goals rule to options is contested, and that it is hardly possible to discuss the matter without making reference to the two leading cases on the point, neither of which is mentioned in the Lord Ordinary's Opinion (or, it may be, in the arguments of counsel). The cases are *Advice Centre for Mortgages Ltd v McNicoll*[6] (which rejects the application of the offside goals rule to options) and *Gibson v Royal Bank of Scotland plc*[7] (which rather supports the application).

Fourthly, in terms of clause 15 of the sublease, the defender had a period of only one month in which to exercise whichever of the options he wished to select. Arguably, the clause did not require actual removal of the chalet within a month, although this is uncertain (at the time of the litigation the chalet was still in place), but the defender was bound at least to indicate which option he intended to pursue. This is consistent with the general law in respect of trade

---

1 (1885) 12 R 1222, 1229.
2 We do not therefore agree with the Lord Ordinary's view (at para 22) that 'since he [the owner of the land] had abandoned any right of property in the building, he had no right to prevent the defender, as subtenant and owner, removing it'. More is said below about the supposed abandonment of the right of property.
3 Although, as we have seen, not on the pursuer as owner of the land.
4 Paragraph 26. For the offside goals rule, see, eg, K G C Reid, *The Law of Property in Scotland* (1996) paras 695–700.
5 (1876) 4 R 236.
6 [2006] CSOH 58, 2006 SLT 591; for commentary, see *Conveyancing 2006* p 104.
7 [2009] CSOH 14, 2009 SLT 444; for commentary, see *Conveyancing 2009* pp 34–37.

fixtures, where the right of severance must be exercised either during the lease or within a short period of its termination.[1] There is no information from the report as to whether this tight timetable was complied with.

Finally, there is the question of ownership, which was the subject of the first of the pursuer's two conclusions. In the head lease it was provided that, following erection of the chalets, 'the tenants shall be entitled to sell houses to third parties (who shall become their sub-tenants in respect of the solum of each house) as tenants' improvements without granting title to the land upon which they stand'. The idea underlying this clause, that the landlord should own the land and the tenant the chalets, was given further expression in the sublease, clause 7 of which provided, succinctly, that 'the said bungalow shall be deemed to be an improvement to the subjects by the sub-tenant and shall remain the property of the sub-tenant'. The Lord Ordinary's analysis was as follows:[2]

> The question however arises, standing the law of accession, what is the extent of that right of property? In my opinion, what the head landlord intended was that the subtenant should have the right to occupy the chalet during the currency of the head lease, that he should retain ownership of the materials in the structure, and that he should be obliged to remove the chalet, and so retain ownership of the materials, at the termination of the head lease and the sublease.

It is implicit in the Lord Ordinary's Opinion that he regarded the head landlord's intentions as having been achieved.[3] This, however, may be doubted. Accession can neither be prevented nor undone by contract. In matters of accession the parties' intentions are simply not relevant.[4] 'Trade fixtures' – fixtures attached by a tenant but which are severable at the end of a lease – accede in the normal way notwithstanding their function or their necessarily temporary status.[5] In the course of argument, counsel for the defender conceded that accession had operated in respect of the chalet.[6] The concession was properly made. It is simply not possible for a building, or the materials in a building, to be in separate ownership from the land.[7]

---

1 Reid, *Law of Property* para 586.
2 Paragraph 23.
3 For example, at para 22 the Lord Ordinary states that the head landlord had 'abandoned any right of property in the building'. At para 26 he refers to 'the right of property in the chalet conferred on Mr Gilchrist'.
4 *Shetland Islands Council v BP Petroleum Development Ltd* 1990 SLT 82, 94 per Lord Cullen. If a tenant has a contractual right to remove (ie to sever) something, that does not mean that he already owns it.
5 *Brand's Trs v Brand's Trs* (1876) 3 R (HL) 16. This was a change from the previous law: for a full account, see K G C Reid, 'The Lord Chancellor's Fixtures' (1983) 28 *Journal of the Law Society of Scotland* 49. The Lord Ordinary in *Van Lynden v Gilchrist* may have been misled by Lord McLaren's view in *Ferguson v Paul* (1885) 12 R 1222, 1227, in respect of the exercise of the tenant's right of severance, that 'the materials then either revert to the tenant who brought them to the ground or they may be held to have remained vested in the tenant from the beginning, in consequence of the agreement that he should remove them'.
6 Paragraph 11.
7 Unless they are moveable, such as the curtains in a house. A limited exception for heritable property exists in the law of the tenement.

ELECTRONIC DELIVERY OF PAPER DOCUMENTS

Introduction

A unilateral document does not take effect until delivery.[1] In the case of electronic documents, delivery, naturally enough, is by electronic means.[2] But the position in respect of 'traditional' (ie paper or equivalent) documents has been a matter of controversy and uncertainty. The decision in *Park Ptrs (No 2)*,[3] in particular, had an unsettling effect on practice by holding that the faxing of a final letter of acceptance of missives did not, at least in the ordinary case, count as delivery of the letter; instead actual delivery, by hand or post, was needed in order for the contract to be concluded. These controversies and uncertainties are stilled by s 4 of the Legal Writings (Counterparts and Delivery) (Scotland) Act 2015. With effect from 1 July 2015[4] it has been competent to deliver a paper deed or document by electronic means.

The standard case: delivery of a copy of the document

In the standard case, what must be delivered is a copy of the document, by which is (presumably) meant the document in its signed form.[5] It would not, therefore, be sufficient to send the mere text of the document as a Word document. What is needed is an electronic reproduction of the document as signed, such as a scanned PDF or fax.

Once the copy has been made, it is transmitted electronically. Normally, that would be as an e-mail attachment, but s 4 leaves other possibilities open such as physical delivery of a DVD or memory stick or, in the interests of future-proofing, 'by other means but in a form which requires the use of electronic apparatus by the recipient to render the thing delivered intelligible'.[6]

Importantly, there is no absolute right to use electronic delivery. The default method, as before, is physical delivery of the document. The use of electronic delivery requires the agreement of the recipient, both as to the principle and as to the method of delivery in question – or, failing agreement (or if the agreed method proves impracticable),[7] that the electronic delivery employed 'is reasonable in all the circumstances'.[8] The recipient's agreement may not need to be specific to the particular document being sent. In the words of the Scottish Law Commission: 'If for example parties have an established practice of electronic

---

1   W W McBryde, *The Law of Contract in Scotland* (3rd edn, 2007) ch 4.
2   Requirements of Writing (Scotland) Act 1995 s 9F.
3   [2009] CSOH 122, 2009 SLT 871; for discussion, see *Conveyancing 2009* pp 85–89.
4   When the Act came into force: see Legal Writings (Counterparts and Delivery) (Scotland) Act 2015 (Commencement) Order 2015, SSI 2015/242.
5   Legal Writings (Counterparts and Delivery) (Scotland) Act 2015 s 4(2)(a).
6   LW(CD)(S)A 2015 s 4(9).
7   The Scottish Law Commission gives the example of the e-mail system having broken down or the recipient's inbox becoming inaccessible, in which case it would be reasonable to send the document by other electronic means such as fax: see *Report No 231 on Formation of Contract: Execution in Counterpart* (2013; available at www.scotlawcom.gov.uk) para 2.70.
8   LW(CD)(S)A 2015 s 4(4), (5). These provisions are modelled on RW(S)A 1995 s 9F(2): see Scottish Law Commission, *Report No 231* para 2.69.

communication between themselves in their dealings, it may be otiose to require them to agree that it be used in each specific transaction'.[1]

Potentially, electronic delivery is available for any conveyancing deed or document, and will be particularly attractive for missive letters. Deeds such as dispositions could also be delivered electronically, as a means of expediting settlement, but – as s 4(6) indeed makes clear – the electronic copy is not the deed itself and so could not be presented for registration. Electronic delivery is also very likely to be used for documents executed in counterpart.[2]

In guidance issued at the time s 4 came into force, the Law Society set out the steps which may in practice need to be taken:[3]

(1) agree in advance between parties' solicitors whether delivery of missives may be by fax, or e-mail attachment, or one of the other methods referred to in section 4(9) of the Act;

(2) agree in advance that on delivery of the document by electronic means, the original document (hard copy) will be forwarded on to the recipient thereafter;

(3) proceed to carry out the electronic delivery;

(4) check thereafter by fax receipt or e-mail read receipt or by physically contacting the recipient solicitors, that the document has been received by them;

(5) forward on the traditional document to the recipient solicitors as soon as possible after the electronic delivery has been carried out;

(6) if no agreement can be reached on the method of delivery then consider utilising the provisions of section 4(5) [allowing delivery by such means as is reasonable] although this may require some careful consideration.

Steps (2) and (5) are a reminder of the need to agree what is to happen to the document itself.[4] In the case of registrable conveyancing documents, at least, the arrangement is likely to be that electronic delivery is to be followed by physical delivery, although of course it is the former that counts as delivery in the legal sense. Physical delivery will always be needed for deeds which are to be registered.

If a deed that is to be registered is delivered *only* electronically, there seems to follow a juridical limbo in which there has been delivery but the delivery fails to attain its chief purpose. In such cases, we suggest, there would be an implied obligation of physical delivery, whether or not electronic delivery has happened.

A special case: delivery of a copy of part of the document

Section 4 gives the option of delivery of a copy of a part only of the document.[5] This is aimed at very long documents which it would be time-consuming, and

1 Scottish Law Commission, *Report No 231* para 2.70.
2 As to which see p 125 above.
3 Law Society of Scotland, *Professional Practice Updates: August 2015* (www.lawscot.org.uk/members/member-services/professional-practice/professional-practice-updates/).
4 LW(CD)(S)A 2015 s 4(7) offers a similar prompt and is without substantive effect.
5 LW(CD)(S)A 2015 s 4(2)(b). The words actually used ('a part of such a copy') seem the wrong way round, appearing to imply that an electronic copy must be made of the whole document out of which only a part will then be sent.

sometimes pointless, to scan or otherwise reproduce, or where the size of the attachment might overwhelm the parties' e-mail system.[1]

There are two qualifications. In the first place, either the intended recipient must agree that only part need be sent, or sending only part must be reasonable in all the circumstances.[2] Delivery by the sending of a part will be particularly attractive to parties who regularly transact together and have built up a relationship of trust such that they do not need to see the full document.[3]

In the second place, the part copied and sent must include the granter's signature and must also be 'sufficient in all the circumstances to show that it is part of the document'.[4] It is enough, therefore, to send only the signature page provided it is clear, from the accompanying text on the page or otherwise, that that page is part of the document in question. The Scottish Law Commission's gloss, however, does little to reassure those who fear the opportunities for fraud:[5]

> Showing that on the balance of probabilities the transmitted part was indeed part of the document actually subscribed by the sender must depend on all the circumstances: it may need as little as the fact that the signing party is designed in the document as one of the parties to it. It may also be by such means as the continuity of pagination between the master text and the sent part, or other uses of the header and footer sections of the whole document.

None of this seems to anchor the signature page very firmly to the rest of the document. Cautious or nervous recipients will want delivery of the full thing.

Finally, whilst the provision says that the whole document does not have to be sent, it is still necessary for the whole document to have been printed off and signed. That having been done, the earlier sheets can, it seems, be binned, especially in a case of execution in counterpart where the counterpart in question is not to form part of the final document.[6] It may be suspected that in practice the printing may not always happen. Whilst that would subvert the execution process, the fact might never come to light.

EXERCISING OPTIONS: THE IMPORTANCE OF WORDS

A party to a contract may sometimes have the benefit of an option. Familiar examples in the field of conveyancing include purchase options or rights

---

1 See eg Scottish Parliament: Delegated Powers and Law Reform Committee, *Stage 1 Report* (2014) para 122, quoting Colin MacNeill of Dickson Minto: 'It is a gross inconvenience to ask a company director to print off 100 pages at 2 o'clock in the morning and then rescan them all to send back, whereas printing off a single signature page to get the deal done is not an inconvenience.'
2 LW(CD)(S)A 2015 s 4(4), (5).
3 Scottish Law Commission, *Report No 231* para 2.76.
4 LW(CD)(S)A 2015 s 4(3).
5 Scottish Law Commission, *Report No 231* para 2.81. As to fraud, see the discussion in Scottish Parliament: Delegated Powers and Law Reform Committee, *Stage 1 Report* (2014) paras 106–129.
6 See p 130 above.

of pre-emption or break options in leases. In *Kinch Ltd v Adams*,[1] the option at stake was a more unusual one. When the purchase of a Glasgow coffee shop was being negotiated, the purchasing company, Kinch Ltd, nervous about funding, managed to include a clause in the missives which allowed it to withdraw from the contract without penalty (other than expenses) provided that this was done by 12 noon on 20 February 2014. Shortly before that date arrived, the purchaser's solicitors sent an e-mail to the seller's solicitors. It began as follows:

> I have received a remarkably long email from my client. In short, my client met with its accountants yesterday and were advised that the property should not be purchased by Kinch Ltd as per the current agreement but by Kinch Investments Ltd (08899815) (see attached). THUS, I understand that my client declines to consent to the missives by noon Thursday 20th February 2014 – although deliberations are ongoing. If certain questions (below) are satisfactorily answered and accepted by my client, new missive conditions could apply on a fresh agreement with my client after Thursday 20th February 2014 and could be signed as early as Thursday 6th March 2014 with an entry date of no later than Tuesday 6th May 2014.

Later the parties were in dispute as to whether, as the purchaser now maintained, this had amounted to a valid exercise of the option to withdraw.

For an option to be properly exercised, scrupulous regard must be paid to any requirements of form. As Lord Hoffmann put it in *Mannai Investment Co Ltd v Eagle Star Life Assurance Co Ltd*, if the clause 'said that the notice had to be on blue paper, it would have been no good serving a notice on pink paper'.[2] There was no requirement as to colour of paper in *Kinch Ltd v Adams*. Indeed there was no requirement as to paper at all. E-mail would do, and hence in sending an e-mail the purchaser was fully compliant in respect of matters of form.

But mere formal compliance is not enough. Care must also be taken with the words used in the notice. The law here has been set out in a number of cases of which *Mannai Investment* is the most important.[3] A flawless notice is not insisted on. But the notice must be clear to a reasonable recipient. The recipient must be left in no doubt that the option in question is being exercised.

How, then, did the notice in *Kinch Ltd v Adams* measure up? There were some obvious difficulties. In place of a direct statement of withdrawal was an account of what the purchaser's solicitor understood ('I understand') to be the client's intention. And what was understood was not that the purchaser withdraws from the contract but rather that the purchaser 'declines to consent to the missives'. This was, as the sheriff[4] pointed out, 'a most peculiar formulation'.[5] The sheriff continued:

---

1 2015 GWD 5-105.
2 [1997] AC 749, 776B. The case was about the exercise of a break option in a lease.
3 Others include *Ben Cleuch Estates Ltd v Scottish Enterprise* [2008] CSIH 1, 2008 SC 252 (*Conveyancing 2007* Case (47)).
4 Sheriff S Reid.
5 Paragraph 38.

Prima facie it is difficult to ascribe any sensible meaning to it. As at the date of the notice, the parties were already contractually bound by the missives. There was no scope or requirement for either party to intimate any form of declinature to consent. *Consensus in idem* had already been reached. Clause 3.6[1] confers a *locus poenitentiae* upon the pursuer. By exercising that right, the pursuer would not have been 'declining to consent' to the missives, but would, in law, have been resiling from a concluded agreement ... The use of the phrase 'declines to consent to the missives' is simply not apt to cover the power of withdrawal conferred by clause 3.6.

These infelicities of expression may already have been enough to invalidate the notice. But the matter was put beyond doubt by the rider, at the end of the same sentence, that 'deliberations are ongoing'. For if deliberations were indeed still continuing, then the notice could not be read as a statement of a final position. As the sheriff put it:[2]

[T]hose words are fatal to the pursuer's assertion that the notice operated as a clear and unambiguous communication of a present withdrawal from the missives ... [I]n my judgment, reading the notice as a whole, it bears to alert the defenders to little more than a current state of thinking on the part of the pursuer which is presently inconclusive, still subject to ongoing 'deliberations' and, logically, remains to be finalised.

Although *Kinch Ltd v Adams* does not make new law, it serves as a reminder of the need to take care with words. The words need not be perfect. That is to require too much of drafting which is often done in haste and without much reflection. And even careful drafting can often be shown to have flaws, at least with the benefit of time and hindsight. But the wording of the notice in *Kinch* fell far below what was needed for the task. Its conversational style was understandable in the context of an e-mail. A notice of withdrawal, however, must be more than a conversation.

FRAUD

Whether conveyancing fraud is becoming commoner would be hard to say without statistics and, as far as we know, statistics are not available. But our impression, and the impression of those we speak to, is that it is indeed becoming commoner, on both sides of the border.

For those who combine intelligence, business acumen, extensive knowledge of conveyancing practice,[3] and evil hearts, there is much money to be made. The fraudsters generally escape with their loot: arrests and convictions are rare.

There are several different types of conveyancing fraud. Here we mention two: setting up a fake law firm, and impersonation of an owner.

---

1 Ie the clause conferring the option to withdraw.
2 Paragraph 35.
3 Many fraudsters, and above all those who set up fake law firms, must have worked in law firms themselves.

Faking law firms

Schubert Murphy v The Law Society[1] was an English case, but the same horror story could happen here. Property in a London suburb, Hadley Wood,[2] was offered for sale, and Mr Kristofi[3] made a successful bid at a price of £735,000. His law firm, Messrs Schubert Murphy, was a genuine law firm. At that point the good news ends.

On 19 May 2010 contracts were exchanged, as the English say. Completion took place two days later, when Mr Kristofi received the keys, and the seller's law firm, Messrs Acorn Solicitors, received the price from Messrs Schubert Murphy. No sooner had the price been paid than Messrs Acorn Solicitors (despite the plural, a one-man firm) disappeared. And with the firm the money, all £735,000, also vanished. Neither the money, nor the man behind the firm, who went by the name of 'John Dobbs', was seen again. 'John Dobbs', of course, was a fake identity.[4] It may be worth mentioning that the fake firm was located nowhere near London, but in Rotherham, Yorkshire. Whether conveyancing fraudsters find advantages in operating at a distance from their victims we do not know.

As 'Mr Dobbs' vanished with the money, the seller's mortgage, which was with Lloyds TSB plc, was never paid off. The sum outstanding on the mortgage was £843,000, so that the property was in negative equity. Indeed, at the time of the sale to Mr Kristofi, Lloyds TSB was already in the final stages of enforcing the mortgage, and on 9 June 2010 an eviction notice was served.

Was the ostensible seller genuine? In other words, was he or she an innocent dupe of 'Mr Dobbs', and genuinely instructed the sale and signed the transfer document?[5] Or had 'Mr Dobbs' impersonated the owner? Information about this is lacking, but there is no suggestion that the ostensible seller was anything other than genuine. Thus it seems that Mr Kristofi did indeed, following completion, acquire ownership of the property. That was not his problem. His problem was that the property was subject to an undischarged mortgage, for a sum greater than the value of the property. What happened to the seller is not known.

A case such as this raises many legal issues. There is the seller's liability to the buyer for failing to give an unencumbered title. There is the possible liability of the buyer's law firm to the client for having failed to obtain an unencumbered title. There is the possible liability of the buyer's law firm to the buyer's lender

---

1 [2014] EWHC 4561 (QB), [2015] PNLR 15.
2 We have never visited Hadley Wood, but one day we must do so because it has some quality irresistible to fraudsters. Another fake law firm case, *Lloyds TSB Bank plc v Markandan & Uddin* [2012] EWCA Civ 65, [2012] 2 All ER 884, also involved a property there. For discussion of that case, see *Conveyancing 2012* pp 146 ff. Hadley Wood was also the base of super-fraudster Ketan Somaia, or 'King Con' as he came to be known: see eg www.theguardian.com/uk-news/2014/jun/13/tycoon-ketan-somaia-guilty-convicted-swindle.
3 That is the spelling given in the reported case. Some other sources have 'Christofi'.
4 The point is not quite clear, but there seems to have been a real solicitor of that name who was retired and whose identity the fraudster stole.
5 A TR1, corresponding to a disposition in Scots law.

for having wrongfully disbursed the mortgage funds.[1] There is the possible liability of the bank that operated the fraudster's account. In the present case, two of these came into play. Mr Kristofi sued Messrs Schubert Murphy, and eventually the case was settled, by the latter's insurer, at the sum of £500,000.[2] It also appears that the fake law firm's bank eventually paid something – the amount is not known – to Mr Kristofi.[3] So Mr Kristofi seems to have recovered most of his loss, but not all.[4] How matters were finally arranged between him and Lloyds TSB is not known.

The action as reported was, however, different. It was an action by the insurer, raised in the name of the insured, Messrs Schubert Murphy, seeking compensation from the Law Society of England and Wales. The basis of the action was that the Law Society had listed the fake law firm on its website, and that Messrs Schubert Murphy had checked the website before proceeding to deal with 'Acorn Solicitors'. The Law Society, pled the claimant, owed a duty of care to ensure that the information on its website was accurate. The case as reported was, in Scots terminology, about relevancy, and the result was that the action was held to be relevant. What happened thereafter we do not know. It should be noted that there was no suggestion that the Law Society was subject to strict liability: the claimants had to establish negligence. That would involve investigation as to how 'Mr Dobbs' had deceived the Law Society.[5]

One lesson from this case is to use the Law Society's 'find a solicitor' service in respect of unfamiliar law firms. This sort of check is not foolproof, as the case shows, but that is no reason not to do it. Of course, it takes a little time, and time is money. Criminals impose costs on everyone, not only on their direct victims.

If fake law firms have yet to arrive in Scotland, they presumably will in due course, though it may be hoped that, since the Scottish legal world is smaller than that of England, the fraud will be a bit harder. We say 'if' but in fact it has already happened, though seemingly not (so far) in conveyancing. In February 2015 the Law Society of Scotland put on its website a case in which an Edinburgh law firm, Capital Defence Lawyers, became subject to identity fraud when they found their details listed on a website for 'Carter Legal Associates'.[6]

---

1 This line of attack has been taken in a number of English cases such as: *Lloyds TSB Bank plc v Markandan & Uddin* [2012] EWCA Civ 65, [2012] 2 All ER 884; *Nationwide Building Society v Davisons Solicitors* [2012] EWCA Civ 1626, [2013] PNLR 12; *Ikbal v Sterling Law* [2013] EWHC 3291 (Ch), [2014] PNLR 9; *Santander UK v RA Legal Solicitors* [2014] EWCA Civ 183, [2014] PNLR 20. This did not happen here, perhaps because Mr Kristofi borrowed, not from a financial institution, but £400,000 from a brother and another £200,000 from a brother-in-law: *Daily Mail* 23 August 2010 (www.dailymail.co.uk/property/article-1305436/How-bogus-solicitors-robbed-735-000-Family-lose-fortune-dream-home-scam.html#ixzz3xFnoRi9z). Assuming that Mr Kristofi borrowed directly from these relations there would have been no *vinculum juris* between these lenders and Messrs Schubert Murphy, unlike the situation in normal residential loan-financing.
2 Paragraph 4. We do not know how this figure was arrived at.
3 Paragraph 4.
4 'He has substantially mitigated, although not entirely avoided, his loss': para 4.
5 Another English case in which a fake firm managed to obtain listing with the Law Society of England and Wales was *Nationwide Building Society v Davisons* [2012] EWCA Civ 1626, [2013] PNLR 12.
6 www.lawscot.org.uk/news/2015/02/fake-law-firms-on-the-rise/.

Impersonating owners

Background

A classic conveyancing scam is to impersonate the owner of property. The two usual ways of turning such an impersonation into money are (i) to sell the property to an unsuspecting buyer or (ii) to borrow from an unsuspecting lender on the strength of a security over the property. Impersonation requires fake ID. But fake ID can be bought. The better the ID, the higher the cost, but the rewards of these scams can be so great that paying a few thousand pounds is as nothing.

If sale is the objective, it will usually be necessary to obtain possession of the target property because otherwise there is the problem of how to show the property to prospective buyers. That presents a hurdle. By contrast, raising a secured loan can often be done without anyone visiting the property.[1] The solution as to possession is simple: look for a property that is on the rental market, and rent it. That will require fake ID and then, when the fraudster immediately thereafter begins to impersonate the owner, new and separate fake ID.

The more valuable the equity left in a property, the greater the profits. There is no point in going through the time-consuming business of impersonation, with all the attendant costs, if the equity is not worth much. So the fraudster needs to look out for properties that have no security over them. This means watching the rental properties that are coming on to the market and checking the Land Register for each. This must be quite an onerous business, given that most rental properties do in fact have standard securities over them; but it would be an unfair world if people did not have to work for their money.[2]

The scam can also work if there is a security, but the sum secured is small or nil. That fact, however, is not easy to discover. Of course, it can be found out once the impersonation is in place because the fraudster can contact the loan company, using the fake ID, though even then there are difficulties. The fraudster, however, wants to know the equity position *before* renting the property, ie before the second fake ID is in place. Thus in practice the existence of a standard security (or mortgage in England) is a fairly high degree of protection against impersonation. A law firm could even consider offering to a client renting out property the option (where there is no security in place anyway) of a nominal standard security in favour of the firm, as an anti-fraud device. Of course, costs would have to be weighed against benefits, and perhaps the idea is fanciful.

This problem of finding properties without a security does not exist in the fake law firm case. As seen above, Acorn Solicitors targeted a property that not only had a mortgage but in fact had no equity at all. So from that point of view, impersonating a law firm is easier than impersonating an owner. But as

---

1 See for instance *Cheshire Mortgage Corporation Ltd v Grandison* and *Blemain Finance Ltd v Balfour & Manson LLP* [2012] CSIH 66, 2013 SC 160 (conjoined cases), discussed in *Conveyancing 2011* pp 118 ff and *Conveyancing 2012* pp 150 ff.

2 Of course, the fraudster could forge a discharge of the security. But that is an extra hurdle, and in practice it seems not to happen in *this* type of fraud. Fraudsters ply their own trades, and whilst forging discharges happens, it happens in a different type of scam. Freddie Fraudster buys a property with a high-percentage loan, keeps up the monthly payments for six months, forges and registers a discharge, sells, and decamps.

against that, of course, setting up a fake law firm brings with it extra costs and an additional layer of necessary expertise.

The Max Hastings case

Max Hastings is a well-known figure, and his name hit the national news in December 2015 when an impersonation fraudster targeted a property owned by his wife. Hastings wrote a long piece about it in the *Daily Mail*,[1] and many other websites carried the story. There has been no litigation yet, as far as we know.

In broad terms, the scam was on the lines just described. Mrs Hastings owned a house in London, as an investment property.[2] It was mortgage-free. The existing tenants moved out in June 2015, and her agents promptly found another, who called himself 'Kevin Hafter'. His ID was fake. He paid the deposit and rent in cash. Almost as soon as he moved in he prepared to sell the house. But he had a problem: sex.

The owner of the target property was female, but he was male, so he would not be able to impersonate the owner directly. He therefore brought in an accomplice, a woman, who impersonated Mrs Hastings. It rather seems as if this was done without forgery: 'We learned' said Max Hastings, 'that a woman from Catford, South-East London, had changed her name to "Penelope Hastings" by deed poll. Having done this, she secured a passport declaring her to be "Penelope Hastings".' One would like to know more. For instance, the deed poll would have given her previous identity. Perhaps that previous identity was false. And one would like to know what happened with her application to the Passport Office, what address she gave, and so on. None of this information is available. But the woman seems not to have been careful: 'The Fraud Squad swiftly traced her to a prison cell, where she is serving a sentence for other offences.' Whether it was she who signed the transfer document, or whether she granted a power of attorney to 'Kevin Hafter', who then signed, is unclear, but the point matters little. Evidently she stayed in the background and it was 'Kevin Hafter' who carried out the sale in a practical sense.[3] Whilst the point is not clear in the on-line sources, we presume that it was he who made off with the money, or the bulk of it.

'Mr Hafter' marketed the property through a well-known firm of estate agents, and used a firm of licensed conveyancers for the legal side. A buyer was found. The transaction completed and the buyer paid the price, £1.35 million, which was never to be seen again.[4]

---

1 *Daily Mail* 12 December 2015 (www.dailymail.co.uk/news/article-3356929/The-thieves-stole-wife-s-house-sold-1-3million.html). The story as set out below is based on the *Daily Mail* account.
2 Inexplicably it was not in Hadley Wood.
3 When selling the property he said that the owner lived in Chicago. If she never showed her face but merely signed something, it is hard to see why he took the trouble to involve her at all. 'Mr Hafter' could have done it all by himself.
4 There is some indication in the *Daily Mail* story that the price was not paid by the buyer's firm to the firm of the bogus seller, but directly by the buyer to 'Mr Hafter' or 'Mrs Hastings': 'He has now vanished with a tax-free million-plus to spend after the young woman he duped paid the money into a Dubai bank account.' If that is so it adds another astonishing fact to the cairn of astonishing facts.

The next chapter of the story is equally remarkable but in a different way. When the firm of licensed conveyancers sought to register the buyer's title, HM Land Registry rejected the application. We have not been able to discover why.

What would have been the situation if the registration application had gone through? Probably the buyer would have obtained a good title,[1] and Mrs Hastings would probably have been paid compensation by HM Land Registry.[2] But because the registration application was rejected, Mrs Hastings remained owner, and the buyer suffered a loss which would not be compensated by HM Land Registry. Whether the buyer might have recourse against her own law firm, or the firm that acted for the fake seller, or anyone else,[3] is at present unclear.

'We were astounded', wrote Mr Hastings, 'to discover that a house could be "sold" without physical possession of the deeds. ... To a layman this seems crazy.' That statement probably does reflect how ordinary clients see matters. And another sentence: 'They set about marketing it, though I would have thought the simplest online check would have shown that the house had recently been let.' This may again reflect client expectations. But it is not what conveyancers or estate agents see themselves as having to check. In any event, there seems to be a muddle here: the fact that a property has been let does not prevent it from being sold. But it seems that non-lawyers may not understand that.

EXERCISE OF SERVITUDES – BY WHOM?

Grant v Cameron

First, some nostalgia. This annual book is based on a seminar which is presented to the legal profession in different parts of Scotland in January and early February of each year; and 2016 marks the twenty-fifth such seminar (although only the seventeenth annual book: the materials for the early years were not published and are now hard to get hold of). In thus celebrating our silver anniversary, we hope we may be forgiven for looking back to the (unpublished) booklet issued on the occasion of our first seminar, in 1992, which surveyed the conveyancing developments of 1991. On p 34 of that booklet can be found the following terse summary of the decision of Sheriff Principal R D Ireland QC in *Grant v Cameron*:

> [T]he defender's croft had a servitude of access 'for all purposes' over a road belonging to the pursuer. The defender turned his croft into a commercial retail concern, with the result that the road came to be used by the general public, but this was held to be within the terms of his grant and hence was not an increase on the burden on the servient tenement.

---

1 'If, on the entry of a person in the register as the proprietor of a legal estate, the legal estate would not otherwise be vested in him, it shall be deemed to be vested in him as a result of the registration': Land Registration Act 2002 s 58(1). This is the 'Midas touch.'
2 Land Registration Act 2002 sch 8 para 1.
3 The *Daily Mail* piece suggests that the letting agents who approved 'Mr Hafter' as a tenant may not have acted with sufficient care in checking his credentials. But even if that is so, it would be a long step to establish a duty of care owed to an eventual buyer.

The case was important because it was not – as it is still not – clear to what extent the holder of a servitude can invite others to make use of it. And our account was terse because we were relying on the brief summary of the case contained in *Greens Weekly Digest*;[1] in those pre-internet days it was much harder than it is today to lay hands on a copy of the full Opinion. A few years later Professor Roderick Paisley, whose sleuthing in pursuit of sheriff court decisions has enriched our annual seminars throughout the years,[2] did better, as he usually does. The Opinion in *Grant v Cameron* was tracked down and reproduced, with an erudite commentary, in the volume of *Unreported Property Cases from the Sheriff Courts* which he and Sheriff Douglas Cusine edited in 2000.[3] Armed, now, with the full Opinion, we can improve on our account of 25 years ago.

The defender, a Mr Angus Cameron, owned a croft house and croft land at Easter and Wester Achvraid in Flichity, Strathnairn. The pursuers were Sir Patrick and Lady Grant, the owners of Tomintoul House. Their complaint was that Mr Cameron had taken to advertising on Moray Firth Radio and in a local newspaper inviting the public to visit Achvraid Farm Nursery, situated on Mr Cameron's croft, at weekends from 10 am to 6 pm. The public were invited to 'take a run into the hills' to buy a variety of hardy plants and fresh vegetables, to view rare breeds of farm animals, to enjoy the scenery of the valley, and to take walks and roam over the hillside. Access to the croft was over a private road belonging to Sir Patrick and Lady Grant. Concerned at the threatened disruption to the solitude of their weekends, they sought interdict against the proposed use.

The servitude was contained in a feu disposition of 1983. This conferred:

A right of access for all purposes from the B851 public road to the boundary of the feu by the existing roadway coloured blue on the said plan subject to a liability to share in the maintenance and repair of the said roadway according to user along with the other parties making use of the said road …

The case turned on the meaning of 'for all purposes'. Did this confer an unrestricted right, including a right to the public at large, or did it, as the Grants argued, refer merely to the type of traffic that was permitted? The sheriff principal took an expansive view:[4]

The solicitor for the pursuers contended that the words 'all purposes' in the feu disposition referred to the purposes for which the road was to be used, namely for foot passage, animals, and carriages and was confined to what he described as 'personal' traffic as opposed to the unlimited traffic which would be attracted to the croft and in effect make it a place of public resort. I see no justification for reading the words 'all purposes' in such a narrow way and there is to my mind no distinction

1 1991 GWD 6-328.
2 Including this year. As well as *Reid v Aberdeen Cafe Co Ltd*, discussed below, Professor Paisley also found and tracked down the papers in four other cases: *Barton v McAllister* (Case (12)), *Gardner v Kerr* (Case (14)), *Fowlie v Watson* (Case (15)), and *Mitchell v Reilly* (Case (25)). None is on the Scottish Courts Website and all would have disappeared but for Professor Paisley's energetic pursuit.
3 R R M Paisley and D J Cusine (eds), *Unreported Property Cases from the Sheriff Courts* (2000) p 264.
4 *Unreported Property Cases* p 266.

between use of the road for 'personal' purposes and the use by the public in order
to gain access to the croft.

The interim interdict would therefore be recalled.

The underlying law

Except where the grant of servitude provides otherwise, the default rule seems
to be that servitudes can be exercised by (a) the owner of the dominant tenement;
(b) the owner's tenants and the holders of certain other subordinate real rights;
(c) the owner's family; and (d) an indeterminate range of other invitees including
visitors, whether personal or professional (such as friends, doctors and postmen).
The scope of (d) will vary from case to case. In their authoritative work on
Servitudes and Rights of Way, Cusine and Paisley write that 'the granter of a
servitude of access should expect much more use by third parties where a road
serves a shopping and leisure complex, compared with a house'.[1] But even the
former is unlikely to allow unlimited public rights. A servitude is not a public
right of way. And even on the wording in *Grant v Cameron* the sheriff principal
was careful to emphasise that 'there is no question of any grant of a right to the
public to use the road, as opposed to the grant of a mere licence for the purposes
of buying the defender's produce'.[2]

The default rule can, of course, be varied by the deed of servitude, although
relatively speaking this is unusual. In *Grant v Cameron* the effect of the wording
was to increase the *range* of those entitled to use the servitude although not, it is
thought, the *volume* of traffic which was permitted.[3] Different wording would have
a different effect. And if the range can be increased by express language, so also
it can be restricted. For an example of such restriction, however, it is necessary to
turn to another, and more recent, act of exhumation by Professor Paisley.

Reid v Aberdeen Cafe Co Ltd

If *Grant v Cameron* seems an elderly authority, it is a spritely youngster compared
to a case recently uncovered by Professor Paisley from the archives of the *Press
and Journal*. *Reid v Aberdeen Cafe Co Ltd* was decided in Aberdeen Sheriff Court on
22 February 1881. The sheriff substitute was John Dove Wilson, a distinguished
jurist who was later to hold a chair of law at Aberdeen University and to serve
as Storr's lecturer at Yale in 1895–96.[4] Thanks to Professor's Paisley's persistence,

1 D J Cusine and R R M Paisley, *Servitudes and Rights of Way* (1998) para 1.60.
2 *Unreported Property Cases* p 266.
3 This, however, is uncertain. The sheriff principal was plainly enthused by the decision of the
   House of Lords in *Alvis v Harrison* 1991 SLT 64, another decision of 1990 which found space in
   our first annual volume. For a discussion by Paisley and Cusine, see *Unreported Property Cases*
   pp 267–68.
4 See A H Millar (revised R Shiels), 'Wilson, John Dove (1833–1908)', in *Oxford Dictionary of National
   Biography* (2004) vol 59, 605–06. Some of the Storr's Lectures were published and repay study: see
   J Dove Wilson, 'Historical development of Scots law' (1896) 8 *Juridical Review* 297; 'The reception
   of the Roman law in Scotland' (1897) 9 *Juridical Review* 361. Having been a student in Berlin as a
   young man, Dove Wilson returned to Germany in the 1890s to study Roman law at Leipzig and
   was responsible for reviving its teaching at Aberdeen University.

the case appears in *Greens Weekly Digest* for 2015,[1] and the full Opinion is now available on Westlaw. It is thus, in a sense, a case of 2015.

The case concerned a temperance café and associated lecture rooms in Aberdeen, a city well known for its hostility to alcoholic refreshment. The premises were accessed from Union Street by a private lane known as The Adelphi, over which there was a servitude of way.[2] The servitude had been granted in 1822 and gave the 'liberty and privilege' of passage to 'disponees and tenants, but to no other persons'. In the action, the owner of the servient tenement, Miss Agnes Reid, sought a declarator that the access could be used only by the owners of the café and their tenants.

Professor Paisley has researched the back story.[3] It appears that Miss Reid was put up to the action by the owners of a number of pubs who previously had had their licences objected to by the temperance café. The café managers had run an aggressive and successful campaign to stop workers in Aberdeen having to go to premises selling alcohol if they wanted a meal and so had broken the monopoly of the bar owners. In revenge, the publicans had conducted a title investigation and then sought the assistance of Miss Reid as owner of the servient tenement in the access to the café. The evident aim was to put the café out of business.[4]

Given the restrictive terms of the servitude, it is hardly surprising that the action succeeded. As Sheriff Dove Wilson explained:

> The defenders' right being one of servitude, it falls, in a question with the pursuers' right, which is one of property, to be strictly construed. ... The words defining the persons who could use the servitude are 'the disponees and their tenants, but no others'. The words are thus taxative, and limit the use to those only who may fairly fall within the definition of 'disponees or tenants'. The visitors to the cafe or lecture rooms cannot come under the first alternative and it would only be through a forced construction that they could be brought under the second. The word 'tenants' may possibly be held to be used in the titles in a popular and wide sense, and it might easily be held to include the members of the tenants' families and their servants, or even others staying in the house, but it would be difficult to get much beyond this latitude, and to make them cover the use of the servitude for everybody whom the owners chose to invite or induce to come upon their premises. Such a construction would seem to be clearly beyond what was intended, and no possible latitude given to the word 'tenants' could include within it such a multitude.

1 2015 GWD 12-205. It is also mentioned briefly in R R M Paisley, 'The demon drink and the straight and narrow way: the expansion and limitation of praedial servitudes', in H Mostert and M J de Waal (eds), *Essays in Honour of C G van der Merwe* (2011) 193, 212–13.
2 For the Adelphi, see http://mcjazz.f2s.com/AdelphiCourt.htm. The name is taken from that of the Adelphi in London, located off The Strand. The London Adelphi was laid out by the brothers John and Robert Adam and the name commemorates this relationship: Adelphi is Greek for 'brothers'.
3 We are grateful to him for sharing the results with us.
4 From the report, however, it seems that the café had a frontage to the street, which would have allowed access in that way. It was for this reason that the sheriff substitute ruled out the possibility of an implied servitude.

The decision had an unexpected sequel.[1] Having confirmed that she had what we would call today a ransom strip, Miss Reid decided to cash it in by allowing the café to acquire from her a servitude sufficiently broad to allow public access. So the owners of the café in *Reid v Aberdeen Cafe Co Ltd*, no less than the owner of the nursery in *Grant v Cameron*, finished up with a servitude which allowed access by the public at large.

Access rights under the Land Reform (Scotland) Act 2003

To some extent, these battles of the past have been overtaken by the access rights conferred on the public at large by part 1 of the Land Reform (Scotland) Act 2003. But only to some extent. Statutory access rights are subject to important limitations. They cannot, for example, be exercised by motorised vehicles.[2] Nor can access be taken so close to a house as to interfere with privacy.[3] Today, statutory access rights might come to the assistance of the patrons of the Aberdeen temperance café, at least if the access was sufficiently distant from Miss Reid's house and if the café still existed, which it does not.[4] It would do nothing for the bucolic motorists seeking the balm of the hardy plants, rare breeds of animal, and open countryside offered by Mr Cameron's croft.

BUYING FROM A DISCHARGED BANKRUPT

Background

Introduction

Buying from a trustee in sequestration is one thing. Buying from an undischarged bankrupt is something very different, and obviously the basic advice is simple: don't – except with the concurrence of the trustee in sequestration. But what about buying from a *discharged* bankrupt?[5] The law in this area is by no means straightforward.

The twin cases of *Fortune's Tr v Medwin Investments Ltd*[6] and *Fortune's Tr v Cooper Watson Ltd*[7] have clarified, and perhaps even changed, one aspect of the law. The two cases involved essentially similar facts, and the parties were represented by the same advocates in each case and were heard by the same judge (Lord Jones), who issued virtually the same Opinions in each, so for all practical purposes they can be regarded as a single case. But before we can reach the facts of *Fortune*, some legal background is necessary.

---

1 Again we are grateful to Professor Paisley for the information.
2 Land Reform (Scotland) Act 2003 s 9(f).
3 LR(S)A 2003 ss 6(1)(b)(iv), 7(5). The leading case is *Gloag v Perth and Kinross Council* 2007 SCLR 530, discussed in *Conveyancing 2007* pp 127–35.
4 Professor Paisley tells us that it is now a warehouse.
5 Or transacting in other ways, such as taking a standard security or other subordinate real right.
6 [2015] CSOH 139, 2015 GWD 34-552.
7 [2015] CSOH 140, 2015 GWD 34-553.

Vesting in the trustee in sequestration

When someone is sequestrated, the whole estate is vested in the trustee.[1] But that does not necessarily mean that the trustee in sequestration immediately obtains a completed title. Whether that is so, depends on the type of property in question. For corporeal moveables, the trustee does receive a completed title. The same is true for monetary claims, so that if, for instance, John Smith owes the bankrupt £10,000, that claim is fully vested in the trustee, even without intimation. But for property held on registered title, most obviously land, the position is different.[2]

For land, the sequestration operates as a general conveyance in favour of the trustee. It is powerful in that it conveys *all* heritable property, without the need to specify what property the debtor in fact has, but it is not exempt from the basic principle of land law: no real right until registration. The real right of ownership – *dominium* – remains, for the time being, in the debtor. That does not mean that the immediate 'vesting' of the heritable property is without effect. Far from it. The trustee acquires the right to control and deal with the property. The trustee is an uninfeft proprietor (or, to use the correct term since feudal abolition, the unregistered holder), and can, as such, either complete title in his or her own name as trustee, or dispone (without first completing title) to a purchaser.[3]

It might be supposed that trustees in sequestration will do one or other of these things fairly swiftly, so that the period during which the bankrupt still has the real right of ownership of the heritable property will be brief. Whilst we know of no statistics on the point, our impression is that in fact trustees in sequestration are often strangely inactive, ie for substantial periods – even years – they neither sell the heritable property nor complete a title to it in their own name. Why this should be, we do not know.

Protection against dealings by the debtor

Since the sequestration does not, in and of itself, deprive the debtor of the real right of ownership of heritable property, and since the period during which title is still held by the debtor may, as just mentioned, be a substantial one, what is to stop the debtor from dealing with such property, most obviously by selling it?[4] The 1985 Act has two provisions that bear on this issue. One is s 32(8), which says that 'any dealing of or with the debtor relating to his estate vested in the trustee ... shall be of no effect in a question with the trustee'. The other is

---

1 Bankruptcy (Scotland) Act 1985 s 31. This and other references given below are likely to change soon because a Bankruptcy (Scotland) Bill is currently before the Scottish Parliament, to repeal and replace the 1985 Act. It is, however, a consolidation measure, meaning that no substantive changes to the law should ensue. For instance, whilst the wording of the proposed s 78 of the Bill differs somewhat from s 31 of the 1985 Act, the differences are not material. The same is true of other provisions of the 1985 Act that are mentioned in *Fortune*.

2 Other examples of registered property include ships, company shares, patents etc. The rules about completion of title to such assets cannot be entered into here.

3 Until the Bankruptcy and Diligence etc (Scotland) Act 2007 the trustee could do either, immediately. That Act added two subsections into s 31 of the 1985 Act (s 31(1A) and (1B)) whereby the trustee must wait at least 28 days. This is an issue to which we return later.

4 That is to say, selling without the trustee's consent. A sale with the trustee's consent would be unobjectionable.

s 14. This says that the sheriff clerk or (depending on the circumstances of the case) the Accountant in Bankruptcy must 'forthwith' send to the Keeper a notice about the sequestration for recording in the Register of Inhibitions, such recording having 'the effect as from the date of sequestration of an inhibition'.[1] Although these two provisions to some extent overlap, the first is wide in its scope whereas the second is relevant only to heritable property and, more specifically, only to such dealings as would be affected by an inhibition. Moreover, there may be differences as to consequences. Transactions in breach of inhibition are not void but voidable, but the consequences of breach of s 32(8) may be voidness. Authority on these issues is spare, and whilst the *Fortune* case mentions the link between s 14 and s 32(8), it does not, we think, shed much light on the matter.

Section 14 and the deemed inhibition

For the time being we focus on the deemed inhibition that arises from a s 14 notice, which tends to be more important in practice than s 32(8), at any rate as far as heritable property is concerned, and which was central to the *Fortune* litigation.

The deemed-inhibition effect lasts for three years.[2] Within that time the trustee should normally have dealt with the heritable property. Nevertheless, the legislation allows the s 14 notice to be extended by a new recording, this lasting for a further three years.[3]

What if the trustee forgets to record a notice of renewal – and there is still unrealised heritable property in the estate to which the trustee has not completed title? This may seem unlikely, but, likely or not, it is a situation addressed by a specific statutory provision. Section 44(4) of the Conveyancing (Scotland) Act 1924 says:

> No deed, decree, instrument or writing granted or expede by a person whose estates have been sequestrated under the Bankruptcy (Scotland) Act 1856, or the Bankruptcy (Scotland) Act 1913 or the Bankruptcy (Scotland) Act 1985 … shall be challengeable or denied effect on the ground of such sequestration if such deed, decree, instrument or writing shall have been granted or expede, or shall come into operation at a date when the effect of recording … under subsection (1)(a) of section 14 of the Bankruptcy (Scotland) Act 1985 the certified copy of an order shall have expired by virtue of subsection (3) of that section, unless the trustees in such sequestration shall before the recording of such deed, decree, instrument or writing in the appropriate Register of Sasines have completed title to such land, lease or heritable security by recording the same in such register …

Fortune was to a large extent about this provision.

---

1 The notice may (depending on the circumstances) be either (i) a notice that sequestration has been ordered or (ii) a notice that there is a pending sequestration petition, the outcome of which is, as yet, undecided. Thus the appearance in the Register of Inhibitions of a s 14 notice does not necessarily mean that the person in question has been or will be sequestrated.
2 Bankruptcy (Scotland) Act 1985 s 14(3).
3 B(S)A 1985 s 14(4). For discussion of how these periods are to be calculated, see W W McBryde, *Bankruptcy* (2nd edn 1995) para 5-36.

The litigation in *Fortune*

The facts

Mr Fortune was sequestrated in December 2010. His estate was substantial, and included at least twelve heritable properties. In March and April 2014 Mr Fortune (i) granted standard securities over four of these properties to Medwin Investments Ltd, (ii) granted dispositions in respect of another three to the same company, and (iii) granted dispositions of another five properties to Cooper Watson Ltd. All these deeds were registered in the Land Register. What Mr Fortune's relationship with these companies was is not clear, but we know that the narrative clauses in the dispositions to Cooper Watson Ltd were 'certain good and onerous causes', 'certain good causes and no consideration', and 'certain good causes'.[1] None of these properties had previously been sold by the trustee in sequestration. In these actions the trustee in sequestration sought reduction of the various deeds.

Assuming that Mr Fortune had by then been discharged, which seems probable, was there anything untoward in his transacting with the properties? It is sometimes supposed that the discharge of a bankrupt reinvests him or her in any unrealised property. That is not so. Subject to one or two qualifications,[2] the estate as at the date of sequestration, plus any estate acquired after that date but before discharge, remains subject to the sequestration and remains realisable by the trustee. Whether Mr Fortune knew this is unclear. He might have assumed that, since he was discharged,[3] and since the years had passed without the trustee in sequestration having sold the properties, they were now his to do with as he chose.

Given that Mr Fortune ought not to have been transacting with these properties,[4] how was it that he was ostensibly able to do so? Had a s 14 notice been recorded in the Register of Inhibitions, in December 2010, as the legislation says must be done 'forthwith'? Had there been a renewal in December 2013? Had the trustee completed title? The surprising answer to these questions is: no, and no, and no. But although the notice was not recorded in the Register of Inhibitions in December 2010, as it should have been, it was eventually so recorded in February 2014.[5] That created a logical puzzle. A s 14 notice expires,

---

1 Paragraph 2. (All references, including this one, to the *Fortune* cases are references to both cases, the judgments being practically identical.) The second of these formulae was used for three of the deeds. No information about the cause of granting is known about the other dispositions, or about the standard securities.

2 One of which is in s 39A of the B(S)A 1985, which is about property that is the debtor's home. One of the properties may have been Mr Fortune's home, but the rest cannot have been within the scope of s 39A. In any event, s 39A was not invoked by the defenders. Another possibility is what is called abandonment. Given the time that had passed, the possibility that the properties had been abandoned by the trustee (and hence at Mr Fortune's disposal once again) is an interesting one. But the defenders did not seek to plead abandonment.

3 As mentioned above, however, the case does not say expressly whether Mr Fortune had been discharged. We assume that he had been: it would only be in very unusual circumstances that a person sequestrated in December 2010 would still be undischarged by March 2014.

4 Other than with the trustee's concurrence, which did not happen.

5 The date of recording seems to have been the subject of some confusion (see in particular para 9), but the court finally concluded that the notice was recorded in February 2014: see para 26.

not three years from the date that it is recorded, but three years from the date of sequestration.[1] So the notice recorded in February 2014 expired in December 2013: it was, so to say, born expired. This extraordinary situation could never have been contemplated by those who drafted either the bankruptcy legislation or s 44 of the Conveyancing (Scotland) Act 1924.

Arguments for the defenders

The defenders were the grantees of the dispositions and standard securities. Their case was mainly based, unsurprisingly, on s 44(4) of the Conveyancing (Scotland) Act 1924 (quoted above). The Lord Ordinary[2] rejected this argument. The precise *ratio decidendi* in this respect may perhaps be open to some debate but we would identify two aspects. One is that s 44(4) protects a grantee from an expired notice. Here the notice, having been 'born expired', had never validly existed at all, with the result that the s 44(4) protection was never engaged.[3] The other is that s 44(4) protects grantees from challenge 'on the ground of such sequestration' and in the view of the Lord Ordinary there existed a challenge that was not 'on the ground of such sequestration', namely the 'offside goals' challenge: we discuss this further below.

The position taken by the Lord Ordinary on the first point might perhaps be questioned.[4] It seems to mean that grantees may be worse off without a s 14 notice than with one. For if there is a s 14 notice, grantees may eventually obtain the shelter of s 44(4) of the 1924 Act, but if there is no s 14 notice, grantees can never obtain that shelter. If that is what is being said, it might be criticised as a little topsy-turvy.

The defenders also argued that the effect of s 44(4) was to terminate the vesting of the properties in the trustee.[5] The Lord Ordinary had no difficulty rejecting this argument, surely correctly. Where s 44(4) operates to protect a grantee, the effect will be that that particular property will cease to be part of the sequestrated estate,[6] but that happens only on a property-by-property basis and only as and when a deed is registered. It is surely clear beyond peradventure that s 44(4) could have no further effect than that.

Arguments for the trustee

The trustee argued that 'Mr Fortune had "no title" to dispone the properties ... Therefore, the dispositions are voidable.'[7] We do not find this easy to follow. If Mr Fortune had no title, the consequences would, presumably, not have been that the deeds would have been voidable but that they would have been void.

---

1 This is clear from s 14. In the normal case the issue is of limited significance, because in the normal case the notice will be recorded 'forthwith' as required by the legislation.
2 Lord Jones.
3 See in particular paras 20 and 21.
4 If we have understood it correctly, which we may not have.
5 Paragraph 27.
6 Assuming that the deed is a disposition. If the deed creates a subordinate real right, the effect of s 44(4) is that the property would remain part of the sequestrated estate but subject to the subordinate real right.
7 Paragraph 11.

But in any event Mr Fortune was and continued to be the heritable proprietor of the properties (a fact due to the inaction of the pursuer).

The trustee also argued that s 32(8) of the 1985 Act ('any dealing of or with the debtor relating to his estate vested in the trustee ... shall be of no effect in a question with the trustee') applied so as to invalidate the deeds. As mentioned above, there is a considerable overlap between that provision and the deemed-inhibition effect conferred by a s 14 notice.[1] Where s 44(4) of the 1924 Act applies, it will, we think, protect the grantee from both s 14 and s 32(4) of the 1985 Act. If that is right, and if the Lord Ordinary was right in his view that the grantees were not protected by s 44(4), it would seem to follow that the trustee should have won on the s 32(8) argument. But as far as we can see that conclusion was not drawn. The precise meaning and scope of s 32(8) have long been uncertain, and despite the *Fortune* case that may continue to be so.

The argument that ultimately won the twin actions for the trustee was that the deeds were 'offside goals'. The offside goals rule is, roughly speaking, that if X has a personal right to acquire property from Y, and Y wrongfully conveys to Z, and Z knows about X's prior personal right, then Z's title is voidable at X's instance.[2] As applied to the facts of the *Fortune* case, the Lord Ordinary took the view that the trustee had a personal right to acquire the various properties, that the deeds by Mr Fortune to the two companies were wrongful, that the two companies were aware of the trustee's rights, and that accordingly the various deeds were all offside goals and thus voidable at the trustee's instance.

In itself this is a strong argument. If it has a weakness it would seem to lie in s 44(4). That provision says that deeds may not be challenged 'on the ground of such sequestration'. But the offside goals rule argument here is based four-square on 'the ground' of the sequestration. It is precisely because of the sequestration that the offside goals rule is applicable.[3] So s 44(4) would seem to exclude the offside goals rule.[4]

The trustee also argued that s 44(4) was inapplicable for another reason: 'Parliament intended that s 44(4)(c) should operate for the protection only of parties acting in good faith.'[5] This is surely stateable, and, if sound, would presumably have been enough to win the case for the trustee without reference to the offside goals rule. But as far as we can see it was not one of the reasons that the Lord Ordinary gave for rejecting the applicability of s 44(4).

Some conclusions

There are such thickets of detail in this case that one can lose sense of direction. So here are one or two attempts to draw some overall conclusions.

---

1 The Lord Ordinary at paras 35 and 36 discusses how s 14 and s 32(8) can be, as he puts it, 'reconciled', but what is said is perhaps too brief.
2 See eg K G C Reid, *The Law of Property in Scotland* (1995) paras 695 ff.
3 The Lord Ordinary takes a different view (para 28) but we do not see on what basis.
4 Of course, as indicated above, the Lord Ordinary considers s 44(4) not to have been engaged because of the 'expiry' issue, but as mentioned we are not wholly persuaded by that argument.
5 Paragraph 13.

In the first place, the case decides, for the first time, that someone acquiring property from a discharged bankrupt will obtain only a voidable title if aware that the property was part of the sequestrated estate, regardless of whether a s 14 notice is in place. That result is in itself a reasonable one, but whether it is what was intended by those responsible for s 14 of the 1985 Act and s 44(4) of the 1924 Act seems far from certain.

In the second place, it is unfortunate that the trustee overlooked the requirement to record a s 14 notice 'forthwith', especially in a case where the sequestrated estate contained numerous heritable properties. How often this failure takes place we do not know for there are, we think, no statistics available, but from anecdotal evidence we believe that the failure is by no means rare. That seems unacceptable.

In the third place, the statutory rules[1] about the interim protection of the estate, ie protection against unauthorised dealings by the debtor (whether undischarged or discharged), do not come out of this case with flying colours. It is not clear why there are two rules rather than one. It is not clear how the two rules relate to each other. It is not clear what the consequences are of a breach of the rule in s 32(8). It is doubtful whether a deemed inhibition is technically a good method of providing interim protection. And the scope of s 44(4) of the 1924 Act is less than clear. Some good-quality technical law reform is needed.

Lastly, the Lord Ordinary makes a point which has, we think, not been noticed before.[2] The Bankruptcy and Diligence etc (Scotland) Act 2007[3] amended s 31 of the 1985 Act so as to ensure that the trustee cannot immediately sell or complete title in his or her own name. The reason for this amendment was to protect buyers (and other grantees) from being wrong-footed by the unexpected sequestration of a seller (etc) before the buyer (etc) can complete title. The amendment imposed on the trustee a 28-day handicap,[4] during which time the trustee could neither sell nor complete title.[5] This 28-day protected period runs from the date of the recording of the s 14 notice. That means that, if no s 14 notice is recorded, the handicap stays in place. That in itself is an interesting and important point. But matters may go even further. What if (as in *Fortune*) no s 14 notice is recorded within the three-year period beginning with the date of sequestration? If that means that no s 14 notice can be recorded thereafter (which is at least one interpretation of the decision in *Fortune*), the trustee would face a major problem, being unable either to complete title or to dispone to a buyer. We do not say that that would definitely be the result, but there is certainly an argument that it would be the result. It was not an argument, however, that the defenders in *Fortune* sought to run.

1　That is to say ss 14 and s 32(8) of the 1985 Act. We call them 'interim' because they become irrelevant once the trustee has sold, or has completed title in his or her own name.
2　Paragraph 10.
3　Section 17.
4　The change derived from the proposals in Scottish Law Commission, *Discussion Paper No 114 on Sharp v Thomson* (2001).
5　Buyers (etc) now have the possibility of further protection through an advance notice.

TENEMENTS AND OTHER DEVELOPMENTS

Common parts: repairs or alterations?

In flatted properties some owners may be keener on change than others. That was the position at 4–8 Cleveden Road, Glasgow, a villa which had been divided into four flats. The owner of one of the flats carried out a number of 'improvements' to the common parts. In particular, he –

- changed the back doorway at the rear of the house;
- changed the exterior lighting at the rear;
- painted the interior passage in a different colour;
- removed a light switch from the passage and replaced it with a sensor and a blank light switch plate; and
- affixed CCTV cameras to the outside walls at the rear.

In carrying out this work he had the consent of the owners of two of the other flats. The owner of the fourth flat, who was often abroad and could be difficult to contact, did not give his consent.

When disputes arise in respect of works carried out in tenements, the issue is usually about who is to pay. In the present case, however, the objection was more fundamental. As the owner of the fourth flat had not agreed to the works, they should not, in his opinion, have been carried out at all. Accordingly, he raised an action in which he sought to interdict the improving owner from carrying out alterations or modifications to the common parts and ordaining him to remove the CCTV cameras and replace the light switch. The case is *Mitchell v Reilly*.[1]

The improving owner had two main defences.[2] The first was concerned with the title conditions affecting each of the flats. These allowed the owners of a majority of the flats to decide what mutual repairs were needed, and to carry the repairs out. In the present case, the necessary majority had been obtained. Therefore, said the defender, the work was lawfully done.

As so stated, this defence had an obvious weakness. Majority decision-making was permitted only in respect of 'repairs'. But most or all of the work went further than that. 'It is important to note', said the sheriff,[3] 'the difference between alterations and modifications on the one hand and repairs on the other hand. In my view the former alter in some way the nature or condition of something … while repairs return it to its original nature'.[4] Which of these categories applied to the defender's works? Most were clearly of the nature of

---

1 11 July 2006, Glasgow Sheriff Court. Although decided almost a decade ago, this case has only just come to our attention. We are grateful to Professor R R M Paisley for tracking down the judgment.

2 There were three others, all weak, and all dismissed by the sheriff. These were (i) that the alterations were *de minimis*; (ii) that the common-law principle requiring unanimity in respect of common property had been displaced, for tenements, by ss 4 and 7 of the Tenements (Scotland) Act 2004; and (iii) that requiring the improvements to be removed was an interference with the defender's right to the peaceful enjoyment of his property conferred by art 1 Protocol 1 of the European Convention on Human Rights.

3 Sheriff P Bowman.

4 Transcript p 5.

alterations rather than simple repairs; only the repainting seemed classifiable as a repair. Not even this was allowed by the sheriff, however. In the sheriff's opinion, all of the work amounted to alterations. The first defence therefore fell to be rejected.

It seems worth adding that the result would have been the same if the titles had been silent and the default repair regime of the Tenement Management Scheme had applied.[1] This allows owners to make a majority decision to carry out maintenance to 'scheme property',[2] which includes property owned in common.[3] But 'maintenance' does not include alterations or improvements. The definition in the TMS is:

> 'maintenance' includes repairs and replacement, the installation of insulation,[4] cleaning, painting and other routine works, gardening, the day to day running of a tenement and the reinstatement of a part (but not most) of the tenement building, but does not include demolition, alteration or improvement unless reasonably incidental to the maintenance.

Painting, it will be seen, is classified as 'maintenance' and so would be covered by a majority decision. But none of the other works carried out by the defender could be classified as 'maintenance'.

There was also a second defence. The defender accepted, as he was bound to, the general principle of the common law that alterations to common property require the agreement of everybody.[5] But to this long-established rule a small number of exceptions exist, of which the most important is the exception in favour of necessary repairs.[6] The work in the present case, it was argued, fell into that category. This defence too was rejected, and rightly so, by the sheriff. This was mainly on grounds of lack of specification: 'the defender does not explain on record what the necessity which required the work to be done was or how it was addressed'.[7] But of course it must also fail for the more fundamental reason, already mentioned, that the work in question did not amount to 'repairs'.

The message from *Mitchell v Reilly* is stark and simple. In respect of common property in a tenement it is necessary to observe a sharp distinction between repairs and alterations. Repairs can typically be sanctioned by a majority of owners, whether under the titles or the TMS; and if repairs are 'necessary' even

1 The Tenement Management Scheme ('TMS') is set out in sch 1 to the Tenements (Scotland) Act 2004.
2 TMS rr 2.5, 3.1(a).
3 TMS r 1.2(a).
4 The installation of insulation would normally be classified as an improvement rather than as maintenance. It is included within the definition of 'maintenance' only because of the evident desirability of encouraging owners to insulate their homes.
5 This rule was first authoritatively articulated in George Joseph Bell, *Principles of the Law of Scotland* (4th edn, 1839; reprinted Edinburgh Legal Education Trust, 2010) § 1075. The defender also relied on a passage in W M Gordon, *Scottish Land Law* (2nd edn, 1999) para 15-18 allowing unilateral action in order to protect the common property; but the context is not works in relation to the property.
6 Bell, *Principles* § 1075: 'necessary operations in rebuilding, repairing, etc are not to be stopped by the opposition of any of the joint-owners'.
7 Transcript p 7.

unilateral action is permitted.[1] But alterations usually require the agreement of everyone. This is not new law, of course. The rules can be traced back to Bell's *Principles* in the 1830s.[2] But of this old law *Mitchell v Reilly* provides a modern, and a timely, reminder.

Appointing factors

There is more than one way to appoint a manager or factor. In modern developments the titles will often provide a rule, such as appointment by a majority of owners or by the owners' association (if there is one). And the first factor may have been appointed by the developer, as is permitted for a limited period by means of a so-called manager burden,[3] and then have continued in office as a result of the enthusiasm or, more likely, the apathy of the owners. Where there are no title provisions, as typically in older properties, legislation steps in to provide a default rule. For tenements this is rule 3.1(c) of the Tenement Management Scheme[4] which allows a 'scheme' (ie majority)[5] decision to be taken to appoint (or dismiss) a manager on such terms as may be determined. For non-tenemental properties, there is a parallel rule in the Title Conditions (Scotland) Act 2003 which allows a majority of owners to appoint (or dismiss) a manager.[6]

Whether a factor is appointed under the titles or under the default law, it is important that the relevant rule is properly complied with and that some sort of record is kept. Otherwise the factor may encounter difficulties in recovering for the cost of his services or for expenditure incurred on repairs and other matters. A difficulty of this kind arose in *Cumbernauld Housing Partnership Ltd v Davies.*[7] The pursuers acted as factor for a tower block in Cumbernauld known as Scott House. The defender, who owned a flat on the eleventh floor, was liable under the titles for 1/45 of the cost of maintaining the common parts. When the defender failed to make payment in respect of outstanding costs, the pursuers raised an action for payment. The amount due had mounted up over the years, and the sum sued for was £9,574.50.

The titles regulated the factor's appointment. They gave an initial option to Cumbernauld Development Corporation, the developers, to act as factors, and it seemed that this option had been taken up. Subsequently, the pursuers had acquired the property rights of the Development Corporation in respect of Scott House, a disposition in their favour being recorded in 2000. The precise nature

---

1 Although the cost of unilateral repairs is no longer recoverable: see Tenements (Scotland) Act 2004 s 16.
2 Bell, *Principles* §§ 1074–1078.
3 Title Conditions (Scotland) Act 2003 s 63.
4 The Tenement Management Scheme ('TMS') is set out in sch 1 to the Tenements (Scotland) Act 2004.
5 TMS r 2.5. This can, however, be displaced by a different rule in the titles: see Tenements (Scotland) Act 2004 s 4(4).
6 Title Conditions (Scotland) Act 2003 s 28. This only applies to 'communities', ie to a group of properties which is subject to community burdens: see s 26(2) and, for discussion of this important default regime, G L Gretton and K G C Reid, *Conveyancing* (4th edn, 2011) paras 14-15–14-17.
7 [2015] CSIH 22, 2015 SC 532. The Opinion of an Extra Division of the Court of Session was given by Lord Brodie.

of these rights is unclear from the report, but seems unlikely to have included the right to act as factor. Finally, the owners themselves had the power under the titles, by majority, to appoint a factor, although it is unclear whether this power had ever been exercised. The position on the ground was that the pursuers acted as factor, and had done so for a number of years. The basis of their appointment, however, seems to have been uncertain.

This uncertainty was seized upon by the defender. The pursuers, it was argued, had failed to prove that they had been appointed factor at the times when the relevant sums became due; hence they had no title to sue. Before the sheriff, this argument succeeded and the defender was assoilzied. But when the pursuers appealed to the Inner House, the defender abandoned this particular defence. In the view of the Inner House, she was right to do so:[1]

> [T]here was undisputed evidence that the pursuers have been acting as factors of the property since 2001 and that the defender had dealt with them as such (indeed that can be taken to have been admitted). To the extent to which the precise mechanism by which they became factors was properly an issue, and we do not see that it was, the pursuers have the benefit of the presumption *omnia rite et solemniter acta praesumuntur*, that is it is presumed that acts done have been done legally and regularly, until their illegality or irregularity is proved (Dickson, *A Treatise on the Law of Evidence in Scotland*, para 114(4)).

The onus of proof, in other words, lay with the defender and not with the pursuers. It was for the defender to show, if she could, that the pursuers had not been properly appointed as factors. This is a line of reasoning which will bring comfort to factors everywhere.[2]

Recovery of repair costs: 5 years or 20?

Suppose that repairs are carried out to the common parts in a tenement or other development. The factor or an owner, weary with the effort already expended, turns to the other owners for reimbursement of their share of the costs. Some pay at once. Some drag their heels but eventually are prevailed upon to write a cheque. A small but recalcitrant minority ignore all letters, e-mails, and knocks on the door. How long does the factor or owner have to recover the costs? Or, to put the question in another way, is the amount due subject to the short or to the long negative prescription?

This was another issue which arose in *Cumbernauld Housing Partnership Ltd v Davies*.[3] The sums sued for were, in some cases, older than five years but not older than twenty. If the long negative prescription applied, recovery could

1 Paragraph 12.
2 Further comfort may sometimes be found in s 65 of the Title Conditions (Scotland) Act 2003, which provides that, 'Where, immediately before the appointed day [28 November 2004], any person is, by virtue of any real burden or purported real burden, ostensibly the manager of related properties that person shall be deemed to have been validly appointed as such'. Despite the reference to the appointed day, s 65 has no particular connection with the abolition of the feudal system – a connection suggested by the Inner House at para 12.
3 [2015] CSIH 22, 2015 SC 532. This case was discussed above in relation to a different point.

be made in full; if the short negative prescription applied, all sums which had been outstanding for more than five years would have to be written off (unless prescription had been interrupted in some way).

The defender, naturally, argued for the five-year prescription. This was on the basis of paragraph 1(g) of schedule 1 to the Prescription and Limitation (Scotland) Act 1973, which applies the five-year prescription to contractual obligations. The pursuers, who were factors, pointed to paragraph 2(e) of schedule 1, which excludes from the short prescription – and hence, by necessary implication, applies the long prescription to – 'obligations relating to land'. Neither argument, however, was satisfactory, as the Inner House pointed out. As the defender's liability arose under a real burden and not a contract, paragraph 1(g) did not apply. And while it might be plausible to characterise that liability as an obligation relating to land, paragraph 2(e) was itself subject to paragraph 1(ac), and it was paragraph 1(ac) – overlooked by both sides – which contained the key to the whole question.

Admittedly, a degree of perseverance was needed to get to the right answer. Paragraph 1(ac) applies the five-year prescription to 'any obligation to pay a sum of money by way of costs to which section 12 of the Tenements (Scotland) Act 2004 (asp 11) applies'. Section 12 of the 2004 Act applies to 'relevant costs', and 'relevant costs' are defined, in s 11(9), to mean, as respects a flat –

(a) the share of any costs for which the owner is liable by virtue of the management scheme which applies as respects the tenement (except where that management scheme is the development management scheme); and
(b) any costs for which the owner is liable by virtue of this Act.

'Management scheme' is defined in s 27 as meaning –

(a) if the Tenement Management Scheme applies in its entirety as respects the tenement, that Scheme;
(b) if the development management scheme applies as respects the tenement, that scheme; or
(c) in any other case, any tenement burdens relating to maintenance, management or improvement of the tenement together with any provisions of the Tenement Management Scheme which apply as respects the tenement.

Finally, 'tenement burden' means any real burden which affects the tenement or any sector in the tenement.[1]

Out of this torrent of words an answer emerges surprisingly easily. The tower block in which the defender owned a flat was, like almost all tenements, governed by a mixture of real burdens (ie 'tenement burdens') and the TMS, and so fell within paragraph (c) of s 27. The obligation on the defender to contribute to common repairs was imposed by a real burden and hence was a 'relevant cost' (ie a 'share of any costs for which the owner is liable by virtue of the management scheme which applies as respects the tenement'). And since it was a relevant

---

1 Tenements (Scotland) Act 2004 s 29(1).

cost, the five-year prescription applied by virtue of paragraph 1(ac) of schedule 1 to the Prescription Act. Hence the pursuer could not sue for any sum which had been outstanding for more than five years.

The Inner House followed these steps, and reached this conclusion, without the aid of counsel or indeed of anything else.[1] A passage in the Scottish Law Commission's *Report on the Law of the Tenement*, which would have been of considerable assistance, appears not to have been drawn to the court's attention.[2] Although the rule which the Inner House uncovered applies only to tenements, there is a separate (and straightforward) provision in a different Act which makes the recovery of maintenance and other costs in non-tenemental properties also subject to the five-year prescription.[3] As the Inner House noted, there are sound reasons for applying the short prescription to cases such as this. If the underlying obligation to the roofer or builder prescribes after five years,[4] it would be surprising if the same cost should continue to be recoverable among the owners themselves for twenty years. '[A] construction of the 1973 Act which has the result that what are essentially tradesmen's bills do not prescribe before the passage of 20 years seems extravagant.'[5]

From the point of view of factors and owners who carry out repairs, the lessons of the decision in *Cumbernauld Housing Partnership Ltd v Davies* are both important and obvious. Where an owner refuses to pay his or her share, it is unwise to delay too long before taking steps for recovery. One step which can be, and quite often is, taken is to register a notice of potential liability for costs against the title of the recalcitrant flat.[6] This is a waiting game. A notice does not of itself lead to payment. But when the flat changes hands, the incoming owner will insist on having the payment (and notice) discharged, for the effect of the notice is otherwise to extend liability to that owner. One cannot, however, wait for ever. The notice expires after three years though it can be renewed.[7] More importantly, the notice has no effect on the running of prescription. That had been another point at issue in *Cumbernauld Housing Partnership*. Prescription is interrupted where the creditor makes a 'relevant claim',[8] and in addition to its core meaning of the raising of a court action 'relevant claim' includes 'the execution by or on behalf of the creditor in an obligation of any form of diligence directed to the enforcement of the obligation'.[9] It was argued for the pursuers that the notice of potential liability for costs which had been registered over the defender's flat was a 'form of diligence' and hence that it interrupted prescription. The court had little difficulty in rejecting what was evidently a tenuous argument.[10]

1 Paragraphs 17–20.
2 Scottish Law Commission, *Report No 162 on the Law of the Tenement* (1998) para 8.23.
3 Title Conditions (Scotland) Act 2003 s 18.
4 Ie under Prescription and Limitation (Scotland) Act 1973 sch 1 para (g).
5 Paragraph 17.
6 T(S)A 2004 ss 12(3), (4), 13.
7 T(S)A 2004 s 13(3).
8 Prescription and Limitation (Scotland) Act 1973 s 6(1)(a).
9 PL(S)A 1973 s 9(1).
10 Paragraphs 21–25.

Finally, mention should be made of s 4A of the Tenements Act. Where an owner will not pay, s 4A allows the local authority to step in and pay for him, after which it can seek to recover the cost from the owner. This is a new provision which only came into force on 1 April 2015.[1] It is to be hoped that local authorities will be willing to use it.[2]

DEBTOR PROTECTION AND THE ENFORCEMENT OF STANDARD SECURITIES

Introduction

The Conveyancing and Feudal Reform (Scotland) Act 1970 made vast improvements to the law of heritable security. But it was not perfect, for nothing in this world is perfect, except the beloved to the lover.[3] Most significantly, the Act's enforcement provisions were unsatisfactory. No one has ever really been able to make sense of them, the reason being, we think, that in the final analysis they did not fully make sense.[4] It might have been hoped that over time matters would have improved but, on the contrary, they have simply become worse. The provisions aimed at protecting debtors in residential cases,[5] however well meant and beneficial,[6] add to the complexity and unclarity of the basic enforcement rules with an additional layer of complexity and unclarity. The Scottish Law Commission intends to tackle the law of standard securities. Anyone who has tried to understand the law about enforcing standard securities will welcome that.

Every year brings a crop of cases on enforcement, and there were two of particular significance in 2015, both about the modern debtor-protection rules.

Westfoot: the protection of corporate debtors

What happened?

European Property Holdings Inc was exotic. It was incorporated in Panama and had its head office at 1461 First Avenue, 360 New York, New York. But on a closer view, it was, perhaps, not quite so exotic. Michael Karus, a name well known in Edinburgh legal circles, was its director.[7]

---

1 It was added to the Tenements (Scotland) Act 2004 by the Housing (Scotland) Act 2014 s 85(1)(b), with effect from 1 April 2015: see Housing (Scotland) Act 2014 (Commencement No 2) Order 2015, SSI 2015/122, art 2.
2 For statutory guidance on this power by the Scottish Government, see p 113 above.
3 Retreating from love to legislation, high claims might be made for some enactments, such as (to keep within the UK) the Bills of Exchange Act 1882 and the Marine Insurance Act 1906. But even those statutes, beautiful though they are, have faults.
4 The unaccountable decision not to repeal and replace the Heritable Securities (Scotland) Act 1894 is another source of ongoing difficulty.
5 Mortgage Rights (Scotland) Act 2001, Home Owner and Debtor Protection (Scotland) Act 2010, and their amendments to the 1894 Act and the 1970 Act.
6 Of course opinions will inevitably differ on this last point.
7 On Mr Karus, see eg www.edinburghnews.scotsman.com/news/crook-karus-bid-to-sell-homes-cheap-to-partner-1-3471187. See also *Playfair Investments Ltd v McElvogue* [2012] CSOH 148, 2012 GWD 30-611 (*Conveyancing 2012* Case (74)).

EPH owned residential properties at 6B Gloucester Square, Edinburgh and 14/2 Gloucester Place, Edinburgh. Both were let to tenants. In April 2013 EPH borrowed £285,000 from an English finance company, Westfoot Investments Ltd, and granted standard securities over the two properties. The loan was to be repaid after six months. 'To be repaid', however, is not the same as 'was repaid'. Nothing was repaid. By May 2015 the amount due, with post-default interest piling up,[1] was £486,825.82.

The lender's law agents must have realised that enforcement might not be simple. The borrower was a foreign company without a UK office.[2] The properties were residential, and they took the cautious view that the debtor-protection rules would apply. They were thorough – impressively so. They made postal service of calling-up notices at the New York office. Service failed, the two notices being returned marked 'Not Deliverable as Addressed – Unable to Forward'.[3] They sent these to the Extractor of the Court of Session, for 'Walls of Court service'. They served notice on the tenants in the two properties.[4] They sent a notice under s 11 of the Homelessness etc (Scotland) Act 2003 to the City of Edinburgh Council. Despite the failure of the service of the calling-up notice, they sent a further letter to the New York office by recorded delivery mail, setting out the position thus far, and reminding EPH it was in continuing default.[5] Information about the interest and charges due, to date, were specified in the letter. A copy of the agreement was enclosed. In the letter the lender indicated a continuing willingness to find a financial accommodation, even at that late stage, and gave details of organisations EPH could approach for debt advice, including Citizens Advice Scotland, the City of Edinburgh Council, the Law Society of Scotland and the Scottish Government website. No reply was received.

Finally the present action was raised to enforce the securities: *Westfoot Investments Ltd v European Property Holdings Inc.*[6] Despite the previous silence, EPH now defended the action. We will not go through the detail of whether the lender had sufficiently complied with the requirements of the legislation: unsurprisingly it was held that it had, and decree was granted in its favour. Nor

---

1 The arrangement about non-default interest is interesting. The whole interest for the six months was deducted from the loan at the outset, so that though the advance was £285,000, the sum paid over by lender to borrower was less than that. How common arrangements of this sort are we do not know.

2 Whether the lender considered this issue when the loan was made we do not know. But foreign corporations can easily throw up problems when they are involved in property transactions here. The many issues include the following. Does the corporation actually exist? Has it the capacity to enter into foreign-property transactions? Does it really have the legal address it says it has? Are its directors really those that it says are its directors? Is it involved in some process analogous to liquidation, etc? In short, due diligence in relation to foreign corporations is more onerous than it is for UK corporations. Moreover, in this respect some foreign legal systems are more problematic than others.

3 Nothing is said in the case about whether postal service was attempted at the company's official address in its place of incorporation, Panama. It is hard to imagine that the transaction had been entered into without obtaining that address.

4 Conveyancing and Feudal Reform (Scotland) Act 1970 s 19A, sch 6 form BB.

5 2015 SLT (Sh Ct) 201: para 15 of the findings in fact.

6 2015 SLT (Sh Ct) 201, 2015 Hous LR 57.

will we discuss the evidence taken, including the odd fact that the only witness for the defender seems to have been Mr Karus's wife, who was not even, it seems, an employee, director or secretary of the company.[1]

Debtor protection

The importance of the case lies in the sheriff's view that the situation was not one to which the debtor-protection legislation applied.[2] The legislation in question is the Mortgage Rights (Scotland) Act 2001 and the Home Owner and Debtor Protection (Scotland) Act 2010, both of which make significant amendments to the Heritable Securities (Scotland) Act 1894 and the Conveyancing and Feudal Reform (Scotland) Act 1970. The sheriff's view is important because it has been generally understood that the test for the applicability of the legislation is whether the property in question is residential. The legislation refers to 'land used to any extent for residential purposes'.[3]

A different view was taken by the sheriff in *Westfoot Investments Ltd*, and for this he adduced some strong arguments. The first was a policy-based approach to the interpretation of the legislation:[4]

> Core to the suite of reforms is the protection of the debtor or entitled proprietor's home which may be imperilled, to the prejudice of a range of other entitled persons living there as their home, by a precipitate action for possession and ejection. In my opinion, the sole beneficiaries of the legislation are debtors who own their home *and use it* as a security for debt, home owners who allow the home they mostly live in *to be used* as security for someone else's debt, occupiers whose home is not otherwise protected by legislation and entitled residents who live solely or mainly in a home used by a debtor or proprietor to secure a debt. This latter group includes former estranged partners of debtors and/or proprietors who have used the security subjects as a home, for at least 6 months, before separation, who have children from their relationship with the debtor or proprietor, under the age of 16, also living with them in the security subjects as their home. However, corporate borrowers that grant standard securities over their residential property assets and use these as collateral security, to raise capital on the financial markets, are not included within the scope of the protection created.

To this the sheriff adds two textual arguments. One concerns s 24(7)(e) of the 1970 Act, which says that account must be taken of 'the ability of the debtor and any other person residing at the security subjects to secure reasonable alternative accommodation'. The sheriff observes that this 'only makes sense if referred to natural not legal persons, who are also debtors. A legal entity such as the defender does not have a home, in the sense it would require to find alternative

---

1 Paragraph 11: 'She is a trainee solicitor with Hughes Dowdall. She is married to Michael Karus who is a director of the defender company. She has no official connection with the defender company.'
2 The sheriff was T Welsh QC.
3 Conveyancing and Feudal Reform (Scotland) Act 1970 s 24(1A). See also Heritable Securities (Scotland) Act 1895 s 5A.
4 Paragraph 26.

accommodation, in the event of an action for possession and ejection being granted over property it owns.'[1]

The other textual argument (albeit less weighty because it refers to a requirement of secondary rather than primary legislation) is that creditors are required to 'consider the affordability of any proposal for the debtor taking into account, where known to the creditor, the debtor's personal and financial circumstances'.[2] This, commented the sheriff, is 'targeted at natural persons in financial trouble rather than illiquid or insolvent corporate borrowers'.[3]

This line of argument (which we have not set out in full) would seem to be technically *obiter*, because the pleadings of both parties, the pursuer as well as the defender, assumed that the protective legislation was indeed applicable. Further, *obiter* remarks at the level of the sheriff court do not, in the usual case, carry much weight. But the sheriff's argument is powerful and we would not be surprised if it were to be followed in future cases.

From a practical standpoint, it clearly makes sense, in cases of this type, to undertake enforcement on the assumption that the protective legislation does apply, notwithstanding the *Westfoot* decision. But once the matter gets to court, and is defended, the lender can argue not only that the enforcement is squarely compliant with the protective regime but also that the protective regime does not apply anyway.

Ejection

Section 5 of the Heritable Securities (Scotland) Act 1894 makes provision for the ejection of a defaulting debtor where the debtor is in 'personal occupation'. One of the defender's arguments was that s 5 could not apply, because a body corporate cannot be in 'personal occupation' of anything. That defence, ingenious but unsound, was not accepted by the sheriff, albeit for an unexpected reason. He said that if s 5 meant that a body corporate (juristic person) could not be ejected, that would breach the human rights[4] of the pursuer. To avoid such a result, he concluded that 'personal occupation' must be read as meaning 'occupation'.[5]

We think, with respect, that that must always have been the meaning. Reading the 1894 Act as a whole, the contrast to 'personal occupation' is 'let out to a tenant'. Hence a body corporate has always been able to be in 'personal occupation' of property within the meaning of the statute.[6]

The sheriff went on to say that, since in this case the property was let out, the question of ejecting the debtor could not arise anyway, so that quite apart from the human rights point the debtor's argument was irrelevant: 'It seems to me in a practical sense there is nothing for sheriff officers to eject, as it is neither

1 Paragraph 25.
2 Applications by Creditors (Pre-Action Requirements) (Scotland) Order 2010, SSI 2010/317, art 3(1)(e).
3 Paragraph 26.
4 European Convention on Human Rights, Protocol 1, art 1.
5 Paragraph 33.
6 Others have taken a similar view. For instance, W M Gloag and J M Irvine, *Law of Rights in Security* (1897) p 99 interprets 'personal possession' in the 1894 Act as meaning 'natural possession'. A juristic person can have natural possession of property.

averred nor proved, that the subjects are actually occupied by the defender. It was accepted by the pursuer that the premises are tenanted.'[1] That is surely correct.[2]

Swift Advances: debtor protection and negative equity

Suppose that there is negative equity. Does that affect the way that the debtor-protection legislation[3] applies? That issue was fought all the way up to the Inner House in *Swift Advances plc v Martin*,[4] a case that was in many ways strange.

The story in outline

Mr and Mrs Martin owned a house over which there was a secured loan with Britannia Building Society.[5] Wishing to borrow further sums on the security of the property, they turned to Swift Advances plc. The property was valued at £750,000, and on that basis a loan was obtained from Swift in the amount of £426,000. This was in 2007. The loan was repayable over 25 years. What happened to the money is one of the mysteries of the case. It was not used to pay off the Britannia loan, for when the current litigation occurred the Britannia standard security was still in place. Another mystery is that this 25-year loan of £426,000 was given to a couple who were, or were soon to become, pensioners.[6]

The Martins fell into arrears almost immediately,[7] and by the time of the proof in the action the amount due had, with accumulating interest, risen from £426,000 to £638,000. Swift raised an action to enforce the security by sale.[8] The action was defended on the basis that the protective legislation barred such enforcement. The Martins were unsuccessful before the sheriff. They appealed to the sheriff principal, and lost again.[9] They then appealed to the Inner House where they have now lost yet again.

The defence in outline

Two protective conditions must be satisfied before a court can order the sale of residential property for the purposes of enforcing a security.[10] In the first place, the creditor must comply with certain 'pre-action requirements'. In the second

---

1   Paragraph 34.
2   But it may be wondered why the interlocutor said: 'Ordains the Defender to vacate said subjects and to flit and remove themselves, their servants, employees, *tenants, sub-tenants* and others …'?
3   Mortgage Rights (Scotland) Act 2001, Home Owner and Debtor Protection (Scotland) Act 2010, and their amendments to the Heritable Securities (Scotland) Act 1894 and the Conveyancing and Feudal Reform (Scotland) Act 1970.
4   [2015] CSIH 65, 2015 Hous LR 50. The court comprised Lord Brodie, Lady Dorrian and Lord Malcolm, the Opinion being delivered by Lord Malcolm.
5   The amount owed to Britannia Building Society is not known. The court comments, at para 40, that 'the amount due to the first charge holder was never fully explored'.
6   'They are in receipt of pension income only and, leaving aside the said subjects, have no funds to meet their obligations to Swift' (para 3).
7   The loan was in 2007 and by the following year they were already in arrears: see para 3.
8   Yet another mystery about the case is what the Britannia Building Society was doing, or rather was not doing. The Britannia loan was also in arrears: see para 3. In such cases the normal practice is for the forced sale to be pushed through by the first security holder.
9   There seem to be no reports of the case when it was before the lower courts.
10 Conveyancing and Feudal Reform (Scotland) Act 1970 s 24(5).

place, it must be 'reasonable in the circumstances of the case' for the court to make the order. The Martins' defence was that neither of these conditions had been satisfied.

The first condition: the pre-action requirements

The pre-action requirements are set out in s 24A of the Conveyancing and Feudal Reform (Scotland) Act 1970.[1] Two were said to be relevant in the present case – those set out in subsections (3) and (4):

> (3) The creditor must make reasonable efforts to agree with the debtor proposals in respect of future payments to the creditor under the standard security and the fulfilment of any other obligation under the standard security in respect of which the debtor is in default.
> (4) The creditor must not make an application under section 24(1B) of this Act if the debtor is taking steps which are likely to result in –
>   (a) the payment to the creditor within a reasonable time of any arrears, or the whole amount, due to the creditor under the standard security; and
>   (b) fulfilment by the debtor within a reasonable time of any other obligation under the standard security in respect of which the debtor is in default.

The Martins had urged on Swift an arrangement which, the Martins said, was designed to maximise Swift's prospects of recovery. Rather than attempt to sell the property on the open market, they proposed to sell it to their daughter and son-in-law, for £300,000. From this sum it would first be necessary to clear the Britannia loan; the rest would be available for Swift. The proposal, as we understand it, was that in exchange for this partial payment Swift would not only discharge the security but cancel the remainder of the debt (ie more than half the debt). An alternative way of proceeding would have been to discharge the security, making it possible for the daughter and son-in-law to acquire a title free of the Swift security, but not to cancel the balance of the debt. In practice these two possibilities would very likely have come to much the same thing, since apart from the property the Martins appeared to have had no means of paying the debt. Nevertheless it is important to note that these two possibilities are separate and distinct. As far as we can see, the negotiations between the parties discussed only the first (discharge of the security and of the whole debt).

So reasonable, indeed so favourable, was this proposal that for Swift to refuse it would, said the Martins, be a breach of subsections (3) and (4) of s 24A. Swift – unsurprisingly – did not see matters in quite this light. One difficulty was a disagreement as to the value of the property. It was common ground that this had declined markedly since 2007, but Swift thought it was worth £500,000 rather than the £300,000 at which the Martins proposed to sell to their relatives.[2] At root, however, the difficulty was the negative equity. Whatever the property's

---

1 This is supplemented by the Applications by Creditors (Pre-Action Requirements) (Scotland) Order 2010, SSI 2010/317.
2 Paragraph 38.

value really was, it was far less than was needed to pay off the loan to Swift. Did the pre-action requirements in subsections (3) and (4) require Swift to sign up to an arrangement which fell so far short of full recovery? Swift argued that they did not.

The Inner House agreed with Swift:[1]

> Nothing in the above provisions prevents court action if, after appropriate communications, it is clear that the debtor simply cannot comply with his obligations in full. The pre-action requirements introduced by the 2010 Act in respect of residential borrowing are designed to ensure that there is a genuine exploration of the possibility of an arrangement being reached whereby, in due course, the default can be remedied, albeit this may require indulgence on the part of the creditor. The whole tenor of s 24A(3) and (4) is of discussions aimed at an alternative agreement whereby the debtor's obligations can be fulfilled, for example, on the basis of a lower monthly payment extending over a longer period. There is nothing to suggest that a proposal to pay only a fraction of the sum due must be accepted, or that it can stop the raising of court proceedings. This is consistent with the government guidance, which provides assistance on what the reasonable creditor is expected to do, for example, extend the repayment period; change the type of repayment from interest plus capital to interest only; or capitalise the arrears on the security.

The second condition: reasonableness

Even if the pre-action requirements have been attended to, the court may still not order sale unless 'it is reasonable in the circumstances of the case to do so'.[2] Swift argued that it was reasonable to seek the best price for the property and that only a sale in the open market could achieve that. For their part the Martins said that there was no realistic prospect of a higher price being obtained than that which was being offered by their daughter and son-in-law.

Again the court found for Swift. Among the factors which the legislation required courts to consider in assessing reasonableness was 'the ability of the debtor to fulfil within a reasonable time the obligations under the standard security in respect of which the debtor is in default'.[3] Yet 'Swift was faced with an insistence that it should discharge the debtors' obligations in return for a fraction of the indebtedness (the amount due to the first charge holder was never fully explored), all based on an offer which fell far below earlier expert valuations, and also Swift's own valuation'.[4] During prolonged negotiations Swift had shown 'remarkable patience and tolerance, even when faced with somewhat intemperate correspondence'.[5] It was not unreasonable that Swift should now be allowed the chance to expose the property to the market.[6]

---

1 Paragraph 27.
2 CFR(S)A 1970 s 24(5)(b).
3 CFR(S)A 1970 s 24(7)(b).
4 Paragraph 40.
5 Paragraph 41.
6 For a somewhat similar approach, albeit in respect of different legislation, see *Cheltenham and Gloucester plc v Krausz* [1997] 1 WLR 1558 (CA) (which was cited in *Swift*) and especially the remarks by Phillips LJ at 1564.

THE SECRET FLAT

The facts

The facts of *Chalmers v Chalmers*,[1] insofar as they can be determined from what the Lord Ordinary[2] described as the 'cobweb of conflicting evidence' at proof,[3] were remarkable. Paul and Therese Chalmers were husband and wife and also partners in a house-rental business known as Rentier Property. As Rentier Property was a partnership, title to the various Rentier houses was taken, on behalf of the firm,[4] in the name of Mr and Mrs Chalmers or sometimes of Mr Chalmers alone. The business was run by Mr Chalmers, and Mrs Chalmers played little or no part in it.

When Mr Chalmers went to work in Dubai in 2007, the marriage, which by then had lasted for almost 30 years, began to break down. By the time, however, that divorce proceedings started, in 2012, Mrs Chalmers had found out about a secret flat, following title investigations by her solicitor. It turned out that in 1998 title to a flat at 38 Hotspur Street, Glasgow had been registered in Mrs Chalmers' name but without her knowledge. The flat had been bought by Mr Chalmers, partly using Rentier Property money and partly money of his own. The flat did not become part of the Rentier portfolio. It did not appear in the partnership accounts, and the rental income was paid to Mr Chalmers and not to Rentier Property. One of the reasons for this method of doing things may have been to avoid paying income tax on the rental income.[5]

The Chalmers had two children, a son and a daughter, and in 2006 a disposition was drawn up which disponed the flat at Hotspur Street to the son, Chris, who at that time was aged 18. The disposition was registered after some delay, on 9 April 2008.[6] Once again, the transaction was organised by Mr Chalmers, who also signed the disposition as a witness. The signature of Mrs Chalmers, however, was forged – by whom has not been determined. When asked during the proof whether he had forged his wife's signature, Mr Chalmers responded: 'I cannot recollect'.[7] The reasons for the transfer are not entirely clear. In part it seems to have been a 'normal' transfer of assets from a parent to a child; a different property was to be given to the Chalmers' daughter later on. But it may also have reflected the deteriorating relationship between husband and wife. In any event, nothing changed on the ground as a result of the transfer. The flat continued to be rented out, and the rental income was paid to Mr Chalmers and not to Chris. It was to be a number of years before Chris came to use the flat for himself.

None of this was known to Mrs Chalmers at the time. It appears that solicitors acted, first in the purchase of the flat and later in its transfer to Chris,

---

1 [2014] CSOH 161, 2015 SCLR 299 rev [2015] CSIH 75, 2015 SLT 793, 2015 Hous LR 82.
2 Lord Boyd of Duncansby.
3 [2014] CSOH 161, para 69.
4 Whether this was done expressly or relied on inference, perhaps with the aid of s 21 of the Partnership Act 1890, is not known.
5 [2014] CSOH 161, para 81.
6 One reason for the delay may have been the death of the solicitor who was acting in the transaction.
7 [2014] CSOH 161, para 11.

without taking instructions from Mrs Chalmers or verifying that those who purported to speak on her behalf were authorised to do so.[1] We refrain from comment.

When she finally found out about the flat, at the time of the divorce action in 2012–13, Mrs Chalmers added appropriate averments to her divorce pleadings.[2] Shortly afterwards, on 12 November 2012, the couple entered into a minute of agreement in respect of the matrimonial property. Among its terms was a transfer by Mrs Chalmers of all her rights in Rentier Property. Each party renounced any further rights against the other. A few days later Mrs Chalmers raised an action of reduction of the disposition against her son, from whom she was now estranged.

The law

It is worth pausing to consider the legal implications of the facts just described. Two issues arise in particular. First, did Mrs Chalmers become owner when, in 1998, a disposition of the flat in her favour was registered in the Land Register? And second, did ownership then pass to her son, Chris, when a disposition in his favour was registered in 2008? Neither issue seems to have been considered in the litigation which was to follow; yet they are fundamental to an understanding of the facts, and indeed of the questions which were to be litigated.

The answer to the first question is perhaps less clear than one would wish. It is true, of course, that Mrs Chalmers' name was entered on the Land Register as proprietor. And it is also true that, by s 3(1)(a) of the Land Registration (Scotland) Act 1979, the Keeper's 'Midas touch' operates so that the person registered as owner becomes owner. But is it certain that registration, in a legal sense, had taken place? Under the Land Registration Rules, an application for registration must be made 'by the person in whose favour a real right will be created', ie in this case by Mrs Chalmers.[3] And behind this requirement is a general principle of property law that the transfer of ownership requires the consent of the transferee as well as of the transferor.[4] But no consent was given by Mrs Chalmers; nor did she apply for registration. In those circumstances, can the Keeper's act in entering her name in the Register properly be classified as an act of registration?[5] If not, ownership remained with the granter of the disposition and did not pass to Mrs Chalmers. On balance, however, it seems likely that ownership did pass

---

1 [2014] CSOH 161, para 44.
2 [2015] CSIH 75, paras 4–6. This did not appear from the Lord Ordinary's Opinion.
3 Land Registration (Scotland) Rules 1980, SI 1980/1413, r 9(1). These were the Rules in force in 1998. This was the equivalent of the warrant of registration in the Register of Sasines, which in turn was the equivalent of the former instrument of sasine.
4 There must be *animus acquirendi dominii* (intention to acquire ownership) on the grantee's side, as well as *animus transferendi dominii* (intention to transfer ownership) on the granter's side: see K G C Reid, *The Law of Property in Scotland* (1996) para 613.
5 After all, under the 1979 Act there are other reasons why an entry might be made on the Register, namely rectification and the entering of an overriding interest. The suggestion here, however, is that the entering of Mrs Chalmers' name was not authorised by any of the provisions of the Act.

to Mrs Chalmers,[1] and this was taken for granted by the Inner House when the Lord Ordinary's decision went on appeal.[2]

No such doubts affect the second transfer. Even assuming Mrs Chalmers to have been owner, the fact that her signature was forged means that the disposition was void. Nonetheless, registration transferred ownership. Why? This time, unlike the last, a proper application was made on behalf of a grantee (Chris Chalmers) who consented to the acquisition. And, that having been done, the Keeper's Midas touch did the rest. On 9 April 2008, therefore, Chris Chalmers became owner of the flat.[3]

The result

The Lord Ordinary refused the reduction and dismissed the action. Although the fact of forgery was not in dispute, there was, he said, a discretion to refuse reduction which it would be appropriate to exercise on the ground that the pursuer was personally barred.[4] On the one hand, the pursuer had sought to gain advantage by raising the action of reduction only after the signing of the minute of agreement put the flat beyond the reach of her husband. On the other hand, the defender, while not blameless, had not been part of the fraud and was now living in the flat as his home.[5]

The result attracted criticism at the time,[6] and it has now been reversed by the Inner House.[7] In the end of the day, the Inner House saw the matter as quite simple:[8]

> In our opinion, a forged disposition is a nullity. It is wholly void, not merely voidable. … Only in exceptional circumstances may a forged disposition have any effect, the exceptional circumstances being where the person whose signature has been forged expressly or impliedly authorises or adopts the forged signature as his or her own.[9] Furthermore, we consider that the system of Scottish land registration could be subverted if it were possible to forge a signature on a disposition which was duly

1 On the basis that primary legislation (s 3(1)(a) of the LR(S)A 1979) trumps secondary (r 9(1) of the Land Registration Rules).
2 [2015] CSIH 75, para 28.
3 Had this second transaction taken place after the Land Registration etc (Scotland) Act 2012 came into force, the result would have been different. Under the 2012 Act, unlike the 1979 Act, a forged disposition does not transfer title.
4 [2014] CSOH 161, paras 86–93.
5 It was also argued for the defender that Mrs Chalmers' title to the flat had been merely as a partner of, and so on behalf of, Rentier Property. In terms of the minute of agreement she had given up any interest in Rentier Property. Hence she had no title to sue. The Lord Ordinary disposed of this argument by finding that the flat was not held on behalf of Rentier Property. The point was not pursued in the appeal.
6 *Conveyancing 2014* pp 196–200; D J Carr, 'Is there an equitable exception to reduction for forgery?' (2015) 19 *Edinburgh Law Review* 273.
7 [2015] CSIH 75, 2015 SLT 793, 2015 Hous LR 82. This was an Extra Division comprising Lady Paton, Lady Smith and Lord Drummond Young. The Opinion was given by Lady Paton.
8 [2015] CSIH 75, paras 23–24.
9 The authorities cited here were: *Mackenzie v British Linen Co* (1881) 8 R (HL) 8; *Muir's Exrs v Craig's Trs* 1913 SC 349, 354–55 per Lord President Dunedin; *Dodd v Southern Pacific Loans Ltd* [2007] CSOH 9, 2007 GWD 21-352; J Rankine, *A Treatise on the Law of Personal Bar in Scotland* (1921) 209; W Gloag, *Contract* (2nd edn, 1929) 546.

registered, and then put forward equitable circumstances supporting a contention that the forged disposition should not be reduced, with the ultimate result (in the context of land tenure) depending upon the discretion of the court. In the present case, there is no evidence that the pursuer expressly or impliedly authorised or adopted as her own the forged signature on the 2006 disposition. We therefore agree with counsel for the pursuer that the Lord Ordinary erred in law by adopting the approach of an exercise of discretion. The deed is null and of no effect, and the pursuer is entitled to decree of reduction.

The Inner House added that, even if there had been a judicial discretion in the matter, it did not consider that it had been properly exercised by the Lord Ordinary. In particular, the Lord Ordinary was wrong to conclude that the action of reduction had come as a sort of 'ambush' of Mr Chalmers after the divorce proceedings were concluded. On the contrary:[1]

> The pursuer, having been kept in ignorance about Hotspur Street by her husband but having been told about it by her lawyer, openly brought the question of Hotspur Street to the attention of Mr Chalmers (and the court) three months before the divorce was finalised. It seems to us that the pursuer was taking such steps as she could to highlight and ventilate the question of Hotspur Street, rather than keeping quiet about it in the divorce action. The person who was being unforthcoming about Hotspur Street was, in our view, Mr Chalmers. It seems to us that the pursuer, having received no information, explanation, or averments about Hotspur Street, went on to conclude her divorce as best she could on the material available. If Mr Chalmers considered that the minute of agreement was not fair or reasonable, he could have sought to have it set aside or varied (Family Law (Scotland) Act 1985 s 16(1)(b)) (but did not).

The future

We have no doubt that the decision of the Inner House is correct. Its implications for the parties, however, are a little harder to determine. The disposition is void, but is the Register now inaccurate as a result? That depends on the transitional provisions contained in the Land Registration etc (Scotland) Act 2012. These say that where, immediately before the designated day (8 December 2014), the Register was inaccurate but could not be rectified, the Register ceased on the designated day to be inaccurate.[2] The inaccuracy, in other words, was cured.

What, then, was the position in respect of the flat immediately before the designated day? That the Register was inaccurate in showing the son, and not his mother, as owner cannot now be disputed; for the disposition was void, and that was so even before the decree of reduction was pronounced.[3] But as the son was a proprietor in possession, rectification could only have taken place to his prejudice on a small number of grounds, of which the only one likely to be of relevance was that the inaccuracy was caused by his fraud or carelessness.[4] Whether that was so – whether the son was complicit in the forgery of the

---

1 [2015] CSIH 75, para 30.
2 Land Registration etc (Scotland) Act 2012 sch 4 para 22.
3 Reductions of void (as opposed to voidable) deeds are merely declaratory in effect.
4 Land Registration (Scotland) Act 1979 s 9(3)(a)(iii).

disposition or at least careless in not uncovering it – we do not know. If it was, the Register remains inaccurate and can be rectified now. But if not, the Register ceased to be inaccurate on the designated day and the son's title today is good beyond challenge.[1] Mrs Chalmers would then seem to have a claim against the Keeper for indemnity for the value of the property.[2] Whether, in that event, the Keeper might have a right of relief against any other party is not an issue we seek to explore here.

PROPERTY TAXES IN SCOTLAND[3]

There must have been times when it did not look like a good idea to introduce the first purely Scottish national taxes for 300 years on April Fools' Day 2015. But introduced they were; on 1 April 2015, stamp duty land tax ('SDLT') was switched off in relation to land in Scotland[4] and land and buildings transaction tax ('LBTT') was switched on.[5] And on the same day, Scottish landfill tax came into operation.[6] Some things, including the ability to report and pay online, were ready by the skin of their electronic teeth; and indeed teething problems continue to emerge, particularly in relation to LBTT on more complex transactions.

However, Scottish taxes and the structure to administer them are up and running; and the devolution of further tax powers operates as a one-way valve, with more to come in the near future. But the bulk of tax law will continue to come from Westminster for many years into the future; advisers and their clients will thus need to have regard to developments from Holyrood, Westminster, two tax administrations, and courts in both jurisdictions.

One area of taxation affecting land which may be liable to substantial change is local taxation, including council tax and business rates. The Scottish Government's response to the final report of the Commission on Local Tax Reform is awaited.[7]

---

1 LR(S)A 2012 sch 4 para 22.
2 LR(S)A 2012 sch 4 para 23. In principle, the amount due would appear to be the value of the property because, by the date on which indemnity became due (8 December 2014), Mrs Chalmers would have been entitled (but for her son having been in possession) to the return of the flat free (it seems) of any claim by her former husband.
3 This part is contributed by Alan Barr of the University of Edinburgh and Brodies LLP.
4 By the Scotland Act 2012, Section 29 (Disapplication of UK Stamp Duty Land Tax) (Appointed Day) Order 2015, SI 2015/637.
5 Land and Buildings Transaction Tax (Scotland) Act 2013 (Commencement No 1) Order 2014, SSI 2014/279; Land and Buildings Transaction Tax (Scotland) Act 2013 (Commencement No 2) Order 2015, SSI 2015/108.
6 UK landfill tax was disapplied in relation to disposals on or after 1 April 2015 by the Scotland Act 2012, Section 31 (Disapplication of UK Landfill Tax) (Appointed Day) Order 2015, SI 2015/638. See also the Devolution of Landfill Tax (Consequential, Transitional and Savings Provisions) Order 2015, SI 2015/599. Its Scottish equivalent was commenced by a series of SSIs: Landfill Tax (Scotland) Act 2014 (Commencement No 1) Order 2014, SSI 2014/277; Landfill Tax (Scotland) Act 2014 (Commencement No 2) Order 2015, SSI 2015/17; Landfill Tax (Scotland) Act 2014 (Commencement No 3 and Transitional Provisions) Order 2015, SSI 2015/109.
7 See Commission on Local Tax Reform, *Just Change: A New Approach to Local Taxation* (2015; http://localtaxcommission.scot/download-our-final-report/).

Land and buildings transaction tax

Rates

As the time approached for the introduction of LBTT, there was a series of hokey-cokey announcements about the rates of LBTT. As John Swinney[1] was forced to react to the somewhat surprising changes to SDLT announced with immediate effect in the Autumn Statement of 2014, the rates of LBTT originally announced for residential property were revised before the tax came into effect. The eventual rates from 1 April 2015 (applying only to the slice above the relevant threshold) are as follows:[2]

Consideration	Rate
Up to £145,000	Nil
£145,001 – £250,000	2%
£250,001 – £325,000	5%
£325,001 – £750,000	10%
Over £750,000	12%

The rates originally proposed for purchases of non-residential and mixed property came into effect without further alteration, as follows:[3]

Consideration	Rate
Up to £150,000	Nil
£150,001 – £350,000	3%
Over £350,000	4.5%

For non-residential leases, likewise, there was no change to the rates originally announced, which are 0% on a net present value up to £150,000 and 1% on the amount above that threshold.[4]

Broadly the result of the changes in Scotland and the rest of the UK mean that on a similar purchase consideration for residential property, less LBBT is payable than SDLT up to £333,000, and more is payable above that figure. As a result there was an acceleration of the settlement of high-value transactions before 1 April

---

1 Cabinet Secretary for Finance, Employment and Sustainable Growth in the Scottish Government.
2 Land and Buildings Transaction Tax (Tax Rates and Tax Bands) (Scotland) Order 2015, SSI 2015/126, art 2, sch, table A.
3 Land and Buildings Transaction Tax (Tax Rates and Tax Bands) (Scotland) Order 2015 art 3, sch, table B
4 Land and Buildings Transaction Tax (Tax Rates and Tax Bands) (Scotland) Order 2015 art 4, sch, table C

2015. This is a partial explanation for the shortfall in expected LBTT revenues in the first year of operation of the tax, that shortfall being particularly evident in the early months of the tax.[1]

The order of events was that the UK Autumn Statement of 2014 followed the original announcement of LBBT rates by the Scottish Government. In 2015, the UK Autumn Statement was delivered on 25 November, while the Scottish Budget was presented on 16 December.[2] The Scottish Budget confirms that the basic rates for LBTT as set out above are to remain unchanged in 2016–17 – although there is another regular opportunity for changes to UK taxation in the 2016 Budget. The framework of changes to Scottish taxation does not as yet include the possibility of changes just before the start of the tax year (as provided at UK level by the Budget) and it will be interesting to see whether such a reactive process is considered necessary if, for example, there were to be significant changes to stamp duty land tax in the March 2016 Budget.

Additional homes supplement

Such a reaction was evident in relation to a change to SDLT announced in the UK Autumn Statement of 2015. This was an additional SDLT charge of 3% on second homes, whether on holiday homes or on buy-to-lets. While there is clearly no commitment or permanent intention that LBTT should reflect all changes in SDLT (and indeed the basic rates now reflect considerable differences in tax on the same consideration at certain points, particularly for expensive houses), it was clearly considered that this increase should be mirrored in Scotland. Thus from 1 April 2016 there is to be an increase in LBTT for the purchase of certain residential property. This is described as the 'additional homes supplement'. It does not apply at all to the rare occasions where the purchase price is £40,000 or less; but it will apply at 3% on all consideration above that. At that level, on the purchase of a first home, LBTT would be at a 0% rate.

The absence of a 0% rate, once £40,000 has been exceeded, involves something of a return to the former 'slab' system that the more progressive LBTT was designed to remove on its introduction: a reform so attractive that it was immediately followed in the rest of the UK for SDLT. Although LBTT was intended to represent a distinctly Scottish approach to taxation, the additional homes supplement represents a small point of convergence between the tax treatment of residential property of Scotland and the rest of the UK. Indeed, the LBTT and SDLT charges on second homes and buy-to-lets are identical in the £40,000 to £125,000 price range. Interestingly, one consequence of both SDLT and LBTT using a supplemental slab is that it remains marginally cheaper to acquire buy-to-let properties in Scotland costing between £125,000 and £333,000.

There is to be consultation on this change, which will require primary legislation. It is to be hoped that that this will include discussion of the reliefs that will be necessary to ensure that important developments such as those in

---

1 Revenue Scotland publish monthly statistics on returns made and tax collected: see www.revenue. scot/about-us/publications/statistics.
2 *Scotland's Spending Plans and Draft Budget 2016–17* (www.gov.scot/Resource/0049/00491140.pdf).

the private-rented sector are not disadvantaged as compared to the rest of the UK, and that taxpayers buying a new house do not find themselves affected by the supplement if there is a minor delay in selling their old house. It is also to be hoped that administrative burdens are kept to a minimum. A short Bill – the Land and Buildings Transaction Tax (Amendment) (Scotland) Bill – was introduced to the Scottish Parliament on 27 January 2016 and completed its Parliamentary passage on 8 March. The Bill, soon to be Act, adds a new schedule 2A to the Land and Buildings Transaction Tax (Scotland) Act 2013.

The new supplement is to be charged as follows:[1]

Consideration	Existing LBTT rates	Additional homes supplement
Up to £40,000	0%	3% (if total consideration exceeds £40,000)
£40,000 – £145,000	0%	3%
£145,001 – £250,000	2%	3%
£250,001 – £325,000	5%	3%
£325,001 – £750,000	10%	3%
£750,000 and above	12%	3%

Sub-sales: from relief to penalty

It was always intended that LBTT should not have a general sub-sale relief. The relief under SDLT (which was not in fact expressed as a relief) was seen as the source of a great deal of tax avoidance, and was in recent years heavily restricted to prevent the more egregious forms of avoidance which had purportedly arisen (although many 'schemes' remain open to challenge through the courts).[2] Thus the Land and Buildings Transaction Tax (Scotland) Act 2013 lacks the general provisions which apply for SDLT to allow sub-sales and assignations of rights which complete on the same day as the original transaction to escape a double charge to tax.

Indeed the position in Scotland is actually worse than that because of s 14(1)(c) of the 2013 Act. Section 14 defines 'substantial performance' of a transaction, which is the event that stimulates the need to report and pay for LBBT purposes; and in terms of s 14(1)(c), a contract is substantially performed when, among other events, 'there is an assignation, sub-sale or other transaction (relating to the whole or part of the subject matter of the contract) as a result of which a person other than the original buyer becomes entitled to call for a conveyance to that person'. This means that not only is there no general relief

---

1 *Scotland's Spending Plans and Draft Budget 2016–17* ch 2.
2 Finance Act 2003 ss 44–45A, sch 2A.

for such a transaction in Scotland, but that by entering into such a transaction a buyer will bring forward the deemed completion of his original transaction – even if the sub-sale relates to only a small part of the purchase subjects and the sub-sale is not due to complete (as inevitably would be the case) until at least the date of the completion of the original transaction. It is hard to believe that it was deliberate policy to replace a relief by a penalty; it looks more like an unintended consequence of copying and pasting from a different part of the SDLT legislation.

Sub-sales: limited relief for commercial developments

The Scottish Government did, however, respond to substantial lobbying that a limited form of sub-sale relief was appropriate for some commercial developments. The result was the Land and Buildings Transaction Tax (Sub-sale Development Relief and Multiple Dwellings Relief) (Scotland) Order 2015.[1] This inserts a new schedule 10A into the 2013 Act, providing what is termed a 'targeted relief'. The target demands that the second of two connected transactions leads to a significant development of the subjects of the second transaction.

The requirements for the relief commence with the need for a qualifying sub-sale: the buyer under a contract (the 'first buyer') must contract to sell all or part of the subject-matter of the contract to a second buyer.[2] As with the original relief in the SDLT regime, it is then a requirement that the substantial performance or completion of the first contract take place at the same time as, and in connection with, the substantial performance or completion of the second contract.[3] So a gap between the original purchaser acquiring the property and selling it on will prevent the relief from taking effect.

There is also a further requirement that 'significant development for commercial purposes of the subject-matter of the qualifying sub-sale' will be completed within five years from the date on which the first buyer entered into the qualifying sub-sale.[4] That leads to the need for further definitions.[5] So 'development' –

    (a) means the building, on the subject-matter of the qualifying sub-sale, of buildings including educational, sports and leisure, residential, retail, office or industrial buildings (but not agricultural buildings, mining or engineering works (other than wind farms) or plant and machinery), and

    (b) includes the redevelopment of such buildings, where the redevelopment works carried out are comparable in scale or cost to the construction of such buildings.

'Significant development' means 'development that is significant having regard to, among other things, the nature and extent of the subject-matter of the qualifying sub-sale and to the market value of that subject-matter'.

---

1 SSI 2015/123.
2 Land and Buildings Transaction Tax (Scotland) Act 2013 sch 10A (inserted by Land and Buildings Transaction Tax (Sub-sale Development Relief and Multiple Dwellings Relief) (Scotland) Order 2015, SSI 2015/123, art 7 para 3.
3 LBTT(S)A 2013 sch 10A para 4(1)(a).
4 LBTT(S)A 2013 sch 10A para 4(1)(b), (3).
5 LBTT(S)A 2013 sch 10A para 7.

Any relief is given in relation to the first transaction. Full relief is given if the whole subject-matter of the first transaction is sold on, while partial relief is available where only part is the subject of the sub-sale.[1] There are provisions for withdrawing the relief in whole or in part where the anticipated development does not take place.[2] Although the initial proposal that the relief should not be available until the development had taken place was withdrawn, commercial developers still consider that the relief is very restricted.

Other reliefs

The same Order which introduced the restricted sub-sale relief also makes minor modifications to multiple dwellings relief[3] to make clear that the minimum prescribed amount of relief is a percentage of the amount that would be payable in respect of the dwellings but for the relief, and not a percentage of the amount that would be payable in respect of the dwellings and the remaining property.[4]

Reflecting a new relief introduced for SDLT, the Scottish Government introduced an exemption from LBTT for land transactions transferring property on the conversion of an authorised unit trust to, or its amalgamation with, an open-ended investment company. Exemption is given where the units of the unit trust are extinguished and the unit holders receive as consideration shares in the company, in proportion to their holdings of units in the trust. A similar exemption is given where there is an amalgamation of a unit trust with an open-ended investment company.[5]

Scottish landfill tax

The Scottish version of landfill tax took over on 1 April 2015. Apart from commencement orders and other necessary preliminary statutory instruments, a series of measures was brought into effect to facilitate its introduction. Thus the Scottish Landfill Tax (Qualifying Material) Order 2015[6] provides the list of materials, in eight groups and some with conditions, which qualify for the lower rate of Scottish landfill tax. The Scottish Landfill Tax (Exemption Certificates) Order 2015[7] makes provision for the issue of exemption certificates by Revenue Scotland to various, mainly public, bodies, who may be required to deal with landfill in certain circumstances.

Tax rates for 2015–16 were set by the Scottish Landfill Tax (Standard Rate and Lower Rate) Order 2015[8] at £82.60 per tonne (standard rate) and £2.60 (lower rate). In the Scottish Budget it was confirmed that the rates are to be increased to the

---

1 LBTT(S)A 2013 sch 10A paras 9, 10.
2 LBTT(S)A 2013 sch 10A paras 13–15.
3 As to which see LBTT(S)A 2013 sch 5.
4 Land and Buildings Transaction Tax (Sub-sale Development Relief and Multiple Dwellings Relief) (Scotland) Order 2015 arts 8, 9.
5 Land and Buildings Transaction Tax (Open-ended Investment Companies) (Scotland) Regulations 2015, SSI 2015/322.
6 SSI 2015/45.
7 SSI 2015/151.
8 SSI 2015/127.

planned UK rates for 2016–17, which are £84.40 (standard rate) and £2.65 (lower rate). This is designed, at least in part, to prevent 'waste tourism'. There is a slight divergence in detail in that the credit rate for the Scottish Landfill Communities Fund (SLCF) is to be maintained at 5.6%, which exceeds the planned UK credit rate of 4.2%.[1]

Tax administration

Revenue Scotland was set up in advance of the introduction of the two fully devolved taxes, and the structure for tax administration was laid down in the Revenue Scotland and Tax Powers Act 2014.[2] The Act was brought into force by a series of commencement orders.[3]

Further statutory instruments have dealt with a number of administrative matters. These include the Revenue Scotland and Tax Powers Act (Privileged Communications) Regulations 2015;[4] the Revenue Scotland and Tax Powers Act (Fees for Payment) Regulations 2015[5] (which apply a surcharge for payment of tax by credit card); the Revenue Scotland and Tax Powers Act (Postponement of Tax Pending a Review or Appeal) Regulations 2015[6]; the Revenue Scotland and Tax Powers Act (Interest on Unpaid Tax and Interest Rates in General) Regulations 2015[7] (which set out formulae for interest on unpaid tax); the Revenue Scotland and Tax Powers Act (Record Keeping) Regulations 2015[8] (which make provision about records which must be kept for landfill tax and also for LBTT transactions which are not notifiable); and the Revenue Scotland and Tax Powers Act (Reimbursement Arrangements) Regulations 2015[9] (which describe the provisions which must be included and the other conditions that must be met in relation to claims for overpaid tax, to prevent unjustified enrichment arising).

UK taxes on land

Annual tax on enveloped dwellings

Additional taxes on residential property, particularly where held other than by an individual, continue to advance; and the meaning of 'high value' in this context continues to diminish. Thus the annual tax on enveloped dwellings ('ATED')[10] applies now (2015–16) to dwellings with a value above

---

1 *Scotland's Spending Plans and Draft Budget 2016–17* ch 2.
2 See *Conveyancing 2014* pp 217–18 for early developments, and the Revenue Scotland website (https://www.revenue.scot/) for further details.
3 Revenue Scotland and Tax Powers Act 2014 (Commencement No 1) Order 2014, SSI 2014/278; Revenue Scotland and Tax Powers Act 2014 (Commencement No 2) Order 2014, SSI 2014/370; Revenue Scotland and Tax Powers Act 2014 (Commencement No 3) Order 2015, SSI 2015/18; Revenue Scotland and Tax Powers Act 2014 (Commencement No 4) Order 2015, SSI 2015/110 (which brought the final provisions of the Act into force).
4 SSI 2015/38.
5 SSI 2015/36.
6 SSI 2015/129.
7 SSI 2015/128.
8 SSI 2015/130.
9 SSI 2015/131.
10 Finance Act 2013 part 3, schs 33–35; see *Conveyancing 2013* pp 206–07.

£1 million;[1] in 2016–17 this threshold will come down to £500,000, increasing considerably the number of properties affected.[2] The amounts of the annual charge have also been increased considerably.[3] There are to be some new reliefs from the ATED regime: subject to conditions, it will not apply from 1 April 2016 to equity release schemes (home reversion plans), certain property development activities, and properties occupied by employees.[4]

Capital gains tax on disposals by non-residents

It has been a principle – and rather an unusual one as compared to other countries – that UK capital gains tax has not been chargeable on assets disposed of by non-residents, other than assets used in a UK business. As part of the package of measures introduced along with the ATED, this principle was eroded for high-value residential property owned other than by individuals.[5] And as with ATED itself, the threshold for increased CGT charges for residential property owned by non-individual entities is being lowered to £500,000 by 2016–17.[6] As announced in the 2014 Autumn Statement, it has now been further eroded in respect of any dwelling owned by a non-resident, including individuals, executors and trustees. The details are contained in a vast schedule to the Finance Act 2015, making extensive amendments and inserting new sections and schedules into the Taxation of Chargeable Gains Act 1992.[7] Gains that would be liable to CGT as part the ATED regime (generally at the same or a higher rate) or to CGT or corporation tax as disposals of assets used in a UK trade are excluded.[8] Various unit trusts and similar collective investment schemes are also excluded.[9]

The charge is to apply to disposals of dwellings and associated land, including dwellings in the process of being constructed.[10] There are various exclusions for school residences, hospices, prisons, hotels, student accommodation and the like.[11] Tax is only to be charged on gains accruing after 5 April 2015. The default method of calculation involves rebasing the value by a deemed disposal on that date and charging the increase since then; there is an alternative of a straight-line apportionment of gains over the whole period of ownership.[12] The rate of

1 Finance Act 2014 s 109.
2 Finance Act 2014 s 110.
3 See amendments to Finance Act 2013 s 99 by Finance Act 2015 s 70, increasing the charges due at each band by 50% above the rate of inflation.
4 *Spending Review and Autumn Statement 2015* (https://www.gov.uk/government/publications/spending-review-and-autumn-statement-2015-documents) para 12.2.
5 See *Conveyancing 2013* pp 206–07 and *Conveyancing 2014* p 216.
6 Finance Act 2015 s 38, sch 8, amending Taxation of Chargeable Gains Act 1992 ss 2C, 2D.
7 Finance Act 2015 s 37, sch 7. Overall this Act was a very large piece of legislation which went through Parliament shortly before it was prorogued for the General Election, with minimal Parliamentary scrutiny.
8 Taxation of Chargeable Gains Act 1992 s 14B, The provisions of the 1992 Act in this and the following notes were added by the Finance Act 2015 sch 7.
9 TCGA 1992 ss 14F, 14G.
10 TCGA 1992 sch B1 para 4(1).
11 TCGA 1992 sch B1 para 4(3)–(11).
12 On all of this, see TCGA 1992 sch 4ZZB (the increasingly impenetrable numbering perhaps indicating the need for a consolidation of the 1992 Act).

tax payable depends on whether the disposal is by an individual, a trust or a company.

It is possible that the dwelling being sold could qualify as the individual's principal private residence. New provisions are inserted to remove or restrict PPR relief where the individual concerned does not actually occupy the dwelling in question for at least 90 days in a tax year.[1]

One particular point to note is that a disposal must be reported within 30 days of settlement of the disposal transaction.[2] Payment of any tax due can generally be deferred until the normal due date for CGT (31 January after the year of assessment for individuals); but this reporting deadline is very much earlier than applies for other disposals potentially liable for CGT, and applies whether or not any tax is actually payable. Further, there is a separate proposal to bring forward the date of payment of CGT generally on the disposal of residential property, so that at least a payment on account has to be made within 30 days of the date of settlement. This, however, is not scheduled to come into effect until 2019.

Inheritance tax

Although most changes in UK tax affecting residential property have tended to involve increases in taxation, one forthcoming change works in the opposite direction. The inheritance tax residence nil rate band will eventually provide an additional nil rate band of up to £175,000. When combined with the normal nil rate band of £325,000 this will produce a total of £500,000, or up to £1 million for married couples and civil partners. The new nil rate band will apply where a dwelling is left to descendants. The increase is hedged with conditions, notably a tapering reduction where the deceased's total estate exceeds £2 million, and is being phased in over four years from 2017–18. It is a complex additional relief which will probably be available to relatively few estates.[3]

The summer Budget following the 2015 election announced a consultation on the proposal to bring the ownership of residential property through sophisticated structures by non-domiciled people seeking to avoid IHT back into charge, in a similar way to direct ownership. ATED was introduced to discourage this. However, HMRC's research suggests that the IHT saving often outweighs the ATED charge and reliefs from ATED often apply in any event.[4]

Income tax: reliefs in respect of rent

A further improvement for those letting out rooms in their houses is the first increase for many years in the level of rent-a-room relief, which exempts from

---

1   TCGA 1992 ss 222A–222C, 223A, and other provisions inserted by Finance Act 2015 s 39, sch 9.
2   Taxes Management Act 1970 s 12ZB (inserted by Finance Act 2015 sch 7 para 43).
3   See Finance (No 2) Act 2015 s 9, inserting ss 8D–8M into the Inheritance Tax Act 1984.
4   See *Technical briefing on foreign domiciled persons/Inheritance Tax residential property changes* (2015; https://www.gov.uk/government/publications/technical-briefing-on-foreign-domiciled-personsinheritance-tax-residential-property-changes). At the time of writing the consultation had yet to appear.

tax gross amounts up to the specified level. This level increases from £4,250 to £7,500, with effect from 2016–17.[1]

A consultation took place on the 'wear and tear' allowance currently available to landlords. This takes the form of a deduction of 10% from gross rents. The intention is that this should be replaced with a relief that enables all landlords of residential dwellinghouses to deduct the costs they actually incur on replacing furnishings in the property. After the consultation, this replacement will be brought into effect from April 2016.[2]

In a phased change, buy-to-let landlords are to be restricted in the amount of interest relief that they can claim. Finance costs will be restricted to a basic-rate tax reduction only by 2020–21, but this restriction will commence in 2017–18 when only 75% of finance costs will be eligible for full relief, the balance getting only a basic-rate reduction. The proportion eligible for full relief goes down to 50% in 2018–19 and 25% in 2019–20, before being removed entirely in the next tax year.[3]

The Scotland Act 2012 and the Scotland Bill

The Scottish rate of income tax will come into effect on 6 April 2016. Under changes introduced by the Scotland Act 2012[4], the basic, higher and additional rates of income tax are reduced by 10 percentage points and the Scottish rate of income tax is then added back to the reduced amount. The resulting rate is then applied to non-savings income. The Scottish Government has announced that for 2016–17, the Scottish rate of income tax will be 10%, thus maintaining the overall rate for Scottish taxpayers at the same level as in the rest of the UK.[5]

It is important to note that income from land is treated as coming from a property business and is thus not categorised as savings income. The Scottish rate will affect the rental profits of Scottish taxpayers wherever their property business is located; but it will not affect the profits from a Scottish property business unless the owner of that business is a Scottish taxpayer.

Extensive amendments are contained in the Scotland Bill, currently before the UK Parliament, and may come into force as early as 2017–18. Under these proposed changes to the Income Tax Act 2007, a Scottish rate resolution may set for Scottish taxpayers a Scottish basic rate and other rates and the thresholds which are to apply for each rate. There is to be no 'lockstep', so some rates could be increased and some decreased as compared to UK rates, new rates could be introduced, and the thresholds could be set at different levels from those applying in the rest of the UK.[6]

---

1 Income Tax (Limit for Rent-a-Room Relief) Order 2015, SI 2015/1539.
2 *Reform to the Wear and Tear Allowance - summary of responses* (2015; https://www.gov.uk/government/consultations/replacing-wear-and-tear-allowance-with-tax-relief-for-replacing-furnishings-in-let-residential-dwelling-houses).
3 Finance (No 2) Act 2015 s 24, inserting ss 272A, 272B, 274A and 274B into the Income Tax (Trading and Other Income) Act 2005 and making similar changes for property partnerships in the Income Tax Act 2007.
4 Scotland Act 2012 ss 25–27, amending the Income Tax Act 2007 s 6.
5 *Scotland's Spending Plans and Draft Budget 2016–17* ch 2.
6 Scotland Bill cls 13–15, amending the Scotland Act 1998 and the Income Tax Act 2007.

In taxes directly affecting land, any tax on the commercial exploitation of aggregates (currently aggregates levy in the UK) will join LBTT and Scottish landfill tax to become a fully devolved tax.[1]

---

1 Scotland Bill cl 18 (inserting s 80M into the Scotland Act 1998) and cl 19.

❧ PART V ❧
TABLES

TABLES

CUMULATIVE TABLE OF DECISIONS ON VARIATION OR DISCHARGE OF TITLE CONDITIONS

This table lists all opposed applications under the Title Conditions (Scotland) Act 2003 for variation or discharge of title conditions. Decisions or expenses are omitted. Note that the full opinions in Lands Tribunal cases are usually available at http://www.lands-tribunal-scotland.org.uk/records.html.

Restriction on building

Name of case	Burden	Applicant's project in breach of burden	Application granted or refused
Ord v Mashford 2006 SLT (Lands Tr) 15; *Lawrie v Mashford* 21 December 2007	1938. No building.	Erection of single-storey house and garage.	Granted. Claim for compensation refused.
Daly v Bryce 2006 GWD 25-565	1961 feu charter. No further building.	Replace existing house with two houses.	Granted.
J & L Leisure Ltd v Shaw 2007 GWD 28-489	1958 disposition. No new buildings higher than 15 feet 6 inches.	Replace derelict building with two-storey housing.	Granted subject to compensation of £5,600.
West Coast Property Developments Ltd v Clarke 2007 GWD 29-511	1875 feu contract. Terraced houses. No further building.	Erection of second, two-storey house.	Granted. Claim for compensation refused.
Smith v Prior 2007 GWD 30-523	1934 feu charter. No building.	Erection of modest rear extension.	Granted.
Anderson v McKinnon 2007 GWD 29-513	1993 deed of conditions in modern housing estate.	Erection of rear extension.	Granted.
Smith v Elrick 2007 GWD 29-515	1996 feu disposition. No new house. The feu had been subdivided.	Conversion of barn into a house.	Granted.

Name of case	Burden	Applicant's project in breach of burden	Application granted or refused
Brown v Richardson 2007 GWD 28-490	1888 feu charter. No alterations/new buildings.	Erection of rear extension.	Granted. This was an application for renewal, following service of a notice of termination.
Gallacher v Wood 2008 SLT (Lands Tr) 31	1933 feu contract. No alterations/new buildings.	Erection of rear extension, including extension at roof level which went beyond bungalow's footprint.	Granted. Claim for compensation refused.
Jarron v Stuart 23 March and 5 May 2011	1992 deed of conditions. No external alteration and additions.	Erection of rear extension.	Granted. Claim for compensation refused.
Blackman v Best 2008 GWD 11-214	1934 disposition. No building other than a greenhouse.	Erection of a double garage.	Granted.
McClumpha v Bradie 2009 GWD 31-519	1984 disposition allowing the erection of only one house.	Erection of four further houses.	Granted but restricted to four houses.
McGregor v Collins-Taylor 14 May 2009	1988 disposition prohibiting the erection of dwellinghouses without consent.	Erection of four further houses.	Granted but restricted to four houses.
Faeley v Clark 2006 GWD 28-626	1967 disposition. No further building.	Erection of second house.	Refused.
Cattanach v Vine-Hall	1996 deed of conditions in favour of neighbouring property. No building within 7 metres of that property.	Erection of substantial house within 2 metres.	Refused, subject to the possibility of the applicants bringing a revised proposal.
Hamilton v Robertson, 10 January 2008	1984 deed of conditions affecting 5-house development. No further building.	Erection of second house on site, but no firm plans.	Refused, although possibility of later success once plans firmed up was not excluded.

Name of case	Burden	Applicant's project in breach of burden	Application granted or refused
Cocozza v Rutherford 2008 SLT (Lands Tr) 6	1977 deed of conditions. No alterations.	Substantial alterations which would more than double the footprint of the house.	Refused.
Scott v Teasdale 22 December 2009	1962 feu disposition. No building.	New house in garden.	Refused.
Rennie v Cullen House Gardens Ltd 29 June 2012	2005 deed of conditions. No new building or external extension.	Extension of building forming part of historic house.	Refused.
Hollinshead v Gilchrist 7 December 2009	1990 Disposition and 1997 feu disposition. No building or alterations.	Internal alterations.	Granted.
Tower Hotel (Troon) Ltd v McCann 4 March 2010	1965 feu disposition. No building. Existing building to be used as a hotel or dwellinghouse.	No firm plan though one possibility was the building of flats.	Granted.
Corstorphine v Fleming 2 July 2010	1965 feu disposition. No alterations, one house only.	A substantial extension plus a new house.	Granted.
Corry v MacLachlan 9 July 2010	1984 disposition of part of garden. Obligation to build a single-storey house.	Addition of an extra storey.	Refused.
Watt v Garden 4 November 2011	1995 disposition. Use as garden only.	Additional 2-bedroom bungalow.	Granted but with compensation.
Fyfe v Benson 26 July 2011	1966 deed of conditions. No building or subdivision.	Additional 3-bedroom house.	Refused.
MacDonald v Murdoch 7 August 2012	1997 disposition. No building in garden.	Erection of 1½-storey house.	Refused.
Trigstone Ltd v Mackenzie 16 February 2012	1949 charter of novodamus. No building in garden.	Erection of 4-storey block of flats. Parking of 2 cars.	Refused.
McCulloch v Reid 3 April 2012	2011 disposition. No parking in rear courtyard.	Erection of two houses.	Refused.

Name of case	Burden	Applicant's project in breach of burden	Application granted or refused
Trustees of John Raeside & Son v Chalmers 2014 GWD 35-660	1989 disposition. Agricultural purposes only.	Erection of mews house in back garden.	Granted.
Sinton v Lloyd 11 June 2014	Instrument of sasine of 1813 prohibiting building.	Erection of new house and extension of existing house.	Granted.
MacKay v McGowan 2015 SLT (Lands Tr) 6	Feu disposition prohibiting building.	Erection of two-storey extension.	Granted in respect of new house (only).
Ferguson v Gunby 2015 SLT (Lands Tr) 195	1972 deed of conditions preventing alterations.		Granted.

Other restrictions on use

Name of case	Burden	Applicant's project in breach of burden	Application granted or refused
Church of Scotland General Trs v McLaren 2006 SLT (Lands Tr) 27	Use as a church.	Possible development for flats.	Granted.
Wilson v McNamee 16 September 2007	Use for religious purposes.	Use for a children's nursery.	Granted
Verrico v Tomlinson 2008 SLT (Lands Tr) 2	1950 disposition. Use as a private residence for the occupation of one family.	Separation of mews cottage from ground floor flat.	Granted.
Whitelaw v Acheson 29 February and 29 September 2012	1883 feu charter. Use as a single dwelling; no further building.	Change of use to therapy and wellbeing centre; erection of extension.	Granted subject to some restrictions.
Matnic Ltd v Armstrong 2010 SLT (Lands Tr) 7	2004 deed of conditions. Use for the sale of alcohol.	Use of units in a largely residential estate for retail purposes.	Granted but restricted to small units and no sale of alcohol after 8 pm.
Clarke v Grantham 2009 GWD 38-645	2004 disposition. No parking on an area of courtyard.	A desire to park (though other areas were available).	Granted.

Name of case	Burden	Applicant's project in breach of burden	Application granted or refused
Hollinshead v Gilchrist 7 December 2009	1990 disposition and 1997 feu disposition. No caravans, commercial or other vehicles to be parked in front of the building line.	Parking of cars.	Granted and claim for compensation refused.
Perth & Kinross Council v Chapman 13 August 2009	1945 disposition. Plot to be used only for outdoor recreational purposes.	Sale for redevelopment.	Granted.
Davenport v Julian Hodge Bank Ltd 23 June 2011	2010 deed of conditions. No external painting without permission.	Paint the external walls sky blue.	Refused.
Duffus v McWhirter 2014 GWD 34-647	2005 disposition prohibiting commercial use.	Commercial equestrian use.	Refused.

Flatted property

Name of case	Burden	Applicant's project in breach of burden	Application granted or refused
Regan v Mullen 2006 GWD 25-564	1989. No subdivision of flat.	Subdivision of flat.	Granted.
Kennedy v Abbey Lane Properties 29 March 2010	2004. Main-door flat liable for a share of maintenance of common passages and stairs.	None.	Refused.
Patterson v Drouet 20 January 2011	Liability for maintenance in accordance with gross annual value.	None, but, since the freezing of valuations in 1989, ground floor flats had reverted to residential use.	Variation of liability of ground floor flats granted in principle subject to issues of competency.
Melville v Crabbe 19 Jan 2009	1880 feu disposition. No additional flat.	Creation of a flat in the basement.	Refused.

Sheltered and retirement housing

Name of case	Burden	Applicant's project in breach of burden	Application granted or refused
At.Home Nationwide Ltd v Morris 2007 GWD 31-535	1993 deed of conditions. On sale, must satisfy superior that flat will continue to be used for the elderly.	No project: just removal of an inconvenient restriction.	Burden held to be void. Otherwise application would have been refused.

Miscellaneous

Name of case	Burden	Applicant's project in breach of burden	Application granted or refused
McPherson v Mackie 2006 GWD 27-606 rev [2007] CSIH 7, 2007 SCLR 351	1990. Housing estate: maintenance of house.	Demolition of house to allow the building of a road for access to proposed new development.	Discharged by agreement on 25 April 2007.

Applications for renewal of real burdens following service of a notice of termination

Name of case	Burden	Applicant's project in breach of burden	Application granted or refused
Brown v Richardson 2007 GWD 28-490	1888 feu charter. No buildings.	Substantial rear extension.	Refused.
Council for Music in Hospitals v Trustees for Richard Gerald Associates 2008 SLT (Lands Tr) 17	1838 instrument of sasine. No building in garden.	None.	Refused.
Gibson v Anderson 3 May 2012	1898 disposition. No building other than 1-storey outbuildings.	2-storey house.	Refused; burden varied to allow limited building.
Macneil v Bradonwood Ltd 2013 SLT (Lands Tr) 41	Mid-Victorian feus limited building at foot of garden to 1 storey.	1.5-storey houses.	Refused; burden varied to allow the proposed houses.
Cook v Cadman 20 December 2013	1876 feu prevented building.	4 additional houses.	Refused; burden varied to allow the proposed houses.

Applications for preservation of community burdens following deeds of variation or discharge under s 33 or s 35

Name of case	Burden	Applicant's project in breach of burden	Application granted or refused
Fleeman v Lyon 2009 GWD 32-539	1982 deed of conditions. No building, trade, livestock etc.	Erection of a second house.	Granted.

Applications for variation of community burdens (s 91)

Name of case	Burden	Applicant's project in breach of burden	Application granted or refused
Fenwick v National Trust for Scotland 2009 GWD 32-538	1989 deed of conditions.	None. The application was for the complete discharge of the deed with the idea that a new deed would eventually be drawn up.	Refused.
Patterson v Drouet 2013 GWD 3-99	1948 deed of conditions apportioned liability for maintenance in a tenement on the basis of annual value.	Substitution of floor area for annual value.	Granted; compensation refused.
Gilfin Property Holdings Ltd v Beech 2013 SLT (Lands Tr) 17	1986 deed of conditions apportioned liability for maintenance in a tenement on a percentage basis rooted in rateable value.	Substitution of a more equitable apportionment.	Granted.
Stewart v Sherwood 7 June 2013	1986 deed of conditions.	Addition of a prohibition on letting.	Granted except in one respect.
Scott v Applin 16 May 2013	2005 deed of conditions.	Removal of requirement that the full-time manager should be resident.	Granted.
McCabe v Killcross 2013 SLT (Lands Tr) 48	Feu dispositions from 1976	Altering apportionment of liability for maintenance following division of one of the flats.	Granted except in one respect.

Personal real burdens

Name of case	Burden	Applicant's project in breach of burden	Application granted or refused
Grant v National Trust for Scotland 8 August 2014	Conservation agreement from 1962 prohibited non-agricultural use.	Building of houses.	Granted in part.

Servitudes

Name of case	Burden	Applicant's project in breach of burden	Application granted or refused
George Wimpey East Scotland Ltd v Fleming 2006 SLT (Lands Tr) 2 and 59	1988 disposition. Right of way.	Diversion of right of way to allow major development for residential houses.	Granted (opposed). Claim for compensation for temporary disturbance refused.
Ventureline Ltd 2 August 2006	1972 disposition. 'Right to use' certain ground.	Possible redevelopment.	Granted (unopposed).
Graham v Parker 2007 GWD 30-524	1990 feu disposition. Right of way from mid-terraced house over garden of end-terraced house to the street.	Small re-routing of right of way, away from the burdened owner's rear wall, so as to allow an extension to be built.	Granted (opposed).
MacNab v McDowall 24 October 2007	1994 feu disposition reserved a servitude of way from the back garden to the front street in favour of two neighbouring house.	Small re-rerouting, on to the land of one of the neighbours, to allow a rear extension to be built.	Granted (opposed).
Jensen v Tyler 2008 SLT (Lands Tr) 39	1985 feu disposition granted a servitude of way.	Re-routing of part of the road in order to allow (unspecified) development of steading.	Granted (opposed).
Gibb v Kerr 2009 GWD 38-646	1981 feu disposition granted a servitude of way.	Re-routing to homologate what had already taken place as a result of the building of a conservatory.	Granted (opposed).

Name of case	Burden	Applicant's project in breach of burden	Application granted or refused
Parkin v Kennedy 23 March 2010	1934 feu charter. Right of way from mid-terraced house over garden of end-terraced house.	Re-routing to allow extension to be built, which would require a restriction to pedestrian access.	Refused (opposed).
Adams v Trs for the Linton Village Hall 24 October 2011	Dispositions of 1968 and 1970 reserved a servitude of access.	Re-routing to a route more convenient for the applicant.	Granted (opposed).
Brown v Kitchen 28 October 2011	1976 feu disposition reserved a servitude of pedestrian access.	Re-routing to the edge of the garden.	Granted in principle (opposed) subject to agreement as to the widening of the substitute route.
Hossack v Robertson 29 June 2012	1944 disposition reserved a servitude of pedestrian access.	Re-routing to end of garden to allow building of conservatory.	Granted (opposed).
Cope v X 2013 SLT (Lands Tr) 20	Servitude of access.	Substitute road.	Granted (opposed).
ATD Developments Ltd v Weir 14 September 2010	2002 disposition granted a servitude right of way.	Narrowing the servitude so as to allow gardens for proposed new houses.	Granted (unopposed).
Stirling v Thorley 12 October 2012	1994 and 1995 dispositions granted a servitude of vehicular access.	Building a house on half of an area set aside for turning vehicles.	Refused (opposed).
Colecliffe v Thompson 2010 SLT (Lands Tr) 15	1997 disposition granted a servitude of way.	None. But the owners of the benefited property had since acquired a more convenient access, secured by a new servitude.	Granted (opposed).
G v A 26 November 2009	1974 disposition granted a servitude of way.	None. But the owners of the benefited property had since acquired a more convenient access (although not to his garage).	Granted (opposed) but on the basis that the respondent should apply for compensation.

Name of case	Burden	Applicant's project in breach of burden	Application granted or refused
Graham v Lee 18 June 2009	2001 disposition granted (a) a servitude of way and (b) of drainage.	None.	(a) was granted provided the applicants discharged a reciprocal servitude of their own, and compensation was considered. (b) was refused.
McNab v Smith 15 June 2012	1981 disposition granted a servitude of vehicular access for agricultural purposes.	None. But the owner of the benefited property could access the property in a different way.	Granted (opposed) but, because works would be needed to improve the alternative access, on the basis of payment of compensation.
Stephenson v Thomas 21 November 2012	1990 disposition granted a servitude of vehicular access.	None. But the owner of the benefited property could access the property in a different way.	Refused (opposed) on the basis that there were safety concerns about the alternative route and the benefited proprietors were proposing to revert to the original route.
McKenzie v Scott 19 May 2009	Dispositions from 1944 and 1957 granted a servitude of bleaching and drying clothes.	None. But the servitude had not in practice been exercised for many years.	Granted (opposed).
Chisholm v Crawford 17 June 2010	A driveway divided two properties. A 1996 feu disposition of one of the properties granted a servitude of access over the driveway.	None. But the applicant was aggrieved that no matching servitude appeared in the neighbour's title.	Refused.
Branziet Investments v Anderson 2013 GWD 31-629	1968 disposition granted a servitude of vehicular access.	Narrowing the servitude to 5 metres so as to allow rear gardens for new houses.	Granted (opposed) except that at either end the width was to be larger.
Mackay v Bain 2013 SLT (Lands Tr) 37	Servitude of pedestrian access over the front garden of applicant's property (1989).	None.	Refused (opposed). The servitude was the only means of access to the respondents' front door.

Name of case	Burden	Applicant's project in breach of burden	Application granted or refused
Pollacchi v Campbell 2014 SLT (Lands Tr) 55	Servitude of vehicular access.	Re-routing to allow creation of garden.	Refused.
Yule v Tobert 2015 GWD 39-620	Servitude of vehicular access over yard (1984).	None, but dominant proprietor wished to use access to allow teachers at his nursery to park.	Refused application to restrict servitude to residential purposes.
United Investment Co Ltd v Charlie Reid Ltd 2016 GWD 1-13	Servitude of vehicular access (1963).	Major redevelopment of site.	Granted (opposed) but subject to the possibility of compensation if loss in value to the benefited property could be shown.

CUMULATIVE TABLE OF APPEALS

A table at the end of *Conveyancing 2008* listed all cases digested in *Conveyancing 1999* and subsequent annual volumes in respect of which an appeal was subsequently heard, and gave the result of the appeal. This table is a continuation of the earlier table, beginning with appeals heard during 2009.

Aberdeen City Council v Stewart Milne Group Ltd
[2009] CSOH 80, 2009 GWD 26-417, 2009 Case (6) *affd* [2010] CSIH 81, 2010 GWD 37-755, 2010 Case (9) *affd* [2011] UKSC 56, 2011 Case (13)

AMA (New Town) Ltd v Finlay
2010 GWD 32-658, Sh Ct, 2010 Case (8) *rev* 2011 SLT (Sh Ct) 73, 2011 Case (1)

Blemain Finance Ltd v Balfour & Manson LLP
[2011] CSOH 157, 2012 SLT 672, 2011 Case (69) *affd* [2012] CSIH 66, [2013] PNLR 3, 2012 GWD 30-609, 2012 Case (70)

Brown v Stonegale Ltd
[2013] CSOH 189, 2014 GWD 2-27, 2013 Case (71) *affd* [2015] CSIH 12, 2015 SCLR 619, 2015 Case (85)

Chalmers v Chalmers
[2014] CSOH 161, 2015 SCLR 299, 2014 Case (22) *rev* [2015] CSIH 75, 2015 SLT 793, 2015 Hous LR 82, 2015 Case (27)

Cheshire Mortgage Corporation Ltd v Grandison; Blemain Finance Ltd v Balfour & Manson LLP
[2011] CSOH 157, 2012 SLT 672, 2011 Case (69) *affd* [2012] CSIH 66, [2013] PNLR 3, 2012 GWD 30-609, 2012 Case (69)

Christie Owen & Davies plc v Campbell
2007 GWD 24-397, Sh Ct, 2007 Case (53) *affd* 18 Dec 2007, Glasgow Sheriff Court, 2007 Case (53) *rev* [2009] CSIH 26, 2009 SLT 518, 2009 Case (82)

Collins v Sweeney
2013 GWD 11-230, Sh Ct, 2013 Case (3) *affd* 2014 GWD 12-214, Sh Ct, 2014 Case (4)

Compugraphics International Ltd v Nikolic
[2009] CSOH 54, 2009 GWD 19-311, 2009 Cases (22) and (90) *rev* [2011] CSIH 34, 2011 SLT 955, 2011 Cases (21) and (74)

Co-operative Group Ltd v Propinvest Paisley LP
17 September 2010, Lands Tribunal, 2010 Case (36) *rev* [2011] CSIH 41, 2012 SC 51, 2011 SLT 987, 2011 Hous LR 32, 2011 Case (38)

Cramaso LLP v Viscount Reidhaven's Trs

[2010] CSOH 62, 2010 GWD 20-403, 2010 Case (58) *affd* [2011] CSIH 81, 2011 Case (57) *rev* [2014] UKSC 9, 2014 SC (UKSC) 121, 2014 SLT 521, 2014 SCLR 484, 2014 Case (31)

EDI Central Ltd v National Car Parks Ltd

[2010] CSOH 141, 2011 SLT 75, 2010 Case (5) *affd* [2012] CSIH 6, 2012 SLT 421, 2012 Case (4)

ELB Securities Ltd v Love

2014 GWD 28-562, 2014 Case (38) *affd* [2015] CSIH 67, 2015 SLT 721, 2015 Hous LR 88, 2015 Case (66)

Euring David Ayre of Kilmarnock, Baron of Kilmarnock Ptr

[2008] CSOH 35, 2008 Case (82) *rev* [2009] CSIH 61, 2009 SLT 759, 2009 Case (93)

Frank Houlgate Investment Co Ltd v Biggart Baillie LLP

[2013] CSOH 80, 2013 SLT 993, 2013 Case (61) *affd* [2014] CSIH 79, 2014 SLT 1001, 2015 SC 187, 2014 Case (65)

Martin Stephen James Goldstraw of Whitecairns Ptr

[2008] CSOH 34, 2008 Case (81) *rev* [2009] CSIH 61, 2009 SLT 759, 2009 Case (93)

Hamilton v Dumfries & Galloway Council

[2008] CSOH 65, 2008 SLT 531, 2008 Case (37) *rev* [2009] CSIH 13, 2009 SC 277, 2009 SLT 337, 2009 SCLR 392, 2009 Case (50)

Hamilton v Nairn

[2009] CSOH 163, 2010 SLT 399, 2009 Case (51) *affd* [2010] CSIH 77, 2010 SLT 1155, 2010 Case (44)

Hill of Rubislaw (Q Seven) Ltd v Rubislaw Quarry Aberdeen Ltd

[2013] CSOH 131, 2013 GWD 27-545, 2014 Case (11) *affd* [2014] CSIH 105, 2015 SC 339, 2014 Case (10)

Hoblyn v Barclays Bank plc

[2013] CSOH 104, 2013 GWD 26-533, 10313 Case (51) *affd* [2014] CSIH 52, 2014 GWD 30-376, 2014 HousLR 26, 2015 SCLR 85, 2014 Case (60)

Holms v Ashford Estates Ltd

2006 SLT (Sh Ct) 70, 2006 Case (40) *affd* 2006 SLT (Sh Ct) 161, 2006 Case (40) *rev* [2009] CSIH 28, 2009 SLT 389, 2009 SCLR 428, 2009 Cases (19) and (52)

Hunter v Tindale

2011 SLT (Sh Ct) 11, 2010 Case (16) *rev* 2011 GWD 25-570, Sh Ct, 2011 Case (19)

K2 Restaurants Ltd v Glasgow City Council
[2011] CSOH 171, 2011 Hous LR 171, 2011 Case (20) *affd* [2013] CSIH 49, 2013 GWD 21-420, 2013 Case (5)

Kerr of Ardgowan, Ptr
[2008] CSOH 36, 2008 SLT 251, 2008 Case (80) *rev* [2009] CSIH 61, 2009 SLT 759, 2009 Case (93)

L Batley Pet Products Ltd v North Lanarkshire Council
[2011] CSOH 209, 2012 GWD 4-73, 2011 Case (62) *rev* [2012] CSIH 83, 2012 GWD 37-745, 2012 Case (43) *rev* [2014] UKSC 27, 2014 SC (UKSC) 174, 2014 SLT 593, 2014 Case (39)

Liquidator of Letham Grange Development Co Ltd v Foxworth Investments Ltd
[2011] CSOH 66, 2011 SLT 1152, 2011 Case (64) *rev* [2013] CSIH 13, 2013 SLT 445, 2013 Case (47) *rev* [2014] UKSC 41, 2014 SC (UKSC) 203, 2014 SLT 775, 2014 Case (70)

Livingstone of Bachuil v Paine
[2012] CSOH 161, 2012 GWD 35-707, 2012 Case (12) *rev* [2013] CSIH 110, 2013 Case (9)

Luminar Lava Ignite Ltd v Mama Group plc
[2009] CSOH 68, 2009 GWD 19-305, 2009 Case (91) *rev* [2010] CSIH 1, 2010 SC 310, 2010 SLT 147, 2010 Case (77)

McGraddie v McGraddie
[2009] CSOH 142, 2009 GWD 38-633, 2009 Case (60), [2010] CSOH 60, 2010 GWD 21-404, 2000 Case (48) *rev* [2012] CSIH 23, 2012 GWD 15-310, 2012 Case (38) *rev* [2013] UKSC 58, 2013 SLT 1212, 2013 Case (32)

MacQueen v MacPherson
3 October 2014, Oban Sheriff Court, 2014 Case (2) *rev* [2015] CSIH 60, 2015 GWD 26-449, 2015 Case (4)

McSorley v Drennan
May 2011, Ayr Sheriff Court, 2011 Case (14) *rev* [2012] CSIH 59, 2012 GWD 25-506, 2012 Case (6)

Mehrabadi v Haugh
June 2009, Aberdeen Sheriff Court, 2009 Case (17) *affd* 11 January 2010 Aberdeen Sheriff Court, 2010 Case (15)

Mirza v Salim
[2013] CSOH 73, 2013 GWD 17-348, 2013 Case (65) *rev* [2014] CSIH 51, 2015 SC 31, 2014 SLT 875, 2014 SCLR 764, 2014 Case (67)

Moderator of the General Assembly of the Free Church of Scotland v Interim Moderator of the Congregation of Strath Free Church of Scotland (Continuing)
[2009] CSOH 113, 2009 SLT 973, 2009 Case (96) *affd* [2011] CSIH 52, 2011 SLT 1213, 2012 SC 79, 2011 Case (77)

Morris v Rae
[2011] CSIH 30, 2011 SC 654, 2011 SLT 701, 2011 SCLR 428, 2011 Case (39) *rev* [2012] UKSC 50, 2013 SC (UKSC) 106, 2013 SLT 88, 2013 SCLR 80, 2012 Case (41)

Multi-link Leisure Developments Ltd v North Lanarkshire Council
[2009] CSOH 114, 2009 SLT 1170, 2009 Case (70) *rev* [2009] CSIH 96, 2010 SC 302, 2010 SLT 57, 2010 SCLR 306, 2009 Case (70) *affd* [2010] UKSC 47. [2011] 1 All ER 175, 2010 Case (52)

Orkney Housing Association Ltd v Atkinson
15 October 2010, Kirkwall Sheriff Court, 2010 Case (21) *rev* 2011 GWD 30-652, 2011 Cases (22) and (41)

Pocock's Tr v Skene Investments (Aberdeen) Ltd
[2011] CSOH 144, 2011 GWD 30-654, 2011 Case (40) *rev* [2012] CSIH 61, 2012 GWD 27-562, 2012 Case (36)

R M Prow (Motors) Ltd Directors Pension Fund Trustees v Argyll and Bute Council
[2012] CSOH 77, 2012 GWD 21-438, 2012 Case (44) *affd* [2013] CSIH 23, 2013 GWD 12-260, 2013 Case (44)

R & D Construction Group Ltd v Hallam Land Management Ltd
[2009] CSOH 128, 2009 Case (8) *affd* [2010] CSIH 96, 2010 Case (4)

Regus (Maxim) Ltd v Bank of Scotland plc
[2011] CSOH 129, 2011 GWD 27-600, 2011 Case (52) *affd* [2013] CSIH 12, 2013 SC 331, 2013 SLT 477, 2013 Case (43)

Rivendale v Keeper of the Registers of Scotland
30 October 2013, Lands Tribunal, 2013 Case (35) *affd* [2015] CSIH 27, 2015 SC 558, 2015 Case (29) and (84)

Royal Bank of Scotland plc v Carlyle
[2010] CSOH 3, 2010 GWD 13-235, 2010 Case (67) *rev* [2013] CSIH 75, 2014 SC 188, 2014 SCLR 167, 2013 Case (75) *rev* [2015] UKSC 13, 2015 SC (UKSC) 93, 2015 SLT 206, 2015 Case (91)

Royal Bank of Scotland v O'Donnell
[2013] CSOH 78, 2013 GWD 19-388, 2013 Case (59) *affd* [2014] CSIH 84, 2014 GWD 33-641, 2014 Case (54)

Royal Bank of Scotland plc v Wilson

2008 GWD 2-35, Sh Ct, 2008 Case (61) *rev* 2009 CSIH 36, 2009 SLT 729, 2009 Case (75) *rev* [2010] UKSC 50, 2011 SC (UKSC) 66, 2010 SLT 1227, 2010 Hous LR 88, 2010 Case (66)

Salvesen v Riddell

[2012] CSIH 26, 2012 SLT 633, 2012 SCLR 403, 2012 HousLR 30, 2012 Case (51) *rev* [2013] UKSC 22, 2013 SC (UKSC) 236, 2013 SLT 863, 2013 Case (50)

Scottish Coal Company Ltd v Danish Forestry Co Ltd

[2009] CSOH 171, 2009 GWD 5-79, 2009 Case (9) *affd* [2010] CSIH 56, 2010 GWD 27-529, 2010 Case (3)

Sheltered Housing Management Ltd v Bon Accord Bonding Co Ltd

2007 GWD 32-533, 2006 Cases (24) and (35), 11 October 2007, Lands Tribunal, 2007 Case (21) *rev* [2010] CSIH 42, 2010 SC 516, 2010 SLT 662, 2010 Case (25)

@Sipp (Pension Trustees) Ltd v Insight Travel Services Ltd

[2014] CSOH 137, 2014 Hous LR 54, 2014 Case (42) *rev* [2015] CSIH 91, 2016 SLT 131, 2015 Case (51)

Smith v Stuart

2009 GWD 8-140, Sh Ct, 2009 Case (2) *affd* [2010] CSIH 29, 2010 SC 490, 2010 SLT 1249, 2010 Case (10)

STV Central Ltd v Semple Fraser LLP

[2014] CSOH 82, 2014 GWD 16-299, 2014 Case (61) *affd* [2015] CSIH 35, 2015 SLT 313, 2015 Case (59)

Tenzin v Russell

2014 Hous LR 17, Sh Ct, 2014 Case (51) *affd* [2015] CSIH 8A, 2015 Hous LR 11, 2015 Case (43)

Thomson v Mooney

[2012] CSOH 177, 2012 GWD 39-769, 2012 Case (63) *rev* [2013] CSIH 115, 2014 GWD 14-263, 2013 Case (74)

Tuley v Highland Council

2007 SLT (Sh Ct) 97, 2007 Case (24) *rev* [2009] CSIH 31A, 2009 SC 456, 2009 SLT 616, 2009 Case (48)

Wright v Shoreline Management Ltd

Oct 2008, Arbroath Sheriff Court, 2008 Case (60) *rev* 2009 SLT (Sh Ct) 83, 2009 Case (74)

TABLE OF CASES DIGESTED IN EARLIER VOLUMES BUT REPORTED IN 2015

A number of cases which were digested in *Conveyancing 2014* or earlier volumes but were at that time unreported have been reported in 2015. A number of other cases have been reported in an additional series of reports. For the convenience of those using earlier volumes all the cases in question are listed below, together with a complete list of citations.

Chalmers v Chalmers
[2014] CSOH 161, 2015 SCLR 299

Drimsynie Estate Ltd v Ramsey
[2014] CSOH 93, 2015 SCLR 58

Frank Houlgate Investment Co Ltd v Biggart Baillie LLP
[2014] CSIH 79, 2015 SC 187, 2014 SLT 1001

Gyle Shopping Centre General Partners Ltd v Marks & Spencer plc
[2014] CSOH 122, 2015 SCLR 171

Hill of Rubislaw (Q Seven) Ltd v Rubislaw Quarry Aberdeen Ltd
[2014] CSIH 105, 2015 SC 339

Hoblyn v Barclays Bank
[2014] CSIH 52, 2014 GWD 30-376, 2014 Hous LR 26, 2015 SCLR 85

MacKay v McGowan
2015 SLT (Lands Tr) 6

McWatters v Inverclyde Council
2014 SLT (Sh Ct) 155, 2014 Hous LR 70

Mathers v Keeper of the Registers of Scotland
2015 SLT (Lands Tr) 109

Mirza v Salim
[2014] CSIH 51, 2015 SC 31, 2014 SLT 875, 2014 SCLR 764

Sauchiehall Street Properties One Ltd v EMI Group Ltd
2015 Hous LR 24